JOHN PAUL II'S
BOOK OF
SAINTS

MATTHEW BUNSON
MARGARET BUNSON
STEPHEN BUNSON

FOREWORD BY
EDOUARD CARDINAL GAGNON

Our Sunday Visitor Publishing Division
Our Sunday Visitor, Inc.
Huntington, Indiana 46750

Pictures used in this book are from a variety of sources. Pictures from *Faces of Holiness,* © 1998 by Our Sunday Visitor Publishing, are used with permission of author Ann Ball. The picture of Blessed Marie Rivier was provided by the Sisters of the Presentation of Mary, Methuen Province, with permission by Sister Helen Bissionnette, P.M., Provincial Superior. The copy of R. Masutti's original painting of Blessed Marie-Louise Trichet was provided by the Daughters of Wisdom and is used with permission. The original is in the house of the Daughters of Wisdom in Turin. The picture of Marcel Callo was supplied by Rudolf A. Haunschmied, Mauthausen Aktiv Gusen, and is used with permission. The picture of Iwene Tansi was provided by Chidi Denis Isizoh. The pictures of Blesseds Elias del Socorro Nieves, Maria Teresa Fasce, and Anselm Polanco were provided by the Postulator General of the Order of St. Augustine and are used with permission. Other pictures are from the Our Sunday Visitor files.

The authors and publisher are grateful to all copyright holders without whose material this book could not have been completed. If any copyright materials have been inadvertently used without proper credit being given in one manner or another, please notify Our Sunday Visitor in writing so that future printings of this work may be corrected.

Our Sunday Visitor Publishing Division
Our Sunday Visitor, Inc.
200 Noll Plaza
Huntington, IN 46750

International Standard Book Number: 0-87973-934-7
Library of Congress Catalog Card Number: 98-67328

Cover Design by Monica Watts

934

PRINTED IN THE UNITED STATES OF AMERICA

DEDICATION

This book is dedicated to the memory of Dr. Rafael Zamora, of Aguadilla, Puerto Rico, sine qua non.

ACKNOWLEDGMENTS

There are many individuals to whom special gratitude is owed for their assistance and cooperation in the completion of this work. Without their charity and generosity this book would not have been possible. Particular gratitude must be given to the Congregation of the Causes of Saints and to the literally dozens of postulators of the saints and beati presented in this work; they are an inspiration to all for their faithful service to the Church and their patience and devotion in laboring on behalf of the truly remarkable men and women who have been raised to the altars by Pope John Paul II. We are indebted to His Eminence, Edouard Cardinal Gagnon for his kindness and inestimable aid. We also thank: Robert Lockwood, Publisher of Our Sunday Visitor for his enthusiasm and confidence; Greg Erlandson, Editor-in-Chief of Our Sunday Visitor; Jackie Lindsey, Acquisitions Editor; and Lisa Grote, Editor, whose labors have improved this and many other books. Additional thanks are owed to: Author Ann Ball for contributing pictures from her book *The Faces of Holiness* and to the Orders, institutions, and individuals who contributed pictures; Mark Thiel; Edward Wells; Kim Clanton-Green; Marie Cuglietta; the staffs of several libraries, including Marquette University and Sahara West Library; His Excellency, Most Reverend Daniel Walsh of the diocese of Las Vegas for his good office, and Rev. Joseph Anthony and Rev. Thomas Duff, O.S.M.

The Church proposes the example of numerous saints who bore witness to and defended moral truth even to the point of enduring martyrdom, or who preferred death to a single mortal sin. In raising them to the honor of the altars, the Church has canonized their witness and declared the truth of their judgment, according to which the love of God entails the obligation to respect his commandments, even in the most dire of circumstances, and the refusal to betray those commandments, even for the sake of saving one's own life.

Veritatis Splendor (91.3)

The martyrologium *of the first centuries was the basis of the veneration of the saints. By proclaiming and venerating the holiness of her sons and daughters, the Church gave supreme honor to God himself; in the martyrs she venerated Christ, who was at the origin of their martyrdom and holiness. In later times there developed the practice of canonization, a practice which still continues in the Catholic Church and the Orthodox churches. In recent years the number of canonizations and beatifications has increased. These show the vitality of the local churches, which are much more numerous today than in the first centuries and in the first millennium. The greatest homage which all the churches can give to Christ on the threshold of the third millennium will be to manifest the redeemer's all-powerful presence through the fruits of faith, hope, and charity present in men and women of many different tongues and races who have followed Christ in the various forms of the Christian vocation.*

Tertio Millennio Adveniente (37)

TABLE OF CONTENTS

PART ONE:
THE SAINTS OF POPE JOHN PAUL II / 11

PART TWO:
THE BEATIFIED OF POPE JOHN PAUL II / 85

FOREWORD

Beatifications and canonizations have been an outstanding feature of Pope John Paul II's magisterium during the twenty years of his pontificate. It is fitting that we be invited to get acquainted with the women and men the Holy Father proposes as models for us to imitate and as patrons on whom we can rely in forwarding our praises and requests to God and in helping us in our necessities.

This is done here through a collection of well-researched and finely-drawn portraits of people who are close to God and also closer to us than we would expect.

Officially proclaiming blesseds and saints has not been something marginal or occasional in the Pope's pastoral solicitude. In fact, the centuries-old practice has been seen by him as a most effective means to carry out his mission as Vicar of Christ and head of the Church — a mission that entails the triple power and duty to govern, to teach, and to sanctify.

To govern the Church means to be responsible for its unity and dynamism. For canonizations and beatifications the Holy Father invites faithful from all places to gather in unity and proclaim the same faith. Those present and those who follow the event from afar are led to understand that one does not become a saint in isolation but as an active member of the Body of Christ, in what the Credo calls the Communion of Saints.

Unity is possible only by the interaction of the diverse functions and charism of bishops, priests, and religious or lay men and women. All have a special role in giving the Church its vitality, making it present in all fields of human endeavor. The condition is that talents and creativity be at the service of charity and tend to one final purpose of glorifying the Lord. By raising to the glory of the altar some of her sons and daughters, the Church tells us that they have done precisely that.

As head of the Church, the Pope has also revealed himself to be a great leader for humanity. He has never missed an occasion to remind those responsible for the government of nations that there are God-given values to be protected. He is listened to when he receives them in audience or makes it a duty to meet them in his journeys.

Official representatives of nations attend beatifications because the new saints are from their country and they cannot but realize the great part they have played for the common good of society by unselfish dedication to popular education, the care of the needy, social and rural development, and other similar causes. The Holy Father never misses telling them that it is the Holy Spirit who has sustained their generosity, their faith in the human person, their awareness of the needs of their brothers, their spirit of initiative, and most of all the holiness of life which has brought success to their efforts.

Pope John Paul II is a great teacher, taking the Gospel to the limits of the earth, never caring about his health or security. *Gospel* means "Good News," and what better "News" can we receive than that of being shown that the Holy Spirit is ever active and powerful in bringing out the best in us and drawing us to perfection.

After he has officially affirmed the holiness of a servant of God and granted the faculty to render him a public cult, the Holy Father always comments on the liturgical texts and explains how holiness is simply putting God's Word into practice. His homilies, showing how the saints have lived the Word of God in the variety of their personalities, their outstanding virtues and their accomplishments, have become a unique commentary on the Scriptures.

In what is called the mission of sanctifying are included the mission of leading the Church in prayer and that of caring for the sanctity of the Church and its members. John Paul II is a man of prayer and it can be seen wherever he goes, and preserving the beauty and purity of the Liturgy has been one of his concerns. Beatifications are an invitation to pray, following the example of the new saints, and they add a dimension to divine cult by making us render homage to God for his saints and together with them.

Beatifications are also a reminder of our call to perfection. Vatican II has reaffirmed the actuality of the vocations of the people that the Pope wants to propose as models — people who are close to us and have been in duties and situations similar to ours.

I remember well having had, twenty years ago at the Committee for the Family, a long conversation with the Archbishop of Hanoi, at a time when the Church in Vietnam was already under a regime of persecution. He was almost miraculously allowed to attend a Synod of Bishops. Knowing the tremendous problems he had to face, we asked him what we could do for him. To our surprise he answered: "Send us lives of saints!" He explained that his people need more than anything else to see that it is possible to follow in Christ's footsteps and to remain faithful even when it requires heroism.

The Pope too has found that the usual pretext to resist Christ's call to obey his Father's commandment is to say that His Church's ideal of virtue, of moral behavior and self-renouncement, is out of reach for most of us. How often, in encounters with family groups, retreats for youth or even for priests and religious have I heard the response: "This is impossible, Christ cannot demand so much. This is not for people like me." Beatifications are the Pope's answer to our lack of confidence in God's overwhelming grace, in the power of the Holy Spirit who dwells in us and "makes the impossible, possible" to quote Pope Paul IV.

The great variety of gifts and personalities in the new saints and blesseds shows that the Holy Spirit is never inactive. They come from the most diverse social and cultural backgrounds; they have had important functions or simple, ordinary lives; their pilgrimage on earth has been long or short; they have lived in poverty or in affluence. And they invite all of us to strive toward perfection.

They have certain common features. In the last ten years I have been what is called the *"cardinal ponens,"* that is, the relator presenting to the Collge of

Cardinals the conclusions of the long work involved in Causes of Saints before they make a final recommendation to the Holy Father on validity of the case. In all the Causes a reality I have always encountered is that the saints have been accepted to bear the Cross of Christ. The cross of daily fidelity to the simple duties of one's state, the cross of physical pain supported with peace or even joy, the cross of spiritual suffering in periods of doubt or the conscience of our human frailty, the cross of sharing in and trying to alleviate the suffering of others, the cross of misunderstanding and even persecution.

Another common feature is the simplicity and humility with which they have accepted the common devotions to the Child Jesus, to the Eucharist, the Passion, the Sacred Heart, the Blessed Mother in her diverse mysteries, to Saint Joseph or some other favorite saint. There they have found the strength to bear the Cross and the inspiration for the accomplishments in which they have become instruments of divine love.

The degree of intimacy with Christ they have attained can be traced back, for instance, to the first spiritual experience of their communion or to the long hours they have spent in adoration before the Tabernacle.

Pope John Paul II has made us the gift of proposing to us models and intercessors for all occasions. Among the holy men and women introduced to us in this book, the Spirit might make some seem more akin to us, more relevant to our conditions and aspirations. The broad panorama offered by the authors should encourage us to study more in-depth the action of grace in one or the other. They have the merit of making us proud of our Church and more confident in our call to imitate our Savior a little more every day.

✠Edouard Cardinal Gagnon
December, 1998

INTRODUCTION

The Saints and Blesseds of the pontificate of Pope John Paul II have been our constant companions for these past many months. It has been an honor and a privilege to record their lives, their contributions to the world, and their spiritual splendors.

The Holy Father seeks to remind the world that the glory of the Church is not limited to one or two continents or countries nor to a specific age in human history. The faith is found throughout the whole of the world and has a relevance and meaning to all human beings in every setting and era and from every ethnic, cultural, and economic background. Many of the Saints and Blesseds walked upon the earth during our lifetime, assuring us that the age of miracles and holiness is not a thing of the past, but alive, vital, and still having an impact on the modern world. While they may be different in the details of their lives, each one of these remarkable human beings brought their individual talents to bear on the tasks at hand, responding to grace and the Will of God with heroic generosity and fidelity. We pray that the spirit of these holy men and women will inspire the faithful throughout the Church in the days to come.

We have also experienced the kindness and generosity of postulators and the men and women who are carrying on the labors, spiritual visions, and heroism of these Saints and Blesseds in completing this work. Their kindness and encouragement reflect the ideals of their founders, and their participation in this work had added to our edification and growth in the faith.

Editorial Note:

Owing to the considerable multiplicity of spellings of the names and places of origins among the Saints and Blesseds of Pope John Paul II, this work utilizes the English spelling and version of most place and personal names. Most of the names are well-known, but some are relatively obscure, necessitating spellings and presentations that are more accessible to all readers. Additionally, the excerpts used throughout the text are taken directly from the addresses, homilies, and writings of Pope John Paul II. As these are official texts, no attempt has been made to edit or revise the specific language used, as customarily found in papal documents such as those published by *L'Osservatore Romano*, though some stylistic changes have been made for consistency and for American-English spelling. Cross-references have been used throughout for greater ease in finding a specific Saint or Blessed under one of the many alternate names by which they are commonly known.

PART ONE:
THE SAINTS OF
POPE JOHN PAUL II

". . . we have become sharers in this mission of the prophet Christ, and in virtue of that mission we together with him are serving divine truth in the Church. Being responsible for that truth also means loving it and seeking the most exact understanding of it, in order to bring it closer to ourselves and others in all its saving power, its splendor and its profundity joined with simplicity. This love and this aspiration to understand the truth must go hand in hand, as is con-firmed by the histories of the saints in the Church. These received most brightly the authentic light that illuminates divine truth and brings close God's very reality, because they approached this truth with veneration and love — love in the first place for Christ, the living Word of divine truth, and then love for his human expression in the Gospel, Tradition, and theology."

Redemptor Hominis (19.2*)***

The saint of the "Little Way," Aegidius was sometimes called Giles Mary of St. Joseph. He was a Franciscan flame of charity who changed the city of Naples, Italy, forever. Humble, serving in the capacity of a simple lay brother,

AEGIDIUS MARY OF ST. JOSEPH PONTILLO

(D. 1812)

LAY RELIGIOUS

Aegidius went about his daily routine with calm and resolve, even though his journeys took him into the lepers' domain where he performed nursing activities among the abandoned.

Aegidius was born on November 16, 1729, in Taranto, Apulia, Italy, was baptized Francis, and was raised in a simple, devout community where he matured in the faith and in awareness of the needs of families in his region. He made his living as a rope maker in his hometown even as he developed an awareness of a religious vocation and of profound spiritual aspirations.

Aegidius matured into the sort of soul that needs no special titles or honors in order to serve and care for the lost or forgotten of his era. He was drawn to the ideals of St. Francis of Assisi, *il Poverello*, and in 1754, Aegidius made his application to the Discalced Friars Minor of St. Peter of Alcántara in Naples. Because he lacked the formal education necessary to train for the priesthood, Aegidius was received as a novice lay brother. After making his vows as a Franciscan, Aegidius was assigned as a porter, a gate-keeper, at the seminary. His position put him in contact with many Neapolitans, and allowed him to perform his charitable acts. The Franciscans at the seminary recognized Aegidius's piety and faithful service, but even they did not know the scope of his activities or the day-to-day valor he displayed.

Skilled in caring for the sick, Aegidius brought a tender concern to the men and women who learned to seek him out at his post. He was busy every day with the wounded or diseased, and he walked outside the city limits offering aid and comfort to the most pitiful people in the region. In keeping with the spiritual legacy of St. Francis, Aegidius made certain to wash and minister to all lepers who needed his aid. He refused no one in his solicitous ministry.

Aegidius lived entirely for service to his fellow human beings, reaching the age of eighty in an endless ministry of compassion and care. He met the assorted ills of his own age by sacrificing his time and energies in face-to-face confrontations with pain and suffering. The Neapolitans, and then people from other regions, looked upon him as the patron of the sick and despised.

When Aegidius died while at prayer in Naples on February 7, 1812, thousands mourned his passing. Vast crowds, surging to display grief, overwhelmed

Aegidius's funeral with their sorrow. His Cause was opened soon after his death, and he was beatified in 1888 by Pope Leo XIII.

Pope John Paul II canonized Aegidius on June 2, 1996. At his canonization ceremony Aegidius was praised as a glory of the Franciscan crown, a humble follower of Christ and *il Poverello* who left the indelible mark of his love and sanctity on the city of Naples and on the modern Church.

Foundress and Royal Religious

Wreathed in mists of legend and time, the royal dynasties of the Middle Ages may seem remote, but the men and women who ruled in that age were very real. Most of the royal lines have vanished through the centuries, especially as the maps of Europe have been redrawn by wars and treaties, with individual rulers remembered only as dim symbols or insignias of certain eras. The modern world rushes toward its own destiny quite unaware of the tragedies and miracles that took place during the Middle Ages more than five hundred years ago.

AGNES OF BOHEMIA

(D. 1282)

FOUNDRESS

Still, Agnes of Bohemia emerges from the shadows of those forgotten ages, bringing to the Church a most remarkable image of faith, trust, and resolve. Agnes was a princess, the daughter of King Ottocar, the ruler of Bohemia — now a part of the modern Czech Republic — and Queen Constance, who was the daughter of the king of Hungary. Agnes was born about 1205 in the city of Prague and is often called Agnes of Prague by historians.

The education of Agnes took place at Trebnitz, where she was placed in the care of the Cistercian Nuns. Such an education was a requirement of Agnes's rank and future role in the society of the time. Agnes was treated kindly in the convent and there she received the grace of a religious vocation.

Royal protocol came between Agnes and her vocation. At the age of three, Agnes was betrothed to Prince Boleslaus, following customs of the period. When Boleslaus died very young, Agnes was betrothed to Prince Henry, the son of Emperor Frederick II of the Holy Roman Empire. Henry married an Austrian duchess instead. Soon after, Frederick himself asked for her hand in marriage, and Agnes was betrothed for the third time by her royal father.

Despite her strict upbringing and her filial duties to her parents, Agnes responded to her religious vocation and refused to accept marriage to the emperor. When the court officials urged her to go to the emperor, Agnes refused, and she appealed to Pope Gregory IX, asking him to intercede for her through an annulment of the betrothal. Upon hearing of Agnes's refusal, Emperor Frederick II was incensed but said, "If she had left me for a mortal man, I would have taken vengeance with the sword, but I cannot take offense because in preference to me she has chosen the King of Heaven." Frederick released her.

Related to St. Elizabeth of Hungary on her mother's side, Agnes knew that this former queen had become a tertiary and then a nun at Marburg. The courts of Europe were quite shocked by this royal dedication, and they wondered what could have prompted such a drastic retreat into the religious life. Agnes understood that St. Elizabeth was responding nobly to the grace of God, something that she planned to imitate with the same enthusiasm. In 1225, the Friars Minor had arrived in Prague, introducing the Franciscan spirit to the capital. Agnes was drawn to that spirit and allowed it to form her aspirations.

She obtained a grant of land from her brother, King Wenceslaus I, and on the property she erected a Franciscan hospital for the poor and needy. Agnes then established the Confraternity of the Crusaders of the Red Star to staff the hospital and the attached clinics.

In 1234, Agnes founded a Poor Clare Convent, St. Savior, in Prague. In order to make sure that the true rule and ideal of the Poor Clares was instilled in St. Savior's, Agnes wrote to St. Clare of Assisi, asking her aid in this endeavor. St. Clare responded by sending five nuns from Assisi to establish the rule and the cloister routine successfully. Agnes and St. Clare never met face to face, but they corresponded by letter for two decades. These letters have been preserved by the Franciscan Order. Agnes entered St. Savior on Pentecost Sunday, 1234, and remained cloistered for almost half a century. In time she became abbess of the convent and was revered as a model of religious.

Almighty God blessed the sacrifices and devotion that Agnes demonstrated with her religious life. Countless men and women of all ranks looked to Agnes as an example of dedication and piety, and she symbolized the beauty of the cloister and prayer for her own era. Given the gifts of healing and prophecy, Agnes experienced ecstasies and union with God. She also predicted events happening in the world, including her brother Wenceslaus' victory over the duke of Austria. This saintly princess remained a Poor Clare for forty-six years. She died in the St. Savior Convent in Prague on March 6, 1282.

Pope John Paul II canonized her on November 12, 1989, in Rome, declaring: *"Agnes of Bohemia, although she lived in a period far removed from ours, still remains a shining example of the Christian faith and heroic charity, which invites us to reflection and imitation . . . she is an example of courage and spiritual help for the young people who generously consecrate themselves to the religious life; for all those who follow Christ; she is a stimulus of charity practiced toward everyone with total dedication, overcoming every barrier of race, nation or mentality; she is the heavenly protectress of our difficult daily journey. To her we can therefore turn with great trust and hope."*

Founder of the Gray Brothers and Sisters

Some human beings are born with unique visions of life and the world — they see the mortal journey of men and women as a treasure that unfolds splendors in the soul. These special individuals, usually given the grace of talents and spiritual insights, soar as comets through the dark skies of modern disbelief, illuminating for all to see the love of God. Albert Chmielowski, called *"the Brother of Our Lord"* by Pope John Paul II, was a radiant example of these unique souls.

ALBERT CHMIELOWSKI

(D. 1916)

FOUNDER

Born Adam Chmielowski in Igoalomia, Poland, on August 20, 1845, Albert lived during a turbulent era in European history. He felt committed to the people and events of his own age from his earliest years, and lost a leg while taking part in an insurrection for Poland's freedom when he was seventeen. Later Albert turned to art as a form of expression, and he gained considerable popularity and fame.

Albert lived in Krakow, Poland, where he had countless friends and demonstrated a gentle charm and an astute awareness of the stark tragedies of modern society — tragedies that preyed upon the young, the needy, and the helpless. He continued painting, but in his soul he heard a call to yet another form of service for the Lord. Albert realized that he was being called to unite himself to Christ in serving his fellow human beings in the world.

Seeking to respond by deepening his spiritual life, he entered the Franciscans as a member of the Third Order, gave up any thought of continuing his painting, and embraced the spirit of St. Francis of Assisi. Known as Brother Albert, he centered his labors on the poorest and most destitute in Krakow.

In 1887, Albert donned a coarse gray habit and founded what came to be called the Brothers of the Third Order of St. Francis Servants of the Poor. These religious were called the Albertines in his honor, and in 1891 he established a similar congregation for women. They organized shelters and soup kitchens and undertook other charitable enterprises for the poor and the abandoned. The "Gray Brothers" and "Gray Sisters," as they are also known, took up Albert's dream of becoming the brothers and sisters of all whom they served.

Albert preached that one of the greatest calamities of the time was the fact that the majority of human beings refused to see the truly wretched state of modern society, thereby absolving themselves of the fundamental obligation to strive to correct these evils. Thus, he took it upon himself to do what he could on behalf of the defenseless. He died at work in Krakow on Christmas Day, in 1916.

Pope John Paul II canonized Albert on November 12, 1989, declaring that this new saint understood the necessity of *"giving one's soul."* The Holy Father also honored Albert's *"tireless, heroic service on behalf of the marginalized and the poor."*

Pope John Paul II has long been an admirer of the spiritual legacy of the man he called the *"Brother of Our Lord."* He wrote a sensitive and dramatic play about Albert in 1949. The Holy Father's play is scheduled to become a motion picture. Pope John Paul II beatified a spiritual daughter of Albert Chmielowski, Maria Bernardina Jablonska, on June 6, 1997. At Albert's beatification by Pope John Paul II, held in June, 1993, the Holy Father said: *"Holiness is a particular likeness to Christ. A likeness through love."*

Alphonsus Rodriquez ❦ **See Jesuit Martyrs of Paraguay.**

Andrew Dung Lac ❦ **See Martyrs of Vietnam.**

Andrew Kim and Companions ❦ **See Martyrs of Korea.**

Model Religious

When Almighty God chooses certain men and women to serve as spiritual vessels of the faith, he lovingly provides them with special graces and earthly friends to aid them in their tasks and apostolates. Claude de la Colombière was such a "faithful servant and perfect friend." He was the spiritual director of St. Margaret Mary Alacoque and one of the leaders in the spread of the devotion to the Sacred Heart. Claude also has the distinction of being a "dry" martyr of England, a valiant soul who suffered at the hands his English captors and then survived in order to achieve the Will of God on earth.

CLAUDE DE LA COLOMBIÈRE

(D. 1682)

RELIGIOUS

Claude was born at Saint-Symphorien d'Ozen, near Lyons, France on February 2, 1641, and was formally educated at the Jesuit College in Lyons. Receiving the grace of a religious vocation and having developed a knowledge of the spiritual life, he entered the Society of Jesus in 1659. He was sent to Avignon and Paris for advanced studies by the Jesuits, and was ordained to the priesthood in the society. Claude then served as tutor to the son of the powerful French minister Colbert, acquiring as well a reputation as a preacher.

In 1675, Claude became the superior of Paray-le-Monial College, demonstrating academic brilliance and an intense loyalty to the precepts of the faith. While serving at Paray-le-Monial, he met St. Margaret Mary Alacoque. He became her confessor and aided her in spreading devotion to the Sacred Heart of Jesus. In a vision, St. Margaret Mary was told that Claude was Christ's "perfect friend . . ." and that Claude's gift was "to lead souls to God."

He then was assigned by the order to England to serve as a chaplain to Mary Beatrice d'Este, the duchess of York. When, however, the Titus Oates Plot was launched (the spurious claim purported by Titus Oates that a vast Jesuit conspiracy was at work to assassinate King Charles II and install his brother the duke of York — the future King James II — on the throne and to bring England back to the Catholic Faith), Claude was falsely charged as a participant during the hysteria that gripped the kingdom. These charges were made because of the resentment caused by Claude's loyal service to the duchess of York and his respected position in her court. Claude was imprisoned and was harshly treated before receiving banishment from England. He never recovered from the torments that he endured at the hands of the English, who singled him out because he was a Jesuit.

He was able to return to Paray-le-Monial in 1679, where he was welcomed as a "dry" martyr for the faith. This meant that he had suffered every indignity and cruelty but had not shed his blood, nor had he suffered execution. Claude remained in poor health, physically broken by his many ordeals. He died of hemoptysis (coughing up blood from the lungs) on February 15, 1682, and his sufferings were widely known within the Church of his era. Pope Pius XI beatified him on June 16, 1929.

Pope John Paul II canonized Claude in Rome on May 31, 1992, declaring that: *"The past three centuries allow us to evaluate the importance of the message which was entrusted to Claude. . . . In a period of contrasts between the fervor of some and the indifference or impiety of many, here is a devotion centered on the humanity of Christ, on his presence, on his love of mercy and on forgiveness . . . devotion to the Heart of Christ would be a source of balance and spiritual strengthening for Christian communities so often faced with increasing unbelief over the coming centuries. . . ."* The Holy Father also declared Claude the true Jesuit, the *"companion of St. Ignatius"* in fidelity and honor.

Claudine Thévenet ❧ **See Mary of St. Ignatius Thévenet.**

Foundress of The Little Sisters of Our Lady of Sorrows

The youngest foundress of a religious congregation and given a very short time on earth, Clelia Barbieri stands today as a truly remarkable woman who followed her vision and remained faithful to Christ in all things.

She was born in Budrio, Emilia, Italy, on February 13, 1847, the daughter of Joseph and Hyacintha Nanetti Barbieri. Her father died in 1855, leaving her family endangered financially, and Clelia had to assume many responsibilities at an early age.

She became a catechist for the local parish, even though there was political un-

CLELIA BARBIERI

(D. 1870)

FOUNDRESS

from *Faces of Holiness*

St. Clelia Barbieri

rest and an anti-religious feeling sweeping through the area. The local pastor encouraged Clelia to start educating young women as well, and a friend, Teodora Baraldi, joined her in the task. The Little Sisters of Our Lady of Sorrows developed from Clelia's efforts, and another young woman, Orsola Donati, aided in the founding of the congregation on May 1, 1868. The archbishop of Bologna, Lucida Maria Cardinal Parocchi, blessed the Little Sisters and their work. The members of Clelia's congregation are also called the "Minims of Our Lady of Sorrows." In 1949 the institute was given pontifical status and was attached to the Servite Order. The Minims work in Europe, Tanzania, and India.

Clelia understood the modern demands upon religious and, accordingly, she designed the congregation as both an active and a contemplative apostolate. Dedicated to Christ in the Holy Eucharist, Clelia received many mystical graces. She had prayed that God would "make me burn with love," and she demonstrated this love with unique fidelity to the everyday, parish-level activities that brought the faith to her neighbors. Clelia died very suddenly on July 13, 1870, at the age of twenty-three, at Budrio. Her biography was written by Giorgio Cardinal Gusmini from 1914-21, and the faithful of the region honored her immediately, calling Clelia "the mother."

Pope John Paul II canonized Clelia on April 9, 1989, declaring that *". . . Clelia Barbieri is not the fruit of a particular school of spirituality but the genuine product of that first and fundamental school of holiness which was the parish church of her village. The Eucharist is the theological location both of the mystical experiences of Clelia — from the first Communion to the termination of her life — and of that reality which she herself will name the glorious inspiration, the charism of foundation. From the devotion to the Eucharist springs forth her multiple charitable activities in the form of evangelization and education, assistance and immediate intervention on behalf of the poor, the sick, the margialized, by means of a simple and ingenious creativity which makes her worthy of the title given to her by her people: 'Mother,' 'Mother Clelia.' "* The Holy Father praised Clelia's devotion to the Holy Eucharist which was her *"glorious inspiration, the charism of foundation,"* and reminded the members of Clelia's congregation present at the ceremony that their foundress had promised: *". . . I will always be with you and never abandon you."*

Model Religious: The Little Beast of Burden

The insignias of souls united to God are most often gentleness, kindness, and good humor, especially about the frailties of the human experience. Such holy men and women, having no need for the poses and demands of the world, can move freely as friends of God. Crispin of Viterbo was such a friend.

Born in Viterbo, Italy, on November 13, 1668, Crispin grew up in the city. At the age of five, he was consecrated by his mother to the Blessed Virgin. His mother fostered in him a special devotion to the Blessed Virgin Mary and was his first teacher of the faith. Crispin was so spiritually advanced as a child that the villagers affectionately called him *il Santorello,* the little saint.

CRISPIN OF VITERBO

(D. 1750)

RELIGIOUS

A glimpse of a procession of Friars Minor Capuchin inspired Crispin to embrace the religious life. He was accepted into the Franciscans as a lay brother assigned to menial tasks. In this capacity, Crispin called himself "the little beast of burden of the Capuchins." This was not a complaint but a simple statement of his humble status in the order. He served as a cook in the Viterbo Capuchin monastery. He was then assigned to other tasks in Tolfa, Rome, and Albano. Going about his chores without a hat, Crispin was asked by a passerby why he went on his rounds bare headed. "An ass," Crispin replied, " does not need a hat," confirming his own nickname.

Crispin modeled his life on that of St. Felix of Cantalice, using that saint as a model of perfection. He grew in holiness and wisdom and soon attracted the notice of men and women outside of his community, who visited Crispin for his counsel and guidance. He also began to receive visits almost every day from bishops, cardinals, and others of note, and was even consulted by the Holy Father. He did not take their ranks and titles too seriously, viewing them instead as children of God who needed reminders about the eternal aspects of salvation and the need for self-awareness and truth. Crispin brought a heavenly perspective on human affairs to people of all ranks.

When Crispin became infirm due to age, austere penances, and labors, he was sent to Rome to rest. He died there on May 19, 1750, surrounded by his mourning Franciscan companions and leaders of the Church. This hidden, humble, lay brother had touched the lives of hundreds, without fanfare, without the obvious trappings of world power. Crispin had communicated his wisdom, fervor, and devotion face to face with those who sought him out. He was a font of spiritual perfection, and his body, discovered still remarkably preserved, is enshrined under a side altar in the Capuchin church in Rome. He was beatified by Pope Pius VII in 1806.

Pope John Paul II canonized Crispin on June 20, 1982, the first saint raised to the altars in this pontificate. During the ceremonies, the Holy Father praised this humble monk as a giant of the spiritual life, a gentle soul who perceived the secrets of the saints and perfection.

Dominic Ibañez de Erquicia 🕭 **See Martyrs of Japan.**

Members of the Order of Preachers

The Martyrs of Vietnam include members of the Order of Preachers, the Dominicans, who gave their lives and truly suffered in the missions of Vietnam during the persecutions that took place in that kingdom. King Tu-Duc ruler of the

DOMINICAN MARTYRS OF VIETNAM

(D. 1856-1862)

🕭

MARTYRS

central region of Vietnam — known also as Tonkin, Indo-China, and Assam — ascended to the throne in 1848. He followed the pattern of religious persecution set by his anti-Christian predecessors and then increased the scope and fury of such programs. His persecutions continued until 1862 when he was compelled to sign a peace treaty with France and Spain that demanded an end to the oppression and the protection of European missionaries and their converts.

The persecution of the European missionaries had been both merciless and efficient. In 1848, a price was set on the heads of foreign missionaries, and in 1851 it was decreed that all European and native priests were to be slain. By 1855, Christians were commanded to abjure the faith, and rewards for European missionaries were offered everywhere. In July, 1856, wholesale massacres of Christians began, resulting in such atrocities as the burning of entire Christian villages and their inhabitants.

Although Dominicans faced torture, imprisonment, and martyrdom in Vietnam before 1856, the Dominican Martyrs of this era are especially honored. Bishops Joseph Diaz Sanjuro, Jerome Hermosillo, and their fellow Dominicans were slain during the reign of Tu-Duc. Some were tortured to death, strangled, or abused until they died. Included in this list are:

Dominic Kham Viet Pham, Joseph Khang, Melchior Garcia Sampedro, Dominic Ninh, Lawrence Ngon, Luke Thin Viet Pham, Joseph Tuc, Paul Duong, Thomas Khuong, Dominic Cam, Joseph Tuan Van Tran, Dominic Huyen, Dominic Toai, Dominic Mau, Vincent Duong, Peter Tuan, Peter Dung Van Dinh, Peter Da, Dominic Nhi, Andrew Tuong, Dominic Nguyen, Vincent Tuong, Dominic Mao.

The fervor and fidelity of these martyrs has long brought fame and honor upon the Dominicans. They were canonized by Pope John Paul II on June 19,

1988, among one hundred seventeen Martyrs of Vietnam. As members of the Order of Preachers, however, they deserve special recognition. (See Martyrs of Vietnam for additional details.)

Carmelite Martyr

The ferocity of the Holocaust of World War II left the world stunned, and it is still difficult for people to comprehend the bestiality and horror unleashed by the Nazis across Europe. Almost an entire generation perished as victims or as soldiers on the battlefields of the world at war. Among these victims were truly gifted souls who brought to the faith remarkable brilliance, fidelity, and valor.

EDITH STEIN

(D. 1942)

MARTYR

The Church honors Edith Stein as one of those rare souls cut down by a reign of terror that remains today as an insignia of consummate evil. Teresa Benedicta of the Cross, this convert, was one of the most brilliant philosophers of the modern era, but she died in Auschwitz concentration camp as a victim of the faith of her fathers.

Edith was born in Breslau, Germany, on October 12, 1891, the youngest of seven children in a prominent Jewish family. Edith abandoned Judaism as early as 1904, becoming a self-proclaimed atheist. Her brilliant intellect was seeking truth, and she entered the University of Göttingen, where she became a protégé of the famed philosopher Edmund Husserl. She was also a proponent of the philosophical school of phenomenology both at Göttingen and Freiburg in Breisgau. She earned a doctorate in 1916 and emerged as one of Europe's brightest philosophers. One of her primary endeavors was to examine phenomenology from the perspective of Thomistic thought, part of her growing interest in Catholic teachings. Propelled by her reading of the autobiography of St. Teresa of Ávila, she was baptized on January 1, 1922. Giving up her university post, she became a teacher in the Dominican school at Speyer, receiving as well in 1932 the post of lecturer at the Educational Institute of Munich, resigning under pressure from the Nazis, who were then in control of Germany.

In 1934, Edith entered the Carmelite Order. Smuggled out of Germany into the Netherlands in 1938 to escape the mounting Nazi oppression, she fell into the hands of the Third Reich with the Nazi occupation of the Netherlands in 1940. Arrested in 1942 with her sister Rosa (also a convert) as part of the order by Hitler to liquidate all non-Aryan Catholics, she was taken to Auschwitz, and, on August 9 or 10, 1942, she died in the gas chamber there. In the years after the war, her extensive spiritual and philosophical writings were collected and published, receiving promotion by the *Archivum Carmelatinum Edith Stein* at Louvain, Belgium. Her Cause was formally opened in 1962.

Pope John Paul II canonized Edith on October 11, 1998, praising the Carmelite martyr for her fidelity to the truth and to the love of Christ.

"The spiritual experience of Edith Stein is an eloquent example of . . . extraordinary interior renewal. A young woman in search of the truth has become a saint and a martyr through the silent workings of divine grace: Teresa Benedicta of the Cross, who from heaven repeats to us today all the words that marked her life: 'Far be it from me to glory except in the Cross of our Lord Jesus Christ.' Dear brothers and sisters! Because she was Jewish, Edith Stein was taken with her sister Rosa and many other Catholic Jews from the Netherlands to the

Edith Stein, canonized October, 1998

concentration camp in Auschwitz, where she died with them in the gas chambers. Today we remember them all with deep respect. A few days before her deportation, the woman religious had dismissed the question about a possible rescue: 'Do not do it! Why should I be spared? Is it not right that I should gain no advantage from my Baptism? If I cannot share the lot of my brothers and sisters, my life, in a certain sense, is destroyed.'

". . . This woman had to face the challenges of such a radically changing century as our own. . . . The modern world boasts of the enticing door which says: everything is permitted. It ignores the narrow gate of discernment and renunciation. I am speaking especially to you, young Christians . . . . Your life is not an endless series of open doors! Listen to your heart! Do not stay on the surface, but go to the heart of things! And when the time is right, have the courage to decide! The Lord is waiting for you to put your freedom in his good hands."

Founder of the Congregation of the Oblates of Mary Immaculate

The hallmarks of the true Christian are courtesy, respect for the dignity of others, and fidelity to the truths of the faith. Such virtues distinguish the great saints of every era, men and women who achieved perfection and carried Christ's message to the world with grace and winning charm. Eugene de Mazenod was just such an ambassador of the faith, and his legacy of courtesy and nobility is inspiring new generations.

EUGENE DE MAZENOD

(D. 1861)

FOUNDER

This saint was born Charles Joseph Eugene de Mazenod in Aix, Provence, France, on August 1, 1782. A son of a devout noble family, he had to endure exile in Italy because of the terrors of the French Revolution.

Although he was the last of his noble line, Eugene studied for the priesthood and was ordained at Amiens on December 21, 1811. He served in parishes in Aix, where he was moved by the plight of the faithful as a result of the revolution. Gathering a small group of missionaries, Eugene sent them into the rural areas of Provence to instruct the local populace. The Missionary Oblates of Mary Immaculate, the outcome of this original group of home visitors, became a congregation on January 25, 1816. Pope Leo XII gave it his final approval as the Congregation of the Oblates of Mary Immaculate on February 17, 1826.

Eugene also aided his uncle, the aged archbishop of Marseilles, in administering that archdiocese and succeeded him in that see. He was initially consecrated a titular bishop in early 1837, succeeding his uncle in 1851. Pope Pius IX bestowed the pallium upon him. As archbishop of Marseilles, he displayed a brilliant grasp of political and religious affairs and an almost heroic fidelity to the faith. His main focus was on Church renewal and reform, and he introduced the theological system of St. Francis de Sales into Marseilles. He also protected the young people of his region and declared apostolic freedom again and again in the face of adamant civil powers trying to repress the Church in France.

Eugene served the Holy See as well as his own archdiocese. He took an active role in the solemn definitions of the dogma of the Immaculate Conception in 1854 and supported papal infallibility with elegance and firmness. He was created a Peer of France, the result of his valiant service to his native land. This honor demonstrated Eugene's remarkable ability to maintain the virtues and ideals of the faith without alienating those with opposite views. He was always staunch in his defense, but he offered opponents courtesy, respect, and charity. He was slated to receive yet another sign of the Holy See's approval, the rank of cardinal, but he died on May 21, 1861, in Marseilles before he could be elevated to the Sacred College of Cardinals. Eugene was beatified by Pope Paul VI in 1975.

His remains were enshrined in the cathedral of Marseilles, mourned by the thousands who attended his funeral. The Oblates carried his visions and ideals into more than fifty countries of the world, raising up outstanding religious and setting into motion innovative and inspiring institutions and programs. Today, there are more than five thousand members worldwide, including many bishops and one cardinal, Francis Eugene George, archbishop of Chicago, who was made a cardinal by Pope John Paul II in 1998.

Pope John Paul II canonized Eugene de Mazenod on December 3, 1995. At the ceremony, Eugene was praised for his vision, tenacity, and exquisite conformity to the Will of God. His nobility allowed him to transcend the social, political, and religious barriers of his turbulent era, and his fidelity to the faith provided him with a charity that communicated Christ's love to one and all.

Love and its natural outpouring in charity can serve as vital forces for good in human existence. In the souls united to Christ, love becomes a living flame that ignites the heart and mind and leads to sacrifice, dedication, and the surrender of self. Such a living flame was Eustochia Calafato, the Franciscan foundress of Messina, whose life was marked by remarkable events and filled with signs of God's love.

EUSTOCHIA CALAFATO

(D. 1468)

RELIGIOUS

Born in Annunziata in 1434, Eustochia was the daughter of Bernardo and Macaldo Romano Colonna. A legend concerning Eustochia's birth states that she was born in a stable because her mother, a prominent noblewoman, had been directed to deliver the child there. Eustochia was baptized Smeralda, Sicilian for Emerald.

She was raised in the faith by her fervent mother and received the grace of a religious vocation at an early age. Seeking to understand God's Will, Eustochia had a vision of Christ Crucified and was inspired to enter the Poor Clare Convent of Santa Maria di Basicó, despite the opposition of her own brothers. They became enraged and threatened to burn down the convent, forcing Eustochia to placate them. In 1414, however, seeing her determination, her brothers finally relented.

Taking vows and receiving the name Eustochia in religion, she entered into a strict ascetical life centered on the Holy Eucharist. She became somewhat disappointed, however, with the Poor Clares of that convent, as they did not practice an extreme penitential life within the cloister. Eustochia sought another convent in which to serve as a Poor Clare. She received permission from Pope Callistus III to join a community where reforms were being implemented. Eustochia went into Santa Maria Acommodata Convent and was soon joined by others who valued her vision. Her niece, Paula, and her own sister entered as well.

Eustochia served as superior and faced such difficulties and obstacles that she appealed to the Holy See for redress. She had great devotion to the Passion of Christ, and she spent her nights in prayer before the Blessed Sacrament. The sick and needy of Messina benefited from her charity, and in 1463 they flocked to Montevergine, also called Monte della Vergini, the "Maiden's Hill," where she built a cloister large enough to accommodate her community. The people of Messina considered Eustochia their patroness, especially in times of earthquake.

She reportedly died at Montevergine on January 20, 1491, but may have died earlier. Eustochia's body remains incorrupt. In 1777, the senate of Messina voted to make two visits a year to her tomb, where her body is still exposed for veneration. Pope John Paul II canonized Eustochia at Messina on June 11, 1988. He declared: *"St. Eustochia is a splendid example. . . . Learning assiduously in the school of Christ Crucified, she grew in knowledge of him and, meditating on the splendid mysteries of grace, she conceived a faithful love for him. For our saint, the cloistered life was not a mere flight from the world in order to take refuge in God. Through the severe asceticism which she imposed upon herself, she certainly wanted to be united to Christ, gradually eliminating whatever in her, as in every human person, was fallen; at the same time, she felt united to all.*

"From her cell in the monastery of Motevergine she extended her prayer and the value of her penances to the whole world. In such a way she wanted to be near to each brother and sister, alleviate every suffering, ask pardon for the sins of all."

Colombian Bishop

The Catholic Faith has blossomed through the centuries in Latin America, bringing to the Church and to the faithful great luminaries of the spirit who have enriched society and the common good. The spirituality of the Augustinian Order, serving in Latin America and imprinting religious values and graces, has contributed to the growth of the faith in that part of the world by providing entire generations of Catholics with counsel and guidance. These two great traditions of service combined in the education and

EZEKIEL MORENO Y DIAZ

(D. 1906)

BISHOP

sanctification of Ezekiel Moreno y Diaz, a Colombian prelate who sacrificed himself for others throughout his life.

Ezekiel was born in Alfaro Tarazona, Colombia, on April 9, 1848, where the faith was a strong presence in the lives of the people. He was raised devoutly and trained in the Church's doctrines. Receiving the grace of a religious vocation, Ezekiel entered the Augustinian Recollects, drawn to the spirituality of that ancient order. He was ordained and assigned to Augustinian apostolates, displaying fervor and dedication in each undertaking. Ezekiel was elevated to the episcopacy

Ezekiel Moreno y Diaz

and was consecrated the titular bishop of Pinara on October 23, 1893. On December 2 of that year, he was named the bishop of Pasto, a diocese erected in Colombia in 1859. Pasto was still a relatively new diocese (established by Pope Pius IX in 1859), located at the base of La Galera volcano. Here Ezekiel distinguished himself through his care for the needs of his flock, his charity, and his generosity. He died in Montegudo on August 19, 1906, and was mourned by the faithful in the entire region.

Pope John Paul II canonized Ezekiel in Santo Domingo during a visit to the Dominican Republic, on October 11, 1992. At the ceremony, Ezekiel was revered for his fidelity to Christ, his consummate episcopal charity, and his personal holiness.

"Padre Maestro"

The unselfish, committed educators of the Church's religious orders shine as beacons for each new generation of the faith, and they illuminate the paths of rededication necessary if the young people of this age are to be intellectually and morally prepared for their Christian vocations in the world. Francis Anthony Fasani was a teacher, and he understood the implications of educating the young. He was also a true spiritual son of St. Francis of Assisi and an ardent defender of the Blessed Virgin Mary under her title of the Immaculate Conception.

Born at Lucera, Italy, on August 6, 1681, he is sometimes honored in devotions as Francis of Lucera. The son of Joseph and Isabella Della Monaco

FRANCIS ANTHONY FASANI

(D. 1742)

❦

RELIGIOUS

Fasani, he was baptized Donato Antonio Giovanni, and was called *Giovanniello*. Francis' father died when the child was only ten, and Francis was sent to study under the Franciscans, the Friars Minor Conventual, in Lucera, after his mother remarried. There his spirituality and maturity were recognized, and there he received the grace of a religious vocation. At the age of fifteen, Francis joined the Franciscans. He went to Monte St. Angelo Gorgano for religious training and preparation for seminary. His devotion to the Immaculate Conception was profound, and his fidelity to the rule and spirit of St. Francis awed all who came across his path. Francis Anthony completed his seminary training as a Franciscan and his studies for the priesthood, and was ordained a priest at the tomb of St. Francis of Assisi on September 19, 1705.

He then returned to the university to further his knowledge of the faith, earning a doctorate in theology in Rome. His first assignment, in 1707, was to teach philosophy in the St. Francis Convent in Lucera. Within a short time he had earned the title of "Padre Maestro," owing to his learning and erudition, but especially because of his perfect imitation of St. Francis of Assisi.

Through the years, he fulfilled many positions in the Order, including superior and then provincial. He was also a remarkable preacher who took pains to reach the hearts of young and old. Conducting charities, Francis started a Christmas collection for the poor and spent hours caring for local prisoners, who were treated badly by officials in the region. He was deeply committed to the Most Blessed Sacrament and fostered devotion to the Immaculate Conception, and he was one of the first in Italy to conduct novenas to the Blessed Virgin under this title. He preached throughout Italy for thirty-five years, was gifted with many spiritual graces, and even predicted his own death at Lucera on November 29, 1742.

Pope Pius XII beatified Francis Anthony in 1957. Pope John Paul II canonized him on April 13, 1986, honoring him as a glory of the Franciscans and as a promoter of the Immaculate Conception and Our Lady.

Apostolic Missionary, Founder of the Stigmatine Congregation

On their journeys through life and the world, human beings are often gifted by the companionship or the inspiration of soaring, generous men and women who bear the marks of eternity. Such rare souls are not awed by the pomp and power of the world but hold their gaze upon eternal horizons, receiving mystical graces from their union with God in prayer. They live in the human world, but they are transformed by love and set others on fire with their examples and their patient suffering for the salvation of souls.

GASPAR BERTONI

(D. 1835)

MYSTIC

Gaspar Bertoni carried the insignias of eternity throughout his life. A founder, mystic, and preacher, he became "an authentic image of the crucified and risen Christ." His spiritual sons in the Stigmatine Congregation today carry that same image to the faithful in Italy, the United States, Brazil, Canada, Chile, the Ivory Coast, England, Tanzania, Thailand, and the Philippines.

Gaspar was born at Verona, Italy, on October 9, 1777, the son of Francis and Brunora Ravelli Bertoni. His father was a prosperous lawyer and notary. He was baptized the day after his birth, in keeping with the deep faith of his family, and he had a happy childhood save for the death of his beloved sister. Gaspar was educated at home and then at St. Sebastian's School, where Jesuits served on the faculty. The Jesuit Order had been suppressed in 1774, and the Jesuits had to find employment in other institutions. The Marian Congregation was also involved in Gaspar's training.

Gaspar Bertoni

On the day of his first Holy Communion, Gaspar received his first mystical experience and the grace of a priestly vocation. He entered the seminary and was in his first year when the revolutionary troops of France entered northern Italy in 1796. These troops occupied Verona on June 1, 1796, and remained entrenched there for two decades. Wanting to alleviate the sufferings caused by such an occupation, Gaspar joined the Gospel Fraternity for Hospitals, an association dedicated to the care of the sick and wounded, and he cared for the victims of the war. He was ordained to the priesthood on September 20, 1800.

One of Gaspar's first priestly ministries was to serve as a chaplain to the sisters founded by St. Magdalen Canossa. He aided Leopoldine Naudet and Teodora Campestrini, (whose Causes have been opened by the Church) in discerning the Will of God in their lives as well. Gaspar demonstrated unflinching loyalty to the pope during these difficult days, becoming famous as a spiritual director and preacher.

When Pope Pius VII was seized by the French and removed to a place of imprisonment at the command of the French emperor Napoleon Bonaparte, Gaspar was a conspicuous leader in the European-wide movement to offer prayers and support for the captive pontiff. He also established Marian Oratories, organized free schools for disadvantaged youngsters, and became the spiritual director for the diocesan seminary.

In 1816, just one year after the final defeat of Napoleon at the famed battle of Waterloo, Gaspar was at last able to found the Stigmatines, with the aim of having them serve as "Apostolic Missionaries for the assistance of the bishops." Sts. Mary and Joseph were designated as patrons of the congregation. The Stigmatines, the Congregation of the sacred Stigmata of Our Lord Jesus Christ, was founded on November 4, 1816. One year later, Pope Pius VII conferred upon Gaspar the title of "Apostolic Missionary."

Gaspar also spread devotion of the Espousal of Mary and Joseph and of the Five Wounds of Christ. His physical sufferings began in 1812, when he suffered an attack of fever following an ecstasy. At the end of his life, these physical trials increased, and he endured three hundred operations on his infected right leg, calling his hospital bed "the School of God." Gaspar continued to inspire and guide others throughout his physical ordeals. He offered his life as an oblation, even as he served as the "angel of counsel" for many. Gaspar's death on Sunday, June 12, 1835, brought a great response from the faithful of Verona and Rome. He was beatified by Pope Paul VI in 1975. Pope John Paul II canonized him on November 1, 1989, declaring: *"It is significant to note that St. Gaspar Bertoni drew up a project of Christian life which foresaw for all people, regardless of their state of life, the call to holiness; not only for priests, but also for husbands and wives, following the example of the Holy Couple of Nazareth. It was a call to youth, to workers, and to every other type of person."*

Royal Patroness and Defender of the Faith

The men and women on the thrones of European countries of the past were raised to act only for God and their people. Personal desires and ambitions were denied them as part of the royal privileges, and they were expected to endure all things. Hedwig, queen of Poland, was a monarch raised in this traditional manner. Also revered as Jadwiga, she is one of the most honored saints of her homeland because she sacrificed her personal happiness with a devout heart.

HEDWIG

(D. 1399)

❧

LAY

RELIGIOUS

Hedwig was born in Buda, Hungary, in 1374, the daughter of King Louis of Poland. At the age of nine she was betrothed to William, duke of Austria, and she came to love him. The Diet, or parliament of Poland, did not have romantic ideals and did not consider Hedwig's personal needs as vital elements of the succession to the throne. The members of the Diet ruled against the marriage and the subsequent alliance with Austria, and they dissolved the betrothal without allowing Hedwig a personal opinion. William then tried to elope with her, hoping to force the Diet into accepting him, but he failed in his efforts.

In 1384, ten-year-old Hedwig was crowned the queen of Poland. From the moment of her coronation, she understood the duties of the crown, surrendered any thought of marrying William, and accepted the Will of God that she should serve her people. In 1386, she married Grand Duke Ladislas Jagiello of Lithuania, forming a political alliance that served both countries well. Before the wedding, tradition reports that Hedwig covered herself with a thick black veil and went to the cathedral of Krakow. There she prayed for courage and resolve and to receive the grace to keep to the obligations of her station in life. Hedwig left the black veil draped over the crucifix in the cathedral to symbolize her acceptance of her own cross. She was still a child, but she knew enough about crowns and courts to recognize her own destiny. This act was a token of

Hedwig, Queen of Poland, by Marcelo Bacciarelli

her surrender to God's Will for her and for her people.

Hedwig was married to the Grand Duke in a wedding ceremony that was the social highlight of the era. For Hedwig, the wedding symbolized in a new and terribly personal way the sacrifices that she was being called to make for her country.

Jagiello's father had died in 1377, and the new duke faced a rival for the throne of Lithuania, a cousin named Vytautas. By marrying Hedwig, he consolidated his political position and became the king of Poland. A pagan, Jagiello agreed to have himself and the entire population of Lithuania baptized if he married Hedwig. He also agreed to compensate William, duke of Austria, for losing his regal love.

Both Hedwig and Jagiello faced difficulties because of the political unrest in the region. Aided by Hedwig, Jagiello baptized the people of Lithuania; thus, the Teutonic Knights, who were attacking both countries, could not use the excuse that they were invading a pagan country or one with a pagan king. The kingdom soon became one of the truly devout Christian regions in Europe, remaining firm in the faith into the modern age. Having offered her title, her talents, and her entire life to service of Christ, Hedwig obtained permission from Pope Boniface IX to establish a faculty of theology at Krakow University and instituted programs for the sick and poor of many nations, putting her devotion to Christ into charitable actions.

Hedwig and her firstborn child, a daughter, died in childbirth in Krakow on July 17, 1399. She was beatified in 1896 by Pope Leo XIII, and was honored for her commitment to the duties of her throne and the demands of her station as a royal.

Pope John Paul II canonized Hedwig on June 8, 1997, on the Blonia Esplanade in Krakow, in the presence of more than one and a half million of her devout countrymen and women. There the Holy Father declared: *"I thank Divine Providence that this privilege has been given to me, that I have been allowed to fix my gaze, together with you, on this figure who reflects the splendor of Christ, and to learn what it means to say 'the greatest thing is love. . . .' She gave the whole nation the example of love of Christ and of man, of man who is hungry for faith and knowledge, as he is also for daily bread and clothing. God grant that this example will also be drawn from today, so that the joy of the gift of freedom may be complete."*

Carmelite Founder of the Congregation of St. Teresa

One of the great obligations of each and every Christian is to carry the Light of Christ into the world. Each human being is asked to be a Christ-bearer, an instrument of goodness, charity, and truth in an age plunging into mediocrity and sterility of the spirit. It takes a particularly courageous individual to carry such commands into the common arena of competing ideas and values, but the Light of Christ must illuminate the growing shadows and the mists of doubt and confusion. Henry de Ossó y Cervelló of Spain accepted the obligation, and in a turbulent era he responded with generosity, fervor, and innovative methods of reclaiming souls. His Carmelite spirit served as the impetus for his personal holiness and for his remarkable achievements in the world.

HENRY (ENRIQUE) DE OSSÓ Y CERVELLÓ

(D. 1896)

FOUNDER

He was born in Vinebre, a small town in Tarragona province, Spain, on October, 16, 1840, the son of Jaime and Micaela de Ossó y Cervelló. His mother fostered his priestly vocation, but his father was opposed to such a career and sent Henry to an uncle to study the textile business. Henry was only twelve when he made this move to Quinto de Ebro, and within a few months became seriously ill. Henry's father tried again to apprentice him elsewhere, this time in Reus, but once more illness brought the boy home.

In September, 1854, Henry's mother died of cholera in a terrible epidemic. He was sent again to Reus by his father, but he fled the textile training by going to Montserrat Monastery. His brother, James, found him there and took him home, and Henry's father recognized the possibility of a priestly vocation for Henry. Moved by a lecture on the life of St. Teresa of Ávila, Henry took the decisive step of entering the priesthood. He studied at Barcelona and Tortosa and was ordained on September 21, 1867, and celebrated his first Mass at Montserrat. One of his classmates was Blessed Emmanuel Domingo y Sol.

Henry declared that the life of St. Teresa of Ávila had spurred his priestly vocation, and he took upon himself the arduous task of reforming and renewing the faith in Spain. Appointed a teacher of mathematics in the Tortosa seminary, he continued his apostolate of preaching and missions until the local bishop removed him from his faculty obligations, which allowed Henry to dedicate himself full-time to education and catechetics. He was tireless in his efforts, using modern methods to appeal to young and old, and he established many programs, including the Institute of Josephine Brothers and the Teresian Missionaries. The Company, or Congregation of St. Teresa, was his crowning achievement. This congregation was dedicated to forming "Teresians" who would carry the Carmelite spirit into the world, and the congregation received papal approval in 1877, extending its mission to Algiers in 1885. Today these sisters serve in Spain, Portugal, Africa, and Mexico.

Henry also recognized the growing impact of the press on the society of his day, and viewed the arena of communication as a distinct apostolate that had to be undertaken by the faithful. A prodigious writer, Henry started a weekly publication, *El Hombre (The Man)*, and another called *El Amigo del Pueblo (The Friend of the People)*. This was followed by *Revista Teresiana (The Teresian Review)*, a magazine of Carmelite tradition that became popular in Spain. Henry understood and praised the unique apostolate of women in the world, and he offered them specialized publications on prayer and the spiritual life.

Henry hoped to establish a foundation for men, the Josephites, but he was not able to achieve this goal. He went to Valencia to see Blessed Emmanuel Domingo y Sol, and on January 27, 1896, suffered a stroke. He died soon after in Gilet and was buried there. In July, 1908, his remains were transferred to the chapel of the Company of St. Teresa in Tortosa.

Pope John II beatified Henry in 1979 and canonized him in Madrid on June 16, 1993, declaring that this new saint was faithful to God's call, understanding that his *"first and fundamental contribution to the building of the Church itself"* was his own holiness. The Holy Father said that the Catalan province of Spain could rejoice in a son who served as a symbol of the spiritual wealth of the faith in the region.

Martyr of the Confessional

History is filled with the tragedy of religious strife and the sorrowful willingness of many believers to slaughter their doctrinal opponents. A priest named Jan Sarkander stands today as a canonized image of the tragedy of such Christian disunity. His courage, his fidelity, and his sense of decency should illuminate the new debates about faith and church membership. His example pleads eloquently for unity in Christ.

JAN SARKANDER

(D. 1620)

MARTYR

Jan was born at Skotschau, Silesia, in the modern Czech Republic, on December 20, 1576, where he was raised devoutly. During those years, the region was deeply divided by the Protestant Reformation and the lingering hostility of the Hussites, zealous reformers who fought a long and bitter war with orthodox Catholics and who plunged Bohemia and Moravia into chaos and war.

Jan was educated by the Jesuits at the Society's college in Prague, in the modern Czech Republic, and went to the seminary to complete his studies. In 1607, he was ordained a priest at Grozin, where he was already demonstrating holiness and a staunch loyalty to Catholic doctrines and ideals.

His first assignment in 1613 was to Boskowitz, where he served as a curate. Jan was then transferred to the town of Holleschau, in the diocese of Olmütz, in modern Slovakia, in 1616. As he tried to serve the Catholic people of the region, he was continually harassed by a local land owner, Bitowsky von Bystritz, who intended harm to the Church. Jan was not intimated by the land owner, and his constancy and courage made Bitowsky a fervent and unforgiving enemy. Jan was undaunted, and with the aid of Jesuit priests, he converted two-hundred Hussites and Bohemian brethren. His patron in this ministry was Baron von Labkowitz of Moravia.

The eruption of the Thirty Years War in 1618 engulfed Hollenschau and the faithful. Protestants raised armies to put down Catholic authorities and occupied Hollenschau, prompting Jan to go to Krakow, Poland, for a time. He could not leave his parishioners defenseless, however, and resolved to stand with them no matter what perils came his way. Jan returned to Hollenschau and faced the Protestant insurgents.

In 1620, Polish troops moved into the region, and Jan, carrying the Blessed Sacrament, went to the military commanders to plead for the safety of Hollenschau. His courage saved the region from further bloodshed, and the people gave thanks to God for being spared the same ravages that were destroying so much of Europe.

Bitowsky von Bystritz, however, realized that this act of bravery on Jan's part provided him with a ready excuse for revenge. The land owner denounced Jan as a Polish spy and traitor. Jan's protection of Hollenschau was used as evidence, and he was arrested and taken to Olmütz. There a committee of Protestants employed terrible punishments to make Jan break the confessional seal and condemn Baron von Labkowitz. The torture was attended by a Catholic judge, Johann Scintilla, who reported the grim proceedings to Franz Cardinal von Dietrichstein.

Jan was placed on the rack, and on three separate days he was racked for two or three hours at a time. When he remained true to his priestly vows and did not incriminate Baron von Labkowitz, the Protestants soaked Jan in sulfur and feathers and set him on fire. Pitch and oil were hurled at him to increase the burns.

Even after such horrific tortures, Jan did not break his silence, and he was thrown into cell by his frustrated captors. There he lingered in agony for almost a month, receiving additional cruelties by the guards. He finally died on March 17, 1620, and immediately was declared a martyr for the faith. His remains were placed in the cathedral of Olmütz, and he was beatified in 1859 by Pope Pius IX.

Pope John Paul II canonized him at Olomouc, in the Czech Republic on May 21, 1995, and during the ceremonies Jan's fearless defense of the faith and his overwhelming charity were honored. Jan was praised for his suffering in order to protect the confessional seal. His courage and his charitable ministry to his parish were declared hallmarks of his holy life.

Thaumaturgist and Foundress

Jeanne Delanoue enjoyed success in the secular world, but she responded to Christ's call and entered into a life of service and sacrifice. In turn, God gave her many graces, including those of a thaumaturgist, a miraculous healer. In the service of Christ, Jeanne led countless other young women to religious commitment prompted by the Holy Spirit.

JEANNE OF THE CROSS DELANOUE

(D. 1736)

FOUNDRESS

Born in Samur, Anjou, France, on June 18, 1666, Jeanne was the youngest of twelve children in the Delanoue family. Her father was a draper, and her mother operated a religious-goods business in Samur. Bright and ambitious, Jeanne took over the religious business when her mother died in 1691, and proved quite capable of assuming the rough-and-tumble competition in that era. Jeanne earned the respect of other tradespeople by being a wise and shrewd woman who understood the value of work and profits.

Jeanne's life took an abrupt turn, prompted by the Holy Spirit. During the season of Pentecost, in 1698, Jeanne experienced two separate revelations about the truth of human life and labors. She had a vision and heard the pious exhortation of a widowed pilgrim from Rennes, a woman named Frances Souchet. The two events changed Jeanne's outlook on life entirely. Her concern about profits and success paled in the light of Christ's command of charity. Her tidy life, bound by customs, traditions, sales, and net gains, seemed a sterile wasteland when she took a hard look at the suffering around her.

Jeanne closed her shop, much to the astonishment of her neighbors, and began to visit the poor, the sick, and the abandoned. The orphans of Samur were her special concern, and she furnished three houses donated by admiring benefactors, turning them into havens for all in need. More and more companions joined Jeanne in her apostolate, including her niece. In 1704, with her young relative and two trusted members of her group, Jeanne founded the Sisters of St. Anne of Providence of Samur. Jeanne became Jeanne of the Cross.

Two years later, encouraged by St. Louis de Montfort, Jeanne leased a large house from the Oratorians. She began caring for children, poor women, and the sick of Samur. Obstacles did not deter her, and she received canonical approval from the bishop of Angers. She also practiced penance and mortification and was revered for her miracles of healing. By 1721, her sisters were starting new foundations throughout France. She died in Fencet on August 17, 1736.

Pope Pius XII beatified Jeanne in 1947. Pope John Paul II canonized her on October 31, 1982, the same day that the pontiff canonized St. Marguerite Bourgeoys. The Holy Father called Jeanne *"a great prodigy of charity,"* declaring that *"when we proclaim the holiness of Jeanne Delanoue, it is important to try to understand the spiritual secret of her peerless dedication. It does seem that her temperament led her to an interest in the poor through sentimentality or pity. But the Holy Spirit himself led her to see Christ in the poor, the Christ-Child in their children — she had a particular devotion to him — Christ the friend of the poor. Christ himself, humiliated and crucified. And with Christ she wished to show to the poor the tenderness of the Father. To this God she had recourse with the audacity of a child, expecting everything from him, from his Providence, the name with which she designated her homes and her foundation from their very origin, the Congregation of St. Anne of Providence. Her constant devotion to Mary was inseparable from that of the Blessed Trinity."*

Members of the Society of Jesus

Americans remain remarkably unaware of the martyrs of the New World. Few Catholics in the United States know anything about the more than one hundred missionaries and their companions who died bringing the Gospel of Christ to the uncharted wilderness of the continent. The Americas were a grand stage for the spreading of the faith from the first appearance of Europeans in the north and the south. Countless men and women laid down their lives in these Americas so that their blood could nourish conversions and bring about graces for all believers.

JESUIT MARTYRS OF PARAGUAY

(D. 1628)

MARTYRS

The Jesuit Martyrs of Paraguay belong to this illustrious honor roll of the Christian faith. They were three native Paraguayans who traveled from the estuary of the La Plata River, beyond the Mbaracayu Mountains, even to the areas now part of southern Brazil. Entire villages and communities came into existence because of their efforts, and they brought a message of love and spiritual union to the native populations. The leader of these three Jesuit missionaries was Roch Gonzalez, and he was accompanied by Alphonsus Rodriguez and John de Castillo. They are the first American martyrs raised to the altars, beatified in 1934 as the Martyrs of Paraguay.

Roch Gonzalez was born in Anuncíon, Paraguay, in 1576 to a noble Spanish family. Educated well, he studied for the priesthood and was ordained at age of twenty three. He joined the Society of Jesus, the Jesuits, in 1609, and immediately became a forceful advocate of the so-called reductions (from the Spanish *reducciónes*, or settlements), the Jesuit missions where native Americans lived in self-sufficient communities free from the exploitation that was a sad aspect of Spanish colonial activities in South and Central America. He headed the first reduction in Paraguay and founded six others in the Paraná and Uruguay River areas. Dedicated to the care of all the Paraguayan tribes, Roch and his companions opposed strongly the colonial policies of Spain, the operations of the Inquisition, and the enslavement of the native peoples.

In 1626, Roch joined his Jesuit companions, Alphonsus and John, in founding a new reduction, called All Saints. Working together, the missionaries decided to expand their efforts and involve other, more distant tribes. Roch and Alphonsus went to Caaró, in what is now a region in the southern tip of the nation of Brazil. There they opened All Saints chapel and began mission programs.

Roch found himself the target of a local medicine man's hatred. While they tried to make friends, the Jesuits were rebuffed and resented. On November 15, 1628, Roch was hanging a small bell at the Church of All Saints. One of the henchmen of the medicine man came up from behind and struck Roch with a hatchet. Alphonsus was attacked as well, and his body was placed in the chapel beside Roch. The henchmen then set fire to the chapel. John received word of the martyrdom two days later. He was himself attacked soon after — the native tribesmen bound him and then stoned and beat him to death.

The three Jesuits were beatified in 1934 by Pope Pius XI as the Martyrs of Paraguay, the first American martyrs to be so honored. Pope John Paul II canonized Roch and his companion martyrs in Asunciòn, Paraguay, on May 16, 1988, calling them models of holiness for all Christians. The Holy Father said: *"Neither the obstacles of the wilderness, the misunderstanding of people, nor the attacks of those who saw their evangelizing activity as a threat to personal interests, could intimidate these champions of the faith. Their unreserved self-offering led them to martyrdom. . . . The entire life of (Roch) Gonzalez de Santa Cruz and his companion martyrs was completely characterized by love: love for God and, in him, for all people, particularly the most needy, those who did not know of Christ's existence or had not yet been liberated by his redeeming grace . . . the fruits did not take long in coming. As a result of their missionary activity, many people abandoned pagan worship to open themselves up to the light of the true faith."*

John de Castillo ❧ **See Jesuit Martyrs of Paraguay.**

JOHN OF DUKLA

(D. 1484)

RELIGIOUS

Franciscan Missionary

There are human beings on earth who do not take this world seriously. They are not blinded by the world's lights nor consumed by its appetites. They recognize that they are pilgrims journeying through time and existence and are moving steadily, irrevocably to eternal realms. John of Dukla had this unique knowledge, this awareness of pilgrimage, and he served only one master, Jesus Christ.

John was born in Dukla, Galicia, Poland, circa 1414 in a vast farming area where the faith was practiced devoutly and men and women labored long and hard. John learned the faith and the virtues from those who understood the earth as God's creation and lived with the stately procession of the seasons of the year.

John was an intensely prayerful man, and he began his religious life as a hermit, living away from the world in silence and in secret places of contemplation. In time he came to understand that he was to minister to the world and to the souls seeking salvation. Accordingly, John entered the Conventual Franciscans and was ordained. From 1440 to 1463 he labored as a preacher, and he was elected superior of the monastery because of his holiness and sound judgment.

After serving his term in the monastery, John traveled as a missionary to the area of Lvov, in the Ukraine. There a group of Observant Franciscans, called the Bernardines, were conducting their ministries. John was attracted by the Bernardine spirit and transferred to that branch of the Order.

Combining the contemplative and active life styles, John was able to continue his recollected prayer and yet serve the needs of the faithful of the area. He preached everyday, heard confessions, and radiated the light of Christ in activities. People recognized his intense holiness and flocked to him in the confessional, listening intently as well when he preached in the churches.

He was stricken with blindness in the last years of his life, but he did not retire from his pastoral duties. John preached and found his way to the confessional by groping along the pews. He died in Lvov, on September 29, 1484, a beloved priest and a mourned counselor, and his remains were buried in the local cemetery. In 1945 his body was taken to Rzeszow and then to Dukla, where the Bernardine Fathers serve as custodians of his shrine. He was beatified in 1733 by Pope Clement XII.

Pope John Paul II canonized John in Krosno, Poland, on June 10, 1997, during a visit to that country. The pontiff prayed at John's tomb, pronouncing that *"Blessed John earned fame as a wise preacher and zealous confessor. Crowded around him were people hungry for sound doctrine of God, to hear his preaching or, at the confessional grill, to seek comfort and counsel. . . . The written accounts say that despite old age and his loss of sight, he continued to work, and asked to have his sermons read for him so as to be able to go on. He would grope his way to the confessional so as to be able to convert and lead them to God."* The canonization ceremony was witnessed by half a million people, and the Holy Father stated that John of Dukla served only Christ, adding: *"Imitating without reserve the example of his Master and Lord, he desired above all to serve. In this consists the Gospel of wisdom, love, and peace. He gave expression to this Gospel in the whole of his life."*

God has his own "friends," and few of these are in the media spotlight as they toil day after day to alleviate the suffering in the world. Known only to those whom they serve, they are sometimes revered and sometimes mocked and despised. Often when such "friends" die, the world suddenly wakens to its loss, to the realization that holiness and genuine charity have passed from the earth.

JOHN GRANDE (ROMAN)

(D. 1600)

RELIGIOUS

John Grande, who called himself "the Sinner," was just such a "friend of God." He lived in another era, in another clime, but his deeds transcend cultural and national traditions to whisper truths to the people of each new age.

John was born in Carmona, Andalusia, Spain, on March 6, 1546. He went to Seville at the age of fifteen where he apprenticed in the linen business with a relative before returning home to start his own business. At age twenty-two, he was drawn to the religious life, and seeking total union with God, he gave away his possessions and became a hermit near Marcena.

He left his hermitage when he discovered the suffering of people around him. He went to Jerez de la Frontera where he cared for prisoners for three years and called attention to the terrible conditions in a local hospital. With the patronage of a wealthy couple in the area, John established a new hospital which he affiliated with the Order of Hospitalers. He became a member of the Order, bringing his unique abilities and virtues to the Order's various ministries.

Blessed with mystical gifts, John foretold the destruction of the Spanish Armada. He continued to care for prisoners and orphans and established projects and institutions for their nurturing. At the same time, he demonstrated holiness and inspired all who came into contact with him. John did not expect gratitude from those he served. He also did not give in to the officials who resented the standards that he imposed upon them and their charitable institutions.

John gave dowries to poor young women so they could find husbands, and he fed and clothed prisoners and fugitive Spaniards from Cadiz. In 1600, a plague struck Jerez de la Frontera, killing three hundred citizens in a day. John devoted his time and energies to caring for such victims, eventually falling ill himself. He died on June 3, 1600 at Jerez de la Frontera, mourned by all who had long regarded him as the guardian of Jerez. He was beatified in 1853 by Pope Pius IX.

Pope John Paul II canonized John on June 2, 1996. At the ceremony, John was honored not only for his heroic service to others but for his intense prayer life that served as a wellspring of grace, energies, and compassion. "John the Great Sinner" is a favorite saint of Spain.

Martyr of China

John Gabriel Perboyre, the Vincentian martyr of China and that nation's first saint, competed with his beloved brother, Louis, in all things. This familial bond led, in turn, to one of the most heroic displays of Christian fortitude on record.

John Gabriel was born on January 6, 1802, in Le Puech, in the diocese of Cahors in southern France, the son of Pierre and Marie Rigal Perboyre. One of eight children in the family, John had great devotion to his brother, Louis. but he also served as a model for their childhood companions.

JOHN GABRIEL PERBOYRE

(D. 1840)

MARTYR

John Gabriel attended a preparatory school with Louis at Montauban, and there he received the grace of a religious vocation. John Gabriel joined his brother and entered the Congregation of the Mission of St. Vincent de Paul in December, 1818. Two years later, he made his vows as a Vincentian and studied for the priesthood. He was ordained in Paris and then assigned to the seminary at Saint-Fleur where he taught dogmatic theology.

In 1832, John became assistant director of the Vincentian novitiate in Paris, but his heart was in the missions of China. Louis had sailed to these missions and had died there, prompting John to take his brother's place in this foreign assignment. He requested that he be allowed to go to the Far East, and he received such permission in 1835. John Gabriel left Europe on March 21 of that year and arrived in Macao on August 29. There he studied Chinese and adjusted to the new climate and the exotic culture.

He began his mission in June, 1836, and two years later was assigned to Hebei, or Hou-Pé, in the area of the Yangtze Lakes, where he taught the faith and watched with growing concern the mounting official attitude of hostility toward Europeans and the Christian religion. England had attacked China in 1839 as part of the terrible First Opium War, and the Chinese were retaliating against missionaries throughout the land. John Gabriel tried to carry on his labors by avoiding the authorities, but he was betrayed by a neophyte catechist. He was arrested and brought to trial at Cha-Yuen-Keu on September 16, 1839.

Stripped of his priestly garments, he was clothed in rags and dragged from village to village, facing new tribulations and renewed charges. John was tortured at each new hearing; he was regularly hanged by his thumbs and beaten with bamboo rods.

In the face of inhuman cruelty, John Gabriel did not swerve from his love of Christ or the Chinese faithful. He endured his torments with resignation to God's Will, giving praise even as his life was drained in excruciating suffering.

Upon reaching the town of Wuhang, John Gabriel was condemned to death after even more torture. He and seven criminals were executed on September 11, 1840. John Gabriel was tied to a cross on the crest of a hill called "the red mountains," and strangled with a rope. He was declared venerable by Pope Gregory XVI in 1843, and was beatified by Pope Leo XIII on November 9, 1889. Pope John Paul II canonized John on June 2, 1996, declaring his heroism and generosity in service, even unto death.

Physician of Naples

The books of saints and martyrs are filled with exciting examples of men and women who left their homes, families, and friends to perform the tasks designated for them by God and by charity. But there are other kinds of saints in the modern world, inspiring individuals who do not seek cloisters, hermitages, or the far-flung missions. They bring a special grace to their normal activities, elevating their skills and concerns to a level of service that gives praise to God and brings unique graces into the world of human affairs.

JOSEPH MOSCATI

(D. 1927)

PHYSICIAN

Joseph Moscati was a physician of Naples, Italy, who understood the way of service and the sanctification of the everyday routines of life. A man of intense prayer, his chapel was a classroom or clinic.

Joseph was born in Benevento, Italy, on July 25, 1880, where he was raised devoutly in a troubled political era that caused much suffering for the poor of the land. Joseph had a keen interest in medical matters from an early age and began the formal study of medicine in Benevento and then Naples. He furthered his studies in local schools and at Naples University, where he received a medical degree with a specialty in research.

Joseph became famous for his medical skills and soon was appointed a professor at the university. An inspiration for young doctors, he sought always to bring Christ into the realm of medicine and conducted himself with amiable piety. He emulated Christ by using his skills and knowledge to benefit those who were without the means to afford adequate medical care.

Joseph spent many hours each morning conducting clinics for the poor in the region and assisting them with programs to improve the living conditions and the health of their children. Prompted by his piety and the faith, he tried especially to better conditions for the families condemned to live in the slums of the area around Naples. His presence in these wretched communities prompted other leaders to take an interest, especially in the welfare of the very young children of the city. The squalor, filth, and despair of the Neapolitan slums were exposed by Joseph, who made an effort to instill order, cleanliness, and, above all, Christian charity to the sick, abandoned, and destitute. Joseph did not use his position in society for his own benefit but labored among the poor until his death on April 12, 1927. He was beatified by Pope Paul VI in 1975 as a model of medical charity.

Pope John Paul II canonized Joseph on October 25, 1987. At the ceremony, the new saint was honored for his dedication and his sanctification of ordinary tasks assumed by caring people. Joseph is revered as a physician who carried Christ into the hovels of Naples, an individual who understood that each human being on earth must use his or her individual gifts to serve God and better the lives of those in need. The pope added:

from Faces of Holiness

Dr. Joseph Moscati

"In his constant rapport with God, Moscati found the light to better understand and diagnose illnesses and the warmth to be able to draw near to those who, in their suffering, looked for sincere participation on the part of the doctor assisting them.

"From this deep and constant reference to God he drew the strength that sustained him and that allowed him to live with the honesty and rectitude in his delicate and complex setting, without giving in to any form of compromise. He was a Head Physician in the hospital, but without ambition for positions: if he was appointed to them, it was because his merits could not be denied, and when he occupied them, it was with total integrity and for the good of others."

Theatine Cardinal

Truly brilliant, gifted individuals are chosen by God to place their abilities and talents at the service of the Church and the faithful around the world. Joseph Maria Tomasi, a prince of the Church, was such a man. Obedient to the Will of God, Joseph Maria learned to serve in the vaulted corridors of power and in the cramped catechetical centers of poor parishes. A Theatine cardinal and a scholarly mystic, Joseph Maria was also a confessor to Pope Clement XI (r. 1700-1721).

JOSEPH MARIA CARDINAL TOMASI

(D. 1713)

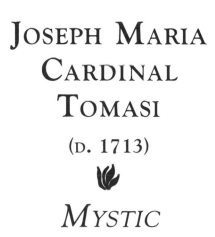

MYSTIC

He was born in Alicata, Licata, Sicily, on September 12, 1649, the son of the Duke of Palermo, and was destined by his princely family for court service. But he received the grace of a religious vocation, and joined the Clerks Regular of the Theatine Order at Palermo on March 24, 1665. In order to become a Theatine, Joseph Maria had to renounce his princely titles and privileges in favor of his brother. He was professed on March 25, 1666.

Sent to Messina to continue his studies, Joseph Maria was stricken with poor health. He recovered and went on with his seminary training at Ferrara, Modena, Rome, and Palermo. He was ordained a priest on December 25, 1673. The years that Joseph Maria spent in seminary brought him considerable attention because of his intellectual prowess and his skills in language. He knew Greek, Ethiopian, Arabic, Syriac, Chaldaic, and Hebrew, converted one of his professors from Judaism through his intellectual sincerity and faith, and specialized in the study of Scripture, the Psalms, and Patristic writings. He wrote many treatises and liturgical works, including an edition of Augustine's *Speculum,* an *Antiphonarium,* the *Codices Sacramentorum,* and a *Psalterium.* Many of his works appeared under the pseudonym of J.M. Carus. He taught that true wisdom rests in the restoration and maintenance of past revelations and knowledge, not just in the embrace of new information alone.

Also revered for his holiness and spiritual graces, Joseph Maria was summoned to the Vatican by Pope Innocent XII (r. 1691-1700) in 1697, and he was appointed theologian to the Congregation of Discipline of Regulars in 1704. Joseph Maria became confessor to Cardinal Albani and ordered him under pain of mortal sin to accept the papacy as Pope Clement XI in 1700. He was, in turn, forced to accept the cardinalate in 1712 from Pope Clement XI on the same condition.

Joseph continued his labors for the Church, but he also experienced visions, cared for the poor, taught catechism to children, and was famed for the abiding pastoral concerns he took for his titular parish in Rome. As his mystical experiences increased, he was known to perform miracles of healing and was provided with many abilities of prayer and grace. Joseph Maria died in Rome on January 1, 1713, and was mourned by all of Rome, from the pope and College of Cardinals to the humblest and poorest of the Eternal City. He was beatified in 1803 by Pope Pius VII.

Pope John Paul II canonized Joseph Maria on October 12, 1986. During the ceremonies the holy prince of the Church was lauded as a true servant of Christ and the "prince of liturgists." His mystical graces and his total surrender to Christ mark him as one of the unique saints of his century.

Capuchin Franciscan

Every human being on earth has at least one secret ambition, one silent dream that haunts the everyday tedium and teases the senses. Some may dream of being adventurers, caped-crusaders, movie stars, stellar athletes, or astounding scientists. Almighty God sometimes asks very special souls to relinquish their secret ambitions in order to serve him and the Church. The manner in which such souls put aside their own desires serves often as the foundation for their perfection.

LEOPOLD CASTRONOVO (MANDIC)

(D. 1942)

CONFESSOR

Leopold Castronovo was such a human being, such a special soul. A Franciscan confessor and spiritual director, he had to surrender his heart's fiercest desire in order to accomplish God's Will in his life, and with this obedience he brought untold graces to the people who came into his presence.

He was born on May 12, 1866, in Castelnuovo, on the southern tip of Dalmatia, Croatia, the son of a devout local Croat family. The twelfth child born to the Mandics, he was baptized Adeodatus. Though always small in stature (he stood four feet five inches as an adult), his faith spanned the world. He wanted to be a foreign missionary, declaring that in his heart and mind he was always "beyond the seas."

Leopold entered the Capuchin Franciscans at Udine, Italy, in response to the grace of a priestly vocation, and he was professed in the Order in 1885. Entering the Franciscan seminary, Leopold completed his studies and was ordained a priest in Venice in 1890. He was given various assignments in the Order's houses, and was sent to Padua in 1906.

World War I shattered Italy and the rest of Europe in the following decade. Leopold was taken prisoner by Austrians and spent one year in a camp where he ministered as a priest to his fellow inmates. When he was released, Leopold asked to be sent to the foreign missions, but he was assigned by his superiors to various houses, where he labored as a confessor and spiritual director. Leopold's holiness, and his unique insight into human souls, led his superiors to make such a decision. He possessed a remarkable ability to discern graces and was much needed in the ongoing care of the faithful. Despite his longing for mission duty, Leopold served as a spiritual director and confessor for the next four decades of his life.

Leopold was always frail, and he suffered from severe stomach ailments and chronic arthritis. These conditions were aggravated by his unending labors in parish confessionals, though Leopold did not complain and did not seek rest. In time, he walked with a pronounced stoop, and arthritis crippled his hands severely. He maintained his grueling schedule and kept his devotion to Our Lady of Sorrows. Leopold had not given up his desire for the foreign missions, but he had resolved to accept the Will of God. He died in Padua on July 30, 1942, in the midst of the Second World War. His funeral was attended by the many souls who had been touched by his pastoral gifts. Beloved and deeply respected in Rome, he was beatified by Pope Paul VI in 1976.

Pope John Paul II canonized Leopold on October 16, 1983, declaring him the saintly hero of the confessional. The Holy Father added: *"His greatness lay . . . in immolating himself, in giving himself, day after day, for the entire span of his priestly life, for fifty two years. . . ."* The pope called Leopold *"the confessor"* who was *"a missionary in another sense."*

Foundress of the Canossian Daughters of Charity

At some point each man and woman on earth seeks a way of starting over, of putting all things right, by mustering the courage to achieve the good works that were originally intended. A new beginning. Life does not allow many new beginnings, and yet, a few individuals have had the daring to turn their back on all the familiar aspects to seek unknown horizons.

MAGDALEN OF CANOSSA

(D. 1835)

FOUNDRESS

At the start of the nineteenth century, a woman named Magdalen of Canossa made a new beginning in her young life, and this dramatic turn of events both confounded her world and brought consolations to the young of her generation. Seeing Christ Crucified, Magdalen could not respond by doing anything less. She united herself to Christ and began an apostolate of total charity.

She was born Magdalen Gabrielle in Verona, Italy, on March 1, 1774, the daughter of the Marquis Ottavio of Canossa and Marchioness Maria Teresa Szlugh. Her father was a naturalist and geologist, a descendant of an ancient aristocratic family. Her mother was a court attendant and lady-in-waiting to Empress Marie Therese's court in Vienna, Austria. When Magdalen was only five, her father died suddenly. While her mother followed all appropriate customs of mourning and maintained the family estate, when she remarried two years later she left Magdalen and her four siblings in the care of their uncle Jerome and the estate servants.

Magdalen suffered a number of major illnesses as a child, but her strength increased as she matured. Uncle Jerome and others discovered as well that she had dedicated herself to Christ and intended to embrace the religious life. She made a prolonged retreat at a nearby Carmelite convent, and for a time she wanted to be a Carmelite. This proved impossible when she assumed the burdens of the family estate at age nineteen. Magdalen proved herself to be a skilled administrator, even when Napoleon, some of his officers, and a troop of his cavalry arrived at her castle door seeking lodgings. The French leader called Magdalen "an angel" and treated her with much respect throughout his stay.

By 1803, Magdalen's family members had started to assume responsibilities for the affairs of the estate. She was free to start her own apostolate, which centered on needy children and on the dream of providing every young boy or girl an education. She opened a school in 1805 in an abandoned Augustinian monastery, reportedly ceded to her by Napoleon, who was now Emperor of France. The young women who joined her in the school became the first sisters of her congregation, the Canossian Daughters of Charity. Magdalen started the congregation in 1808 and saw her sisters laboring in Bergamo, Milan, Trent, and Venice. Today there are about 4,000 members of the congregation, with 395 houses in many countries.

She displayed great holiness in this work, using what she called "the fire" of charity to aid others. Spiritually, Magdalen was a gifted mystic, known to have received many graces. She experienced ecstasies and visions, and she was said to levitate during prayer. A model of charity, she also suffered severe physical problems in her later years, bearing them heroically. Magdalen died in Verona on April 10, 1835, and her remains were enshrined in a marble sarcophagus. She was beatified in 1941.

Pope John Paul II canonized Magdalen of Canossa on October 2, 1988, saying that her life was Christ's alone. The Holy Father declared: *"When she realized the frightful sufferings which material and moral misery had spread among the population of her town, she saw that she could not love her neighbor 'as a lady,' that is by continuing to enjoy the privileges of her social class, and merely sharing her possessions without giving herself . . . charity consumed her like a fever, charity towards God, driven to the heights of mystical experience; charity toward her neighbor, carried to the furthest consequences of self-giving to others. . . ."*

Marek Krizin ❧ **See Martyrs of Kosice.**

Foundress of the Congregation of Notre Dame of Montréal

The New World, a panorama of wilderness and splendor, beckoned explorers and adventurers who blazed new trails and opened rare vistas. In their wake came stalwart missionaries who trekked across the crests and valleys to bring the Gospel of Christ to the native peoples of the untamed continent. In time, of course, entire families entered the New World hoping to put down roots and to start new cities in the

MARGUERITE BOURGEOYS

(D. 1700)

❧

FOUNDRESS

uncharted lands. The families entering Canada in the seventeenth century changed the frontier forever because they brought culture, traditions, human ambitions, and dreams into the wilderness of the Americas.

Heroic men and women blazed new trails in this undertaking, but these were highways of the spirit, the paths of devotion that nurtured the faith and inspired true acts of charity. Marguerite Bourgeoys was one those early heroic individuals, and in time she would be called "the Mother of the Colony" because her love embraced all who dared to face the challenges of the frontier. The foundress of the Congregation of Notre Dame of Montréal, she was an indomitable pioneer in education in Canada.

She was born in Troyes, France, on April 17, 1620, the sixth child of twelve in the family of Abraham Bourgeoys and his wife, Guillemette Garnier. Raised devoutly and educated by her family, Marguerite enjoyed a healthy, happy childhood. Her father was a wax-chandler in Troyes. At age twenty, Marguerite received the grace of a vocation during her prayers on the Feast of Our Lady of the Rosary, and applied at the convents of the Carmelites and the Poor Clares. She was not accepted. Marguerite was, at the time, a Sodalist, attached to the convent of Augustinian Canonesses. A priest in whom she confided her disappointment, Abbé Gendret, advised her that God perhaps had chosen her for an active apostolate.

In 1653, Paul Chomody de Masonneuse, the governor of the French settlement in Canada, then a fort called Ville-Marie, arrived in Troyes to visit his sister, an Augustinian Canoness. He was introduced to Marguerite and decided that she was the woman destined to start educational programs in Ville-Marie, the site that rose in subsequent years as the city of Montréal. Marguerite accepted the governor's invitation and set sail in June, 1653, landing in Québec in September and going overland to Ville-Marie with vigor and hope.

There were two hundred people living there at the time, and the fort was equipped with a small hospital and a Jesuit mission chapel. Marguerite looked after the colony's children and helped in the school, which was located in a stone stable. She had an assistant, but she realized that more young women were needed for the apostolate. Marguerite returned to Troyes to recruit other teachers, including her friend Catherine Crolo. She returned with three young women and expanded the school to meet the needs of the growing colony. When the Iroquois War ended in 1667, Marguerite, seeing the city of Montréal taking shape in the wilderness, added classes for Indian children and introduced a Marian Sodality.

In 1670, she returned to France to recruit more teachers and to receive a letter of patent, an authorization from King Louis XIV for her school. Marguerite brought six more young women with her, and this last contingent made it possible for her to start the Congregation of Notre Dame, canonically erected by the Bishop of Québec, Blessed François de Laval, in 1676. Marguerite envisioned an active apostolate and had to stand firm over the years to keep her sisters from being enclosed or amalgamated with the Ursulines. The sisters endured life without formal religious profession until 1698. The rule and constitution were formally approved on June 24 of that year.

Marguerite endured fires, the deaths of two of her sisters — including her niece — and extreme poverty. Marguerite did not distinguish between the races in her apostolate, and she set a precedent in the New World when she received two Iroquois young women dedicated to Notre Dame de Bon Secours. On Mount Royal in Montréal, she also opened a school for Indian girls. That school moved to Sault au Recollect in 1701 and to the Lake of the Two Mountains in 1720.

In 1689, she was invited by Bishop de Saint-Vallier to start a house of the congregation in Québec. Though advanced in age, she made the long journey to Québec on foot. Four years later, Marguerite was allowed to resign as the superior of the congregation. She was seventy-three, and she had given her life to the people of Montréal, all the while demonstrating unfailing devotion to the faith and to the apostolate of her congregation.

In 1699, Marguerite's health had declined and she prayed that she might die in the place of the young novice mistress of the congregation who was seriously ill. The young novice mistress recovered, and three days later, on January 12, 1700, Marguerite died serenely. She was declared venerable in 1878 and beatified in 1950 by Pope Pius XII.

Pope John Paul II canonized Marguerite on October 31, 1982, declaring that *"in particular she contributed to building up that new country (Canada), realizing the determining role of women, and she diligently strove toward their formation in a deeply Christian spirit. . . . Marguerite Bourgeoys deemed it no less indispensable to do all in her power to lay the foundations for sound and healthy families. She had then to contribute to the solution of a problem very particular to that place and time. . . . Marguerite Bourgeoys went in search, with her great educative know-how, of robust French girls of real virtue. And she watched over them as a mother, with affection and confidence, she received them into her home in order to prepare them to become wives and worthy mothers, Christians, cultured, hard-working, radiant mothers."*

Foundress of the Sisters of Charity

As nations emerge and evolve, a certain awareness of the historical precedents of the founding of such states develops as well. The great nation of Canada, sharing the North American continent with the United States and Mexico, is one of the countries of the world that can trace its faith and moral values directly to the tenets and traditions of the Catholic Church. Although political and military interventions ended the domination of the original

MARGUERITE D'YOUVILLE

(D. 1771)

FOUNDRESS

Marguerite D'Youville

devout French colonizers, the Catholic Faith bequeathed by these pioneers has not been diminished by time. One major demonstration of this lasting legacy is the numbers of saints and blesseds raised to the altars by Pope John Paul II.

The first Canadian elevated to the rank of saint is Marguerite d'Youville, called by Pope John XXIII the "Mother of Universal Charity." She was born Mary Marguerite Dufrost de Lajemmerais in Varennes, Canada, on October 15, 1701, to Christopher and Renée de Varennes Dufrost de Lajemmerais. Her brother was Lavérendrye, the famed explorer who discovered the Rocky Mountains.

Marguerite was educated by the Ursulines in Québec but at age twelve had to return home to aid her widowed mother. In 1722, she married François d'Youville and bore him six children, four of whom died young. François was engaged in the illegal liquor trade and was a wastrel. He treated Marguerite rather indifferently, but when he fell ill, she cared for him for two years until he died in 1730. Marguerite had to take up a small trade in order to support her children and to pay off her dead husband's debts. At the same time, she was caring for the poor.

While working and raising her remaining sons, who became priests, Marguerite still found time and energy to support the Confraternity of the Holy Family in Québec. She had particular devotion to the Eternal Father, trusting in his divine providence. During this period, Marguerite was also able to save a local hospital, originally founded in 1694. She administered the hospital and gathered companions to form a new congregation designed to offer the people of Québec medical care imbued with Christian charity. The women lived in a small house, and in June, 1753, received permission to incorporate their activities. On August 25, 1755, Marguerite and her companions received a gray habit. (The rule of the Sisters of Charity, called the Gray Nuns, had been approved years before.)

In 1747, Marguerite was given charge of General Hospital in Montréal. Under her leadership the hospital cared for disabled soldiers, epileptics, the aged, the insane, the incurables, and lepers, providing as well a haven for orphans and abandoned children. Hôtel Dieu, as it was called, rose as a medical testimony of

Christian virtue. The sisters made clothing for military troops in order to maintain themselves and their patients. During the French and Indian War, as the Seven Years' War was called in North America, Marguerite cared for English prisoners captured by French forces. She also defended the institution against meddlesome government bureaucrats who would have limited her charity.

When the hospital was destroyed by fire in 1766, Margaret knelt in the ashes to sing the *Te Deum*, accepting the terrible loss with religious calm. She died on December 23, 1771, in Montréal. Declared venerable in 1890 by Pope Leo XIII, she was beatified in 1959 by Pope John XXIII.

Pope John Paul II canonized Marguerite on December 9, 1990, declaring that *"More than once the work which Marguerite undertook was hindered by nature or people. In order to work to bring that new world of justice and love closer, she had to fight some hard and difficult battles."* The Holy Father added that Marguerite's holiness *"continues to bear fruit."*

Mark Krizevcanin ❧ See Martyrs of Kosice.

Foundress of the Sisters of Our Lady of Consolation

One of the pressing needs of modern society is the presence of people of good will who also know what they are doing. Only those who bring realistic concerns and skills to the challenges facing today's world will succeed in accomplishing much-needed ministries in this era. Maria Rosa Doloribus Molas y Vallvé understood full well what was needed in her age. She is called by many an "apostle of mercy," and she could be styled "the apostle of practicality and common sense" as well. One of the premier reformers and champions of the poor, Maria Rosa was intelligent, alert, and willing to adapt her Christ-centered ministry to meet the growing needs around her.

MARIA ROSA DOLORIBUS MOLAS Y VALLVÉ

(D. 1876)

❧

FOUNDRESS

She was born in Reus, Spain, near Tarragona, in the northeastern part of the nation, on March 24, 1815. Her parents operated a small store in Reus, and Maria Rosa was raised in a very devout environment. When she was seventeen, Maria Rosa's mother fell victim to an outbreak of cholera and died. Maria Rosa had long desired a religious vocation, but now her father would not allow her to leave home. She remained with her father until she was twenty-six. Then she went to join a group of nuns operating a hospital and almshouse. Maria Rosa demonstrated not only religious virtues as a nun but a practical awareness of order, discipline, and the need for administrative skills in providing care to the sick and needy.

Her greatest trial in this area came when she was made superior of the House of Mercy in Tortona, Spain, a dumping ground for the mentally ill. There were three hundred inmates in that institution, and the medical care being administered was inadequate and injurious to the patients. Maria Rosa established modern methods of hygiene, proper medical procedures, and common-sense order to the entire institution. She separated the vulnerable infants and established wards that employed medical standards and improved care.

For eight years Maria Rosa maintained an institution that met the improved medical requirements of the time. She then discovered that the congregation in which she was professed was not constituted in a valid manner. Debating their next move, Maria Rosa and twelve companions placed themselves under the jurisdiction of the local bishop. He had witnessed Maria Rosa's dedication, administrative skills, and personal holiness and had no doubts about allowing her to found the Sisters of Our Lady of Consolation in 1857. These sisters were organized to care for people everywhere, and they have focused on the poorer regions of the world, carrying on Maria Rosa's apostolate of mercy.

Maria Rosa did not confine her work to the hospital — she also served as a mediator in disputes, and in 1843, she crossed a military battle line in order to negotiate a cease fire during an attack on the city of Reus. Maria Rose died in Tortona on June 11, 1876, and was beatified in 1977 by Pope Paul VI.

Pope John Paul II canonized Maria Rosa on December 11, 1988: *"The existence of this woman, imbued with charity, totally committed to the neighbor, is a prophetic proclamation of the mercy and consolation of God. . . . The life of Maria Rosa, spent in doing good, translated for the people of her time and for those of today into a message of consolation and hope . . . . Mother Maria Rosa is one of those persons chosen by God to proclaim to the world the mercy of the Father. She had the charism to be an instrument of reconciliation and of spiritual and development."*

Lawrence Ruiz and Dominican Religious

MARTYRS OF JAPAN

(D.C. 1630)

🔥

MARTYRS

In times past, men and women dared to sail half way around the world to seek the salvation of souls. Their sacrifices, sometimes ending in the ultimate surrender of their lives, are difficult to understand in this day and age when most people will not walk across the street to speak the Good News of Christ. What modern Catholics do not grasp is the simple fact that the Church would not exist as a universal, vital force in the world if saints and martyrs of old had not made the ultimate offering of their own precious lives. Nor do modern Catholics know that not all of these martyrs were priests or religious, especially in the nation of Japan.

Lawrence Ruiz and his companions are honored as martyrs in Japan. Members of this group were put to death during a five year period, joining thousands who died rather than deny Christ and the faith. This was a time of severe persecution of the Church in Japan, and though the Church was faced with near extinction under the weight of the oppression, it survived and flowered.

Lawrence Ruiz was a layman from Manila in the Philippines. Married and a devout Catholic, he devoted himself to assisting the Dominicans in their mission activities in the Philippines, demonstrating both selfless devotion and courage in often difficult and hostile situations.

As a skilled mariner, Lawrence was asked by the Dominicans to aid them in making a secret voyage to Japan. As the island nation was in the throes of a bitter persecution of the Church, the Dominicans — and Lawrence — were acutely aware that they risked torture and death in order to bring the sacraments to Catholics residing in Japan. Lawrence discussed the voyage with the friars Dominic Ibañez de Erquicia, Jacob Kyshei Tomonaga, and thirteen other members of the Order (including Fathers Michael Anzaraza, Anthony Gonzales, William Cowtet, Vincent Shiwozuka, and Lazarus of Kyoto), agreeing without hesitation to land the Dominicans on the shores of Japan.

The vessel was soon caught in a severe storm at sea and veered off course. After a long ordeal on the high seas, the ship crashed on the shore of Okinawa, which was then under Japanese control. Japanese authorities arrived on the scene quickly and arrested Lawrence and his Dominican passengers.

Every member of the party endured unspeakable torture at the hands of their captors, lingering for many days in abject agony. They were treated with special cruelty for being members of a religious Order. Gradually, one by one, they died from their injuries and the terrible cruelties. Not one abjured the faith, and each displayed astonishing courage, determination, and loyalty to Christ and his Church.

The Martyrs of Japan were canonized by Pope John Paul II on October 18, 1987. The pope had beatified Lawrence and the Dominicans in Manila, the Philippines, in 1981. At the canonization ceremony, the heroism and zeal of these missionaries and their lay companions were honored. These martyrs and their thousands of Japanese comrades in death remain symbols of one of the most remarkable compilations of sacrifice in the history of the Church.

(The Martyrs of Japan canonized by Pope John Paul II should not be confused with the other Martyrs of Japan made famous by the example of St. Paul Miki and his companions. They were martyred in the late sixteenth century and were canonized in 1862 by Pope Pius IX.)

Andrew Kim and Companions, Missionary Martyrs

Few nations on the face of the earth have demonstrated the unique welcoming of Christ and his missionaries as displayed by the Korean people. In most lands, men and women wake up one morning to discover Christians in their midst, hearing the Good News of the Gospel for the first time because missionaries have arrived unbidden on their doorstep. In Korea, the Gospel was known and revered long before any priest dared to enter the country. Actually, the Church was invited into Korea by a convert to the faith.

MARTYRS OF KOREA

(D. 1791-1867)

MARTYRS

The title Martyrs of Korea has been bestowed upon Andrew Kim and 102 companions who died at the hands of brutal opponents of the faith over a period of years. These martyrs represent the more than eight thousand Koreans who died in demostration of the faith in their native land, displaying calm bravery and heroic fidelity.

The Catholic Faith was brought to Korea in a unique fashion, the result of curiosity by the intellectuals of the land who were anxious to learn as much about the outside world as possible. They discovered some Christian books produced through Korea's embassy to the Chinese capital, and one Korean, Niseung-houn, went to Beijing in 1784 to study Catholicism. There he was baptized by Peter Ri. Returning to Korea, he converted many others. In 1791, when these Christians were suddenly viewed as foreign traitors, two of Ri's own converts, Paul Youn and Jacques Kuen, were martyred. This is hardly surprising even though it was tragic. Korea had long been the victim of foreign aggression, in particular by Japan. The Hermit Kingdom — as Korea has traditionally been termed — was always concerned about alien powers overcoming the nation once again. As the Empires of Europe were at that time extending their spheres of influence across Asia, the Koreans were doubly concerned about the Christian faith, seeing it as a prelude to possible Western attack and as a threat to traditional Korean life.

Despite these obstacles, the Catholic Faith endured in Korea so strongly that three years after the martyrdoms of Youn and Kuen, Fr. James Tsiou, a Chinese, entered the kingdom and discovered more than four thousand Catholics awaiting his arrival. He labored in the country until 1801 when Korean authorities martyred him.

Pope Leo XII (r. 1832-1829) established the Prefecture Apostolic of Korea in response to a plea from Korean Catholics who needed a greater Church structure for the growing community. In 1836, Bishop Lawrence Imbert managed to enter Korea, despite the fact that the government had banned all foreign influences and was hostile toward all non-native religions. Others followed the

Bishop Imbert, who labored until 1839 when a full scale persecution claimed his life and the lives of other European missionaries.

Meanwhile, Korean young men who wished to enter the priesthood were sent to Macao, which was owned by China but administered by Portugal. There they were trained and ordained. Andrew Kim Taegon was the first native priest ordained. He returned to Korea in 1845 and was martyred the following year.

Severe persecutions continued, and Korean Catholics fled to the mountainous regions where they established new parishes in exile. In 1864, the Korean government instituted a new persecution, one that claimed the lives of two bishops, six French missionaries, a Korean priest and 8,000 Korean men, women, and children.

Some of the better known martyrs are:

Andrew Kim ☙ The first priest to die for the Catholic Faith in that nation. He is sometimes called Andrew Kim Taegon. Andrew was a member of one of the highest-ranked noble families in Korea. He was educated in the faith, and despite the threat of persecution, he maintained his devotion even when a government-sponsored program began in earnest in 1939 in all regions of the land.

Andrew went to Macao, where he received seminary training and was ordained. He returned to Korea to labor in the missions but was arrested by the authorities almost immediately after reaching his homeland. Joining his countrymen and European missionaries in prison, Andrew was martyred by Korean officials.

Lawrence Imbert ☙ Born in Aix-en-Provence, France, Lawrence entered the Paris Foreign Missions Society and was ordained with the express hope of serving the Church in its distant missions. His aspirations were fulfilled in 1825 when his superiors decided he was ready for missionary work and sent him to China. There he labored for over a decade and proved himself so capable and respected a missionary that he was named titular bishop of Capse.

In 1837, he entered Korea in secret and devoted himself to the very difficult task of assisting the faith in the kingdom. Known as *Bom* among the Koreans, he added his strength to the growing Catholic population, eventually surrendering to Korean authorities in 1839 when the persecutions worsened. Korean Catholics were being tortured to reveal the whereabouts of foreign missionaries, and, rather than have innocent men, women, and children die to shield him, Imbert gave himself up as did Fathers Philibert Maubant and James Honoré Chastan on August 11. After severe beatings, they were beheaded in Gae Nam Do, near Seoul, on September 21, 1839.

Columba Kim ☙ A devout laywoman, Columba was martyred with her sister, Agnes, in 1839. She was twenty-six when arrested. Imprisoned, the women were pierced with red hot awls and scorched without mercy. Stripped of their clothes, they were placed in a cell with male criminals, but, to the surprise of their captors, the prisoners refused to harm them. Columba complained about such treatment for women, even Catholics — who were criminals in the eyes of the Korean government — and the authorities heeded her objection, ceasing the practice. Nevertheless, Columba and Agnes were sentenced to death and were beheaded at Seoul on September 26.

Peter Ryau 🔥 A Christian Korean, Peter was only thirteen when he presented himself to the authorities as was demanded by the law of the land. For what his captors considered obstinate devotion to an outlaw creed, Peter was tortured with such excessive cruelty that his arms and legs were shredded. To demonstrate to the judges the severity of his treatment, Peter pulled away some of his torn flesh and threw it at their feet. The horrified judges were joined by an equally stricken group of on-lookers, and Peter was taken back to the prison and strangled on December 31, 1839.

Companions 🔥 Others are commemorated in this glorious gathering of the blessed, including: thirteen-year-old Peter Yu Tae-Chol, slain for confessing the faith; Anna Pak A-gi, a simple woman who was not advanced in her doctrinal knowledge but went faithfully to death as a disciple of Christ and his Mother; John Nam Chong-sam, a high-ranked noble who served as a model of chastity, charity, and poverty until he was slain; Damien Nam Myong-hyok and Mary Yi Yon-hui, both martyred, were models of family life; and John Yi Kwong-hai, who dedicated himself in celebrating consecration to the service of the Church.

The Martyrs of Korea were canonized by Pope John Paul II on May 6, 1984, in Seoul, Korea. At the ceremony, the Holy Father declared that the Church in Korea was a community unique in the history of the Church. The pope said: *"The death of the martyrs is similar to the death of Christ on the Cross, because, like his, theirs has become the beginning of new life."*

Members of the Society of Jesus

In the past, wars and murders were committed in the name of Christ and were carried out with a stunning ferocity. Marek Krizin, also known as Marek Korosy or Mark Krizevcanin, was a victim of these atrocities committed in the name of religion. With two Jesuit companions, Stephen Pongracz and Melchior Grodecz, Marek was martyred at Kosice, Slovakia, by Calvinist troops invading the region.

MARTYRS OF KOSICE

(D. 1619)

JESUIT CONFESSORS

Marek was from a well-known Croat family. He studied at the Germanicum in Rome and then became a canon in Esztergom, Hungary. Concerned deeply about the loss of the faith in the region around Kosice and inspired by the model of St. Peter Canisius, he accepted assignment to Kosice with the express hope of regaining Catholic vigor among the inhabitants. His Jesuit companions came from different backgrounds. Stephen

Pongracz was a Hungarian, and Melchior Grodecz, also called Melchior Grodziecky, was a Czech.

Taken prisoner by the Calvinist forces, the three priests suffered abuse and torments, but they did not deny the faith. Their captors, enraged by their loyalty to the pope and the Church, killed them. All were honored as martyrs and were beatified in 1905 by Pope St. Pius X. Pope John Paul II canonized them on July 2, 1995, as the Martyrs of Kosice.

"The Apostles bore this witness to Jesus by their words, their example and their blood. After them countless others down the centuries have put these words of Christ into practice, even to the point of making the supreme sacrifice. The Holy Martyrs of Kosice also belong to these noble ranks. By their example and their intercession, they also encourage believers of the present generation not to draw back when faced with the difficulties which faithful adherence to the demands of the faith can occasion."

Martyrs of Paraguay 🔥 **See Jesuit Martyrs of Paraguay**.

Andrew Dung Lac and One Hundred Sixteen Companions

The age of the martyrs did not end with the fall of the Roman Empire. Many men and women willing to make the ultimate sacrifice for the faith have died in the far-flung places of the world in the last few centuries. The Catholic people of Vietnam, for example, were shedding their blood and enduring torments in an era of the world considered one of enlightenment and progress. They were the victims of regimes that suppressed European ideals and religious values that threatened their stranglehold on the land. Vietnam and its neighboring states lived under this terrible cloud of horrors and pain in a modern era where thousands perished

MARTYRS OF VIETNAM

(D. 1798-1861)

MARTYRS

because they dared to seek liberty, faith, and full dignity as human beings.

Andrew Dung Lac and 116 companions suffered martyrdom at the hands of government officials of Vietnam. Bishop Valentine Berriochoa, Théophane Venard, Bishop Jerome Hermosilla, and others were imprisoned and tortured before being executed by the Vietnamese, who were highly inventive in methods of abuse, torment, and humiliation. These officials visited terrible ordeals upon the Catholics in their prisons.

The story of the Catholic Church in Vietnam commenced in 1533 when a Portuguese missionary arrived in the kingdom. An imperial edict against Christianity soon made it impossible for the religion to take root until 1615, when the

Jesuits established a permanent mission in the central region of the kingdom. In 1627, a Jesuit went north to establish another mission, and by the time this missionary, Father Alexander de Rhodes, was expelled in 1630, he had baptized 6,700 Vietnamese. In that same year the first Christian martyr was beheaded. More Catholics were executed in 1644 and 1645.

Father Rhodes returned to Vietnam, but he was banished once more in 1645. He then went to France, where the Paris Seminary for Foreign Missions was founded — the Society for Foreign Missions. Priests trained in the Society soon arrived in Vietnam, and the faith underwent a period of swift growth.

Between 1798 and 1853, a period of intense political rivalry and civil wars in Vietnam, sixty-four known Christians were executed. They were beatified in 1900 by Pope Leo XIII. In 1833, all Christians were ordered to renounce the faith and to trample crucifixes underfoot, and that edict started a persecution of great intensity that was to last for half a century. Twenty-eight martyrs from this era were beatified in 1909. The bishops and priests, Europeans, were given "a hundred wounds," disemboweled, beaten, and slain in a host of terrible ways.

For a brief period in 1841 the persecutions abated as France threatened to intervene with warships, but in 1848, bounties were placed on the heads of the missionaries by a new emperor. Two priests, Fathers Augustin Schöffler and John LouisBonnard were beheaded as a result. In 1855, the persecution gained speed, and the following year wholesale massacres began. Thousands of Vietnamese Christians were slain, including four bishops and twenty-eight Dominicans.

It is estimated that between 1857 and 1862, 115 native priests, 100 Vietnamese nuns, and more than 5,000 of the faithful were martyred. Convents, churches, and schools were razed, and as many as 40,000 Catholics were dispossessed of their lands and exiled from their own regions to starve in the wilderness or in the jungles. The martyrdoms ended with the Peace of 1862, brought about by the surrendering of Saigon and other regions to French colonial forces and the payment of indemnities to France and Spain.

Also called the Martyrs of Tonkin or Annam, the Martyrs of Vietnam include ninety-six Vietnamese, eleven Spaniards, and ten French missionaries. Pope John Paul II canonized them collectively on June 19, 1988. Among the better known martyrs of this group are the following:

Andrew Dung Lac An Tran ❧ A native of Vietnam, Andrew was educated in the faith and ordained a priest. He served in the Catholic missions in Vietnam until the persecutions brought about untold sufferings among the Vietnamese Christians. The priests associated with the Foreign Mission Society of Paris were particularly singled out for harsh treatment, and Andrew was arrested with St. Peter Thi and joined his fellow martyrs in prison. There they endured hideous tortures and abuse. (Missionaries were slain in several hideous fashions, sometimes after months of imprisonment.) Andrew shared his sufferings with St. Théophane Venard, St. Thomas Thien Tran, St. Emmanuel Phung Van Le, St. Hieronymus Hermosila, St. Bishop Valentine Berriochoa, and others. He was beheaded on December 21, 1839.

Andrew Thong Kim Nguyen 🍃 Andrew was born in 1790 in Vietnam and grew up a respected member of his village, even serving as mayor. When the persecutions were started by the Vietnamese government, Andrew was exiled from his village because of his devotion to the Catholic Faith. He died from exhaustion and dehydration during the forced march of all Christian prisoners to Mi-Tho in 1855.

Andrew Trong Van Tram 🍃 A native of Vietnam, Andrew was born in 1817 and, while raised a Catholic, he decided to follow a military career in his native land. He also aided the Paris Foreign Mission Society which was then conducting missionary and parochial operations in Vietnam. Discovered by Vietnamese authorities in 1834, Andrew was stripped of his military rank and put into prison in Hué. The following year Andrew joined his companions in martyrdom after refusing to abjure the faith. His mother was present at her son's death in Hué. Andrew was beheaded, and his mother knelt beside the executioner's block to catch his severed head in her lap.

AnthonyQuynh (Nam) 🍃 Anthony was born in 1768 and studied medicine, becoming a physician. A Catholic, he aided the missionary labors of the Paris Foreign Mission Society in Vietnam and was arrested for his association with the European missionaries in 1838. He was kept in prison for two terrible years. During his imprisonment, Anthony cared for his fellow martyrs and endured many tortures and abuses. He was strangled in prison in 1840.

AnthonyDich Nguyen 🍃 Anthony was a wealthy farmer, much esteemed. He supported the Paris Foreign Mission Society in Vietnam and was a generous patron of the Church. He also sheltered priests who were fleeing the government authorities during the persecutions in that land.

St. James Nam, a priest, sought refuge in Anthony's residence and was hidden for some time. The authorities discovered Anthony's activities and arrested him. After torture and abuse, Anthony was beheaded in 1838.

Augustine Huy Viet Phan 🍃 A companion of St. Nicholas Thé in death, Augustine was born in Vietnam and served for a time as a soldier. A Catholic, he joined fellow soldier St. Nicholas in aiding the missionary labors of the Church. Both were arrested and condemned to death in 1839. They were stretched on a rack and sawed in half.

Augustine Moi Van Nguyen 🍃 Augustine was a native Vietnamese who worked as a day laborer. He studied the faith, became a Dominican tertiary, and was known for his piety and charity. When the persecution of the Church raged in Vietnam, he was ordered by authorities to step on a crucifix as a visible sign of his abjuring the faith. He refused and was strangled.

Augustine Schöffler 🍃 One of the French missionaries to die for the faith in Vietnam, Augustine was born in Mittelbronn, Lorraine, France, in 1822, and studied for the priesthood. After receiving training as a member of the Paris Foreign Mission Society, Augustine was sent to Vietnam in 1848. He was soon caught up in the persecution of that era, and was arrested by the authorities. He was martyred by beheading in 1851.

Bernard Due Van Vo ❦ Bernard was born in Vietnam in 1755 and converted to the faith. After becoming a Catholic, Bernard studied for the priesthood. He was ordained and subsequently served for decades in various missionary labors on behalf of the faith in the country. Bernard was eighty-three when he was arrested and beheaded by government authorities in 1838.

Dominic (Nicholas) Dat Dinh ❦ A native of Vietnam, Dominic embraced the faith and was serving in the army when arrested during the persecutions of the faith by order of the Vietnamese government. Refusing to deny the faith, Dominic was stripped of his military position and strangled in 1839. It is possible that he was a Dominican tertiary.

Dominic Henares ❦ A Spaniard by birth, Dominic became bishop-coadjutor to St. Ignatius Delgado in Vietnam, serving as vicar apostolic of the region. When the government sponsored persecution of the Church started, Dominic was arrested with his catechist, St. Francis Chieu. They were imprisoned and beheaded. Dominic died praising God and proclaiming his faith.

Dominic Trach (Doai) ❦ Dominic was a native of Vietnam, born in 1792. A devout Catholic, he became a Dominican tertiary and became a priest. Ordained for the mission in his native land, Dominic labored in his own country until his arrest in 1842. He was beheaded by the Vietnamese authorities.

Dominic Uy Van Bui ❦ Born in Vietnam in 1813, he lived as a devout Catholic for many years, performing duties as a catechist for the local community. When the persecution erupted in Vietnam, he was seized and ordered to abjure the faith. He refused and was strangled at age twenty-six in 1839.

Dominic Hanh Van Nguyen ❦ A native of Vietnam, Dominic was a devout Catholic and studied for the priesthood. After ordination, he labored in his country for decades. At the time of the severe persecution of the Church in Vietnam, Dominic was arrested and martyred at age sixty-seven.

Dominic Xuyen Van Nguyen ❦ A native of Vietnam, he was ordained for the Dominican missions and gave his life to the cause of advancing the faith among his people. When the persecutions started, he was arrested with St. Thomas Du. They were beheaded.

Emmanuel Trieu Van Nguyen ❦ Born in Vietnam in 1756, he was raised a Christian. After serving in the army, Emmanuel entered the seminary to become a priest of the Paris Foreign Mission Society. He returned to Vietnam after ordination and was arrested while visiting his mother. Taken to a prison, he was beheaded by government officials.

Francis Xavier Can Nguyen ❦ Francis was a native of Vietnam, born 1803 in Sou Mieng, and a catechist. Francis aided the missionary labors of the Paris Foreign Mission Society and was arrested by government authorities. He was strangled in prison when he refused to abjure the faith.

Francis Chieu Van Do ❦ A native of China, Francis was born in 1796, embraced the faith, and then devoted himself to aiding the priests in their Vietnamese mission. He was arrested by government authorities with St. Dominic Henares, a bishop, whom he was serving. They were beheaded together in 1838.

Francis Gil de Frederich 🔥 Francis was born in Tortosa, Spain, in 1702, and was educated at Barcelona. He entered the Dominicans and after his studies was sent to the Philippines as a missionary. After laboring there for a time, in 1732 Francis was assigned to Vietnam. He performed his missionary duties until his arrest in 1742 or 1743 and was martyred by beheading.

Francis Isidore Gagelin 🔥 A French martyr in Vietnam, Francis was born in Montperreaux, France, in 1799 and entered the Paris Foreign Mission Society. He was sent to Vietnam in 1822, and was ordained to the priesthood there. When the government instituted a renewed persecution of the Church, Francis surrendered to authorities at Bong-son. He was placed in a prison, where he was martyred by strangulation in 1833.

Francis Jaccard 🔥 A French martyr in Vietnam, Francis was born in 1799 at Onnion, in Savoy, France. Entering the Paris Foreign Mission Society, he was ordained a priest and was sent to Vietnam in 1826. He labored there until his arrest. He was martyred for the faith by strangulation in 1838.

Francis Trung Von Tran 🔥 A native of Vietnam, Francis was born in Phan-xa in 1825 and embraced the Catholic Faith. A corporal in the Vietnamese army, he was arrested and commanded to abjure Christ. When he refused, he was beheaded at An-hoa in 1858.

Hyacinth Casteñeda 🔥 A Dominican Spanish martyr of Vietnam, Hyacinth was born in Sétavo, Spain. After entering the Dominicans, he was ordained and sent to the mission in China and then to Vietnam. There he was arrested by government authorities and beheaded with St. Vincent Liem in 1773.

Ignatius Delgado y Cebrián 🔥 Ignatius was born in Spain, in 1761. Raised in a prayerful family, he became a professed Dominican. Sent to the missions in Vietnam, he labored for half a century on behalf of the faith. Owing to his skills as a preacher and an administrator, he was named vicar apostolic for the eastern region of that land and consecrated a bishop. Thus, when the persecutions of the faith were launched, Ignatius was arrested by government authorities and placed in a cage for public ridicule. He died in his cage from hunger and exposure. Pope Leo XIII beatified him in 1900.

James Nam 🔥 A native Vietnamese priest, James was associated with the Paris Foreign Mission Society. Arrested in the great persecutions by government authorities, he was imprisoned and beheaded in 1838 with Sts. Anthony Dich and Michael My.

Jerome Hermosilla 🔥 A martyred Spanish Dominican bishop, Jerome was an important leader of the Church in Vietnam during one of its darkest eras. Born in La Calfada, Spain, he was professed as a Dominican and was assigned to the mission of the order in Manila, in the Philippines. There he was ordained, and in 1828, he was sent to Vietnam to serve in the Dominican missions in the eastern region. Jerome succeeded Ignatius Delgado as vicar apostolic. Consecrated a bishop, he was soon singled out for arrest by government authorities because of his prominent position. Imprisoned, Jerome was tortured cruelly and then beheaded in 1861 with Bishop Valentine Berriochoa.

John Dat ❧ A native of Vietnam, he was born in 1764 and was ordained a priest in 1798. Arrested by authorities for preaching the Gospel, he was kept imprisoned for three months before being beheaded in 1798.

John Louis Bonnard ❧ A French Martyr of Vietnam, John was a member of the Paris Foreign Mission Society and thus dedicated to the apostolate in Vietnam. He was arrested by government authorities and beheaded at the age of twenty-eight in 1852.

John Baptist Con ❧ John was a native of Vietnam, born in 1805. A true adherent of the faith, he married and served the Church in his area as a lay catechist. In the midst of the severe persecution of the Church in the country, John was arrested and imprisoned. He was martyred by beheading in 1840.

John Charles Cornay ❧ A French martyr of Vietnam, John was born in Loudon, France, in 1809. Ordained a priest of the Paris Foreign Mission Society, he was sent to Vietnam to work for the faith. He was arrested and kept as a chained prisoner in a cage for three months, and was beaten and beheaded on September 20, 1837.

John Hoan Trinh Doan ❧ John was born about 1789 at Kim-long, Vietnam, and was educated by the missionaries of the Church in that country. Such was his faith that he entered the seminary and was ordained a priest. In 1861 John was arrested by the troops of King Tu-Duc, and executed for the faith. Pope St. Pius X beatified him in 1909.

John Thanh Van Dinh ❧ A native Vietnamese, John served as a catechist with the Paris Foreign Mission Society, laboring to bring the faith to his people. Arrested and tortured, John was martyred for the faith.

Joseph Canh Luang Hoang ❧ Born in 1765, Joseph was a native of Vietnam. He studied medicine and became a Dominican tertiary. As a prominent Catholic, he was arrested by government authorities and beheaded in 1838.

Joseph Fernandez ❧ A Spanish Dominican, Joseph served as provincial vicar in the Vietnamese mission until his death. He was born in Spain in 1775 and entered the Dominicans as a young man. Sent to Vietnam in 1805, he completed his studies and was ordained a priest with the express purpose of serving in that mission. Recognized for his abilities, he was appointed provincial vicar. Unfortunately, he was arrested soon after by authorities and martyred by beheading. He was beatified in 1900 by Pope Leo XIII.

Joseph Hien Quang Do ❧ A native Dominican of Vietnam, Joseph served as a priest in his own land, laboring in the Dominican missions until his arrest by government authorities in 1840. Joseph was beheaded for the faith at Nam-Dinh that same year.

Joseph Khang Duy Nguyen ❧ Joseph is remembered as the servant of St. Jerome Hermosilla, the Dominican bishop in Vietnam. Joseph died for the faith and loyalty to both his employer and the Church. Joseph was born in 1832, eventually becoming an aide to St. Jerome. When the bishop was imprisoned in 1861, Joseph tried to help him escape from his captivity. Caught by the authorities, he was beaten, tortured, and then beheaded.

Joseph Luu Van Nguyen ❦ A native Vietnamese, Joseph was born in 1790 and became a devout supporter of the Church and the Vietnamese missions. Arrested by government authorities, he died of tortures and abuse in a prison in Vinh-long in 1854.

Joseph Marchand ❦ A French martyr, Joseph was a member of the Paris Foreign Mission Society, the congregation that gave so many members to the cause of martyrs. He was born in Passavant, France, in 1803, and entered the Society. Assigned to the missions in Vietnam, Joseph labored there until his arrest in 1835. Joseph was martyred by having his flesh torn apart by tongs.

Joseph Vien Dinh Dang ❦ A native of Vietnam, Joseph was born in 1786 and raised a Catholic. Ordained a priest, he labored in the missions until his arrest. Joseph was beheaded.

Joseph Nghi (Kim) ❦ A native priest, Joseph was associated with the Paris Foreign Mission Society. He was arrested by government authorities during the persecution and was beheaded for the faith in 1840.

Joseph Thi Dang Le ❦ A Vietnamese soldier, Joseph was in the service of King Tu-Duc until his faith was discovered. Arrested, Joseph refused to deny Christ and was garroted in 1860.

Joseph Uyen Dinh Nguyen ❦ A martyr and Dominican tertiary, Joseph was a native of Vietnam, born in 1778. Aiding the missions of the Church, Joseph was arrested by government authorities. He died of torture and abuse in prison in 1838.

Lawrence Huong Van Nguyen ❦ Lawrence was a native of Vietnam, born about 1802. Ordained as a priest and committed to the cause of the Church in his native land, he worked for a number of years until caught up in the persecutions. Arrested and imprisoned, he suffered martyrdom by beheading in 1856.

Luke Loan Ba Vu ❦ A revered, elderly priest who labored many decades for the his people, Luke was born in Vietnam in 1756 and educated in the faith. Called to a vocation, he studied for the priesthood and was ordained. After many long decades of service to the Church and his own people, he was arrested by government authorities and beheaded in 1840.

Martin Tho ❦ A native of Vietnam, Martin suffered martyrdom with aged St. Martin Tinh. Martin was a tax collector and a devout Catholic. During the time of the persecutions, he refused to abjure the faith and was martyred in 1840.

Martin Tinh Duc Ta ❦ A native priest of Vietnam, Martin was executed at the age of eighty. Martin labored for decades in Vietnam before falling victim to the persecution. He died with St. Martin Tho.

Matthew Gam Van Le ❦ Matthew was a native of Vietnam, born in 1812. Joining the Paris Foreign Mission Society, he dedicated himself to promoting the faith. One of his achievements was to bring Christian missionaries from Singapore to Vietnam on his fishing boat. Arrested for such service in 1846, Matthew was tortured and beheaded the next year.

Matthew Alonzo Leziniana ☙ A Spanish Dominican Martyr of Vietnam, Matthew was born in Navas del Rey, Spain. Entering the Dominicans, Matthew was ordained and assigned to the Order's missions in the Philippines. He was then sent to Vietnam. After a period of service, he was arrested and beheaded in a persecution in 1745.

Matthew Dac (Phuong) Nguyen ☙ Matthew was a native Vietnamese. Born in 1801, he served as a catechist for the faith for some years until his arrest by authorities. He was beheaded near Dong-hai in 1861.

Michael HyDinh-Ho ☙ Michael was born about 1808 and was a Vietnamese nobleman in a Christian family. Rising in the royal administration, he became powerful as the superintendent of Vietnam's silk mills. When the persecution brought sufferings to the Church, Michael was not involved at first. He became more and more concerned, however, and began to take a role in protecting the faithful. For this Michael was arrested and beheaded near Hué.

Michael My Huy Nguyen ☙ A native Vietnamese, Michael was the father-in-law of St. Anthony Dich. Married with a family and a farmer by profession, he served the Church with great fidelity. Michael gave special assistance to St. Anthony in his efforts to protect the missionaries during the persecution. When St. Anthony tried to hide St. James Nam in 1838, they were arrested with Michael. All three were martyred.

Nicholas Thé (Duc Bui) ☙ A soldier of Vietnam, Nicholas served the rulers of the country with loyalty until a persecution was launched against the faith. As he was a devout Catholic, Nicholas refused to deny Christ when arrested and was racked and sawed in half for proclaiming the faith.

Paul Tong Buong ☙ A captain of the royal bodyguard of Vietnam, Paul served King Minh-Menh. As a Catholic who supported the programs of the Paris Foreign Mission Society in Vietnam, Paul was arrested in 1832, stripped of his military rank, and imprisoned. Paul suffered for months before being beheaded in 1833.

Paul Hanh ☙ Paul was one of the most unique of the Vietnamese martyrs as he was an outlaw who secretly supported the Christian community. When he was arrested as an outlaw, Paul openly professed his belief in Christ. For this he endured terrible tortures before his beheading near modern Saigon (Ho Chi Minh City) in 1859.

Paul Khoan Khan Pham ☙ Paul was born in Vietnam and studied with the Paris Foreign Mission Society. Ordained, he labored for four decades before his arrest. He was beheaded for the faith in 1840 after enduring two years of extreme abuse in a prison.

Paul Loc Van Le ☙ Paul was a native Vietnamese, born in 1831, and was a veteran of Vietnam's army before studying for the priesthood. Ordained, Paul was soon arrested and beheaded in 1859.

Paul Tinh Bao Le ☙ A priest of the missions of Vietnam, Paul studied for ordination in order to aid the evangelization of his land. When the persecution caught him, he was imprisoned and then beheaded at Sontay in 1857.

Peter Duong Van Troung ❧ A native Vietnamese, Peter suffered martyrdom with St. Peter Truat. They both served as catechists, aiding the European and Vietnamese missionaries in their evangelizing programs. For these acts of loyalty, the two were taken in the persecution of the Church and martyred in 1838.

Peter Hieu Van Nguyen ❧ A member of the Paris Foreign Mission Society, Peter was a native catechist who aided the missions. He was arrested and refused to deny Christ. Peter and two companions were beheaded in 1840.

Peter Francis Néron ❧ One of the French martyrs of Vietnam, Paul was born in Jura, France, in 1818, and studied with the Paris Foreign Mission Society. Ordained in 1848, he was assigned to the missions in Hong Kong and was then sent to Vietnam, where he headed the society's central seminary. When the persecution was launched once more by the Vietnamese government, Peter was arrested. He endured harsh treatment and suffered martyrdom by beheading in 1861.

Peter Quy Cong Doan ❧ Peter was born at Bung, Vietnam, and was a devout Christian. Ordained as a priest, he labored to evangelize his native land until his arrest. He was tortured and beheaded at Chaudoc in 1859.

Peter Thi Van Truong (Pham) ❧ Born in Vietnam in 1763, Peter was a devout priest who labored in the Catholic missions. Elderly at the time of his arrest in 1839, he was beheaded for the faith.

Peter Tuan Ba Nguyen ❧ A martyred priest of Vietnam, Peter was born in 1766. He was ordained to the priesthood and labored many years in the missions. Arrested, Peter would not abjure the faith and was condemned to death. He died in prison in 1838, from wounds received from his captors.

Peter Tuy Le ❧ A native Vietnamese priest, Peter had been raised devoutly and studied enthusiastically for ordination. Many years later in 1833, when Peter was seventy years old, he was arrested and beheaded.

Peter Van Van Doan ❧ Peter was born about 1780 and was dedicated to the evangelization of his native land. To make his contribution, Peter labored as a catechist. Arrested, Peter refused to deny Christ and was beheaded for his heroic loyalty in 1857.

Philip Minh Van Phan ❧ A priest martyr of Vietnam, Philip was born in 1815 and entered the Paris Foreign Mission Society. After studies and ordination, he returned to Vietnam and labored there until his arrest. Philip was beheaded at Vinh-hong in 1853.

Simon Hoa Dac Phan ❧ Simon was a Catholic physician and mayor of his native village in Vietnamwho aided the Paris Foreign Missions Society. Arrested in 1840, he was cruelly tortured and beheaded. Simon was beatified in 1909.

Stephen (Etienne-Theodore) Cuenot ❧ Martyred bishop of Vietnam, a French missionary bishop who gave his life for Christ. Born in Beaulieu, France, in 1802, Stephen was ordained and made a member of the Paris Foreign Mission Society. In 1833, Stephen was made vicar apostolic of Vietnam and was consecrated in Singapore as a bishop. He labored in the missions, expanding the faith, until his arrest in 1861. Stephen died in prison on November 14, possibly by poisoning, just before his slated execution.

Stephen Vinh ✤ Martyred layman of Vietnam and a devout peasant, Stephen was a Dominican tertiary. When he refused to abjure the faith, Stephen was strangled at Ninh-Tai with four companions.

Théophane Venard ✤ A French priest and martyr of Vietnam, Théophane is remembered for his service to the faith and for chanting hymns on the way to his execution. Théophane was born in St.-Loup, France and was raised devoutly in the faith. Aspiring to the missions, he entered the Paris Foreign Missions Society, received seminary training, and was ordained on June 5, 1852, for the Society's missions.

On September 19 of that year, he sailed to Hong Kong, where he labored for the next fifteen months. He was then assigned to Vietnam, to an area called Tonkin at the time. A Vietnamese royal edict condemning Christianity began Théophane's heroic ordeals on the mission. He was forced to hide in Christian villages and to conduct his ministries at night. He was also plagued by serious physical problems, having to summon up courage in order to serve his Vietnamese faithful.

Théophane maintained this grueling labor for almost four years, eluding the Vietnamese authorities that searched for missionaries with a ruthless persistence. He was captured by them on November 30, 1860. Théophane was tried and condemned to death by authoritie, but was not given the grace of a sudden martyrdom. Théophane was put into a cage and abused and tortured. He did not complain, and in a letter to his father he described his coming martyrdom by likening himself to "the spring flower which the Master of the garden gathers for his pleasure."

On February 2, 1861, Théophane was carried to the site of his execution, where, as he described the act in a letter "a slight saber-cut will separate my head from my body." Ill and wounded by his tormentors, Théophane sang hymns on his way to death. When he was slain, his head was placed on a pole and exhibited as a victory for the Vietnamese authorities. His remains were saved and eventually transferred to a shrine in Paris. He was beatified on May 2, 1909.

Thomas De Van Nguyen ✤ A layman of Vietnam, Thomas was a tailor by profession and a Dominican tertiary. Thomas sheltered missionaries and was arrested in 1839 for his activities. He was strangled with four companions for refusing to deny the faith.

Thomas Thien Tran ✤ Also listed as Thomas Dien, Thomas was a seminarian of Vietnam at the time of his martyrdom. He studied with the Paris Foreign Missions Society and was preparing to be ordained when he was arrested in 1838. Thomas was only eighteen when Vietnamese authorities scourged and strangled him.

Thomas Du Viet Dinh ✤ A Dominican tertiary and ordained priest of Vietnam, Thomas labored in the missions in Nam-Dingh. He was arrested in 1839, at the age of sixty-five, and after hideous tortures, he was beheaded.

Thomas Toan ❦ A native of Vietnam, Thomas was laboring as a catechist when arrested in 1840, at the age of seventy-three. Thomas showed signs of apostatizing, however, but he repented this weakness and stayed firm in the faith despite being scourged and exposed to the sun and natural elements for twelve days. Thomas died of his torments, still faithful to Christ.

Valentine Berriochoa ❦ A Spanish martyr, Valentine served as a bishop of Vietnam and was a companion of St. Jerome Hermosilla. Valentine was born in Elloria, Spain, later entered the Dominicans, and became known as an especially devout member of his Order. Professed and ordained, Valentine was sent originally to the Dominican missions in the Philippines, where he distinguished himself by faithful service. In 1858, Valentine was consecrated a bishop and appointed vicar apostolic of the Dominican mission territories of Vietnam.

Upon his arrival, Valentine faced the ordeals of the Vietnamese persecutions and labored under extreme difficulties. He was arrested in 1861, and was imprisoned and tortured with another Dominican bishop, St. Jerome Hermosilla. Valentine was beheaded with St. Jerome. He was beatified in 1909 by Pope St. Pius X.

Vincent Diem The Nguyen ❦ The first Dominican martyr of Vietnam, Vincent was also a noble by birth in his native land. Raised as a Catholic, Vincent became a Dominican and was ordained for the priesthood. He was soon assigned to assist St. Hyacinth Castañcda in his endeavors. Arrested in 1773, Vincent was beheaded with St. Hyacinth.

Vincent Yen Do ❦ A Vietnamese priest, Vincent was ordained in 1808 and labored in the missions until his martyrdom. When the persecutions began in 1832, Vincent went into hiding and managed to conduct his priestly ministry in secret. Betrayed to authorities, Vincent was arrested in 1838 and beheaded.

Pope John Paul II canonized all of the Martyrs of Vietnam on June 19, 1988, praising the courage and loyalty of these stalwart martyrs who aided the faithful of that land during the terrible years of persecution. The Holy Father canonized ninety-six Vietnamese, eleven Spaniards, and ten French martyrs. During the ceremony in St. Peter's Square, he stated:

"The Vietnamese martyrs 'sowing in tears,' in reality initiated a profound and liberating dialogue with the people and culture of their nation, proclaiming above all the truth and universality of faith in God and proposing, moreover, a hierarchy of values and duties particularly suited to the religious culture of the entire Oriental world. Under the guidance of the first Vietnamese catechism, they gave testimony that it is necessary to adore the one Lord as the one personal God who made heaven and earth. Faced with the coercive impositions of the authorities with regard to the practice of the faith, they affirmed their freedom to believe, holding with humble courage that the Christian religion was the only thing that they could not abandon, that they could not disobey the supreme Sovereign: the Lord. Moreover, they vigorously affirmed their desire to remain loyal to the authorities of the country, observing all that is just and right: they also taught that one should respect and venerate one's ances-

tors, according to the customs of their land, in the light of the mystery of the resurrection. The Vietnamese Church, with its martyrs and its witness, has been able to proclaim its desire and resolve not to reject the cultural traditions and the legal institutions of the country; rather, it has declared and demonstrated that it wants to incarnate them in itself, in order to contribute faithfully to the true building up of the country. . . . Once again, we can say that the blood of the martyrs is for you, Christians of Vietnam, a well-spring of grace to make progress in the faith. In you, the faith of our fathers continues and is carried on to new generations. This faith remains the foundation of the perseverance of all those who, considering themselves authentically Vietnamese, faithful to their land, also want to continue to be true disciples of Christ."

Foundress of the The Congregation of the Sisters of Jesus and Mary

The French Revolution unleashed horrors upon the world and threatened the faith in the nation called "the eldest daughter of the Church." The mob-violence, the terrors, and the suffering raised up saints who put aside their instincts for survival to succor a world in turmoil. One woman was Claudine Thévenet, revered today as Mary of St. Ignatius. The Revolution was not some distant peril in her life but an excruciating devastation that formed her into a "messenger of God's mercy and forgiveness."

MARY OF ST. IGNATIUS (CLAUDINE) THÉVENET

(D. 1837)

FOUNDRESS

She was born on March 30, 1774, in Lyons, France, and was baptized Claudine. Raised in a devout family acutely attuned to the injustices of her era, Mary of St. Ignatius saw her brothers, Louis and Francis, taken prisoner by the government authorities. In January, 1794, she saw them paraded to their deaths in Lyons and followed so that she could witness their martyrdoms while comforting them with her loving presence. As they died, Louis and Francis told her that they forgave their captors. They urged her to do the same in a heroic demonstration of charity.

She began her apostolate among the poor and abandoned, focusing on the young women active in the workforce of Lyons. In 1816, after years of labors, she established a pious union with the aid of Father Coindre. This led to the founding of the Congregation of the Sisters of Jesus and Mary two years later. Taking the religious name of Mary of St. Ignatius, she gathered pious companions and formed a community designed to provide young women with a Christian education conformable to their positions in a changing society, while instructing these women in the faith.

In this program Mother Mary of St. Ignatius established boarding schools, academies, and residences for young women of the working classes who had few resources in the secular world. She was a true model of charity, demonstrating as well an understanding of the era in which she lived. Countless young women looked to Mother Mary of St. Ignatius for education, respect, and secure lodgings in a turbulent period. She even conducted residences for ladies involved in the literary profession, a pressing need at the time. The Congregation of the Sisters of Jesus and Mary established houses at Le Puy, Rodes, and Remíremont. The motherhouse had to be established in Rome when the persecutions started in France. The sisters also started a college in Rome, imbued with the foundress's spirit of adapting to new needs.

Mother Mary of St. Ignatius Thévenet went to her reward on February 3, 1837, in Lyons. Ten years later, Pope Pius IX approved the constitution of her congregation. In 1842, members of her community started missions in India and Pakistan, including Bombay, Poonah, Lahore, Simla, and Agra. In 1850, the sisters established a house in Spain, and one was opened in Mexico in 1902. Mother Mary of St. Ignatius' spiritual daughters started their labors in Canada in 1855 and in the United States in 1877.

Pope John Paul II canonized Mother Mary of St. Ignatius on March 21, 1993, declaring her religious life was a "hymn of glory" to Christ and the imitation of the Virgin Mary: *"In the frailty of a child Claudine Thévenet discerned the power of God the Creator, in the child's poverty the glory of the Almighty, who does not cease calling and who calls us to share the fullness of life which he possesses; in the child's abandonment, Christ crucified and risen, who is ever present in his brothers and sisters, the least of people. . . . Her concept of education combines a sense of human realities with a sense of the divine. Were not the homes which she founded for the poorest girls called 'Providences'? Indeed, it was necessary to teach the young girls to manage a good household, doing the smallest chores with as much care and love as the greatest. A burning charity places her at the service of the young with respect and affection in order to permit each one to give the best of herself. . . . She ceaselessly invoked God's goodness."*

Marian Apostle

MAXIMILIAN KOLBE

(D. 1941)

MARTYR

The tragic lesson of World War II has been lost on this generation, which means that this generation may well be forced to relive the horrors of that earlier era of evil. A vile cancer of lies and murder was allowed to grow in the days before World War II and in time that cancer threatened to spread across the earth, spewing terrors and unspeakable acts of human cruelty. Nations were torn asunder before the evil of the Nazis and their allies was defeated, and countless victims perished at the hands of ruthless captors. One man chose to give his life in the brutal surroundings of a Nazi death camp, and he stands before the world today as both an insignia of a terrible age and a magnificent symbol of Christian perfection.His name is Maximilian Kolbe, and he was one of the most talented, tireless, and dedicated men of his time.

He was born in Zdunska-Wola, near Lodz, Poland, on January 7, 1894, and was baptized Raymond. At a very young age, Maximilian had a vision in which the Blessed Mother offered him a life of purity or a life of martyrdom. Fearlessly, Maximilian chose both.

Maximilian Kolbe

On September 4, 1910, Maximilian received the habit of the Conventual Franciscans and the name in religion by which he is revered on earth. He was ordained a priest in Rome in 1918, having earned a doctorate in theology and having funded the Militia of Mary Immaculate to advance Marian devotion. This group is also called the Knights of the Immaculata.

In 1920, Maximilian suffered a bout of tuberculosis and was confined to a convalescent home for two years. Recovered, he returned to Krakow, Poland, and continued his ministry in the Knights of the Immaculata. He then went to Japan and India, spreading the special devotion to those countries.

Recalled to Poland in 1939, Maximilian faced the Nazi occupiers of his homeland, realizing that his apostolate was being targeted. In that year, he was arrested by the Gestapo, but was fortunate enough to be released. In February, 1941, he was arrested again and confined in Warsaw. On May 28, 1941, with two hundred and fifty other prisoners, he was sent to Auschwitz, the Nazi extermination camp. He and the other priest prisoners were singled out for special punishment details and beaten. Throughout, Maximilian assured his companions that the Nazis "will not kill our souls." He added: "And when we die, then we die pure and peaceful, resigned to God in our hearts."

In August, 1941, Maximilian saw a Polish soldier, Francis Gajowniczek, chosen as a victim of retaliatory execution for the escape of a prisoner. He announced to the startled German commandant: "I am a Catholic priest from Poland, I would like to take his place, because he has a wife and children." Francis Gajowniczek was returned to the ranks, and Maximilian became a condemned victim.

With the nine other chosen prisoners, Maximilian was placed in a starvation unit, deprived of food and water. They did not cry or weep but recited the Rosary and sang Marian hymns. A Nazi officer was so impressed by the piety and the courage that he kept careful documentation of the days of suffering. At the end of two weeks Maximilian and three other prisoners were still alive. They were given lethal injections by the camp executioner on August 14, 1941, and their remains were cremated the next day. Maximilian was beatified in 1971 by Pope Paul VI.

Pope John Paul II canonized Maximilian Kolbe as a martyr on October 10, 1982, declaring him the *"Patron of our difficult century."* In describing Maximilian's heroism and devotion, the Holy Father said: *"The reality of death through martyrdom is always a torment; but, the secret of that death is the fact that God is greater than the torment. So then, we have before us a martyr — Maximilian Kolbe — the minister of his own death — stronger still in his love, to which he was faithful, in which he grew throughout his life, in which he matured in the camp at Auschwitz. . . . That maturing of love which filled the whole life of Father Maximilian and reached its definitive fulfillment on Polish soil in the act at Auschwitz, that maturing was linked in a special way to the Immaculate Handmaid of the Lord . . . Maximilian Kolbe, like few others, was filled with the mystery of the divine election of Mary. His heart and his thoughts were concentrated in a particular way upon that 'new beginning,' which — through the work of the Redeemer — was signified by the Immaculate Conception of the Mother of his earthly incarnation. . . . Maximilian Kolbe penetrated this mystery in a particularly profound way and complete way: not in the abstract, but in the life-filled context of the Triune God, Son and Holy Spirit, and in the life-filled context of the divine salvific plan for the world. . . . Once there arose, in the Middle Ages, the legend of Saint Stanislaus. Our time, our age will not create a legend of Saint Maximilian. The eloquence of the facts themselves, the testimony of his life and martyrdom, is strong enough."*

Model Religious and Evangelist

Even great saints of the Church can be placed to rest and then lost in the rapid pace of the centuries' compulsions to progress. Such a saint was Meinard, the Augustinian Apostle of Livonia, the area now called Latvia and Estonia in Europe. Pope John Paul II reintroduced Meinard to the modern Church, thus offering a timeless model of holiness, courage, and dedication on behalf of souls.

MEINARD

(D. 1196)

RELIGIOUS

Meinard was born in Germany, c. 1130. He entered the monastery Segelberg, founded by St. Vicelino and inherited the missionary spirit of that saint and the dedication and valor of the Augustinian Canons Regular, who were outstanding pioneers in many territories of Europe where the light of Christ had only begun to penetrate. Ordained a priest and imbued with zeal, Meinard went to Livonia, which was still a pagan region, and established himself at Ykescola, near Riga, Latvia. Consecrated a bishop in 1186, he was the first prelate of Livonia. In the castle of Ykescola, Meinard formed a community of Canons Regular, and trained members of the community were brought from Segelberg for the new foundation. They aided Meinard in forming a regional clergy and in establishing seminary standards. He was tireless in his efforts to evangelize the region and carefully consolidated the diocesan gains among the local pagans. He forged a solid Christian base before he died, ensuring growth and stability, because he was prudent and alert to the customs and views of the local peoples.

Meinard's successes in evangelization and administration were results of his heroic virtue and spiritual maturity. The graces of Meinard were attested to by Pope Clement III (r. 1189-1191) and Pope Celestine III (r. 1191-1198) in their letters. These pontiffs recognized the need for administrative abilities, coupled with holiness, in establishing new mission territories.

Meinard died in his Livonian castle on August 14, 1196. He was buried there, but his remains were translated from Ykescola to the cathedral of Riga in the thirteenth century. A monument and a sepulcher still honor his memory in the region. During the Reformation of the sixteenth century, with its political and social impacts, Meinard was forgotten by the outside world.

Pope John Paul II reintroduced this missionary giant to the faithful. He canonized Meinard in Riga on September 8, 1993, calling upon the Christians of this era to take up the Cross of Christ and the ministry of evangelization with renewed zeal.

Melchior Grodziecky ❦ **See Martyrs of Kosice.**

Christian Brother

MICHAEL (MIGUEL) FEBRES CORDERO

(D. 1910)

❦

SCHOLAR

Michael Francis Febres Cordero stands before the world as the insignia of fidelity. He did not perish in a martyr's arena; he did not evangelize whole nations. Michael Francis simply fulfilled his religious vocation as a Christian Brother with zealous perfection, becoming a glory for his native Ecuador. He also brought a brilliant and scholarly intellect to the service of the young, providing his pupils with profound horizons of expanding faith.

Michael (Miguel) Febres Cordero

Michael Francis was born in Cuenca, Ecuador, on November 7, 1854, to a prominent family. Crippled from birth, he suffered pain from his malformed feet. This early cross did not embitter him but taught him the saint's joy of suffering. At the age of five, Michael Francis had a vision and started walking for the first time. His family understood this event as a sign of God's favor and raised the boy with care and fervor, calling him Pancho in the family.

In 1863, after being tutored at home, Michael Francis entered the de la Salle Christian Brothers school, demonstrating his brilliance in the classrooms. He received the grace of a religious vocation while at the school, but his family wanted him to pursue a career in the world. In time they settled on a priestly vocation, and sent Michael Francis to the seminary at Cuenca. There he became quite ill.

Michael Francis returned to the Christian Brothers when he recovered, and in 1868, at the age of fourteen, he received the habit. He was the first native Ecuadorian to become a Christian Brother. His novitiate was made in Cuenca because of his poor health, but he flourished and started writing books in his late teens. He published his first book at age twenty, a work dedicated to Spanish grammar, and was a gifted teacher revered for his sense of humor and common sense. His personal prayer life was also intense and served as the basis for his fidelity to his vocation as a Christian Brother.

His research earned him considerable fame, and he became a member of the Academies of France, Ecuador, and Spain. Michael Francis had great devotion as well to the Sacred Heart and to the Blessed Virgin Mary. He imbued his students with the same spiritual graces, not only by instructing them but by serving as a model of such devotions. Men and women in the scientific and educational fields learned to respect Michael Francis and to appreciate the deep spiritual values that prompted all that he accomplished.

In 1907, Michael Francis visited New York, en route to Belgium. There he was asked to translate texts, and there his health deteriorated once more. He went to Premia del Mar, in Spain, to the junior novitiate of his congregation to recover, but the political unrest in that nation swept up both Michael Francis and his students. In July, 1909, when the Spanish nation was overwhelmed by a revolution, Premia del Mar was attacked. Michael Francis took the Blessed

Sacrament from the chapel and led his novices calmly to safety. As a result of these strenuous exertions, he contracted pneumonia and died in Premia del Mar on February 9, 1910. He was mourned by the faithful in many different countries around the world who had given support to his many labors.

On July 21, 1936, Premia del Mar was attacked by Spanish Communists who set fire to the chapel. During the assault, Michael Francis' coffin was opened, and his body was found to be intact. His remains were subsequently returned to Ecuador, and a young crippled boy was miraculously cured by touching the coffin in the procession through the streets of Quito.

Pope John Paul II canonized Michael on October 21, 1984. The Holy Father declared that the Church looks to St. Michael Francis Febres Cordero, the *"apostle of the school, who was also an exemplary missionary, an evangelizer of Latin America. . . ."* The pope added: *"He never hesitated to present an exacting and demanding Christianity to the young men sent to him"* and he *"shared heroically in the sufferings of Christ. . . ."*

Christian Brother

Mutien-Marie Wiaux would have understood the Americans of the past, and he would have won their respect. He is another saint of the "Little Way," the day-to-day struggle of the commonplace with the spiritual life, to fill the things of normal existence with supernatural graces. Mutien Marie was born in Mellet, Belgium, in a village in the French-speaking region, on March 20, 1841. His father was a prosperous blacksmith, and his mother operated a small café located in part of the family residence. The devout family ran a very proper café, and every night ended in the establishment with recitation of the Rosary.

MUTIEN-MARIE WIAUX

(D. 1917)

❦

RELIGIOUS

A leader of the children of the area, Mutien-Marie was educated in the village and then went to work at his father's blacksmith forge; however, he was not physically equipped to follow his father's trade. Rather, he had an abiding interest in the Christian Brothers, who had arrived in the area in 1855. He entered the congregation that same year, recommended by his local pastor. Completing his novitiate at Namur, Mutien-Marie was assigned to St. Bertuin's, a school in Malonne, Belgium.

His first teaching experience ended in disaster, but a Brother Maixentis, who taught art and music, defended Mutien-Marie and had him appointed as his assistant. The young Mutien-Marie set about learning art and music, having

Mutien-Marie Wiaux

no experience in those fields. In time, he played a variety of musical instruments. He also lived the rule of the congregation perfectly for fifty-eight years, serving all that time at St. Bertuin's. When he was not in the classroom, Mutien-Marie labored as a prefect and as a parish catechist. The simple beauty of his life, as noted by Pope Paul VI in his beatification homily for Mutien-Marie, rested in the day-to-day transformations of routine tasks into moments of devotion and true sanctity.

Noted for his dedication to the Blessed Sacrament and to the Blessed Virgin Mary, Mutien-Marie's entire existence was focused on the education of the young men of the region, especially in the fields of art and music. He did not treat these subjects as mere adjustments of life but incorporated them into the human quest for salvation.

He lived his vows with a quiet dignity, refining the religious customs and regulations and transforming them into acts of love. He accepted as well the physical infirmities that plagued him from 1875 until 1906. He spent all of his time praying the Rosary for the Christian Brothers and their charges. The Blessed Virgin remained always at his side. He wrote that Mary was the sure and brief path to intimacy with Christ.

In January, 1917, Mutien-Marie collapsed from a final and severe bout with ill health. He grew weaker steadily until finally, on January 29, he recited a litany and died the next morning. Miracles were quickly attributed to his intercession. A shrine was erected in Malonne, honoring this gentle, caring, Christian Brother. Pope Paul VI beatified him in 1977.

Pope John Paul II canonized Mutien-Marie on December 10, 1989, declaring that Mutien-Marie *"has all the greatness of the humble."* The Holy Father added: *"His message is not expressed in terms of this world's. Rather, he shows his brothers, teachers, and students the true fruitfulness of a life that is humbly offered."*

Foundress of the Sisters of St. Dorothy in Genoa

There are souls in the world who are asked to mature early, to assume tremendous tasks while still young. Such individuals serve as the foundation for an entire generation. They are dependable, practical, and generous. Life has taught them at an early age that only the strong will survive human misadventures. Love has shown them that only charity and concern will heal the wounds of suffering. Paula Frassinetti was a soul trained by tragedy and need early in her life.

PAULA
FRASSINETTI
(D. 1882)

FOUNDRESS

She was born in Genoa, Italy, on March 3, 1809, the only daughter of John and Angela Frassinetti. Paula had four brothers, all of whom became priests. Raised in a devout and happy home, Paula suffered tragedy when her mother died when the girl was only nine years old. Seeking consolation, Paula turned to the Blessed Mother, dedicating herself to Mary.

An aunt came to raise the family but died within three years, leaving Paula to manage the household. She learned her lessons from her father and brothers, who educated her faithfully in home classes. Thus her lifestyle was set early, and each day of her life started with daily Mass. Paula then performed the many chores required in the home. For seven years she followed this routine, maturing in prayer.

At the age of twenty she developed bronchial problems and went to live with her brother, a priest at Quinto, a village on the west coast near Genoa. There she recovered her health and served as the parish housekeeper. Paula also opened a school for poor girls, training them in the spiritual life as she educated them for life in the world. Her brother aided Paula in her labors. As his housekeeper, she demonstrated a prayerful spirit and a genuine concern for the poor of the parish, particularly the young children.

In 1834, Paula founded the Sisters of St. Dorothy in Genoa, a congregation dedicated to the education of poor children. Her spirit brought about many vocations to her congregation and increased the benefits of the poor. Paula confronted the problems facing her new congregation, spending entire nights before the Tabernacle. She saw her sisters expand their labors in Europe, going to Portugal and then to Brazil. In 1835, an epidemic of cholera ravaged northern Italy, and Paula and her sisters served faithfully until all of the victims had received adequate care. The congregation continued to flourish, a sign, Paula said, of the "Will of God."

She worked until 1876, when she suffered a paralyzing stroke. She endured two more such attacks in 1879 and 1882. During her last attack, St. John Bosco came to visit her, announcing her virtues and her coming death. Paula contracted pneumonia and began a rapid decline. She died in Rome on June 11, 1882, and her remains were enshrined at St. Onofria, the Dorothean motherhouse in the Eternal City. In 1906, her body was found to be incorrupt, and it was placed in a silver and crystal casket, a gift from the faithful of Brazil. Paula was beatified in 1930 by Pope Pius XI.

Pope John Paul II canonized Paula on March 11, 1984, declaring: *"Paula Frassinetti is . . . a splendid fruit of the redemption always active within the Church. It has been said that in order to determine if a work is Christian, it is necessary to see if there is the seal of the redeeming Cross. . . . In fact, she was convinced that whoever wants to undertake a path to perfection cannot renounce the Cross, mortification, humiliation, and suffering, which assimilate the Christian to the divine model, who is Crucified. . . . Not only did the Cross not frighten her, but it was for her the powerful spring which moved her, the secret source from which sprang her tireless activity and her indomitable courage."*

Discalced Carmelite, "Martyr of the Confessional"

The friends of God are not perfected by chasing a particular apostolate or vocation. Saints are in a constant state of "becoming" mirrors of Christ, no matter what tasks are given to them, no matter where they are asked to spend their time and energies. Raphael Kalinowski was such a soul; a friend of God who suffered the outrages of the world in his own era but used those experiences to perfect his interior spirit so that he could mirror Christ for his fellow human beings in that world through the Carmelite tradition.

RAPHAEL (JOZEF) KALINOWSKI

(D. 1907)

RELIGIOUS

Raphael was born Josef Kalinowski on September 1, 1835, in Vilna, Lithuania, of Polish descent. Raised in an era of military expansion and unrest, Raphael attended the military academy at Pietroburgo, and, upon graduation, was assigned to Brest, Litowski, in Belarus. An engineer, he attained the rank of captain and witnessed the Czar's occupation of Poland in 1863. He joined the insurrection that developed as a result of Russian military action and was arrested. In 1864, Raphael was sentenced to ten years in the hard-labor camps of Siberia for his part in the uprising.

Released from his imprisonment in 1874, Raphael returned to Poland with a deeply profound spiritual vocation. He taught for a time, and one of his students was August Czartoryski, one of the first Salesians, whose Cause is also open. Drawn to the contemplative life, Raphael entered the Discalced Carmelites in Austria. Completing his novitiate and seminary studies, he was ordained a priest on January 15, 1882.

Raphael was a superb confessor and spiritual director who fought valiantly for Church unity in a troubled era. He also gained considerable fame as a confessor, and he fostered intense devotion to the Blessed Virgin Mary. St. Albert Chmielowski, the founder of the Albertines, met Raphael and was guided by his wisdom.

Raphael died in the Carmelite monastery at Wadowice on November 15, 1907, after decades of faithful service in the confessional and in the direction of souls. He was a spiritual giant of Poland, mourned by the people of that land.

Pope John Paul II canonized Raphael on November 17, 1991, naming him a *"Martyr of the Confessional."* The Holy Father declared as well: *"Ordained a priest, Raphael . . . set to work in Christ's vineyard. He was as esteemed confessor and spiritual director. He guided souls in the sublime knowledge of the love of God, Christ and Our Lady, the Church and neighbour. He dedicated many hours to this humble apostolate. He was always recollected, always ready to make a sacrifice, to fast, to practice mortification. The man* 'conquered by Christ.' *The man whose spirit, after all the difficult experiences of his former life — and even through the experiences which caused him much suffering — discovers the full meaning of the words which Christ spoke in the Upper Room: 'As the father loves me, so also I love you . . . (Jn. 15:9,13).'"* The pope added that with St. Albert Chmielowski, Raphael provided Poland with new horizons of faith, saying: *"These two great sons of the Polish land, who showed the paths to holiness to their contemporaries and to the succeeding generations, ended their lives at the dawn of this century, on the eve of the regained independence of Poland."*

Medical Doctor and Founder

Richard Pampuri, who died during the Great Depression, stands as a model of Christ-like awareness of need and obligations in this world. He also stands as a symbol of generosity of heart. He was born Erminio Filippo Pampuri in Trivolizi, Italy, on August 2, 1897, the tenth child of a prosperous, pious family.

RICHARD PAMPURI

(D. 1930)

FOUNDER

His mother died when he was three, and the child was sent to Torino to live with his grandfather and an aunt. An uncle, Carlo, trained Richard in medical practices, instilling in him a deep love of serving the sick. In 1907, his father was killed in an accident, but his family was so kind and loving that he survived the tragedy with calm.

Putting aside his original desire to become a foreign missionary, Richard entered medical school. Richard's sister entered the convent, and he became a Franciscan tertiary, saluting her for full commitment to the religious life. He also took part in Catholic associations at a time when anticlericalism was rampant in Italy. Conscripted into the army, Richard served in the medical corps in World War I, receiving a decoration for conspicuous bravery.

In 1918, he continued his studies, graduating in medicine and surgery on July 6, 1921. The following year he completed his internship, and in 1923, was registered at Pavia University as a general practitioner and surgeon.

As a student he had been active in the Conference of St. Vincent de Paul and other service organizations. He wrote to his sister, the nun: "Pray that pride, selfishness, and any other evil passion will not prevent me from always seeing the suffering of Christ in my patients, treating him and comforting him."

Richard went to Milan where he founded the Band of Pius X, a group dedicated to medical care for the poor. Richard also raised funds to provide food and clothing for the needy. He was realizing his own religious vocation as well. Entering the Hospitaller Order of St. John of God, he promised: "I want to serve you, God, for the future, with perseverance and supreme love. . . ."

On June 22, 1927, Richard became a Hospitaller of St. John of God, dedicating his medical skills entirely to the service of Christ and his poor. He took his vows on October 28, 1928, and was assigned to a clinic in Brescia. There he continued his apostolate to the poor, earning fame for healing the sick. He was suffering from a severe lung affliction and it worsened. Moved to Milan, he soon developed pneumonia and prophesied when he would die. Correct in his prediction, he expired on May 1, 1930, at the age of thirty-three. Richard was beatified in 1981.

Pope John Paul II canonized Richard on November 1, 1989, declaring that the saint was *"close to our times, but even closer to our problems and our sensibilities."* The Holy Father also said that Richard's life shines with *"the mystery of eternal holiness of the Triune God."* With St. Gaspar Bertoni, canonized on the same day, Richard displayed the content of the evangelical Beatitudes. The pope said: *"They are two witnesses to Christ's love, in different times and different kinds of life."*

Roch Gonzalez 🔥 **See Jesuit Martyrs of Paraguay**.

Religious Pioneer in America

ROSE PHILIPPINE DUCHESNE

(D. 1852)

🔥

FOUNDRESS

The human spirit is indomitable, capable of overcoming time, distances, and physical limitations to demonstrate heroic concerns and values. There are those men and women who do not accept the ready formulas concerning set activities corresponding to the number of decades that they have spent on the earth. Sometimes necessity is the compelling factor, the spur to action that denies frailty, weaknesses, or advanced age. For Rose Philippine Duschene, the impetus was love.

She was born in Grenoble, France, on August 29, 1769, the daughter of Pierre François Duchesne, a prominent lawyer. Her mother belonged to the distinguished Periér family, an ancestor of Casimir Periér, the president of France in 1894.

Desiring a religious vocation, Rose Philippine joined the Visitation Sisters at age seventeen but saw her convent caught up in the tragic persecutions of the French Revolution. The convent was closed, and Rose Philippine was sent home in order to save her life. When the Revolution ended, she returned to the convent, hoping to revive the branch of the Visitation Congregation. Unable to achieve this, she invited St. Madeleine Sophie Barat to assume control of the convent for her own ministry. St. Madeleine could not expand her congregation's work in that fashion and had to declined the offer.

Rose Philippine Duchesne

Rose Philippine had already demonstrated her courage and constancy during a period of intense trial and danger. After being sent home from the convent, she had provided havens for the clergy being hunted by the anti-religious forces and had cared for political prisoners. Recognizing this fortitude and spiritual maturity on the part of Rose Philippine, St. Madeleine invited her to become a member of the Society of the Sacred Heart. On December 31, 1804, Rose Philippine took vows in that congregation, immediately demonstrating her leadership and generosity.

In 1818, when Rose Philippine was forty-nine, she was chosen to lead four companions to the United States, and Bishop Dubourg of New Orleans welcomed her to the city. She did not speak English, but she opened a school in St. Charles, Missouri, and pioneered Indian schools, orphanages, and a Sacred Heart novitiate. She recognized the sacrifices demanded of the Church and missionaries in the New World, saying: "Poverty and Christian heroism are here and trials are the riches of priests in this land."

When Rose Philippine was on the Potowatami reservation, she was unable to learn the tribal language but earned the admiration of the Indians through her holiness and recollections. The Potawatamis called her "the Woman Who Prays Always." She suffered keen disappointments in her labors of more than three decades, but she continued to lead the way in establishing educational and charitable institutions. One after the other, such programs demonstrated the Christian response to human suffering.

Rose Philippine died in St. Charles, Missouri, on November 18, 1852, at the age of eighty-three. A shrine was erected there in her memory, and she was also inscribed in the pioneer Hall of Fame of the State of Missouri. In the process of beatification, the remains of Rose Philippine were exhumed in 1940 and found to be incorrupt. The only true photograph of her was taken on that occasion.

Pope John Paul II canonized her on July 3, 1988, declaring that her: *"whole life was transformed and enlightened by her love for Christ in the Eucharist. During the long hours she spent before the Blessed Sacrament she learned to live continually in the presence of God. . . . The radical commitment of Mother Duchesne to the poor and the outcast of society, remains a very dynamic source of inspiration for her own Congregation, and for all religious today. . . . Her absolutely unique example is valid for all Christ's disciples, especially for those who live in the underprivileged parts of the world."* The Holy Father also said: *"With missionary courage, this great pioneer looked to the future with the eyes of the heart — a heart that was on fire with God's love."*

Trinitarian Tutor and Royal Confessor

The friends of God have been given a simple mandate which in the modern vernacular translates as: "Bloom where you are planted." This means that saints of the world may be called to cloisters, to the far-flung missions, to urban ghettos, or even to the stately environments of the rich and powerful of the world. Each apostolate is unique and grace-filled. Each ministry carries its own temptations, perils, and spiritual rewards. God raises up the souls needed to intervene in human affairs on various levels of society, providing such stalwart missionaries of the spirit with the graces necessary for their part in divine will.

Simon de Rojas was particularly suited for the role that he was destined to play in the life of Spain during a troubled era. He was born in Valladolid, Spain, on October 28, 1552, the third of four children of

SIMON DE ROJAS

(D. 1624)

RELIGIOUS

noble parents, Gregorio Ruiz de Navamanuel and his wife, Costanza de Rojas. Shy and slow, Simon nevertheless was noted for his love of the Blessed Virgin Mary.

Educated and displaying a keen intellect as he grew older, Simon also maintained a profound spirit of recollection. He entered the Trinitarians at the age of twelve and was professed eight years later in the Valladolid Trinitarian monastery. Simon was sent to Salamanca for philosophy and theology training and was ordained a priest in 1577. During this period he dedicated his life to the Blessed Mother.

His academic brilliance and administrative abilities led to his appointment to religious offices in the Trinitarians, and he served as a superior as well. Simon's sermons and obvious piety brought him to the attention of the Spanish court of King Philip III, a deeply religious ruler. Philip was not particularly active, leaving the task of government to the duke de Uceda. The king, however, recognized Simon's holiness and ordered him to serve as confessor to the court. In time, Simon was appointed tutor to the heir, Prince Philip, who inherited the throne as Philip IV in 1621, ruling until 1665. He was also confessor to Queen Isabella of Bourbon.

Simon did not forsake his Trinitarian ministry. He accepted his rule in the court and trained the prince, but he also gave public missions and demonstrated a remarkable zeal in an era of religious and political turmoil. His spiritual insights and intense spirituality radiated a calming, dedicated aura wherever he went. Simon refused two appointments as bishop and gave his personal funds to aid the poor. He was particularly devoted to the Holy Eucharist. He also spread devotion of total consecration to Mary throughout Spain and Germany. Pope Gregory XV (r. 1621-1623) joined in this total consecration. The Holy Father and others of that era looked upon Simon as the St. Bernard of Spain. The "Congregation of the Servants of the Most Sweet Name of Mary," a secular association promoting the Cause, was founded by Simon as well.

Toward the end of his life, Simon was able to spend more time in prayer and private penance. He died in Madrid on September 28, 1624, and was given royal honors and mourned by the people of Spain. Simon was beatified in 1766.

Pope John Paul II canonized Simon on July 3, 1988, declaring that the new saint *"Gave full meaning to his life as a Christian as a priest, in his contemplation of the mystery of the God of Love. Faithful to the redeeming and merciful charism of his Order, 'Father Rojas' — as he was familiarly called by his people — was very aware of all kinds of needs in his neighbor, especially of the poor and the outcast, as he was aware of the needs of Christians imprisoned for their faith. On their part, the poor saw in him their guardian champion and father."* The Holy Father also stated that Simon's active apostolate was *"not an obstacle to his contemplative prayer, nor to his dedication of long periods of time for prayer during the day, and still more during the night after the sung office at midnight."* Pope John Paul II also praised Simon as a true Marian disciple.

Stephan (Stefan) Pongracz ❧ See Martyrs of Kosice.

In the world of souls and the spirit, laurels and crowns are usually won with time and endurance. Yet, even here, there are spiritual prodigies, the very young who soar as eagles toward the sun and others who plod the plains below. Teresa Fernandez Solar, called Teresa of the Andes, was one of these spiritually precocious souls, inflamed by love and filling a remarkably brief life span with edifying heroism.

TERESA (JUANA) FERNANDEZ SOLAR

(D. 1920)

VICTIM SOUL

She was born Juana Enriquita Josephine of the Sacred Hearts Soler in Santiago, Chile, on July 13, 1900. She was the daughter of Michael Fernandez Jaraquemada and Lucia Solar Armstrong of that city. Teresa was well-educated by her parents, and she displayed a unique religious fervor even as a small child.

As she matured, Teresa loved solitude and desired Christ, not the world. She recognized a Carmelite vocation and entered the Carmelite Convent of the Andes on May 7, 1919. She received the habit of Carmel on October 14, 1919, and was given the religious name Teresa of Jesus.

As a Carmelite, Teresa received many mystical graces and displayed a contemplative splendor. In her prayers, Teresa became united to Christ, the Divine Victim. She was enrapt and experienced many spiritual encounters, even as her health failed. She was a victim of immolation for love, suffering from *typho correpta*, a severe form of typhus.

Teresa was professed as a Discalced Carmelite before she died. On April 2, 1920, she received the Last Sacrament, and her profession as a cloistered nun took place on April 6. Six days later she died of love as her last desires were granted to her.

Pope John Paul II canonized Teresa on March 21, 1993, before a crowd of one million of her countrymen in Santiago, Chile. At the ceremony, the Holy Father declared: *"Sister Teresa 'de los Andes,' Teresa of Jesus, is the light of Christ for the whole Chilean Church; the Discalced Carmelite, the first fruit of holiness of the Teresian Carmel of Latin America, today is enrolled among the saints of the Universal Church . . . God made shine forth in her in an admirable way the light of his Son Jesus Christ, so that she could be a beacon and guide to a world which seems to be blind to the splendour of the divine. In a secularized society which turns its back on God, this Chilean Carmelite whom to my great joy I present as a model of the perennial youth of the Gospel, gives the shining witness of a life which proclaims to the men and women of our day that it is in the loving, adoring and serving God that the human creature finds greatness and joy, freedom, and fulfillment. The life of Blessed Teresa cries out continually from within her cloister: 'God alone suffices!' She shouts it out particularly to the young people who hunger for the truth and seek a light which will give direction to their lives. To young people who are being allured by the continuous messages and stimuli of an erotic culture, a society which mistakes the hedonistic exploitation of another for genuine love, which is self-giving, this young virgin of the Andes today proclaims the beauty and happiness that come from a pure heart."*

Théophane Venard ❦ **See Martyrs of Vietnam.**

Valentine Berriochoa ❦ **See Martyrs of Vietnam.**

Dominican Tertiary

There have been periods in world history that can be viewed as considerably more disagreeable than this modern age. Europe endured entire eras in which migrating peoples ravaged countrysides and obliterated cultural and religious institutions and ideals. Just existing in these historical periods was no mean feat. Holding fast to the faith and standing as a beacon of love and charity were acts of heroism that inspired young and old, rich and poor, and preserved Christianity for new generations.

ZDISLAVA DE LEMBERK

(D. 1252)

FOUNDRESS

Zdislava de Lemberk, also called Zdislava Berka, was a woman capable of such acts of valor. A Dominican tertiary and a model lay religious, she embodied Christ to her people in unique and telling ways.

She was born on an unknown date in the thirteenth century in Krizanov, Moravia, now Letomerice, Bohemia (in the modern Czech Republic). Of an aristocratic family, Zdislava was forced to marry a nobleman allied to her clan. Arranged marriages were not designed to provide brides and grooms with romantic joy. The practical nobles of that historical period knew that the offspring of such men and women of rank held the keys to the future. Couples were wed because of their status, their holdings, and their political allegiances, usually to foster peace between factions or to advance a family's cause. Romance had nothing to do with such marriages, and couples accepted their fate and learned to make do with the partners provided for them. Zdislava and her husband resided in a castle at Gabel, and the noble residence became a haven for the people of the surrounding region. Hundreds of local men and women journeyed there in times of trial, assured that Zdislava would find a way to ease their sufferings. When the Mongol invasions of the area brought about upheavals and disaster, refugees swarmed about Gabel. Zdislava cared for them all.

Her husband was so impressed with Zdislava's goodness and compassion that he allowed her to become a member of the Dominican Third Order, a rare privilege in that era. Embracing the tertiary rule and lifestyle, she grew in prayer and received many singular mystical graces and experiences. Zdislava founded St. Lawrence Priory, establishing this religious house as a source of faith in her area. She was also known to have experienced visions and ecstasies.

Zdislava died in 1252 at Jablone, Bohemia, possibly on January 1. She was beatified in 1907 by Pope St. Pius X. Pope John Paul II canonized Zdislava at Olomanc, in the Czech Republic on May 21, 1995, saying: *"St. Zdislava of Lemberk, heroine of charity and the family, is as it were a reflection of Mary. During her life she imitated Mary's tenderness and concern for neighbor, especially the poor and the sick."*

PART TWO:
THE BEATIFIED OF
POPE JOHN PAUL II

"Jesus Christ: though he was rich, he became poor for your sake, to make you rich out of his poverty" (2 Cor 8:9).

". . . This phrase, taken from the Letter of St. Paul to the Corinthians, is a sort of introduction to the Gospel and the parable of the rich man and Lazarus. At the same time the Church, assembled near the tomb of St. Peter, pronounces this phrase while looking to all the Servants of God who are proclaimed blessed. . . . To each of them Jesus showed the way to holiness, first becoming poor and making himself a model for all, he who was the Son of God, of one being with the Father. He revealed the mystery of this poverty which makes one rich to each of the new blessed. In this way he showed each of them the way to holiness. Today the Church rejoices for these sons and daughters who have traveled the way indicated by the Divine Master."

Beatification Mass, October 1, 1983

Founder of the Kolping Societies and Model Religious

In the Germany of the last century there was a priest who spent his energies undoing wrongs and promoting papal teachings on justice. His name was Adolph Kolping, and he was called "the Journeymen's Father," or *Gesellenvater.*

Adolph was born in Kerpen, a village in Germany, on December 8, 1813, and entered the local work force at an early age because of his family's strained economic conditions. As an unskilled laborer, Adolph experienced the cruel realities of working in the plants and factories of Germany at the time.

ADOLPH KOLPING

(D. 1865)

FOUNDER

Always faced with delicate health and physical sufferings, Adolph worked and studied in order to respond to a call to the priesthood. He conducted his seminary studies while earning his own living until his ordination in 1845, using that experience to guide his apostolate. As a priest he began a series of projects to aid the young working men of his area. A choir that he founded developed into the Young Workmen's Society, designed to uplift the moral life of the working classes. The "Kolping Societies" or, as they were called, the *Gesellenvereine,* spread quickly throughout Europe and were popular in America. Adolph formed one in Cologne in 1849 and another in St. Louis, Missouri, in 1856. When he died there were more than four hundred *Gesellenvereine* in the world.

He was also a strong defender of the family, saying: "The first thing that a person finds in life and the last to which he holds out his hand, and the most precious that he possesses, even if he does not realize it, is family life." Adolph placed great value on the sanctification of families.

Always available to the poor and the downtrodden, Adolph spent his life defending their rights and trying to better their working conditions. He was a pioneer in this cause, bringing his own experiences and faith to the work and recognizing the harsh demands of an industrialized people. Adolph died in Cologne on December 4, 1865, and the news of his passing brought thousands of mourners to the large funeral. The working people came to lay him to rest with reverence and genuine grief.

The message that Adolph tried to give the people of his world was prophetic and filled with dire warnings that have been fulfilled in the modern eras. He recognized that even in his own time the world was so secularized, so materialistic, so greed-driven that individual men, women, and children were considered meaningless in the affairs of states and industrialization. Adolph had witnessed as well an onslaught against the Church in his own age. Germany was waging a war of culture against the Catholic Faith, a relentless persecution that tried to force the concept of a Germany united in all things.

Adolph taught the young that such views of faith and the temporal world lead only to a certain sterility, a demeaning of the human soul and he fought to empower working men and women with courage born of Catholic truths and traditions.

Pope John Paul II beatified Adolph Kolping on October 27, 1991, and met with pilgrims who had come to Rome for the ceremony. The Holy Father described Blessed Adolph as a man who *"stood with both feet planted firmly on the earth, and was oriented toward heaven . . . in the world, but not of the world."*

Agatha Phutta **See Martyrs of Thailand.**

Mystic and Model Religious

Some souls lead brief but spectacularly powerful lives. Almighty God entrusts them with a particular task and demands generosity of spirit, providing as well the grace necessary. Agnes of Jesus de Langeac was such a soul. She volunteered at age seven to become "a slave of the Holy Virgin" and performed a singular mission that aided the faith in France.

Agnes of Jesus was born in Puy-en-Velay, France, on November 17, 1602.

At the age of five, she was entrusted to the Congregation of the Holy Virgin for her education and demonstrated great piety. In 1623, Agnes of Jesus followed her desire to become a religious and entered the Dominican Convent at Langeac. There she matured spiritually and was elected prioress four years later. Agnes of Jesus was later deposed from this office, but she accepted that event with calm and grace.

Her devotion to the Blessed Virgin continued, and in 1631, the Blessed Mother of God appeared to Agnes of Jesus, telling her to "Pray to my Son for the Abbot of Prébrac." Agnes of Jesus knew nothing about this abbot, never having met him,

AGNES OF JESUS GALAND DE LANGEAC

(D. 1634)

MYSTIC

but she spent the next three years praying and making sacrifices for the man. She then appeared to the famous abbot and preacher Jean-Jacques Olier, abbot of Prébac during his retreat under the direction of St. Vincent de Paul. Agnes of Jesus met the abbot when he instituted a search for her as a result of her supernatural appearance before him. She told him: "I have received orders from the Holy Virgin to pray for you. God has destined you to open the first seminaries in France."

The abbot was called to Paris in 1634, and Agnes of Jesus, knowing that her mission was completed, died on October 19 of that year.

Pope John Paul II beatified Agnes on November 20, 1994, declaring: *"Truly blessed, Agnes de Langeac was able, without the slightest reservation, to enter into God's plan for her, offering her intellect, will, and freedom to the Son of Man, that he might transform them and harmonize them totally with his own!"*

Agnes Phila ❧ See Martyrs of Thailand.

Evangelizing Prelate

Considered by many to be a remarkable gift from God, Alanus de Solminihac came in to the world possessing extraordinary abilities, a lucid vision, and many graces. He rose to serve the Church with a simple but telling motto: "Faith and Valor." Raised devoutly and educated to confront the swirling social calamities of his own era, he received the grace of a religious vocation.

Alanus was an aristocrat of France, born in the family's castle in Belet on November 25, 1593. Alanus longed to serve as a Knight of Malta, as he was attracted to the military discipline and the courageous commitment of that Order. In 1613, however, at the age of twenty, he entered the Canons Regular of St. Augustine at Chancelade Abbey, near Périqueux.

There he started an intense spiritual life that aided him when he was sent

ALANUS DE SOLMINIHAC

(D. 1659)

BISHOP

to Paris to continue his theological and spiritual studies. In 1623, Alanus returned to Chancelade Abbey where he was installed as superior and entrusted with the enormous task of restoring the Augustinian rules and ideals. His fervor and holiness inspired the members of his abbey to undertake the reformation with zeal. Other religious communities in the region responded with the same ardor.

In 1636, Pope Urban VIII (r. 1623-1644), who recognized the zeal and nobility of Alanus, consecrated him as the bishop of Cahors, France. Alanus brought a spirit of reform to that city, but he also demonstrated a genuine pastoral concern that took him on many face-to-face visits among the people. He attended the council of Trent, and followed the lead of St. Charles Borromeo in enforcing the council's decrees.

Alanus convened a diocesan synod, held an episcopal council, and restored traditions and religious customs. He actually visited each one of his parishes nine times. This was no mean feat, considering that there were eight hundred parishes under his jurisdiction. He also started a priestly seminary, sponsored regular parish missions and charitable organizations, and promoted eucharistic adoration. Three years before his death, Alanus preached at the diocesan jubilee. He died, revered by his contemporaries for his holiness and asceticism, in Mercues, on December 31, 1659.

Pope John Paul II beatified Alanus on October 4, 1981. The Holy Father praised the new blessed as a singular bishop who had *"the courage to evangelize the modern world fearlessly."*

Apostle of Social Justice

The nation of Chile in South America boast natural splendors, a richness of spirit, and a faithful people. This nation also can point with reverent pride to a modern apostle, called "the friend of God and man." A Jesuit priest, Alberto Hurtado Cruchaga used the new modes of communication in the world to foster timeless faith.

Alberto was born in Vina del Mar, Chile, on January 22, 1901, and was raised with an awareness of local injustices and the changing approaches to spreading the doctrines of the Church. His father died when he was young, and his family was poor. Yet he was well-educated, having earned a scholarship and having learned about modern communication methods before entering the Society of Jesus. Ordained in 1933, Alberto made his final vows and began his ministry as a teacher and retreat master. In time he would spearhead the Church's efforts and support social programs in Chile, starting with his best-selling book, *Is Chile a Catholic Country?*

Vivacious, enthusiastic, and open to all, he was a true "Father of Chile," devoted to the poor, especially those who were helpless victims, and he ministered to their needs through charitable projects with a personal commitment based on the faith. He wrote and lectured throughout Chile to awaken the Christian conscience, using his first-hand knowledge and his personal experiences as a missionary to arouse his fellow countrymen. Because of his preaching and ceaseless efforts, Alberto inspired the Christian Democratic Movement in Chile and aided the organization of Christian labor unions that were designed to protect workers from abuse. Many social action groups in Chile, such as *Centro Bellarmino*, *El Hugar de Cristo*, and the Rural Institute for Education, trace their origins to Albert's

ALBERTO HURTADO CRUCHAGA

(D. 1952)

RELIGIOUS

preaching and concern for social justice in the region. He also founded the Chilean Trade Union Association and the journal, *Mensaje*. When Alberto died of pancreatic cancer in Santiago, Chile, on August 18, 1952, at a comparatively young age, thousands came to mourn him and to demonstrate grief for Chile's loss. On his deathbed, he said: "I am happy, Lord."

Pope John Paul II beatified Alberto on October 16, 1994. During the ceremony *"the friend of God and man"* was praised for daring to use modern methods to spread the Gospel of Christ. Alberto was revered for serving as a true pastor of the abandoned and betrayed.

Alfredo Ildephonse Schuster ❧ **See Ildephonse (Alfredo) Schuster**.

Croatian Cardinal

A cardinal of the Church and martyr, Aloysius Stepinac serves as an outstanding example of the valor required of prelates in defending the universality of the Church against the onslaughts of Communist regimes. He served until the end of his life "without hatred towards anyone, and without fear from anyone."

Aloysius Stepinac, called Alojzije in his native Croatia, was born in Krasíc, Yugoslavia, on May 8, 1898. He was educated locally and completed military service in World War I before deciding to study for the priesthood. In Rome, Aloysius studied at the Pontifical Germanicum-Hungaricum College and earned doctorates at the Pontifical Gregorian University. He was ordained a priest on October 26, 1930.

His first assignment was in Zagreb, his archdiocese, as a parish priest, but he distinguished himself by founding the archdiocesan Caritas in 1931. Three years later, at the age of thirty-six, he was appointed coadjutor archbishop of Zagreb. He created twelve new parishes and promoted the Catholic press, defending the rights of the Church during the Concordat between Yugoslavia and the Holy See. Aloysius was consecrated archbishop of Zagreb when his predecessor died on December 7, 1937.

ALOYSIUS STEPINAC

(D. 1960)

MARTYR

The advance of the Nazis alerted Aloysius to the sufferings of refugees, and he founded charitable organizations, including the Action for Assistance for Jewish Refugees in 1938. His writings clearly demonstrate his concerns: "The Catholic Church does not recognize races that rule and races that are enslaved."

Initially optimistic about the Church's position in Croatia when Ante Pavelic and the Ustasha regime came to power, he was soon appalled at the fascist policies of the government and protested the treatment of the Church, Jews, Serbs, and Gypsies, writing on May 23, 1941: "Every day we witness measures that are ever more severe against people who, often, are totally innocent."

World War II brought about terrible ordeals, and Stepinac was most concerned about the plight of Jews and Orthodox Christians. To save as many as possible, he permitted all priests to accept as a convert any Jew or Orthodox Christian without the requirement of special catechetical knowledge and with the understanding that they would return to their original faiths "when these times of madness and savageness are over." At the end of the fighting, Aloysius and his Catholic people found themselves under the control of the Communists. He was arrested in 1945 for speaking out against the murders of priests by Communist militants and for refusing to accept anything less than full freedom for the Church and a continuation of the unity of the Church in Croatia with the Holy See. Aloysius was pressured by Josip Broz Tito, the new Communist leader of Yugoslavia, to create a nationalized Croatian Catholic Church without allegiance to Rome. This he and the other bishops of Yugoslavia refused to do, and so the full fury of the Communists was leveled at Aloysius. He was vilified in the press, ridiculed by Communist spokesmen, and made the target of hate campaigns. Arrested on the spurious charges of war crimes, he was put on trial in September 1946, and sentenced on October 11, 1946 to sixteen years of hard labor for defending the Holy See and Church unity. The Jews of Yugoslavia openly protested this sentence, declaring that Aloysius was one of the few men in Europe who risked all by defending their rights. Aloysius was imprisoned until 1951, when his health deteriorated. He was put under house arrest in Krasíc, but he still managed to write more than five thousand letters and to serve as a priest.

On June 23, 1953, Pope Pius XII elevated Aloysius to the rank of cardinal, citing him as "an example of apostolic zeal and Christian strength." Yugoslavia retaliated against the pope's action by breaking diplomatic ties with the Vatican. Aloysius remained under house arrest until 1959, when he was ordered to testify at the trial of the spiritual director of the seminary.

He refused, citing the abuses he had endured and the need for the freedom of the Church in Croatia. He died on February 10, 1960, almost certainly as the result of poisoning by his Communist captors.

Pope John Paul II beatified Aloysius Cardinal Stepinac on October 3, 1998, at the Marian shrine near Zagreb before 500,000 Croatians and other faithful. The Holy Father declared at this ceremony: *"Blessed Alojzije Stepinac did not spill his blood in the strict sense of the word. His death was caused by the long suffering he endured, the last fifteen years of his life were a continual succession of trials, amid which he courageously endangered his own life in order to bear witness to the Gospel and the unity of the Church. In the words of the psalmist, he put his very life in God's hands (cf. Ps 16 [15]: 5). Very little time separates us from the life and death of Cardinal Stepinac: barely thirty-eight years. We all know the context of his death. Many present here today can testify from direct experience how much the sufferings of Christ abounded in those years among the people of Croatia and those of so many nations on the continent. Today, reflecting on the words of the Apostle, we wish to express the heartfelt hope that after the time of trial, the comfort of the crucified and risen Christ may abound in all who live in this land. For all of us, a particular cause* *for comfort is today's beatification. This solemnity takes place in the Croatian national shrine of Marija Bistrica on the first Saturday of the month of October. Beneath the gaze of the Most Blessed Virgin, an illustrious son of this blessed land is raised to the glories of the altars, on the 100th anniversary of his birth. It is an historic moment in the life of the Church and of your nation. The Cardinal Archbishop of Zagreb, one of the outstanding figures of the Catholic Church, having endured in his own body and his own spirit the atrocities of the communist system is now entrusted to the memory of his fellow countrymen with the radiant badge of martyrdom."*

Poor Clare Mystic and Victim Soul

Every human being born on earth desires peace, and everyone endures what can be called "the longing of the human soul for God." In India, the land of exotic beauty and mystical awareness, a very young woman, Alphonsa Muttathupandatu, opened her soul and life to Christ and started a spiritual journey that serves as a model for the faithful.

ALPHONSA MUTTATHUPANDATU

(D. 1946)

MYSTIC

Alphonsa was born into the Syro-Malabar rite of the Church in Arpukara, India, on August 19, 1910, and she was called Annakutti, or Anna, by her loving family. The child's life changed when her mother died and Alphonsa came to be raised by her aunt, Annamma, who was devout and set in the old customs of the region.

Alphonsa received a good education and she was expected to marry a young man chosen by her family. She refused all offers of marriage, expressing her belief that Christ had called her to the religious life. When pressed by family members to wed, Alphonsa went to the local fire pit, where she intended to burn and disfigure her feet to discourage suitors. She fell into the pit accidentally, however, and suffered severe burns over her entire body.

This act of self-immolation and the resulting tragedy convinced Alphonsa's family that she was adamant in her desire for the convent. She was allowed to recover in peace and was then given reluctant permission to enter the Poor Clares, the Clarist Sisters, a Franciscan tertiary congregation in the Syro-Malabar rite.

Alphonsa became a Poor Clare in 1928 and went to the Clarist Convent to begin her religious training. There she received the name Alphonsa of the Immaculate Conception, and she displayed spiritual maturity and spiritual gifts, including one of prophecy. Alphonsa experienced a vision of St. Thérèse, the Little Flower, and entered into a mystical union in prayer.

She was an exemplary religious, but was also a victim of love. In her daily convent routines, Alphonsa kept the rule faithfully, performing everything necessary to keep herself in a life of dedication, virginity, and prayer. As a religious, Alphonsa matured and also endured great physical suffering. She said that "A day without suffering is a day lost." Alphonsa offered herself as a victim for others until she died on July 28, 1946, at the Clarist convent in Bharananganam. She announced just before her last breath that she was at peace.

The funeral astounded the Clarist Sisters as people of all faiths came to honor the memory of Alphonsa. Her grave became an instant ecumenical pilgrimage destination, and men and women wept over her life and death. They called her "Sister Alphonsa of India."

Pope John Paul II beatified Alphonsa on February 8, 1986, in Changanachery (Kottayam), India, praising her as a victim of love who embraced Christ Crucified. Alphonsa was honored as a pure soul of India who achieved greatness through humility.

Aloysius Orione ✺ **See Luigi (Aloysius) Orione.**

Aloysius Scrosoppi ✺ **See Luigi (Aloysius) Scrosoppi of Udine.**

Aloysius Versiglia ✺ **See Luigi (Aloysius) Versiglia.**

Amalio Mendoza ✺ **See Martyrs of Almeria.**

ANDRÉ BESSETTE
(D. 1937)
✺
MIRACLE WORKER

Thaumaturgist

Almighty God most often chooses the humble, the unassuming, to achieve his divine will. Such a soul was the "Miracle Worker of Montreal," a simple Holy Cross lay brother whose devotion to St. Joseph raised up one of Canada's most venerated shrines.

André was born in St. Gregoire d'Iberville, near Montreal, Canada, on August 9, 1845. He was the son of Isaac and Clothilde Foisy Bessette, baptized Alfred. After moving to Farnham in 1849, André's family suffered a terrible tragedy when Isaac was killed in a logging accident in 1855. André's mother was unable to care for her sons and daughters and put eleven of them up for adoption. She kept André with her and moved to St. Césaire d'Iberville. Two years later, she died also, and the local mayor and his family adopted the boy and raised him in a kindly manner.

In 1863, André moved to the United

States where he worked for four years as a laborer. He returned to Canada where he applied to the Congregation of the Holy Cross and was accepted as a lay brother in 1870. His poor health put his vocation in doubt, but he was allowed to serve as a porter, or door-keeper, at Holy Cross College at St. Césaire. His first miraculous cures date to this initial stage of this religious life.

While he performed the duties assigned to him, André visited many individuals or received them at his post, bringing about phenomenal cures. He also had a sincere desire to establish a unique haven of wor-

Brother André Bessette

ship on Mount Royal, in Montreal, and started fund-raising. André served as a barber for the college students in order to put aside money for his proposed shrine. Successful in raising sufficient money, André laid the cornerstone of the present basilica on August 31, 1924. The original structure on the site was a wooden chapel called St. Joseph's Oratory. André had been guided in his work on the shrine by the announcement by Pope Pius IX (r. 1846-1878), declaring St. Joseph patron of the Universal Church.

André was a famed thaumaturgist, or healer, and he spent many hours at the bedside of the ill throughout the region. He took no credit for the miracles, saying: "I am nothing . . . only a tool in the hands of Providence, a lowly instrument at the service of St. Joseph."

At the basilica of Mount Royal, André received thousands of visitors until his death on January 6, 1937. One million people paid tribute to his remains as he lay in state in the Mount Royal crypt chapel for seven days. The basilica there attracts more than two million pilgrims each year.

Pope John Paul II beatified André on May 23, 1982, declaring:

"Where, then, does his unheard-of radiance, his fame among millions of people, come from? A daily crowd of sick, afflicted, poor of all kinds, and those who were handicapped or wounded by life found in his presence, in the parlor of the college, at the oratory, a welcoming ear, comfort and faith in God, confidence in the intercession of St. Joseph, in short, the way of prayer and sacraments, and with that the hope and often manifest relief of body and soul. Do not the poor today have as much need of such love, of such hope, of such an education in prayer?"

Andreas Carol Ferrari was one of the most beloved cardinals of Milan, Italy, and an outstanding Churchman of his era. A man of power and esteem, he maintained a close relationship with the faithful of the region, young and old, rich and poor. Reflecting Christ's redemptive love, Andreas was a true "Father of Souls."

ANDREAS CAROL FERRARI

(D. 1921)

❧

CARDINAL

He was born in Lalatta di Protopiano, in the diocese of Parma, Italy, on August 13, 1850, the son of Giuseppe and Madellene Langarine Ferrari. They raised him piously and encouraged his vocation. Educated in Parma, Andreas entered the seminary there and was ordained a priest on December 20, 1873. He was appointed the vice-rector of the seminary in that same year and rector in 1876. In 1878, Andreas was made canon of the cathedral and was consecrated bishop of Guastalla in 1890. One year later, Andreas was made bishop of Como, Italy. In 1894, his appointment as archbishop of Milan was announced, and Andreas received the rank of cardinal on May 21, 1894.

He attended the conclave in 1903 as an advisor and conducted three diocesan synods in Milan. Andreas also established a Eucharistic Congress and celebrated the centennial of St. Charles Borromeo, the city's patron saint. Andreas erected many churches, the Catholic University of the Sacred Heart, and charitable institutions. He also organized a committee to care for soldiers and prisoners and was decorated with the Grand Cross of Sts. Maurizio and Lazarro in 1919. He celebrated his twenty-fifth anniversary of consecration in Milan that same year.

Stricken with cancer of the throat, Andreas endured three months of agony as the illness reached its terminal stages. He did not remove himself from the faithful of Milan even in that torturous time, but allowed thousands of Milanese to come to his bedside. His nights and days were filled with such visits, as men and women of all stations and all walks of life stood in line before his residence to bid him farewell in their own words. These deathbed conversations inspired a whole generation of faithful in Milan and brought about a revival of Catholicism in the archdiocese.

At the end, Andreas also wrote a personal

Cardinal Andreas Ferrari

letter of farewell to his people in which he promised his prayers for their salvation. He died on Candlemas Day, February 2, 1921, and he was buried near St. Charles Borromeo, as he had requested.

Pope John Paul II beatified Andreas on May 10, 1987, extolling his faithfulness to Christ, the Good Shepherd, and praising the fervent charity that he demonstrated for his people.

Foundress of the Company of the Cross

Some individuals have a difficult time discerning the Will of God for their lives, always seeking opportunities for service, despite rejections or denials. Angela of the Cross Guerrero Gonzalez sought her destiny with an unending perseverance, coming at last to the founding of a new congregation designed to serve the poor among the poor.

ANGELA GUERRERO GONZALEZ

(D. 1932)

FOUNDRESS

She was born in Seville, Spain, on January 30, 1846, to a family of modest means. Angela had to give up schools because of the family's poverty, and she spent twelve years in a workshop where she made shoes. There Angela displayed such advanced spiritual graces that her employer brought her to the attention of Father Torres Padilla, a priest of Seville known for his piety and spiritual dedication.

Angela recognized that she had been given the grace of a religious vocation, and she attempted to enter the Carmelite cloister in Seville. At first rejected, she eventually was accepted into a convent only to become so ill that she was forced to depart for the sake of her restoring her health. She had a strong desire to live in the world as a religious, and Angela received word from Father Padilla on November 1, 1871, that she should live according to a specific rule of life and should take yearly vows while living as a religious in the service of God and others. On August 2, 1875, the Company of the Cross received its official beginning as a religious congregation dedicated to the care of the sick and poor. During the epidemic of 1876 in Seville, Angela and the other sisters displayed heroic charity in caring for victims in the city. Angela died in Seville on March 2, 1932, mourned by the local citizens and her spiritual daughters.

Pope John Paul II beatified Angela on November 5, 1982, in Seville. A vast crowd rejoiced as the Holy Father raised her to the honor of the altar and praised her for the long dedication, resolve for Christ, and commitment to the religious life and the service of others.

Franciscan Tertiary and Defender of the Poor

Some saints and blesseds consecrated themselves to God in the world, choosing as lay people to bring Christ to their neighbors. Some of these lay people serve with no other credentials than a dedicated heart. Angela Salawa was a Franciscan tertiary of Poland who mirrored the faith as a simple woman of the people.

ANGELA SALAWA

(D. 1922)

LAY RELIGIOUS

Angela was born in Siepraw, Poland, on September 9, 1881, and was raised in a devout family. She moved to Krakow to become a serving woman, and she began to care for young domestic workers of the city, teaching them the faith and protecting them. Her Franciscan spirit inspired her to spiritual maturity and to an heroic apostolate among the needing.

When World War I tore apart her native land, Angela cared for wounded Polish soldiers and gave comfort to all who were afflicted by the military campaigns. Her intense devotion to the Holy Spirit enabled Angela to bring heroic stamina and zeal to all of her good works. She wrote to Christ in her diary: "I want you to be adored as much as you were destroyed." Angela died in Krakow on March 12, 1922, mourned by all those touched by her Franciscan ardor.

Pope John Paul II beatified Angela in Krakow's Market Square on August 13, 1991, announcing: *"This daughter of the Polish people, who was born in nearby Siepraw, was associated for a large part of her life with Krakow. It is in this city that she worked, that she suffered, and that her holiness came to maturity. While connected to the spirituality of St. Francis of Assisi, she showed an extraordinary responsiveness to the action of the Holy Spirit."*

Noble Patroness of the Young

Wars and tribulations sometimes cripple people and cultures, but these same terrible trials can inspire truly generous souls, bringing them into the arena of society in order to rescue their fellow human beings. Such a generous soul was Angela Maria Truszkowska, a remarkable Polish noblewoman who served everyone who came into her sphere of concern. She was the foundress of the Felician Sisters, the highly re-

ANGELA MARIA TRUSZKOWSKA

(D. 1899)

FOUNDRESS

vered Polish Franciscan Congregation, and her Cause was opened by His Eminence, Karol Cardinal Wojtyla, now Pope John Paul II.

Angela was born on May 16, 1825, in Kalisz, Poland, the daughter of prosperous parents, the nobles Joseph and Josepha Truszkowska. She was baptized Sophia Camille and was raised in the Russian-dominated section of Poland. She was never blessed with robust health. Born premature, Angela was placed in an incubator, a unique, advanced invention devised by her mother. Prayers were also said to Our Lady of Czestochowa to save the infant. Angela's childhood was marked by her piety and by her early charitable activities in Kalisz. In her twelfth year, her family moved to Warsaw where she contracted tuberculosis and was sent to Switzerland to recover in a sanitarium.

Her personal life was thus filled with graces and almost miraculous recoveries, and while she endured many physical problems this did not stop her from taking part in various charitable works, including aiding the Society of St. Vincent de Paul. Angela also became a Franciscan tertiary, and in 1857 received the habit when she founded her Franciscan congregation. Because the convent was near the church of St. Felix of Cantalice, the sisters became known as the Felicians.

Within four years, Mother Angela had opened twenty-seven schools, and in 1860 she founded a contemplative branch of the congregation to ensure graces for the active apostolate. The Russian occupation in 1864 saw the Felicians lose everything they possessed because they had cared for wounded Polish soldiers. They were disbanded by the conquerors, but Emperor Franz Josef gave Angela and her sisters refuge in the Austrian sector of Poland. By 1866, the congregation was united in the Austrian area and flowering again. In 1874, Mother Angela sent the first Felician Sisters to the United States. The other houses flourished as well, even in the turmoil of that European era.

By combining the active and contemplative vocations of the congregations, Angela brought all aspects of religious life to bear on the ministry of charity and education. At age forty-four, Angela withdrew from the active leadership of the Felician Sisters because of her increasing deafness. She accepted this retirement as God's Will and served for three decades as a source of grace, inspiration, and prayer.

Angela was diagnosed with stomach cancer in 1899, and her physician was astonished at the amount of suffering that she had borne in silence before receiving medical care. She died on October 10, 1899, in Krakow, Poland. Her remains were enshrined in the Krakow motherhouse.

Pope John Paul II beatified Angela on April 18, 1993, praising her as a glory of Poland and the Church. The Holy Father announced:

"Christ led Mother Angela on a truly exceptional path, causing her to share intimately in the mystery of his Cross. He formed her spirit by means of numerous sufferings, which she accepted with faith and a truly heroic submission to his Will: in seclusion and in solitude, in a long and trying illness and in the dark night of the soul. Her greatest desire was to become a 'victim of love.' "

Dominican Mystic

Also called Anna of the Angels, this blessed was a Dominican mystic of Peru, and she is revered as the second St. Rose of Lima. In her religious life, she combined the fervor of her native people of Peru with the splendid graces that enhanced her contemplative vocation.

ANNA MONTEAGUDO

(D. 1686)

MYSTIC

She was born in Arequipa, Peru, circa 1600, the daughter of Sebastian and Francisca de León Monteagudo. Her parents were Spaniards, and Anna benefited from their social status and their piety. Early in her life, she had great devotion to St. Rose of Lima, and demonstrated a reverence for the contemplative life at the same time. She was well-educated, attending the Dominican Convent of St. Catherine of Siena in Arequipa, where her religious vocation was recognized. The convent, which had been founded in 1577, was reportedly the size of a small city, forming a haven for the devout within its massive walls.

When Anna announced her desire to enter the Dominican convent, her parents did not give their consent willingly, having planned a secular life for their daughter. She did not swerve from her determination, and her parents relented in the face of Anna's obvious religious vocation. She entered the Dominican convent, receiving the religious name Anna of the Angels. After her religious training Anna resided in a small enclosure of the convent, where she matured spiritually.

Gifted with many remarkable graces, Anna demonstrated the ability to give spiritual counsel and to discern prophecies. She became novice mistress of the convent in 1648. There she served as a model of prayer and religious fidelity. She died in St. Catherine of Siena convent on January 10, 1686, having served faithfully for decades.

Pope John Paul II beatified Anna on February 2, 1985 while on a papal visit to Latin America. At the ceremony, Anna was honored for her faithfulness to her religious vows before thousands of her own countrymen. Her graces and gifts did not lead her astray from her commitment to service and to love.

Educator of the Young

For some souls, life is a series of trials and tests of faith that demands endurance. Annunciata Cocchetti was such a soul. She demonstrated with elegant simplicity that each day's crosses can be met with faith and prayer if Christ's love inflames the soul.

ANNUNCIATA
COCCHETTI

(D. 1882)

FOUNDRESS

Annunciata was born in Rovato, Italy, on May 9, 1800, the beloved daughter of a wealthy local family. When her parents died, Annunciata was raised by her grandmother, a noblewoman. This aristocratic relative was very devout and kind and gave Annunciata tender care. The young woman was educated by the Ursuline Sisters until they were suppressed by Napoleon. She was then tutored in her home, and there she recognized her calling to the service of others, particularly to the service of the abandoned girls of her region.

Her grandmother died in 1823, and her uncle insisted that Annunciata move to Milan, where she resided for six years. In 1831, however, given encouragement by her spiritual director, Annunciata went to Cemmo, where she joined Erminia Panzerini. Erminia was living as a religious and conducting a school for girls. Annunciata undertook the same charitable work and placed herself under the direction of Bishop Girolamo Verzeri. With his aid, she founded the Sisters of St. Dorothy of Cemmo. Annunciata was forty at the time. She received her religious training in Venice and then resided in Cemmo in the Val Camonica, near Brescia. There she remained the inspiration and model for her expanding community for another four decades. Annunciata died on March 23, 1882.

Pope John Paul II beatified Annunciata on April 21, 1991. The Holy Father praised the new blessed, saying: *"She expressed her love for God . . . with a fidelity that endured everything, with a strong asceticism which helped her overcome the difficulties she met throughout her daily life."*

ANSELM POLANCO
FONTECHA

(D. 1939)

MARTYR

Augustinian Bishop

The mindless violence of the Spanish Civil War has never been understood by the faithful of America. The war was depicted as glamorous in some American films — films that did not report the anti-Catholic nature of the Communist forces. Anselm Polanco Fontecha was a victim of these forces, and his only crime was being an Augustinian religious of holy repute and a bishop.

Anselm was born in Buenavista de Valdavia, Palencia, Spain, on April 16, 1881. Raised in the faith, he entered the Augustinians at age fifteen in Valladolid, and was educated and ordained for the priesthood. In time he was elected prior of his monastery, a position he held until he was sent to the Augustinian missions in the Philippines as a provincial councilor. Anselm became provincial superior in 1932 and visited China, Colombia, Peru, and the United States.

In 1935, Anselm was consecrated the bishop of Teruel, Spain, and the apostolic administrator of Albarracin. Three years later the city was taken by the revolutionary forces of the Republican Army. Anselm had already signed the collective letter of the Spanish bishops denouncing the persecution of the Church, and he refused to deny that signature or document. He was arrested with Blessed Felipe Ripoll Morata, his vicar general, and shared a prison cell with him for over a year. In 1939, when the Communist-led troops were retreating, Anselm and Blessed Felipe were used as human shields and then shot in a gorge near Gerona, called Can Tretze of Pont de Molins. Their remains are enshrined in the Cathedral of Teruel.

provided by the Order of St. Augustine

Anselm Polanco Fontecha

Pope John Paul II beatified Anselm and Felipe on October 1, 1995, announcing: *"Martyrdom is a particular gift of the Holy Spirit; a gift for the whole Church."* The Holy Father added: *"Anselm Polanco, an Augustinian religious, chose as his Bishop's motto: 'I will most gladly spend myself and be spent for your souls.'"* (See also Felipe Ripoll Morata.)

Apostle to the Poor

Caring souls, those who seek the salvation of their neighbors, will put all things to good use in order to impact upon the world. The abandoned, the used, and the trivial can become formidable weapons in the hands of the friends of God. Such a friend was Anthony Chevrier, a founder of religious congregations and the defender of thousands of the poor who spent his entire priestly life seeking the salvation of souls.

Anthony was born in Lyons, France,

ANTHONY CHEVRIER

(D. 1879)

FOUNDER

on April 16, 1825, baptized Antoine-Marie. After studying for the priesthood, Anthony was ordained in Lyons in 1850.

He was assigned as a curate in a working-class parish where he saw the sufferings of the poor and the disabled. On Christmas, 1856, Anthony received a divine revelation concerning his apostolate, and he vowed then and there to follow Jesus Christ "for the salvation of souls." One of his first charitable projects was for flood relief, and he was encouraged by St. John Vianney, the *Curé* of Ars, to serve as a chaplain for the "Town of Infant Jesus," a massive charitable organization. Anthony remained in this work for three years, learning the depths of poverty in his area and seeking innovative ways of teaching the Gospel and the love of Christ.

Anthony decided to reach the poor by opening a charitable institution in the midst of the suffering people. He purchased an abandoned ballroom in Lyons, called the Prado. There he opened services to aid the sick and poor, calling the work "the Providence of the Prado." He remained in the renovated ballroom for twenty years, joined by others who came to aid him in his apostolate. As a result, Anthony founded his congregation to stabilize and extend their charitable undertakings. He also wrote treatises and devised training programs for priests and seminarians. The Providence of the Prado set a standard for service to the needy of the region, and Anthony was recognized as a spiritual mentor and servant of the poor. He was called upon often to inspire others who were seeking the same ministries. His Society of the Priests of the Prado and the Society of Sisters of the Prado gave themselves entirely to the elderly, the abandoned, and the suffering.

Exhausted by his labors and suffering from painful ulcers, Anthony died in Lyons on October 2, 1879. He was buried in a chapel of the Prado.

Pope John Paul II beatified Anthony on October 4, 1986, in Lyons, praising his holiness and the dedication of this patron of the poor. Anthony was revered for his motto: "To know, to love, to act." His writings testified to the Christian commitment that he made as a priest of the people.

ANTHONY LUCCI

(D. 1752)

❦

BISHOP

Franciscan Reformer

The Church needs bright, quick-witted, holy men and women who can make their way in the world and confound the enemies of the faith. The revered Franciscan Anthony Lucci, a papal aide, a theological luminary, and a bishop dared to use modern approaches to the faithful. Anthony received praise in 1729 from Pope Benedict XIII (r. 1724-1730) who said, while consecrating him a bishop: "I have chosen a profound theologian and a great saint as Bishop of Bovino."

Anthony was born in Agnone, Italy, on August 2, 1681, and was baptized Angelo Nicola. Educated very well by his parents, Anthony entered the Friars Minor Conventual at Isernio. He made his profession as a Franciscan in 1698, and studied at Assisi and in other houses.

Anthony was ordained to the priesthood in 1705 and received his doctorate in theology in 1709. He was then assigned to San Lorenzo Monastery in Naples, where he taught and worked among the people of the city. His contemplative prayer life left its mark upon his ministry, and people recognized his piety and loyalty to the Franciscan ideals and to the faith.

In 1718, Anthony was elected as provincial superior, as a regent of studies, and then as rector of the College of St. Bonaventure in Rome. He served the pope as a theologian in two synods and as a consultor of the Holy Office and then was named bishop of Bovino. Pope Benedict XIII consecrated Anthony on February 7, 1729.

Charity was a hallmark of Anthony's service as bishop. He reformed the clergy and religious with kindness and began a series of campaigns to protect the poor. With Franciscan humility, Anthony served as a simple catechist and prepared children for the sacraments. He established schools and emptied his own episcopal treasury to provide for the needy.

After twenty-three years of service, Anthony died at Bovino on July 25, 1752. He was declared Venerable by Pope Pius IX (r. 1846-1878) in 1847.

Pope John Paul II beatified Anthony on June 18, 1989, stating that Anthony was *"attentive to the signs of the times,"* and served as *"a great tree"* that spread out branches of charitable activities to offer refuge and relief to all in need.

Scalopian Priest and Apostle of Workers

The plight of young men and women in past decades was the motivating concern of the many apostolates of Blessed Anton Maria Schwartz. Even before Pope Leo XIII issued *Rerum Novarum*, Anton labored for workers' unions and protections, starting social and political storms in his own era.

Anton was born in Baden, near Vienna, Austria, on February 28, 1852, the fourth of thirteen children. He was introduced to the musical world by his father and became a singer, attending also the Schotten-gymnasium in Vienna.

In 1869, Anton joined the Scalopian or Piarist Congregation, which was threatened with suppression. Anton left the congregation to study in the seminary in

ANTON

MARIA

SCHWARTZ

(D. 1929)

FOUNDER

Vienna. He was ordained a priest on July 23, 1875, and had to rent vestments and a chalice for his first Mass because he was too poor to purchase them.

Anton was assigned to Marchegg, where he became famous for his vigorous concerns. In 1879, he was named chaplain to the Daughters of Charity Hospital in Vienna-Sechshaus, and there he started his young workers' apostolate. He founded the Congregation of Christian Workers of St. Jospeh Calasanz, also called the *Kalasantiner* in Vienna. Four companions aided him in this founding, and Anton was able to better the conditions of young workers. He also founded an "Oratory for Apprentices," and another for workers, where housing, education, and spiritual instructions were freely available. Anton united himself with striking workers and became the patron of tailors and shoemakers.

In 1908, Anton withdrew from all public controversy, dedicating himself to the workers and their needs. He died on September 15, 1929.

Pope John Paul II beatified Anton on June 21, 1998, declaring:

"In Vienna 100 years ago, Father Anton Maria Schwartz was concerned with the lot of workers. He first dedicated himself to the young apprentices in the period of their professional training. Ever mindful of his own humble origins, he felt especially close to poor workers. To help them, he founded the Congregation of Christian Workers according to the rule of St. Joseph Calasanz, and it is still flourishing. He deeply longed to convert society to Christ and to renew it in him. He was sensitive to the needs of apprentices and workers, who frequently lacked support and guidance. The Holy Father added:

"He leaves us a message: Do all you can to protect Sunday! Show that it cannot be a work day because it is celebrated as the Lord's day! Above all, support young people who are unemployed! Those who give today's young people an opportunity to earn their living help to make it possible for tomorrow's adults to pass the meaning of life on to their children. I know that there are no easy solutions. This is why I repeat the words which guided Blessed Father Schwartz in his many effort: 'We must pray more!' "

Sardinian Virgin

The Church has always honored the devout young women who have fallen prey to sexual predators, bestowing upon these young women the rank of martyr because they rejected the advances of their attackers. Such a martyred virgin was Antonia Mesina.

ANTONIA MESINA

(D. 1935)

MARTYR

Born in Orgosolo, Sardinia, on June 21, 1919, Antonia was raised in a pious family and lived in tightly-knit community that revolved around the Church and the faith. Her life was bound by the seasons, by local customs, and by her parish activities. She grew up in the traditions of work and prayer, but she would never marry or know the joys of womanhood in her hometown. At age sixteen, on May 17, 1935, while walking with a young companion, Antonia was accosted by a male youth, Giovanni-Ignacio Catgui. Antonia's companion ran to the nearby village for help as Giovanni assaulted Antonia. She refused his advances, and in a rage he killed her. Her body bore seventy-four wounds from the stones that he used in his murderous assault.

Antonia's family and neighbors were horrified by the crime and inconsolable over their loss. Giovanni denied his guilt and tried to hide the evidence of his crime. The witness identified him, however, and two days later he confessed to his guilt. Giovanni was tried, condemned, and executed for murdering Antonia. Her remains were laid to rest amid the outpouring of grief by the men and women of the region. All of Sardinia honored this young woman who chose a brutal death before dishonor.

John Paul II beatified Antonia as a martyr on October 4, 1987, praising her innocence, her piety, and her fidelity to purity.

Brazilian Apostle

There are some souls who are so compelling and dynamic that their very presence in a city or region consoles others and gives hope to the faithful. Antoñio de Sant Anna Galvão, a native of Brazil, possessed a remarkable spirit that permeated his life and his apostolate. He was called a "man of peace and charity," and he lived the Franciscan ideals that inspired countless others.

Antoñio was born into a prominent family in São Paulo, Brazil, in 1739. The family lived in the Guaratingueta area of the city famed for religious devotion. Antoñio was raised in a pious household, and at age thirteen was placed in the Jesuit seminary at Belém. In time, his father directed him to the Alcantarine Franciscans, and he entered St. Bonaventure Friary in Macao, Rio de Janeiro, on April 15, 1760.

ANTOÑIO DE SANT ANNA GALVÃO

(D. 1822)

❧

FOUNDER

After completing his novitiate and seminary training, Antoñio was ordained a priest on June 11, 1762. He was assigned to St. Francis Friary in São Paulo, where he served as a porter (or gate keeper), preacher, and a confessor to the local lay men and women. From 1769-1770, Antoñio served as confessor to a unique institution, called a *recolhimento*, a convent of Recollects of St. Teresa in São Paulo. He then aided Sister Helena Maria of the Holy Spirit, a famed mystic, in founding Our Lady of the Conception of Divine Providence in February, 1774. Sister Helena died suddenly in 1775, and Antoñio was the one destined to guide the Recollects.

He wrote the rule for the congregation and built a church and convent dedicated on August 15, 1802. In 1781, Antoñio was named novice master of the Franciscans in Macao, and in 1798 appointed guardian of St. Francis Friary in São Paulo. When it became apparent that Antoñios duties would take him away from São Paulo, the bishop, religious, and laity notified the Franciscans that "None of the inhabitants of the city will be able to bear the absence of this religious for a single moment. . . . " Antoñio remained in São Paulo, holding various posts in the Franciscan Order until his health demanded rest.

In 1811, he found St. Clare Friary in Sorocaba, São Paulo, and then returned to St. Francis Friary. Receiving permission to reside within the Recollect convent, Antoñio died there on December 23, 1822. He was buried in the convent church, and his tomb became an immediate pilgrimage site. Pope John Paul II beatified Antoñio on October 25, 1998, in Rome, declaring that Antoñio *"fulfilled his religious consecration by dedicating himself with love and devotion to the afflicted, the suffering, and the slaves of his era in Brazil."* The Holy Father added: *"His authentically Franciscan faith, evangelically lived and apostolically spent in serving his neighbor, will be an encouragement to imitate this man of peace and charity."*

Christian Brother, "Guide for the Young"

ARNOLD (JULES) RÉCHE

(D. 1890)

RELIGIOUS

The saints of the "Little Way," those holy men and women who attain perfection just by fulfilling ordinary lives, are vitally important today. Arnold Réche was a Christian Brother, revered by his contemporaries as "an ambassador and minister of Jesus Christ," though his life was a matter of quietly fulfilling obligations.

Arnold was born in a simple family in Landroff, France, on September 2, 1838, the eldest of eight children. His parents were Claude and Anne Clausset Réche, and he was baptized Julian Nicholas Réche. Poor, Arnold started working early in life, performing menial jobs in his local area. He was honored even then as an exceptionally pious young man as he had a devout prayer life.

Drawn to the Christian Brothers who were conducting education programs in the town, Arnold asked to enter the congregation and was accepted. He became a novice in November, 1862, and in 1871 made his solemn profession. He then began an academic career that included teaching in the Christian Brothers school in Reims for fourteen years.

Arnold taught advanced students in many subjects, showing skill and concern. The Franco-Prussian War of 1870 involved Arnold and his confreres who cared for the wounded on both sides of the conflict. Arnold served with such distinction that he was awarded the Bronze Cross by the military authorities. At the same time his spiritual maturity and his intense prayer life were manifesting themselves in the congregation.

Arnold was appointed the director of novices in 1877 at the Christian Brothers monastery at Thillois, and in 1885 he went to Courlancy, near Reims, the new formation center. The novices of the congregation received training in docility, personal holiness, and loyalty to the ideals of the Christian Brothers through Arnold's solicitude and example. He had particular devotion to the Sacred Heart and the Passion of Christ, and he devoutly attended daily Mass and community prayer.

Arnold died in Reims on October 23, 1890, some months after being appointed director of the formation center at Courlancy. He suffered a cerebral hemorrhage. Buried in a cemetery in Reims, Arnold's grave was the site of miracles, and soon became a famed pilgrimage destination.

Pope John Paul II beatified Arnold on November 1, 1987, and the prayer prepared for this ceremony called this Christian Brother *"an admirable guide for the young."* Arnold was praised for his manner of sanctifying the everyday aspects of life and transforming them into heroic acts of love.

Asensio Barroso ✤ **See Florentino Asensio Barroso.**

Founder of the Institute of Sisters of the Immaculata

The rural communities that served as vibrant cradles of the faith in past centuries are disappearing in many places of the world today. The simple farm routines and the solitude of nature's wilderness forged remarkable human souls in these places that can still fascinate and inspire new generations. Augustine (or Agostino) Roscelli came out of one of these rural setting with zeal and contemplative wisdom.

AUGUSTINE ROSCELLI

(D. 1902)

FOUNDER

Augustine was born in Casarza Ligure, Italy, on July 27, 1818, to a local farming family. Reserved as a child but bright and sensitive, Augustine's labors involved the care of the farm's sheep flock.

He spent hours with the sheep, learning to pray and to seek union with God. This spiritual union led him to a parish mission in 1835, where he received the grace of a religious vocation. His seminary training was sponsored by generous friends, and Augustine was ordained in 1846.

His first assignment was as a curate of St. Martin d'Albaro, and in 1854 he became pastor of the Church of Consolation. Concerned about the young women of the area, Agustine founded a residential center for them in Genoa and provided intellectual and professional training programs. In 1874, he became chaplain of a provincial orphanage and served as well as a prison chaplain.

His congregation, the Institute of Sisters of the Immaculata, was founded in 1876 to serve in the residential women's centers. He devoted his life to aiding those forgotten or abased by society. Through the years, Augustine became spiritually mature and was especially gifted with the grace of contemplation. These mystical experiences spurred him to ever greater service, and this spirit was imbued in his religious congregation. Augustine died in Genoa on May 7, 1902.

Pope John Paul II beatified Augustine on May 7, 1995, declaring:

"A spiritual feature characteristic of Blessed Agostino Roscelli, founder of the Sisters of the Immaculata, was to work at the service of his brothers and sisters without ever neglecting his interior union with the Lord. The true contemplative is the one who is able to work with greater force and incisiveness for the salvation of souls and the good of the Church. The new blessed's apostolic activity was truly fruitful because it flowed from a genuine mystical and contemplative life. His ardent love for God, enriched by the gift of wisdom, enabled him to give himself as far as possible to serving his neighbor without ever being separated from the Lord."

Augusto Andres Fernández ☙ See Martyrs of Asturias (Turon).

Aurelio María Acebrón ☙ See Martyrs of Almeria.

Dominican Tertiary, "The Man of Mary"

Pompeii, the buried city of Italy, has long fascinated people around the world because of its rare glimpse of life in ancient Rome. The city has been restored, rescued from a timeless tomb by modern archaeologists, and tourists flock to the splendid ruins. What many people do not know is that there is a Pompeii that did not die; a modern city that has undergone all of the pressures of political, social, and religious change. Pompeii is also a city that can claim its own apostle — Bartholomew Longo, the "Man of Mary." Bartholomew was a Third Order Dominican who promoted devotion to Our Lady of the Rosary throughout his life and started a unique Marian devotion.

BARTHOLOMEW LONGO

(D. 1926)

LAY RELIGIOUS

Bartholomew was born in Latiana in southern Italy, on February

11, 1841, the son of a prosperous and devout physician. He was educated by the Scalopian or Piarist priests and then studied law at the University of Naples. On March 25, 1871, Bartholomew became a Dominican tertiary, receiving the name "Brother Rosary." He devoted himself to charitable works until 1872, when he went to Pompeii on a legal matter. There he felt compelled to counteract the growing ignorance of the faith and the rampant secularism in the region.

Bartholomew bought a rather unfashionable painting of Our Lady of the Rosary which he restored and decorated to use in his apostolate. He erected a shrine for the painting and started the Rosary of the Fifteen Saturdays, a unique Marian devotion. The cornerstone of the chapel was laid in 1876. Pope St. Pius X (r. 1903-1914) elevated the shrine to the status of a pontifical basilica, as miracles were reported at the site of the holy image almost immediately.

A noblewoman, Countess Marianna de Fusco, had been aiding Bartholomew in his apostolate. When Bartholomew consulted Pope Leo XIII (r. 1878-1903) about his work, the Holy Father recommended he marry the countess in order to avoid scandal. They were wed and devoted their lives to the people of Pompeii. This ancient ruin of a city experienced a spiritual rebirth because of their devotion. They opened orphanages and did other charitable works, all of which they ceded to the Holy See. In 1906, Bartholomew turned over their entire estate and all properties to the Holy See. Their schools, hospices, and presses are still in operation.

When Bartholomew died on October 5, 1926, his remains were placed in the basilica. A year before he had been made a Knight of the Guard Cross of the Holy Sepulcher. His tomb was prepared beneath the throne in Our Lady's shrine.

Pope John Paul II beatified Bartholomew on October 26, 1980, and in the ceremony he was called the *"Herald of the Blessed Virgin Mary's Rosary,"* and honored for his generosity and lifelong commitment to the faith.

Marian Apostle

During every era men and women are required to speak out against error, injustice, and philosophies that threaten the faith. Bartholomew Maria dal Monte was needed in his own age, and he responded with fervor, eloquence, and a certain charm that led to his being called "the missionary of discretion." An apostle of the Blessed Virgin Mary, Bartholomew defended the faith through a very turbulent time.

Bartholomew was born in Bologna, Italy, on November 4, 1726, the son of Orazio dal Monte and Anna Maria Basani. He was confirmed by Prospero Cardinal Lambertini, who

BARTHOLOMEW MARIA DAL MONTE

(D. 1778)

MISSIONARY

was to become Pope Benedict XIV (r. 1740-1758). As a young man, Bartholomew displayed great discretion and zeal, and he was revered for his dedication.

Trained by the Jesuits at Santa Lucia College, Bartholomew met with St. Leonard of Port Maurice, who encouraged Bartholomew's missionary desires and his priesthood. Bartholomew was ordained on December 20, 1749, and completed a degree in theology. He then began his priestly ministry of parish missions, first in Bologna and then in sixty-two dioceses, as he was a popular and powerful orator.

Parish missions, Lenten retreats, spiritual exercises, and conversions were daily activities for Bartholomew for twenty-six years. He opposed the heresy of Jansenism and the philosophical errors of the Enlightenment of his era, becoming known as "the missionary of discretion." Bartholomew was also devoted to Mary, the Mother of Mercy, and to saving souls.

He recognized the secular forces loose in the world, and he labored unceasingly to give the Church a voice amid the materialism and chaos. Bartholomew also had many spiritual graces. Worn out by the unending demands of his mission schedule, Bartholomew predicted his own death on Christmas Eve. His died in Bologna on December, 24, 1778, as he had prophesied. His remains were enshrined in the basilica of Bologna.

Pope John Paul II beatified Bartholomew on September 27, 1997, in Bologna, stating that Bartholomew's life was modeled on Christ and on divine love. The Holy Father announced: *". . . Blessed dal Monte shines brightly before us as a witness to Christ who was particularly sensitive to the demands of the modern age."*

Hospitaller of St. John and Crusader for Reform

No age of human history has escaped tragedy or violence, and such brutalities can cripple time-honored institutions and traditions. The world in which Benedict Menni lived had been drained and wounded by political and social conflicts. He did not cringe or seek a safe haven but went to do battle with the problems of his age. Devoted to Christ and to the Immaculate Virgin, whom he addressed as "the Queen of Love," Benedict became their champion.

BENEDICT
MENNI

(D. 1914)

❦

RELIGIOUS

He was born in Milan, Italy, on March 11, 1841, and was raised firmly in the Catholic Faith. When he had completed his education, Benedict worked in a bank and became involved in the political upheavals of the time. Drawn into military service, he labored as a stretcher bearer in the Battle of Magenta, witnessing the horrors of war on a close, personal basis.

He was released from military duties

and prayed to know the Will of God for his life. Through prayer, he was led to a local hermit who recognized unique spiritual abilities in Benedict and advised him to become a religious. Benedict entered the Order of the Hospitallers of St. John of God, receiving his habit on May 13, 1860. In 1866, he was ordained a priest in Rome.

On January 14, 1867, Benedict was received by Pope Pius IX (r. 1846-1878), who knew that the father general of the Order had asked Benedict to go to Spain to restore the Order there. The pope said: "Go forth to Spain, my son, and restore the Order in its place of its birth." Benedict had many trials in Spain, including a threat to his life, and he was expelled once for his activities. However he continued his labors and restored the Order in Portugal, Mexico, and Spain. He also founded the Hospitaller Sisters of the Sacred Heart of Jesus with Maria Josefa Recio and Maria Augustias Jimenez. The congregation was founded in Ciempozuelos, Spain, in May, 1881.

While active and crusading for reform and restoration, Benedict was seeking the perfection of the saints. This spiritual charisma transformed his daily activities and ennobled his trials. Benedict died, exhausted by his ministries, in Dinan, in northern France, on April 24, 1914.

Pope John Paul II beatified Benedict on June 23, 1985, observing:

"Father Menni fully understood this need to dedicate one's own life to Christ. He had read and made his own the words of the divine Master which have been proclaimed in the Gospel of this eucharistic celebration: 'Whenever you did things to the least of these my brothers, you did them to me' (Mt 25:40). . . . He is therefore a glory of the Order of the Hospitaller Brothers who have in him a luminous example of the service of the sick, identified with Christ."

Foundress of the Benedictine Sisters of Providence

There are instances in which married couples, inspired by divine grace, give up the conjugal pleasures of their wedded state in order to conform to the Will of God for their salvation. Benedicta Cambiagio Frassinello and her husband put aside their own desires to accomplish particular apostolates.

Benedicta was born on October 2, 1791, in Langasco, near Genoa, Italy, the daughter of Giuseppe and Francesca Cambiagio. The family, devout and faithful, moved to Pavia while Benedicta was still young. There Benedicta, at age twenty, had a profound mystical experience. She devoted herself to prayer and penance and wanted a religious vocation.

BENEDICTA CAMBIAGIO FRASSINELLO

(D. 1858)

FOUNDRESS

She married Giovanni Battista Frassinella on February 7, 1816, in compliance with her family, and the couple lived a normal married life for two years. Then Giovanni, impressed by Benedicta's holiness, agreed to live as brother and sister. The couple was taking care of Benedicta's younger sister Maria at the time. When Maria died of intestinal cancer in 1825, Giovanni entered the Somaschan Fathers and Benedicta became an Ursuline.

One year later, Benedicta became ill and left the convent to return to Pavia, where she began an apostolate among young women of the region. Giovanni was recalled from his monastery to aid in this work, and the couple took vows of perfect chastity. So successful were they in Pavia that Benedicta was appointed "Promoter of Public Instruction." Unfortunately, civil and Church authorities criticized Benedicta because of the unusual relationship she shared with her husband; thus, in 1838 she turned over her work to the bishop of Pavia and withdrew to Ronco Scrivia. There the couple and five companions founded the Congregation of the Benedictine Sisters of Providence and opened a school. Benedicta died in Ronco Scrivia on March 21, 1858.

Pope John Paul II beatified Benedicta on May 10, 1987, declaring that her remarkable piety inspired others to heroic sanctity and to unstinting service of those in need.

Berlin Canon and Foe of Nazis

The rise of Hitler and the Nazi Party engulfed the world in horror and in conflict. Spectacular military campaigns raged across Europe, and it took the combined efforts of the United States, Britain, and their allies to turn back the barbaric tide of Nazism. The Nazis began their cruel assault on faith and human decency in Germany, and they claimed many victims long before their open aggression roused the free world. One of the victims was Bernard Lichtenburg, who chose torment and death rather that surrender the truths of the faith.

BERNARD LICHTENBURG

(D. 1943)

MARTYR

Bernard was born in Ohlau, Silesia (modern east central Europe), on December 3, 1875. He received the grace of a priestly vocation and studied at the seminary in Innsbruck, Austria. He was ordained at the age of twenty-four. Bernard was sent to Berlin, where he studied at St. Hedwig's Cathedral. He was appointed a canon of the cathedral and began his ministry as the Nazis began their vicious campaign for power.

The rise of the Nazis alarmed Bernard, especially as spread through Josef Goebbels's newspaper, *Der Angriff.* Bernard became politically active, and in

1935 he protested the rising tide of Nazism and the persecution of the Jews by going to Herman Göring to make a personal plea for a more humane policy. The Nazis viewed Bernard as naïve and pious at first, dismissing his concerns with nonchalance.

Bernard was not naïve, and he did not intend to stand by idly as the Nazis destroyed Germany and the faith. He continued his confrontations with officials and preached again and again for an awareness of the murderous immorality being institutionalized in the land. He was warned by many but did not falter in his opposition to the Nazi dogmas. He distributed copies of Pope Pius XI's (r. 1922-1939) encyclical *Mit brennender Sorge* ("With Burning Anxiety"), which was banned in Germany.

In 1941, Bernard was arrested and held in appalling conditions for two years. He was then given to the Gestapo for "re-education," the Nazi method of controlling adversaries. On his way to Dachau concentration camp, Bernard, old and ill from abuse, died in a cattle car near the town of Hof on November 5, 1943. More than four thousand mourners attended his funeral in Berlin, despite the Nazi condemnation of his activities and beliefs.

In Berlin on June 23, 1996, Pope John Paul II beatified Bernard with Carol Leisner, another victim of the Nazis, proclaiming:

"On the basis of his clear principles . . . Lichtenburg spoke and acted independently and fearlessly. Nevertheless, he was almost overcome with joy and happiness when his Bishop, Konrad von Preysing, upon his last prison visit at the end of September, 1943, relayed to him a message from my predecessor, Pius XII, in which he expressed his deepest sympathy and paternal appreciation. Whoever is not hampered by cheap polemics knows full well what Pius XII thought about the Nazi regime and how much he did to help the countless people who were persecuted by the regime. For Bernard Lichtenburg conscience was 'the place, the sacred place, where God speaks to man' (Veritatis Splendor, n. 58). And the dignity of conscience always derives from the truth (cf. Ibid, n. 63)."

Passionist Superior

Some individuals are called to fame and power in the world, others to lives that are fulfilled by families, loved ones, and professions that offer comfort and stability. Others are led to Christ's service totally. Bernard Maria Silvestrelli was called to personal sacrifice, and because of his dedication and zeal, he is the glory of the Passionists and hailed as the "Second St. Paul of the Cross."

Bernard was born in Rome, Italy, on November 7, 1831, the third of seven children of Gian Tommasso and Teresa

BERNARD MARIA SILVESTRELLI

(D. 1911)

RELIGIOUS

Silvestrelli. Baptized Cesare, he was raised in a devout Catholic home that trained him in the virtues. Bernard was educated at home, then by the Jesuits, and finally at the Roman College. A brilliant man of remarkable administrative abilities, he originally intended to serve as a civil servant, but he sacrificed all worldly honors when he enter the Passionist Congregation at the age of twenty-two.

Bernard brought his academic background to the task of renewing and expanding the congregation. Ill health forced him to return home for a time, but he continued his studies and was ordained a priest on December 22, 1855. He also returned to the Passionists and was professed on April 28, 1857, receiving the religious name of Bernard Maria of Jesus. One of his novitiate companions was St. Gabriel Possenti.

In 1865, Bernard became the master of the novices at Scala Santa Monastery in Rome, and was named superior of the house when international students were enrolled. In 1875, he became a provincial counselor, and on May 4, 1878, Bernard was elected the superior general of the Passionists. He was an energetic defender of the Passionist ideals, directing restoration and expansion programs and serving as superior general from 1878 to 1889 and from 1893 until 1903.

Bernard died on December 9, 1911, at Morricone Monastery after suffering a fall. His Cause was opened soon after.

Pope John Paul II beatified Bernard on October 16, 1988, praising him for holding *"steadfast in the profession of faith with exemplary strength and generosity."* The Holy Father called Bernard *"an instrument of mercy and grace."*

Bibiana Khamphai ❧ **See Martyrs of Thailand**.

Ursuline of the Little Way

While most religious servants of the Church honor Christ with an active apostolate — a life of visible labor in charitable programs or the missions —

BLANDINA
MERTEN

(D. 1918)

VICTIM SOUL

some unique souls are called to follow a hidden path to the Cross. These men and women labor each day while enduring suffering interiorly. They attain such perfection through the Cross that they are hailed as "Apostles of Suffering." Blandina Merten, an Ursuline nun, was a woman who followed her hidden path with love.

Blandina was born Maria Magdalena Merten on July 10, 1883, in Duppenweiler, Germany. The ninth child of a pious family, she received the grace of a teaching vocation and entered the Ursuline convent. She would serve for only eleven years as an Ursuline, accomplishing no famous activity or goal, and her life was filled with intense physical suffering. She bore her pain in calm silence, demonstrating for the world the spiritual truth that all things, no matter how small, insignificant, or commonplace, can lead souls to God.

After months of ill health and pain, Blandina was diagnosed with a terminal illness. She bore the news with silence and calm, indicating that her desire for union with Christ would be fulfilled. As an Ursuline she relied upon the rules and ideals of her religious life in order to continue teaching without drawing attention to her sufferings. Her teaching vocation was noted for profound concern for each of her students. She did not burden them with her sufferings, did not seek their sympathy. She centered her pain and her hidden torments on the Holy Eucharist and prayers saying: "Whoever loves God does not need to achieve exceptionally elevated actions; it is enough to love." Blandina died in the company of her Ursuline Sisters in Trier on May 18, 1918.

Pope John Paul II beatified Blandina on November 1, 1987, praising her heroism and her fidelity to the "Little Way" of performing all things for love.

Foundress of the Missionary Sisters of the Holy Family

A Church divided is a Church made vulnerable to its enemies in the modern world. The Holy Fathers and many Church leaders of this century have been preaching this truth for a very long time. Recent events, and the terrors of World War II, certainly prove to teach Christians that only in union and solidarity is there common defense. A Polish woman, Boleslawa Maria Lament, taught these same realities. She did not speak in words alone but in deeds that changed the lives of thousands.

BOLESLAWA MARIA LAMENT

(D. 1946)

FOUNDRESS

Boleslawa Maria was born in Lowicz, Poland, on July 3, 1862, and as she matured in the faith and in prayer, she took the motto of St. Ignatius as her own: "All for the greater glory of God."

Boleslawa began her apostolate by establishing Catholic organizations in Lowicz to care for the abandoned or ill. When others came to join her in this ministry, she started the Missionary Sisters of the Holy Family. Her congregation served in St. Petersburg, Mohilev, and Zytomierz. After World War I ended, Boleslawa went to Pinsk, Vilnius, and Bialystak. The times were difficult, and she had to start over on three separate occasions, facing hunger and homelessness because of political unrest.

While Boleslawa concentrated on the forgotten suffering of the modern world, she also felt a need to work for Church unity. She worked ceaselessly to improve relations between Catholics and the Orthodox faithful in Poland. Long before Vatican Council II, Boleslawa was an instrument of ecumenical accord. When she died in Bialystak on January 29, 1946, people of all faiths came to mourn her passing from the world.

Pope John Paul II beatified Boleslawa in Bialystak, Poland, on June 5, 1991. He called the beatification a true pilgrimage to honor Boleslawa, who *"set herself apart by showing sensitivity to human misfortune."* The Holy Father also declared: *"The faithful in Poland and in areas of her apostolate will henceforth be able to acclaim her in liturgical prayer and to follow the example of her life."*

Braulius María Corres Diaz de Cerio ❧ See Martyrs of the Hospitallers of St. John of God.

Foundress of the Ursuline Sisters of Mary Immaculate

Throughout history, certain souls have attracted the attention of others, radiating a light or an aura of unique destiny. Events, even tragedies, intrude at times on the lives of such individuals, but they do not allow such occurrences to deter them, using all for good. They follow wherever God leads, and they come at last to the fulfillment of union and perfection. Brigida of Jesus had this extraordinary aura.

BRIGIDA OF JESUS MORELLO

(D. 1679)

FOUNDRESS

Living in perilous times and experiencing the day-to-day problems, trials, and pains of life, Brigida emerged from each episode of her life purified and radiant. She was born in San Michelle di Pagana, Italy, on June 17, 1610, her parents were Nicolo and Lavinia Borgese Morello, nobles, who had seven children. Brigida was the sixth born to the couple. Well-educated and trained in the faith, her motto even as a child was "to be a saint and to be a religious, in order to become a saint faster."

But the convent was not her only destiny. In October, 1633, Brigida married Matteo Zancari, from Cremona. He lived in Salsomaggiore, an area recovering from the 1630 plague. Brigida and her sister, Agata, aided in this recovery. Two years later, owing to political upheaval, the family had to seek refuge in the castle of Tabiano. The castle came under siege, and Matteo, leading the defenses, became seriously ill with tuberculosis. Brigida collapsed as well. While she recovered, her husband did not.

After mourning Matteo, Brigida dedicated herself to a life of penance and prayer, aided by the Franciscans of Salsomaggiore and the Jesuits of Piacenza. She displayed particular mystical gifts, and served as a prophetess and a miracle worker. When Margherita de' Medici Farnese opened a school for young girls in Piacenza, Brigida was recommended for the position of directress. Out of this apostolate the Ursuline Sisters of Mary Immaculate was founded. The congregation was started on February 17, 1649. In April, 1655, Brigida offered herself as a victim of love. For almost a quarter of a century, Brigida endured a serious illness, borne with joy. She died on September 3, 1679.

Pope John Paul II beatified Brigida on March 15, 1998, declaring: *"In love with God, she was thus ready to open her heart and her arms to brothers and sisters in need."* The Holy Father added: *"A constant invitation to trust in God shines through her. . . ."*

Martyr of China

The Church has been blessed with young men and women who have set sail to distant shores to bring the Gospel to strangers in foreign lands. They labored and died, or they were slain by those who opposed their faith, but they witnessed for Christ. Callisto Caravario, a young missionary in China lived in this fashion, and he died defending the purity of the women in his company.

CALLISTO CARAVARIO

(D. 1930)

MISSIONARY

Callisto was born in northern Italy on June 8, 1903, and moved to Turin with his family as a young boy. Educated in local religious schools, Callisto applied to the Salesians in 1918, and was professed the following year as a member of the congregation. In 1924, he was sent to Shanghai and then to Macao and Timor. In 1929, Callisto was ordained by Bishop Versiglia in Shiu Chow. He then accompanied the bishop on a missionary tour, setting out on February 24, 1930. Two young men and three young women, catechical teachers, were in Bishop Versiglia's party on board a small boat.

On February 25, 1930, Chinese pirates took over the boat, assaulting the women. Callisto and Bishop Versiglia defended them and were beaten for their efforts. Taken on shore by the pirates, the two martyrs knew they would be slain for defending the women in their care. They were shot together, despite Bishop Versiglia's plea that Callisto be spared. The martyrs' intervention did save the young women, and other missionaries looking for the group claimed the bodies of Callisto and Bishop Versiglia. Callisto was buried at the door of the church of St. Joseph in Lin Kong How. His death and the martyrdom of Bishop Luigi Versiglia brought new converts to the faith in that region.

Pope John Paul II beatified Callisto on May 15, 1983, with Bishop Versiglia, saying their martyrdoms served as foundations for the Church in China. The Holy Father honored the martyrs for giving their lives *"for the salvation and the moral integrity of their neighbors."*

Foundress of the Daughters of Jesus

Cándida María Cipitria y Barriola was a visionary blessed with a prophetic view of the modern world who employed new techniques and innovations to empower the Church. Her motto was: "I am for God alone."

CÁNDIDA MARÍA OF JESÚS CIPITRIA Y BARRIOLA

(D. 1912)

FOUNDRESS

Cándida María was born in Berrospe, Andoáin, Guipúzcoa, Spain, on May 31, 1845, and was baptized Juana Josepha Cipitria y Barriola. She grew up in a turbulent period in Spain and recognized the dangers facing Catholics, especially the young, the poor, and the politically powerless. Under the direction of the Jesuit priest Michael Herranz, Cándida started a series of charitable and educational programs. In 1871, she gathered other young women and founded her congregation, The Daughters of Jesus, in Salamanca.

Called *Hijas de Jesus* in Spain, the Daughters of Jesus were the result of Cándida's vision of using modern methods for education. Cándida had witnessed the devastation visited upon the people of Spain, and she designed her congregation to provide educational institutions, retreat houses, medical dispensaries, and social service centers. The congregation spread to Europe, Asia, and South America, inspired by her example. The Daughters of Jesus, approved by Pope Leo XIII in 1902, arrived in the United States in 1950, founding a convent and opening their educational apostolates. Mother Cándida died in Salamanca on August 9, 1912. Mother Cándida's fame grew after her death as the faithful heard of her profound spiritual life. A contemplative, she trusted in Our Lady, whom she called "the Star of our way." Mother Cándida spent long hours in prayer before the tabernacle, and she radiated calm and trust in the Holy Spirit. She also recognized the holiness of Blessed Maria Antonia Bandrés y Elosegui, who was raised to the altars with her.

Pope John Paul II beatified Cándida on May 12, 1996, observing:

"Keeping Jesus' commandments is the supreme proof of love (cf. Jn 14:21). This is how it was understood by Mother Cándida María de Jesús Cipitria y Barriola, who said as a young girl: 'I am for God alone' and at the moment of her death stated once again: 'In all forty years of my religious life, I do not recall a single moment which did not belong to God alone.' Her deep experience of God's love for each of his creatures led her to respond with generosity

and dedication. She concretely expressed her love of others by founding the Congregation of the Daughters of Jesus, whose charism was the Christian education of children and adolescents. The attention she showered on her sisters, the benefactors of her works, priests, students, the needy, to the point of becoming universal, are a visible expression of her love for God, of the radical way she followed Jesus and her total commitment to the cause of his kingdom."

Carlos Eraña Guruceta ☙ **See Martyrs of the Marianists Congregation.**

Carol Leisner ☙ **See Karl Leisner.**

Polish Victim of Communists

When the Berlin Wall was torn asunder in 1989, people around the globe breathed a sigh of relief because it signaled that one of the most hated regimes in the history of the world was finally on the verge of total collapse. The atrocities committed by Communist dictatorships around the globe are well documented, and the prominent victims of the Communists are still heralded. Now the hidden victims, such as Caroline Kozka, are being hailed for their sacrifices and loyalty to the faith. Caroline, a martyred virgin of Poland, was one of the countless victims of the Russian occupation of that country.

CAROLINE KOZKA

(D. 1914)

MARTYR

She was born in Wal-Ruda, Poland, on August 2, 1898, the fourth of the eleven children of Jan and Maria Borzecka Kozka. They resided in a devout rural community of Poland where Caroline was raised as a daughter of the Church. She attended Mass and devotional services and taught catechism, as the local parish was the center of the community's life.

When Caroline was sixteen, she was attractive, lively, and enthusiastic about life and her future. She was denied that future by a Russian soldier. He kidnapped her on November 18, 1914, after she refused his advances. The soldier dragged Caroline to a woods near the village where he assaulted and killed her.

Caroline's body was not discovered for a long time, despite the frantic searches conducted by her family and fellow villagers. On December 4, her body was found, and she was buried two days later in a parish plot at Zabawa. In November, 1917, her remains were solemnly interred, and a cross was erected at the site of her cruel slaying. Caroline was revered as a martyr of purity.

Pope John Paul II beatified Caroline in Tarnów, Poland, on June 10,

1987. Throughout the beatification ceremony, Caroline was honored as a young woman who would never surrender to brutal impurity, even at the cost of her life.

Catherine Marie Drexel **See Katherine Marie Drexel.**

Dominican Tertiary, the "Little Nun"

CATHERINE JARRIGE

(D. 1836)

LAYWOMAN

The modern world looks back at the French Revolution and its Reign of Terror as an era of unbridled cruelty and horror. For the Catholic faithful who had to endure its terrifying spectacles and its relentless pursuit of religious men and women, the Revolution was a nightmare. Few had the courage to proclaim Christ in this dark hour of France, and even fewer dared to protest the hunted priests and religious who were being wantonly slain. Catherine Jarrige, the "Little Nun of the Priests and the Poor" achieved all things for Christ in the midst of the horrors. She dared to keep the faith and to protect all that she held sacred.

She was born on October 4, 1754, in Doumis, France, the youngest of seven children, and as a child was called *Catinon-Menette,* "Cathy the Little Nun" because of her humility and gentle ways. At the age of nine, Catherine was sent to work as a maid, and at thirteen, she suffered the tragic loss of her mother. She learned how to make exquisite lace products as a way of earning a living as a result, and moved to Mauriac to support herself.

Catherine became a Third Order Dominican soon after, adapting to the life of a *menette,* or "little nun." She lived in a small room with her sister and kept a vow of chastity, praying daily with other tertiaries. Her constant companion was the Rosary as she cared for the sick and the poor and sheltered orphans. She worked in this apostolate for many decades, even as political conditions in France worsened around her. As a dedicated laywoman, Catherine was able to serve her neighbors in person, using her skills to aid the poor, especially the sick and elderly.

In 1791, the French Revolution brought terror and death to the Catholic people of the nation. Priests and religious were driven from their institutions and hunted by authorities for cruel punishments. Catherine, alert to the need for havens for priests, started a network of safe houses. She found devout families willing to aid the priests, and she kept such havens supplied with food and clothing. Catherine even managed to provide vestments, hosts, and wine so that the priests could celebrate Mass for the faithful. She endured the years of turmoil, keeping faithful watch on her charges.

After the persecution ended, Catherine resumed her usual ministry among the poor and needy. She also served in prisons and hospitals. She died on July 4, 1836.

Pope John Paul II beatified Catherine Jarrige on November 24, 1996, declaring: *"A Dominican tertiary, the spiritual daughter of St. Catherine of Siena, she preached Christ and his Gospel by her actions. Her message is a message of joy, love, and hope."*

Cecilia Butsi ❧ **See Martyrs of Thailand**.

Martyred Gypsy Layman

Some of the most remarkable and enduring people on the face of the earth are the Gypsies. Legends of their nomadic ways, their life set apart from the modern world, abound. Gypsies have been in Europe and other countries for centuries, always keeping to their own customs and traditions, and are usually the target of animosity or fear by settled towns and villages. The Catholic Faith nurtured by the Gypsies of Europe is little known or understood, but now one of their own has been raised to altars of the Church and hailed as "Blessed." That Gypsy is Ceferino Gimenez Malla, called "El Pele" by his people and respected by Spanish of all walks of life.

Ceferino was born in Fraga, Huesca, Spain, probably on August 26, 1861. He married a Gypsy woman, Teresa Gimenez Castro and lived in Barbastro. Having no children, they adopted a niece, Pepita, and raised her as a devout Catholic.

Ceferino was a respected horse dealer, called the patron of the Gypsies. Though il-

CEFERINO

GIMENEZ

MALLA

(D. 1936)

MARYTR

literate, he was sought as a counsel for the poor and the politically powerful. He continued his religious observances and was revered as a pious Catholic. In July, 1936, Ceferino protested the arrest of a priest by Spanish revolutionary militia and was taken prisoner because of his fervor. Placed in a Franciscan monastery which had been converted into a prison, Ceferino recited the Rosary and incited his guards. One of the leading revolutionists of the area came to Ceferino to warn him to hide his faith, but "El Pele," a daily communicant, even refused an offer of freedom if he would stop reciting the Rosary. Considering devotion to the Blessed Virgin Mary a matter of honor, Ceferino refused to deny the Holy Mother of God. He was not impressed with the threats and lies of the revolutionaries. With great calm, Ceferino continued to recite the Rosary and was singled out for punishment. He was shot to death on August 2, 1936, in the cemetery of Barbastro, and died with his Rosary in his hands, crying: "Long live Christ the King."

Pope John Paul II beatified Ceferino on Sunday, May 4, 1997, declaring him a glory of his people and a glory of the Church. As was noted during the ceremony, Ceferino proved that a *"death for the faith"* is always rooted deeply in a *"life of faith."*

Child Martyrs of Tlaxcala ❦ **See Christopher, Anthony, and John**.

Passionist Missionary to Dublin

A Passionist missionary with the title of "St. of Mount Argus," Charles Houben was a holy man who went where Christ called him for the good of souls and a human being who understood the needs of others.

CHARLES OF MOUNT ARGUS HOUBEN

(D. 1893)

❦

RELIGIOUS

Charles was born in Munstergeleen, in the Netherlands, on December 11, 1821, the fourth of eleven children born to Peter Joseph and Elizabeth Houben. He was baptized John Andrew, and his father recorded the baptism and the family's gratitude to God, as was the pious custom of the time. Charles was a quiet child and a slow learner who worked on his lessons carefully. He received the grace of a priestly vocation early and realized that he had to master his school work.

In 1840, Charles enlisted in the military and spent five years on duty, although he saw only three months active service. When this reserve term ended, he worked in his uncle's mill.

In 1845, he entered the Passionists and was given the religious name of Charles of St. Andrew. He was ordained on February 21, 1852 and was assigned to England, where he remained for five years. In July, 1857, Charles went to serve in a retreat house in Dublin, in an area called Mount Argus. He returned to England for a time in 1866 but then went back to Mount Argus, where he labored and earned the trust of the local people.

Charles was tireless in his efforts to ease the burdens of the poor in his mission. His holiness was recognized by Catholics and non-Catholics alike, and when he died, exhausted by his labors, on January 5, 1893, the entire city mourned his passing. When Charles was beatified, a 103-year-old woman, a living witness of Charles' work who revered his memory, attended the ceremony.

Pope John Paul II beatified Charles on October 16, 1988, with Bernard Silvestrelli. The Holy Father praised Charles's ecumenical labors and his ministry in the Sacrament of Penance, saying that Charles *"was daily concerned with the difficulties of others."*

Child Martyrs of Mexico

The land of Mexico is one of the oldest cultural monuments in the world, filled with people who achieved architectural, metropolitan, astronomical, and military heights before the time of Christ. When the Catholic Faith was introduced into Mexico, it blossomed into a vibrant, living flower that has survived military and political assaults and suppressions. The faith of Mexico was watered with the blood of martyrs in almost every generation, dating back to the Child Martyrs of Tlaxcala: Christopher, Anthony, and John.

CHRISTOPHER, ANTHONY, AND JOHN

(D.C. 1527)

MARTYRS

These young men are believed to be the first laymen to be martyred in the New World. They were slain sometime between 1527 and 1529 in the region of Mexico which is now the diocese of Tlaxcala.

Christopher, called Cristobal in Mexico, was born in Atlihuetza about 1514, the son of an influential native resident and one of his sixty wives. He was sent to the Franciscan mission school nearby, where he became a Catholic. Christopher, zealous in the faith, tried to convert his family and admonished his father for his dissolute lifestyle. His father killed Christopher, who was twelve or thirteen years old, because of these rebukes.

Anthony, called Antonio in Mexico, was born in Tizatlan, circa 1516. He was the son of a local senator and heir to the family fortune. Anthony was baptized at the Franciscan mission at Tlaxcala and was very devout. When the Dominican priest Bernardino de Minaya started his journey to Oaxaca, Anthony volunteered to accompany him into the dangerous territory. He was slain at Cuauhtinchan, near Puebla, in 1529.

John, called Juan in Mexico, was born in Tizatlan, and appears to have been a servant in Antonio's family. When Antonio was baptized, John was at his side. This faithful lad accompanied Antonio and the Dominican missionary to Oaxaca, sharing their fate, and probably died while trying to save his master and friend.

All of the Child Martyrs of Tlaxcala were revered immediately after their deaths. The missionaries gathered up their remains and placed them in the mission church grounds, as the local Christians honored them as true martyrs of the faith in the New World.

Pope John Paul II beatified the three child martyrs at the basilica of Our Lady of Guadalupe in Mexico City, Mexico, on May 6, 1990. The Holy Father praised *"these sons of Mexican soil,"* declaring that they inspired countless generations of Mexico in the panorama of faith through the centuries.

Martyrs of the Catholic Action Movement

When tyrants and despots take control of any nation in the world, they strike hardest at the individuals and organizations that they know will stand firm against their evils. This was especially true in Mexico during the revolution. The Catholic Action Movement did not surrender to the anti-Catholic regime or its demands, and members of the organization went to their deaths rather than yield to corruption. Christopher Magellanes and his twenty-four companions were all part of the Catholic Action Movement martyred for the faith between 1915 and 1937.

CHRISTOPHER MAGALLANES AND COMPANIONS

(D. 1915-1937)

MARTYRS

Among the martyrs were twenty-two devout priests and three laymen — Manuel, David, and Salvador. The martyrs died in different regions of Mexico and at different times, but they were all victims because they refused to allow a godless regime to stamp out the faith. The Mexican authorities were trying to impose a "Mexican Church" on the nation, replacing Catholic bishops with schismatic prelates. Foreign missionaries were expelled, and schools and seminaries were closed by government order. Pope Pius XI (r. 1922-1939) worked with the Mexican bishops to find a way of preserving the faith. In retaliation, the government closed the churches. Priests were hunted down, and devout laypeople were warned to abjure the Church and Christian worship.

Catholic Action responded to the challenge, blunting the message of secular humanism and keeping the faithful inspired. The priests who belonged to Catholic Action were singled out for persecution — fifteen were martyred in Jalisco, four in Zacatecas, and one each in Chihuahua, Colima, Durango, Guanajuato, Guerrero, and Morelos. Most died at the hands of firing squads, and all were tortured hideously before their martyrdoms.

The three laymen, David, Manuel, and Salvador, died with their parish priest, Blessed Luis Batis. All of the martyrs symbolize the other Mexican men and women who made the ultimate sacrifice for the faith during the same period of ordeal.

Pope John Paul II beatified Christopher and his companions on November 22, 1992. The Holy Father praised their *"faithful commitment to the Lord and Church which have been characteristic of the Mexican people."*

Servant of Charity

The visions of the friends of God come as revelations that prompt such men and women to respond to the needs of the Church and their neighbors. Herculean tasks await such heroic souls, but they do not serve alone in accomplishing the charitable works asked of them. Other generous souls respond in kind, aiding the saints and bringing their own unique abilities to the work at hand. Chiara Bosatta de Pianello, sometime called Clara, was just such a faithful servant of the Lord.

Chiara was a spiritual daughter of Blessed Luigi Guanella. She was born Dina Bosatta in Panello Lario, Italy, on May 27, 1858. Chiara and her sister, Marcellina, were two of the first women to support the work of Blessed Luigi among the poor. In 1886, she joined Blessed Luigi's congregation and began her spiritual ministry, receiving the religious name of Chiara.

Chiara had been serving in her local

CHIARA BOSATTA DE PIANELLO

(D. 1887)

VICTIM SOUL

parish as a religious, despite an illness which she had contracted during her care of the poor in her hometown. Blessed Luigi recognized her as a soul especially chosen, saying: "God led her on the way of the strong souls, a life that is difficult and dangerous, he guided her so that her feet would not fail."

Surrendering herself as a victim soul, Chiara labored among the poor until physically incapacitated. She had great spiritual as well as physical suffering but relied upon Divine Providence. Chiara died on April 20, 1887, at the age of twenty-nine.

John Paul II beatified Chiara on April 21, 1991, praising her unending dedication to the religious and charitable ideals of Blessed Luigi and his congregation. The Holy Father also honored Chiara's vocation as a victim soul of love.

Claretian Martyrs ❧ **See Martyrs of Barbastro.**

Sculptor and Model Religious

Artists are revered in almost every age and culture because they bring a rare and unique view of people and the world to bear on life. The holy men and women on earth are also revered because their vision of eternity provides hope and peace among all peoples. Blessed Claudius Granzatto combined holiness with artistry, making him a glory of the Franciscan Order.

CLAUDIUS GRANZOTTO

(D. 1947)

RELIGIOUS

Claudius was born on August 23, 1900, at St. Lucia del Piave, Italy, the son of a poor but devout local family. He lost his father when he was only nine and had to go to work in order to aid the family. At fifteen, he was drafted into the army and served throughout World War I, serving an additional three years in peacetime.

Discharged, Claudius enrolled in the Academy of Fine Arts in Venice. In 1929, he received his degree as a "professor of sculpture," with honors and high praise from instructors. Claudius specialized in sacred art and opened his own studio, making a name for himself because of his skills and sensitivity to his subjects. He felt drawn to the religious life, and he entered the Franciscans to combine his skills with the devotion of the Order. His parish priest, commenting on Claudius's entrance into the Friars Minor, said: "The Order is receiving not only an artist, but a saint. . . ."

Throughout his religious life, Claudius displayed humility and great compassion. He spent hours in prayer and sculpted as part of his daily routines. He predicted, however, "I am leaving on the Assumption." Diagnosed in 1947 as suffering from a brain tumor, Claudius died in Padua on August 15.

Pope John Paul II beatified Claudius on November 20, 1994:

"Love of Christ, 'Son of Man,' and service to God's kingdom are uniquely resplendent in the life of Blessed Claudius Granzotto. The youngest of nine children, he learned at home how to fear God, how to live a sincere Christian life, with generous solidarity, willingness to sacrifice, and love of hard work in the fields. Because of his docility to the Spirit and such an effective family upbringing, the earthly life . . . became a constant pilgrimage towards holiness, to the very peaks of Gospel perfection. A true son of the Poverello of Assisi, he could express contemplation of God's infinite beauty in the sculptor's art, of which he was a master, making it the privileged instrument of the apostolate and evangelization. His holiness was especially radiant in his acceptance of suffering and death in union with Christ's Cross. Thus by consecrating himself totally to the Lord's love, he became a model for religious, for artists in their search for God's beauty and for the sick in his loving devotion to the Church."

Founder of the Congregation of the Daughters of St. Joseph

The sacramental life of the Church sustains the faithful and provides the graces necessary for the Christian apostolate. The saints are founded in the Sacraments, especially in the Holy Eucharist, the great communal celebration that unites all in Christendom and inspire heroic measures of love. Clemente Marchisio was dedicated particularly to the Holy Eucharist, from which he derived the grace of his vocation and his untiring energies for good.

CLEMENTE MARCHISIO

(D. 1903)

FOUNDER

He was born in Racconigi, Italy, on March 1, 1833, and was raised devoutly by his family. Entering the seminary after receiving a call to the priestly life, he was ordained to the priesthood. Clemente conducted his ministry with great devotion from the start, caring for those in want. He founded the Congregation of the Daughters of St. Joseph to serve the needs of the poor, stressing to his congregation the need for devout prayer lives and union with God in order to bring Christ's love into the lives of the people of the region. He became known as a loving father of the poor and a holy man of intense piety. Clemente died in Rivaiba, Italy, on December 16, 1903, mourned by his spiritual daughters and by the thousands that he had aided in his humble apostolates.

Pope John Paul II beatified Clemente on September 30, 1984, honoring this priest-founder as *"the image of Christ the Good Shepherd."* Clemente was praised as a man who attained perfection *"through the Sacrament of the Body and Blood of Christ."*

Clementine Nengapete ❦ See **Maria Clementine Anuarite Nengapete**.

Foundress of the Benedictine Oblates

Some individuals demonstrate a unique capacity for love and goodness. The lives that such souls touch are enriched and purified as a result, and they stand as lights in the gloom to speak of Almighty God's patience and mercy. Treasured by those who came into contact with her was Colomba Joanna Gabriel. She was hailed in her own time as "a woman born for love."

Born to a Polish family in Stanislaviv, now Ivano-Frankivsk, Ukraine, on May 3, 1858, Columba's baptismal name was

COLOMBA JOANNA GABRIEL

(D. 1926)

FOUNDRESS

Joanna Matylda. A noble by birth, she was well-educated, both in local schools and in Leopoli. During this period, Colomba received the grace of a religious vocation and decided upon the Benedictines at Leopoli. She served in that convent for some time but felt the need to conduct programs for the poor, especially vulnerable young working girls.

In 1900, Colomba moved to Rome and two years later went to Subiaco, returning to Rome the following year. Her spiritual director was the Dominican Blessed Hyacinth Cormier, and he guided her as she started teaching catechism and visiting the sick and poor in the parish of the Prati district of Rome. This apostolate led to the founding of the Benedictine Oblates, a secular group. In 1908, Colomba was inspired to found the Benedictine Sisters of Charity as a more permanent institute of charity. Young women entering the new congregation established homes and other charitable programs for the poor people of Rome. Colomba earned the respect and reverence of the Romans as her congregation spread throughout Italy to Madagascar and Romania. Her patrons included Pope St. Pius X (r. 1903-1914) and Pope Benedict XV (r. 1914-1922). Queen Elena of Italy also aided her apostolate.

"The woman born for love" died at Centacelle, a suburb of Rome, on September 24, 1926, mourned by thousands who cherished her vision and her spiritual motherhood.

Pope John Paul II beatified Colomba on May 16, 1993, declaring: *"On the path of suffering the Holy Spirit uprooted her from her homeland, led her to leave everything and begin all over."* The Holy Father praised Colomba's special charism: *"the gift of the active apostolate of charity."*

Member of the Order of Trappists

Cyprian Michael Tansi was a holy and gentle priest, willing to sacrifice himself for good. A Trappist from Nigeria who died in England, he is hailed as "a man of God and a man of the people."

CYPRIAN (IWENE) TANSI

(D. 1964)

❦

RELIGIOUS

Cyprian was born in 1903 in Igboezunu, in southern Nigeria, the son of farmer Tabansi and his wife Ejikweve of the Igbo tribe. Cyprian was called Iwene at birth, and he was sent to a Christian mission at Nduka, in 1909, where he received the name Michael.

Cyprian earned his first teaching certificate at age sixteen, and he taught in Onitsha and Aguleri. In 1925, he entered St. Paul's Seminary in Igboriam and was ordained in Onitsha Cathedral on December 19, 1937. Cyprian started his ministry then as a pastor in Nnewi. In 1939, he was sent to Dunukofia, in the Umudioka region.

There he confronted the myth of the "cursed forest," putting it to rest. He also started the League of Mary and marriage preparation centers. On foot or on bicycle, from village to village, Cyprian traveled endlessly, raising vocations and giving the faith a rebirth. In 1945, he was assigned to Akpu, and four years later went to Aguleri.

In order to assist Bishop Charles Heerey, who wanted to establish a Trappist monastery in the diocese, Cyprian agreed to undertake the necessary training for such a foundation. Accordingly, he left his homeland and went to the abbey of Mount St. Bernard in Leicestershire, England, after making a pilgrimage to Rome in 1950. There he received the religious name, Cyprian, and took his vows on December 8, 1956.

Blessed Iwene Tansi

The plans for the Nigerian Trappist monastic foundation did not materialize, much to the surprise of Cyprian. The Trappists chose the neighboring land of Cameroon instead, causing Cyprian severe suffering; however, he accepted God's Will and continued his cloistered life in a foreign land.

In January, 1964, Cyprian developed an aortic aneurysm while in the Trappist cloister. He did not recover and died on January 20. When his death was announced, people came from far and wide to attend his funeral. Among those in attendance was Father Francis Arinze, the future cardinal of the Church. Cyprian's remains were taken to Onitsha for burial in 1988. They are now enshrined in Aguleri.

Pope John Paul II beatified Cyprian in Nigeria on March 22, 1998. During the ceremony, the Holy Father praised Cyprian as a human being who understood *"true holiness"* and *"true charity."*

Founder of the Carmelite Brothers of Mary Immaculate

The spirit of the Carmelite Order dates to ancient times and embodies particular aspects of Marian devotion, fidelity to the faith, and contemplative worship. Carmel has had an impact on the secular world through the centuries and has served the Church on the frontiers of evangelism. Recent Carmelite testimony and martyrdom has once again brought this ancient tradition to a new flowering. Cyriac Elias Chavara has

CYRIAC ELIAS CHAVARA

(D. 1871)

FOUNDER

raised the banner of the Carmelite spirituality in a new and innovative manner in his own land. A Carmelite visionary and founder, and a devoted son of the Blessed Virgin Mother of God, Cyriac Elias is a model of the fervent charity of Christ. A member of the Syro-Malabar Catholic rite, he instituted a ministry fitted to his era and to his region of the world.

Cyriac Elias was born in Kainakary, in the Malabar region of India, on February 10, 1805. Cyriac Elias was raised by a pious family and as a child was continuously gentle and prayerful. Knowing he had been called to the priestly life, he entered the local seminary and was ordained in 1829.

In 1831, Father Thomas Parukara, the secretary to the vicar apostolic, with Father Thomas Palakal, rector of the seminary, erected the Third Order Discalced Carmelites. Before a formal rule could be drawn up, both Father Palakal and Father Parukara died. Cyriac Elias had moved to Mannara, the site of the congregation, and the burden of the new religious community came to rest upon him. He already had many priest members, and he achieved a formal approbation of a rule in 1855, calling the congregation the Carmelite Brothers of Mary Immaculate. He took vows that same year, on December 8, becoming Cyriac Elias of the Holy Family. Elected superior, Cyriac Elias governed the congregation until his death.

In guiding the apostolates and the expansion of the Carmelite Brothers of Mary Immaculate, he founded six houses. With Father Leopold Beccaro, O.C.D., Cyriac Elias also founded a congregation for women at Koonammavu, bringing dedicated young women of the region into the service of the faith. He was then appointed vicar general of the Syro-Malabar rite in that part of the world. This was yet another burden, as Cyriac Elias had to safeguard ancient rites, stemming schismatic movements of that era.

Cyriac Elias organized both contemplative and active apostolates, distinctly Carmelite and devoted to the Blessed Virgin Mary. Prayerful and guided always by fervent charity, Cyriac Elias saw his congregation become the largest in India, with missions in Tanzania, Somalia, Sudan, and in Europe. He died at Koonammavu on January 3, 1871, after a long illness.

Pope John Paul II beatified Cyriac Elias in Changaachery, India, with Blessed Alphonsa, on February 8, 1986, praising the spiritual heights of Carmel that spurred the new blessed to heroic service.

Cyril Bertram Tejedor ❦ See Martyrs of Asturias (Turon).

Missionary to the Lepers, the "Hero of Molokai"

Few human beings on earth dare to challenge centuries-old traditions or social practices, and even fewer individuals will put themselves deliberately into harm's way for the sake of charity. The term "harm's way" very much describes the dreaded Hansen's Disease, the terrifying condition known throughout the centuries as leprosy. Since biblical days, the lepers of the world have been chased into remote wildernesses, shunned, feared, and hated. Dread cloaked their presence in the world, even as late as the 1880s. Then, in Hawaii, a young man took upon himself a new apostolate; viewing the lepers not as terrifying carriers of suffering and death, but as God's own children. He lived on Molokai with the exiled lepers and then became one of them. The young man was Damien Joseph de Veuster.

DAMIEN DE VEUSTER

(D. 1889)

MISSIONARY

He was born in Tremeloo, Belgium, on January 3, 1840, the son of a prosperous couple. Robust, shy, and yet remarkably adamant about matters of the spirit, Damien followed his brother, Auguste, called Pamphile, into the Congregation of the Sacred Hearts, the Picpus Fathers. He took his final vows on October 7, 1860, and then volunteered as Pamphile's replacement to the Hawaiian missions, even though he had not been ordained. Damien arrived in Honolulu on March 19, 1964, and was ordained two days later in the cathedral.

Assigned to the island of Hawaii, called the Big Island, Damien took up residence at Puna. He then served at Kohala and Hamakua, spending eight years in a mission that covered two thousand square miles of cliffs, ravines, valley, and volcanoes. In January, 1866, the Hawaiian royal government, recognizing that leprosy was spreading through the islands, exiled victims of the disease to a settlement on the island of Molokai. Damien had been caring for some of these lepers on Hawaii, and he said that he had "an undeniable feeling that he should join them."

Damien's prophetic words proved true on May 10, 1873, when he landed

Blessed Damien de Veuster

at Kalaupapa, Molokai, in the company of Bishop Louis Maigret, S.S.C.C. At an earlier meeting, Damien and the Sacred Heart Father had volunteered to go to the leper settlement. Damien, the first one assigned, would remain there for the rest of his short life.

Damien built coffins for the dead and houses for the living, as well as chapels. Going from leper to leper, he washed and bandaged each one. His medical skills were matched only by his fervent charity and his view of the lepers as individuals worthy of respect, kindness, and courtesy. As children of God given a unique and devastating cross to bear in the midst of tropical splendor, these islanders received Damien's total commitment.

In 1876, the first symptoms of leprosy appeared in Damien's left foot. Damien was at peace because he could see the results of his labors, and he was thrilled to see the Franciscan Sisters of Syracuse, led by Mother Marianne Kope, arrive to start an advanced medical clinic. Father Damien died of leprosy on April 15, 1889, and was buried on Molokai. At the request of the Belgian government, his remains were returned to his homeland decades later. Damien, however, is revered in his adopted islands, and he also represents Hawaii in Statuary Hall in Washington, D.C.

Pope John Paul II beatified Damien on June 4, 1995, honoring him as a *"Servant of Humanity"* and an inspiration to the world during his years of ministry on Molokai. His dedication and unfailing devotion also changed the way the world viewed lepers. Simple, adamant in his concerns and care, Damien became the Hero of Molokai.

Holy Ghost Apostle

The Christian faith calls all believers to widen their horizons of the spirit and to develop an awareness of human needs at home or far afield. Daniel Brottier, a French missionary, chaplain, and patron of orphans, is a symbol of such concern. As a member of the Holy Ghost Congregation, he cared for those around him and even for souls in distant Senegal.

DANIEL BROTTIER

(D. 1936)

RELIGIOUS

Daniel was born in La Ferté-Saint-Cyr, France, on September 7, 1876. While growing up the Loire Valley town, Daniel displayed intellectual and spiritual gifts at an early age. He received as well the grace of a priestly vocation and entered the seminary.

Ordained in 1899 for the diocese of Blois, Daniel was assigned as a faculty member of the college of Pontlevoy. He desired missionary work, however, and entered the Congregation of the Holy Ghost at Orly, at age twenty-six. In 1903, Daniel was sent to Saint-Louis in

Senegal. He labored in that mission for eight years, returning to France in 1911 because of ill health.

Because of his devotion to Senegal, Daniel agreed to a request from Bishop Jalabert, the vicar apostolic of the region, to launch a fund-raising campaign to build a cathedral in Dakar. This cathedral would serve as a memorial to the French men and women who died in Africa, a *Souvenir Africain*. Daniel aroused all of France as he raised funds for the memorial which would also honor Africans who had given their lives for France.

During World War I, Daniel served as a chaplain. He was cited for bravery six times and was awarded the *Croix de Guerre* and the medal of the Legion of Honor. He attributed his survival on the front lines to the intercession of St. Thérèse of Lisieux and built a chapel for her at Auteuil in the year of her canonization. Daniel also organized war veterans and assumed the administration of a work called the Orphan Apprentices of Auteuil. At first, he supervised 175 apprentices; later the number increased to 1,408.

On February 2, 1936, Cardinal Verdier of Paris consecrated the cathedral in Senegal made possible through Daniel's labors. This was also the last day that Daniel was able to rise from his bed. He became very ill and died in Paris, France, on February 28, 1936, mourned by all of France. More then 15,000 men and women paid their respects, and Cardinal Verdier preached the funeral homily.

Pope John Paul II beatified Daniel on November 25, 1984, praising his spirit of service, generosity, and true Christian valor that knew no national boundaries or racial designations.

Apostle to Africa and Bishop of Khartoum

The Church is called "universal" because the faith has blossomed on the various continents and in far-flung lands through the centuries. This Catholic Faith did not appear miraculously in the nations of the world, but was carried there by apostles and missionaries. A very special individual, Daniel Comboni, is a modern missionary model. The first bishop of Central Africa, he was the founder of missionary congregations including the Sons of Verona, also called the Verona Fathers, and a pioneer in the African apostolate.

DANIEL COMBONI

(D. 1881)

FOUNDER

Daniel was born at Limone, Lake Gorda, in northern Italy on March 15, 1831. One of eight children, he was the only one to survive to maturity. Daniel was inspired by accounts of the martyrs of Japan, and attended the school operated by Father Nicholas Mazza, who was training missionaries for Africa. After studying for the priesthood, Daniel was ordained in December 1854. He also underwent medical training, and when a plague struck Verona, he aided countless victims.

In September 1857, Daniel and five companions were sent to Africa. They spent three months in Khartoum and then went to the Holy Cross Mission in southern Sudan. There the group was felled by malaria, and Daniel and the survivors had to leave the area in January, in 1859. He returned to Father Mazza's Institute to train more missionaries.

Daniel was one of the first Europeans interested in educating Africans and establishing a native clergy for the continent. He was given seven African slaves, rescued by the British, and he restored several to their villages and educated the rest. With these slaves in mind, Daniel founded the Institute of the

Blessed Daniel Comboni

Good Shepherd for the Regeneration of Africa in 1867, a group called the Comboni Missionaries. Five years later he founded the Verona Sisters to aid the priests in the mission apostolate. He spoke six European languages as well as Arabic and six dialects of Dinko, Bari, and Nuba. From 1867 until his death, Daniel made eight long and dangerous journeys to Africa, working successfully to stem the slave trade. During the Sudan rebellion, some of his priests and nuns were captured by the religious leader of the rebels, the Mahdi. The Mahdi's forces killed Lord Gordon at Khartoum but showed respect for the Catholic religious, who were returned unharmed.

In 1872, Daniel was appointed pro-vicar apostolic of Central Africa, responsible for administering missions in Nubia, Egypt, Sudan, and southward to the region of the Lakes. In 1877 he was named vicar apostolic and was consecrated a bishop, and one year later was involved in relieving Khartoum in a dire famine. He died in Khartoum of malaria on October 10, 1881, and Pope Leo XIII (r. 1878-1903) called his death "a great loss." Other Comboni missionary groups have since been established to carry on his visioned apostolate, and they arrived in the U.S. by 1940.

Pope John Paul II beatified Daniel on March 17, 1996, declaring:

" 'Leading humanity to the light of eternal life': Daniel Comboni's ideal continues today in the apostolate of his spiritual sons and daughters. They still maintain strong ties in Africa, particularly in Sudan, where their founder spent a great part of his energy as a tireless evangelizer and where he died at a young age, worn out by his labors and illness. The unconditional trust he had in the power of prayer (cf. Scritti, n. 2324) is effectively expressed in the 'Cenacles of missionary prayer' which are being set up in many parishes and represent a significant way to promote and renew missionary spirituality."

David Carlos 🔥 See Martyrs of the Scalopian Congregation.

Dermot O'Hurley 🔥 See Martyrs of Ireland.

Spanish Missionary to Guam

This blessed was a noble Spaniard who gave his life as a missionary in Agana, Guam, in the Pacific, bringing the "Good News" of Christ. Courageous, untiring in his efforts, Diego was a pioneer of the faith and a martyr of the Jesuits.

He was born into a noble family of Bourgos on November 12, 1627, and was raised in the faith and in the royal court. Diego was educated by the Jesuits in Madrid, Spain, at the *Colegio-Imperial,* and he entered the Society with a desire to be a missionary in China.

DIEGO ALOYSIUS DE SAN VITORES

(D. 1672)

MARTYR

Ordained in 1651, Diego was assigned to the Philippines nine years later. He arrived in the Philippines in 1662, and on the voyage came into contact with the Marianas Islands. Intent upon starting a mission in the Marianas, Diego volunteered to go there and received permission from King Philip III (r. 1621-1665) in June, 1665. With missionary companions, Diego had a ship built and sailed to Guam, arriving in June, 1668.

Initially successful, Diego and his companions faced opposition eventually from the powerful clans that ruled the region. Missionaries were assaulted and slain, but Diego went from island to island to strengthen the efforts of his fellow Jesuits. On one such journey, Diego met up with a convert who had apostasized. That native cursed Diego and attacked him with a spear. The missionary died on the beach of Tumon, near Agana, on April 2, 1672.

Pope John Paul II beatified Diego with two other Jesuits, Blessed Francis Garate and Blessed Joseph Rubio y Peralta on October 6, 1985. During the beatification, the dedication of Diego to the apostolate of evangelization was honored. Carrying the Gospel of Christ to the world was the paramount impetus of his life. Diego's willingness to risk all for the Marianas served as the fire that illuminated his priestly vocation.

Diego Ventaja Milan 🔥 See Martyrs of Almeria.

Member of the Sisters of Jesus and Mary

Dina Belanger

(d. 1929)

Mystic

It is said that saints and mystics are human beings who have "fallen in love with God." They are men and women who are transfixed, enraptured, and ennobled by their union with the blessed Trinity, and they stand as contradictions to the modern world. Dina Belanger was just such a mystic. She died very young but with the radiance of a chosen soul.

Dina was born in Quebec, Canada, on April 30, 1897, and was raised devoutly by her family. A skilled musician, she was given special training at academies in Canada and in New York. She did not pursue a musical career, however, receiving the grace of a profound religious vocation with an abundance of mystical graces.

In 1920, Dina joined the Sisters of Jesus and Mary, having entered a mystical state of union. She said: "My hunger for the Eucharist is always growing. A day without bread, is it not a day without sunshine, hours in which evening delays in coming?" Dina received many extraordinary mystical gifts, but the essence of her religious life remained union with Christ and surrender to divine love.

She became ill soon after taking vows, and spent her remaining religious life suffering. She clung to Christ, offering all to the Sacred Heart, and calling Jesus "the life of my life." Dina died in Sillery, Canada, on September 4, 1929.

Pope John Paul II beatified Dina on March 20, 1993, saying: *"Her message is handed on to us this evening, brothers and sisters, with a marvelous purity and clarity. Welcoming Jesus in our life, uniting our hearts with his, love of the Blessed Virgin, a fraternal spirit in the community: these are the graces of the Lord through the intercession of Dina Belanger, who leaves us as her last motto: 'To love Jesus and Mary and make them loved.'* "

Dionysius Pamplona ❧ See Martyrs of the Scalopian Congregation.

Apostle of the Blessed Sacrament

Dominic Lentini

(d. 1828)

Priest

Called "an angel of the altar" by all who knew him, this blessed was revered as a model of ministerial priesthood and a man of unstinting generosity and service. Dominic Lentini was born in Lauria, Potenza, Italy, on November 20, 1770, the youngest of five children raised in the faith. He desired a priestly vocation and, at age of fourteen, entered the seminary at Salerno, beginning his studies for the priesthood. He completed his training and was ordained in 1794. He was then sent to his hometown, Lauria, to perform his ministry.

Dominic had an extraordinary devotion to the Blessed Sacrament, keeping vigil and offering adoration whenever possible. He was a model of piety as well in the celebration of Mass. People from the surrounding area came to participate in Dominic's Masses, inspired and spiritually renewed by his devotion and grace. He evangelized Lauria and the entire region and taught everyone to honor Our Lady of Sorrows.

Personally, he was an ascetic, sleeping on the floor, never sparing himself, and practicing severe penances in a spirit of reparation. His purity was evident to all, especially when celebrating the Holy Eucharist or when administering the Sacraments to his parishioners. Dominic also gave everything that he owned to the people of Lauria. He lived humbly and in the spirit of poverty, compelled by the terrible poverty and need that he saw around him.

Dominic died as a simple priest on February 25, 1828, and all of the Potenza region of Italy was devastated by the loss. He had brought angelic goodness and saintly perfection into their lives.

Pope John Paul II beatified Dominic on October 12, 1997, declaring: *"A priest with an undivided heart, he could combine fidelity to God with fidelity to man."* The Holy Father added: *"His total dedication to his ministry made him, in the words of Pope Pius XI, 'a priest rich only in his priesthood.'"*

Tritarian Priest

The young can show the way to Christ, and today's Church is rejoicing in the number of saints and blesseds who made choices of extraordinary valor while still in their tender years of life. Dominic Iturrate Zubero was one of these young, heroic souls. A Trinitarian priest united to Christ, Dominic was from the Basque region of Spain and brought the strong faith of his ancestry to his brief apostolate on the earth.

He was born in Dima, Spain, on May 11, 1901, and he showed devotion to the Blessed Virgin Mary at an early age. Dominic received the grace of a priestly vocation and entered the Trinitarian Order, where he studied in the seminary program. Professed as a Trinitarian, he received the religious name of Domenico Iturrate of the Most Blessed Sacrament, and was ordained to the priesthood. But Dominic would never be allowed to actively pursue his ministry.

DOMINIC ITURRATE ZUBERO

(D. 1927)

RELIGIOUS

He was spiritually advancing toward union with Christ as a Trinitarian. In 1922, Dominic wrote: "Our obedience to God's Will must be total, without reserve, and constant." Guided by his Order, Dominic vowed: "never to refuse God our Lord, but to follow his holy inspiration in everything with generosity and joy." Dominic celebrated Mass as "an act of personal sacrifice in union with the Supreme Victim on behalf of all men." His own life was to become a sacrifice as well. Dominic died in Belmonte, Spain, on April 8, 1927, mourned by his fellow religious and all who knew him.

Pope John Paul II beatified Dominic on October 30, 1983, declaring: *"The faithful fulfillment of God's Will is an aim which in him reached very lofty heights, especially during the last years of his life."* The Holy Father added: *"As a Trinitarian religious, he strove to live according to two central principles of the spirituality of his Order: the mystery of the Holy Trinity and the work of the Redemption, which lead to a life of intense charity."*

Edmigio Rodríguez ❧ See Martyrs of Almeria.

Founder of the Brothers of the Christian Schools

At one time the American Catholics enjoyed one of the largest and most dedicated diocesan school systems in the entire world. The models for these schools were brought by pioneering missionaries and religious from Europe to the New Worldwhere they flourished and nurtured generations of the faithful. One of these models for the American schools was brought from Ireland, de-

EDMUND IGNATIUS RICE

(D. 1844)

FOUNDER

signed by Edmund Ignatius Rice, who founded the Congregation of the Brothers of the Christian Schools. He was a pioneer in Catholic education, but he was a holy, fearless defender of the faith as well.

Edmund was born in Westcourt, Ireland, on June 1, 1762, the fourth of seven sons in a farming family. At age seventeen, he began working at his uncle's import-export business in Waterford, which he later inherited. Married at twenty-five, Edmund lost his wife two years later and was left with a sickly infant daughter. A devout man, Edmund attended Mass and meditated in this time of suffering, also dedicating himself to charitable works. He was living in troubled times, and Ireland faced economic and political storms that had a significant impact on the young and the aged. While Edmund saw all of this, he desired a religious vocation in the contemplative life.

The bishop of Waterford put an end to that attraction when he pointed to the ragged youths in the streets and asked Edmund if he planned to abandon them. Encouraged by Pope Pius VII (r. 1800-1823) and Bishop Hussey, Edmund sold his business, arranged for his daughter's care, and opened his first school in 1802. He had three other schools in operation by 1806, and in 1808 he took the name Ignatius as a religious with companions in a pontifical institute.

He established the "Catholic Model School," and saw the founding of eleven communities in Ireland, eleven in England, and one in Australia, with requests from the United States and Canada. He resigned as Superior General in 1838 and died at Mt. Sion, the site of his first school, on August 29, 1844.

Pope John Paul II beatified Edmund on October 6, 1996, declaring:

"The Spirit eventually led him to the total consecration of himself and his companions in the religious life. Today his spiritual sons, the Christian Brothers and the Presentation Brothers, continue his mission. . . ."

Bishop of Susa, Italy

Edward Joseph Rosaz was one of those unique souls called by God to assume the mantle of episcopal responsibility in a diocese and to guide the faithful. He founded the Sisters of the Third Order of St. Francis of Susa in order to aid in this episcopal ministry.

Edward was born in Susa, near Turin, on February 15, 1830. His parents were hard working and devout, and Edward grew up in the ideals and sentiments of the faith, receiving the grace of a priestly vocation. He entered the seminary and was ordained during a turbulent era in Italy. Edward served in various priestly ministries and apostolates in the region, winning many to the Church. His holiness and zeal were recognized as he was consecrated the bishop of Susa, the historical diocese that had endured political and international problems, and he brought charity and a clear vision to Susa when he was installed.

EDWARD (EDOARDO) JOSEPH ROSAZ

(D. 1903)

🔥

FOUNDER

Edward immediately started a series of renewal programs, instituting charitable programs and focusing on the need for educational facilities to train the young people of the region. The Sisters of the Third Order of St. Francis of Susa were founded by Edward to operate schools and orphanages as part of the renaissance. Recognizing the area's needs, the sisters started hospices and geriatric residences as well. In time they expanded their charitable works to Turin and then to Switzerland. When Edward died in Susa on May 3, 1903, he was mourned by the members of the congregation and by the faithful of the diocese.

Pope John Paul II beatified Edward in Susa on July 14, 1991, and during the ceremony Edward was described as a model of episcopal charity, a man who radiated the redeeming love of Christ for all souls.

Augustinian Martyr of Mexico

Caught up in the reign of terror in Mexico in 1928, Elias del Socorro Nieves, an Augustinian priest, surrendered his own life in service to Christ the King and the faithful of Mexico. He was born on the island of San Pedro, Yuriria, Guanajuato, Mexico, on September 21, 1882. Circumstances delayed his vocation, including a bout of tuberculosis and the death of his father, and it was 1904 before Elias could be admitted to the Augustinian college at Yuriria. He took final vows in 1911, putting aside his baptismal name, Mateo Elias, to become Elias del Socorro. Elias had endured trials and delays in order to realize his eternal vocation, and he would demonstrate the same rigorous character as a priest and as an opponent of the anti-Catholic government of Mexico during the revolution.

ELIAS DEL SOCORRO NIEVES

(D. 1928)

MARTYR

Elias was ordained a priest in 1916 and was appointed parochial vicar of La Cañada de Caracheo, where he won the respect and affection of the local Mexicans. When the Mexican authorities restricted religious services and the activities of priests, Elias refused to allow his care of the faithful to be disrupted. He moved to the hills of La Gavia, making them the base of his clandestine ministry.

Elias and two ranchers were arrested because of this defiance. The ranchers were shot by the soldiers on the way to Cartazar, the local capital. When the leader of the squad taunted Elias with his coming death, referring to the Mass, the martyr exclaimed ": ... to die for the faith is a sacrifice pleasing to God." Elias's last words on March 10, 1928, were: "Long live Christ the King."

Pope John Paul II beatified Elias on Sunday, October 12, 1997 declaring: *"His total trust in God and Our Lady of Christians to whom he was deeply devoted, characterized his whole life and priestly ministry, which he exercised with self-denial and a*

Elias del Socorro Nieves

spirit of service, without letting himself be overcome by obstacles, sacrifices, or dangers. This faithful Augustinian religious knew how to transmit hope in Christ and Divine Providence."

Trinitarian Tertiary

This blessed, Elizabeth Canori Mora, enters the modern scene as a "battered wife" of the eighteenth century, and serves as a patroness of all the women of the world who endure humiliation, degradation, and pain from their spouses.

Born in Rome on November 21, 1774, to wealthy Tommaso and Teresa Primali Canori Mora, Elizabeth studied with the Augustinian Sisters at Cascia, where she excelled in her studies and displayed spiritual maturity. In 1796, she was wed to Cristofora Mora, a young lawyer of Rome. He proved unfaithful and dissolute, and in no time reduced Elizabeth to poverty. She bore him four children, two of whom died in infancy, but she raised her daughters, Marianna and Luciana, by earning a meager living with her own skills.

ELIZABETH CANORI MORA

(D. 1825)

MYSTIC

In 1801, Elizabeth was stricken with a mysterious illness and miraculously cured. She also had a mystical experience that enabled her to counsel others and to spend herself in charitable works. Her home became a haven for the needy and the troubled.

In 1807, Elizabeth became a member of the Trinitarian Third Order, and her fame spread throughout Rome, Albano, and Marino. She predicted that Christoforo would eventually repent and become a devout Catholic.

Elizabeth died on February 5, 1825, in Rome, while being cared for by her daughters. She was buried in the Trinitarian church of San Carlino alle Quattro Fontane. Following her death, her husband gave up his dissolute lifestyle, entered the Triniarian Third Order, and then became a Conventual Franciscan priest.

Pope John Paul II beatified Elizabeth on April 24, 1994, declaring:

". . . An ardent faith and an exceptional mystical experience sustained her during the many difficulties she encountered, both in her married life and in bringing up her children. At every moment, her strength was in prayer. She offered her suffering for the conversion of her husband, Christopher, who after her death became a Conventual Franciscan, dying a holy death in the Lord . . . Elizabeth lived her vocation as wife and mother, as a tertiary in the Trinitarian Third Order, aware that it was her duty to show absolute fidelity to God in her own state of life and always to respect the Commandments. Thus her witness is an invaluable example for Christian spouses. As I recall the new blessed, I am thinking in particular of the Trinitarian Order and of all those whose life is inspired by the luminous example of this faithful Gospel witness."

Foundress of the Sisters of Our Lady of Sorrows

Napoleon Bonaparte is a romantic figure of world history, depicted in histories, novels, and movies as a dashing conqueror and military genius. While his ascent to power put an end to the horrors of the French Revolution, Napoleon was not a dedicated Catholic or even an ally of the faith. In fact, his invasion and occupation of European countries put the Church into considerable danger in some areas, but it also raised up valiant men and women who were daring and innovative in order to serve Christ and their neighbors. Elizabeth Rienzi, was one of these courageous faithful.

ELIZABETH RIENZI

(D. 1859)

FOUNDRESS

Elizabeth, called Elisabetta at Baptism, was born on November 19, 1786, in Saludecio, near Rimini, Italy. Her parents were wealthy and socially prominent, and they raised Elizabeth in a truly devout home. She desired a religious vocation and entered the Augustinian convent at Petrarubbia in 1807, when she turned twenty-one. Elizabeth was not destined to serve as an Augustinian, however. She was not able to start her novitiate or receive the habit because the convent was suppressed by Napoleonic proclamations. Elizabeth returned home and performed charitable works until 1824, and in April of that year she went to Coriano, a town near Rimini, where she became an instructress in a girl's school.

Elizabeth hoped that St. Magdalen of Canossa would take over the school, and she corresponded with the saint, offering her the facility. St. Magdalen of Canossa, however, advised Elizabeth to assume the responsibility herself, especially in view of the precarious political situations in the region. She gathered companions to undertake this ministry, and she studied the religious constitutions of the Canossan and Venerian Congregations.

In 1839, Elizabeth founded the Sisters of Our Lady of Sorrows, a teaching congregation active in Italy, the United States, Bangladesh, Brazil, and Mexico. Elizabeth died on August 14, 1859, and was declared Venerable in 1988.

Pope John Paul II beatified Elizabeth on June 19, 1989, calling the faithful to reflect on her ministry of charity that reflects *"on the life of the Church, considered in her mysterious and unexpected development in time and among mankind. . . ."*

Carmelite Mystic

Elizabeth of the Trinity was a Carmelite nun of the nineteenth and is now revered as one of the great mystical writers of the modern age. People of all faiths look at her life and work and are drawn to her spiritual wisdom, which was founded on the Carmelite tradition and nurtured by her devotion to the Most Blessed Trinity.

ELIZABETH OF THE TRINITY

(D. 1906)

MYSTIC

She was born in Camp d'Avor, Bourges, France, on July 18, 1880. By all accounts she was a rather willful child, even called "a little devil" by relatives until her father died when she was seven. His death made her aware of the spiritual aspects of human existence and the depths of union possible for souls. She also made her First Communion in April, 1891, experiencing a profound spiritual effect as a result of the sacrament.

Raised with her sister, Margaret, by their mother, Elizabeth was given every advantage as a child. She displayed unique musical talents and studied at the Dijon Conservatory, but she did not develop these talents further, making such gifts a sacrifice to God. In turn, she received the grace of a vocation and mystical consolations. Elizabeth was "dwelt in" by the Holy Trinity, and no opposition could keep her from entering Carmel and experiencing the contemplative life. Her mother was vehemently opposed, forbidding such a vocation, but Elizabeth did not falter.

She entered the Carmel of Dijon on August 2, 1901, at the age of twenty-one, receiving the name Elizabeth of the Trinity, but also calling herself *Laudem Gloriae,* "the praise of glory." She received the habit on December 8, 1902, destined to have only four more years on earth.

Her writings are considered spiritual treasures, attesting to the Divine Indwelling in the soul through sanctifying grace. Elizabeth longed "to die not only as pure as an angel but transformed into Christ Crucified." She possessed a rare awareness of the presence of God and the need to unify one's personality in order to offer God praise and service. She was possessed by God in a unique mystical union. Elizabeth also knew that the true spouse of Christ must be immolated with Him. She longed to share her Divine Indwelling and to offer herself as a victim of love.

On July 1, 1903, Elizabeth displayed the first symptoms of Addison's disease, a rare illness of the adrenal glands. She worsened and collapsed three years later, surrendering herself to her coming death. Spiritual pain was added to her severe physical suffering, but Elizabeth did not deny her commitment, announcing: "In the evening of life, nothing remains but love." She died on November 9, 1906, declaring: "I go to the light, to love, to life."

Pope John Paul II beatified Elizabeth of the Trinity on November 25, 1984, declaring that this blessed *"gives witness to a openness to the Word of God . . . truly nourishing with it her prayer and reflection, to the point of finding therein all her reasons for living and of consecrating herself to the praise of the glory of this Word."*

Foundress of the Franciscan Tertiary Sisters of St. Elizabeth

Born into an age of political turbulence and suffering, Elizabeth Vendramini chose to commit herself to the care of others. She demonstrated a remarkable trust in Divine Providence always, founding a vital apostolate in her own troubled era.

ELIZABETH VENDRAMINI

(D. 1860)

FOUNDRESS

Elizabeth was born in Bassano del Grappa, Italy, on April 9, 1790, when political and social forces were competing for power across Europe. Sent to the Augustinian convent for her education, Elizabeth was trained by the nuns until she reached fifteen. She was then considered eligible for marriage but refused such plans because she had received the grace of religious vocation.

In 1820, Elizabeth joined the staff of an orphanage for girls. The Capuchin Franciscans operated the institution, and Elizabeth was trained in the spirit of the Order. She became a Third Order Franciscan and practiced a life of religious consecration.

After arriving in Padua in 1827, Elizabeth worked with children, realizing the need for a religious congregation to take up this ministry. In 1829, she and two companions started a small house that offered free education for needy children. In the next year she was aided by the bishop of Padua in forming the Franciscan Tertiary Sisters of St. Elizabeth; a congregation that followed the rule of the Third Order Regular of St. Francis. The constitutions of the congregation were completed in 1830.

Elizabeth governed the congregation until her death, and saw her sisters adding the apostolate of caring for the elderly and other charitable labors to their original education ministry. Prayerful, trusting always in the Blessed Trinity, Elizabeth served as superior for more than three decades. She died in Padua on April 2, 1860.

Pope John Paul II beatified Elizabeth on November 4, 1990, declaring: *"Today from heaven, Elizabeth exhorts all those who want to give effective spiritual and physical aid to their brothers and sisters to draw their strength from faith in God and the imitation of Christ."* The Holy Father added: *"Blessed Elizabeth teaches us that wherever faith is strong and sure, our charitable outreach to our neighbor will be more daring. Wherever our sense of Christ is more acute, our sense of the needs of our brothers and sisters will be more correct and on target."*

Foundress and Missionary to India

The "now" of life is a unique stepping stone to all the tomorrows given in a single lifetime. Blessed Emilie d' Hooghvorst was a woman who understood the "sacrament of now." She realized early in her life that each hour was an instant in time in which she could serve Christ on earth while her mortal life continued and then in eternity. Trials and tribulations did not make her flee from the "now" of existence, and her love endured through her tomorrows.

EMILIE D' HOOGHVORST

(D. 1876)

FOUNDRESS

She was born on October 11, 1818, in Wegimont, Liège, Belgium, to a noble family. Her father served as the Belgian ambassador to the Vatican, and her home life was centered around the faith. Emilie developed a lasting devotion to the Blessed Sacrament at a young age; she knew enough about events in the world to understand the need for atonement and reparation. She also had a special dedication to Sacred Hearts of Jesus and Mary.

In 1837, Emilie married Baron Victor van der Linden d' Hooghvorst, and they had four children before the baron was stricken with a severe illness. Emilie cared for him tenderly until his death in 1847, exhausted by the demands of such nursing procedures and by the sufferings of a loved one. When the baron died, Emilie knew that she had given him all that she had in his hours of need.

Evaluating the events and the future, Emilie realized that the baron's death demonstrated that she had been set aside by God in order to fulfill his Will. Her personal losses did not matter in the face of such a destiny. Emilie consecrated herself to Christ and set about gathering companions to begin an apostolate of service and reparation. In 1857, Emilie founded the Congregation of St. Mary Reparatrix. She took the religious name of Mary of Jesus. Emilie's two daughters also entered the congregation, but they died young. The congregation was dedicated to reparation and to conducting retreats.

In 1859, Emilie led her sisters to Madras, India, where she founded a mission. She established houses in other Indian cities, and then in Mauritius and La Réunion. The congregation expanded to France, England, Ireland, Italy, and Spain. Her sisters arrived in the United States in 1908.

Emilie's last years were difficult and troubled, and she suffered great spiritual and emotional trials. She died in Florence, Italy, on February 22, 1878, in the company of her son, Adrien.

Pope John Paul II beatified Emilie on October 12, 1997, declaring:

"Widowed and motivated by the desire to participate in the paschal mystery, Mother Mary of Jesus founded the Society of Mary Reparatrix. By her life of prayer she reminds us that in Eucharistic adoration, where we draw from the source of life that is Christ, we find the strength for our daily mission."

Founder of the Congregation of Diocesan Workers

Blessed Emmanuel Domingo y Sol represents one of the finest aspects of the servants of the people of God. Gifted intellectually, he did not hoard his abilities or use them for his own benefit, but spent them on the young of his own era. A founder and patron of youth, Emmanuel was innovative, daring, and astute in judging the needs of young people and in using modern techniques to draw them to Christ.

EMMANUEL DOMINGO Y SOL

(D. 1909)

❦

FOUNDER

Emmanuel was born on April 1, 1836, at Tortosa, Tarragona, Spain. Educated in the local school and then by a tutor, Emmanuel received the grace of a priestly vocation and entered the seminary in October 1851. He was ordained a priest in July, 1860, and started his priestly ministry by giving missions in regional parishes. He then served as a priest in Aldes.

In 1862, his bishop, recognizing Emmanuel's intellectual and spiritual qualities, sent him to the University of Valencia. There he earned a degree in theology, using his education as a lecturer at the Tortosa seminary. At the same time, Emmanuel catechized the young, giving missions to workers and starting *El Congregante,* a publication designed to foster ideals among the youths of the diocese. He also built a theater complex and a sports arena to offer Christian recreational facilities for the young.

Here Emmanuel excelled in winning the trust of the youth of his era. They knew that he was educated and brilliant, but they also understood that Emmanuel knew of their problems and intended to bring them the consoling and inspiring comforts of the faith.

Emmanuel was also a devoted friend of another holy man of that era, St. Henry de Ossó y Cervelló. Emmanuel assisted the saint at his first Mass in 1867, maintaining a close friendship throughout their lives and was at the saint's bedside when he died. In 1881, Emmanuel started the Congregation of Diocesan Workers, a unique group of dedicated individuals to serve in the operation of the local seminary. Recognizing as well the need for a Spanish institution of learning in the Eternal City, Emmanuel founded the Pontifical Spanish College in Rome in 1882. This institution allowed young Spanish seminarians to complete their studies near the Vatican.

By 1909, Emmanuel was well-known and highly-regarded by many, who made unending demands on his time and energies. On January 25, 1909, Emmanuel died in Tortosa. His Cause was opened in July 1946.

Pope John Paul II beatified Emmanuel on March 29, 1987, praising his generosity and priestly ministries, directed toward safeguarding the future of the Church in the care of the young.

Emmanuel Medina Olmos ✿ **See Martyrs of Almeria.**

Emmanuel Segura ✿ **See Martyrs of the Scalopian Congregation.**

Enrico Canadell ✿ **See Martyrs of the Scalopian Congregation.**

Mystic and Camillian Contemplative

Blessed Enrico Rebuschini, was called the "Mystic of the Streets," and he cared for countless young and old by always displaying the love of Christ.

Enrico died as a Camillian priest, a servant of the poor. He was born in Gravedona, on Lake Como, in Italy, on April 28, 1860, the son of a prominent, wealthy family of the region. He desired a religious vocation at an early age, but Enrico was restrained by parental opposition. In accordance with his father's wishes, he attended Pavia University in order to prepare himself for the secular career demanded by his father. He did not remain there because he was horrified by the wanton secular environment and the disregard for the faith.

ENRICO REBUSCHINI

(D. 1938)

MYSTIC

Military service was demanded of him as well, and Enrico fulfilled his obligations and then went to work in a silk plant owned by his brother-in-law. The family had discovered that Enrico was favored by God in unique ways. He was so good, so holy and pure, that his relatives feared that he could not endure the coarse ways of their society and labor sites. In the end, Enrico was sent to the Pontifical Gregorian University, where his family hoped he would thrive.

He returned home because of illness and had to spend a long period in recuperation. As his body mended, his soul blossomed in prayer and mystical gifts as Enrico became united to Christ. He entered the Camillians, Servants of the Sick, in Verona. On April 14, 1889, he was ordained to the priesthood by the future Pope St. Pius X (r. 1903-1914).

Enrico served in various charitable capacities for the Camillians and eventually was assigned to Cremona, where he served from 1903 to 1937 as superior. His gifts of contemplation were so evident that people remarked on his holiness and recollection. Even when involved in the active service of others, Enrico displayed his mystical gifts, reflecting Christ to others. His devotion to the service of the sick was a hallmark of his priestly vocation. The last Mass that Enrico celebrated upon the earth was for the intentions of the sick. He fell ill with bronchial pneumonia and died on May 10, 1938. The people of Cremona mourned the passing of their mystic patron.

Pope John Paul II beatified Enrico on May 4, 1997, declaring: *"Throughout his life Blessed Enrico Rebuschini walked resolutely towards that 'perfection of charity'. . . his firm resolution . . . involved him in a demanding ascetic and mystical journey marked by an intense life of prayer, extraordinary love for the Eucharist and constant devotion to the sick and suffering."*

Member of the Congregation of the Holy Family of the Sacred Heart

The way of "Spiritual Childhood," a humble path of total reliance upon God, was the crowning glory of Blessed Eugénie Joubert. She was born in Isingeaux, France, on February 11, 1876, and she was trained in the faith and in charity by her mother. Realizing a religious vocation, Eugénie entered the Congregation of the Holy Family of the Sacred Heart in 1895. This religious community founded by Marie Ignace Melin, served as catechists for the poor and as devotees to the Sacred Heart of Jesus.

EUGÉNIE JOUBERT

(D. 1904)

🔥

RELIGIOUS

Professed, Eugénie was assigned to missions at Saint-Denis and at Aubervilles. When her health failed, she was assigned to St. Giles Parish in Liège, Belgium. For two years Eugénie suffered a severe illness, responding with good-natured calm and a distinct sense of God's presence. Eugénie also practiced the "Little Way" of total reliance upon God, observing obedience and humility in all things.

Eugénie had a brief trip to Rome before she died in Liège, on July 2, 1904, at the age of twenty-eight. Her silent suffering was at an end.

Pope John Paul II beatified Eugénie on November 20, 1994, announcing: *"Sister Eugénie Joubert, a religious of the Congregation of the Holy Family of the Sacred Heart, is presented to us as a living example of what God works in a human heart. With her too, a Christian upbringing was decisive for all her subsequent activities. Two years before she died, at the end of a brief life devoted in particular to the catechesis of small children, she expressed this heartfelt cry: 'I want to be just like a tiny child carried in her mother's arms.'*

"Christ's kingdom can begin in the heart of a child. This is what Sister Eugénie realized and for this reason she took care in preparing the little ones for their First Confession and First Communion. Each, from the earliest years, is called to witness to the truth. Ceaselessly the Church makes the Lord's words resound: 'Let the children come to me!' (Mt 19:14). She was to continue to do so, for she knew that no human child, however poor or humble he might be, is indifferent to God. Each is called to enter the kingdom and the blessed go before us to show us the way."

Faustina Kowalska ❧ See Maria Faustina Kowalska.

Founder of the Daughters of the Divine Shepherdess

The great Piarist or Scalopian spirit has offered the modern world true spiritual giants of service and dedication over the centuries. Faustino Míguez, a priest of the congregation and a founder, displayed the educational zeal of the Scalopians and the true sense of religious obedience that distinguished his efforts. His entire apostolate was dedicated to the work "of seeking souls and leading them to God."

FAUSTINO MÍGUEZ

(D. 1925)

PIARIST

Faustino was born on March 24, 1831 in Xamirás, a village of Rio Calanova, Orense, Spain. The fourth child of a devout family, Faustino studied Latin and the humanities in Orense. He also received the grace of a religious vocation, being inspired by the spirit of St. Joseph Calasanz and drawn to the Scalopians. Faustino entered St. Ferdinand's novitiate in Madrid in 1850, starting a vocation that would span half a century in the educational ministry.

He was ordained a priest and served the Scalopian institutions in San Fernando, Guanboacoa, Getafe, Monforte de Lemas, Celanova, El Escurial and Sanlúcar de Barrameda. His special concern for the young, and his remarkable kindness, became evident in all of his ministerial assignments. He was tireless in his efforts to open new scientific and cultural horizons for his students, and served as well as a confessor and medical researcher. Faustino opened the Míguez Laboratory in Getafe, one of his great legacies today.

While stationed in Sanlúcar de Barrameda, Faustino became aware of the harsh realities of educational opportunities for women. In order to provide a ministry to train such women, he founded the Calasanctian Institute of the Daughters of the Divine Shepherdess on January 2, 1885. This congregation was devoted to the Blessed Virgin and dedicated to aiding the poor, especially young women. Before he died, Faustino saw the congregation spread to Andalucia, Castile, Galicia, and then to Argentina and Chile in South America.

He was not allowed to remain in Sanlúcar de Barrameda to aid in the formation of the Daughters of the Divine Shepherdess. Assigned once more to Getafe, Faustino obeyed his superiors and resumed his medical studies. He died at age ninety-four in Getafe, on March 8, 1925.

Pope John Paul II beatified Faustino on October 25, 1998, declaring: *"By renouncing his own ambitions, the new blessed followed Jesus the Teacher and dedicated his life to teaching children and young people in the style of St. Joseph Calasanz. As an educator, his goal was the formation of the whole person. As a priest, he continually sought the holiness of souls. As a scientist, he was able to alleviate sickness by freeing humanity from physical suffering."* The Holy Father praised Faustino as *"the very image of Christ, who welcomes, pardons and gives life."*

Spanish Vicar General

The martyrdom of Spain's leading churchmen during that nation's Civil War has never been explained fully for American Catholics, who should understand the true nature of the Communist-led "Republican Army" — savagely anti-Christian. Felipe Ripoll Morata, with his bishop, Blessed Anselm Polanco Fontecha, paid the ultimate price in this tragic political and ideological insanity.

FELIPE RIPOLL MORATA

(D. 1939)

MARTYR

Felipe was born in Teruel, Spain, on September 14, 1878. Raised devoutly, he entered the seminary and was ordained for his diocese. He served as a professor and then as rector of the local seminary. Blessed Anselm Polanco Morata Fontecha, bishop of Teruel in 1935, appointed Felipe as the diocesan vicar general.

When the revolutionary military forces took Teruel in 1938, Felipe stood firm with Blessed Anselm against the godless doctrines of the Republican Army. He was arrested and spent more than a year in prison with Blessed Anselm. In 1939, Felipe and Blessed Anselm were used as human shields for the retreating revolutionaries. They were then taken to a gorge near Gerosa and shot. Their remains are enshrined in the Teruel Cathedral.

Pope John Paul II beatified Felipe on October 1, 1995, declaring that both Felipe and Blessed Anselm chose to stay with the faithful in a time of crisis.

The Holy Father added: *"The new blesseds, before the alternative of abandoning the requirements of the faith, or of dying for it, strengthened by God's grace, put their own destiny in his hands. The martyrs did not defend themselves, not because they thought little of life, but out of their total love of Jesus Christ."* (See also Anselm Polanco Fontecha.)

Fidel Fuido ☙ See Martyrs of the Marianist Congregation.

Salesian Superior and Spiritual Director

The truly great works of the Church demand many willing hands. Men and women may be inspired by the Holy Spirit to undertake charitable apostolates, but they do not succeed in any massive ministry unless they are joined by others with the same level of dedication. St. John Bosco, venerated for his lasting contributions of mercy and care in the world, was aided by another singular soul who responded to the needs of his time and carried the banner of the Salesian Congregation into the world.

His name was Filippo (Philip) Rinaldi, and he was described as a "living image" of Christ. Born in Lu Monferrato, Italy, in 1856, he was only ten when he met St. John Bosco at Mirabello, outside of Turin. Filippo received the blessings of the saintly founder and a priestly vocation as well. He was ordained a Salesian priest on December 23, 1882, in the cathedral of Ivrea.

FILIPPO RINALDI

(D. 1931)

RELIGIOUS

St. John Bosco recognized the extraordinary virtues of Filippo early on and prepared for his unique role in the Salesian community. Nine months after ordination, Filippo was named director of a community and set about expanding the congregation's ministries in Spain and Portugal. He founded twenty-one houses during this period.

In 1901, Filippo returned to Turin to serve as prefect general of the Salesians. He also earned the respect of many individuals and groups for his ministry as a confessor and spiritual director. In 1922, Filippo became rector major of the Salesians, serving in this capacity until his death in Turin on December 5, 1931.

Pope John Paul II beatified Filippo on April 29, 1990, declaring that this third successor of St. John Bosco was worthy of the rank of martyr for the faith. The Holy Father said: *"Don Rinaldi was an especially tireless promoter of the great Salesian Family in its various groups and worked to help it develop more and more into a worthwhile organized and adaptable force for Christian education of youth and of the popular classes."*

Apostle of Our Lady of Pompeii

The disabled and the disadvantaged of past centuries had few champions. While the Church always maintained charitable programs for the sick and the vulnerable, Almighty God also raises up men and women to care for particular victims of society who need special care. Filippo Smaldone was the father of the deaf, blind, and abandoned of his era, sacrificing himself to educate and protect them.

FILIPPO
SMALDONE

(D. 1923)

FOUNDER

Filippo was born in Naples, Italy, on July 27, 1848. He studied for the priesthood at Rossano Calabro, and was finally ordained for the archdiocese of Naples in 1871. Filippo started his ministry by holding evening catechism classes, and during an epidemic, he cared for victims until falling ill himself. Our Lady of Pompeii, for whom Filippo had a special devotion, cured him miraculously.

Interested in the deaf mutes of Naples at an early age, in March, 1885, Filippo went to Lecce, Italy, where he opened an institute for deaf-mutes with Father Lorenzo Apicella. Women dedicated to the care of deaf-mutes aided Filippo and formed the Congregation of the Salesian Sisters of the Sacred Heart. Filippo also opened an institute in Bari and took in blind children, orphans, and the abandoned.

Filippo faced many trials throughout his life, but continued his apostolate. He labored as confessor and spiritual director for priests and founded the Eucharistic League of Priest Adorers and Women Adorers. He also served as the superior of the Missionaries of St. Francis de Sales. Filippo received many honors before dying of a diabetic condition with cardiac complications on June 4, 1923, in Lecce.

Pope John Paul II beatified Filippo on August 16, 1996, announcing: *"He who loves me will be loved by my Father, and I will love him and manifest myself to him (Jn 14:21). Filippo Smaldone, the Lecce priest whose life was marked by constant attention to the poor and extraordinary apostolic zeal, also intensely lived and embodied charity to God and neighbor. This great witness to charity realized he had to fulfill his own mission in Southern Italy, and turned specifically to the care and education of the deaf to give them an active role in society. His intense, unwavering priestly spirituality, nourished by prayer, meditation, and even bodily penance, spurred him to provide a social service open to those advanced insights which true pastoral charity can inspire."*

Fiorentino Felipe ❦ **See Martyrs of the Scalopian Congregation.**

Bishop of Barbastro

Spain has a long and revered history of faith and is often called the "Land of the Mystics." This nation has also endured godless rebellions that have claimed the lives of men and women, the family of faith. A victim of a particularly vicious Communist revolution of the late 1930s, Florentino Asensio Barroso gave his life for the people of God, thus bequeathing not only the faith to future generations, but also the insignia of valor to be cherished and revered by all.

FLORENTINO ASENSIO BARROSO
(D. 1936)

MARTYR

Florentino Asensio was born in Villasexmir, Valladolid, Spain, on October 16, 1877. He studied for the priesthood and was ordained on June 1, 1901. He earned a doctorate at the Pontifical University of Valladolid and began teaching. When his uncle, Cardinal Cos, died, Florentino Asensio became a priest in the cathedral, earning a reputation as a preacher and as a spiritual director for many religious houses in the area. His fame led to his consecration as the bishop of Barbastro on January 26, 1936, where he began programs for the poor.

He had served in this office for a little less than six months when the forces of the Spanish Civil War began their persecutions. As the anti-clerical spirit rose in Barbastro, Florentino Asensio was placed under house arrest on July 20, 1936. On August 8, he was placed in solitary confinement, tortured, and mutilated. Florentino Asensio was singled out for this harsh treatment because of his holiness and reputation as a leader of the Catholic Faith.

On August 9, 1936, Florentino Asensio and twelve others were taken by truck to the local cemetery. They were shot, and when the first salvo did not end the saintly bishop's life, he was shot once again in the temple. His remains were dropped into a common grave but later identified and placed in the crypt of the cathedral. Just before his martyrdom, Florentino Asensio had calmly announced "I am going to heaven."

Pope John Paul II beatified Florentino Asensio Barroso on May 4, 1997, declaring: *"At the last moments of his life, after having suffered lacerating humiliations and tortures, in answer to one of his torturers as to whether he knew the destiny that awaited him, he relied serenely and firmly: 'I am going to heaven.' Thus he proclaimed his staunch faith in Christ, conqueror of death and giver of eternal life."*

The mystical way of prayer is one of sacrifice and silence. Those souls called to this way are blessed in unusual and beautiful fashions, and they teach by their example. A noblewoman, Florida Cevoli is one of these gifted mystics of the past.

FLORIDA CEVOLI

(D. 1767)

REFORMER

She was born an aristocrat in Pisa, Italy, on November 11, 1685, and baptized Lucrezia Elena Cevoli. Florida was educated by the Poor Clares of Pisa, and at eighteen she revealed her desire to enter the cloister. She sought admission to the Poor Clares, the Franciscan Second Order, in Città di Castello.

Her family opposed her vocation, and the Poor Clares were reluctant to accept someone of her rank, especially in the face of her family's lack of consent. However, Florida did not swerve from her calling, and she was finally allowed to enter the novitiate at Città di Castello. Her novice mistress was St. Veronica Giuliani, and Florida was trained to the paths of perfection by this model religious. Even after taking her vows, Florida remained in the novitiate to benefit from Veronica's direction. Her assignment in the cloister was to administer the pharmacy.

In 1727, Florida, who was a true contemplative and humble servant of all, was elected abbess. She had served as vicaress when St. Veronica was superior and was well prepared for this office. Florida restored many customs to the cloister and increased the weekly receptions of the Holy Eucharist by the nuns. She also fed the poor who came to the cloister for aid.

Physically, Florida endured pain and fever throughout her religious life. Yet she never indulged herself, and when she died on June 12, 1767, her confessor said she had expired "out of pure love for God."

Pope John Paul II beatified Florida on May 16, 1993, declaring that her entire life was dedicated to love and service. The Holy Father said that *"Florida was inspired by the Spirit of Truth who leads believers to interiorize the Word of God."*

Patron of Catholic Artists

One of the greatest religious painters of all time and a model of purity and generosity, Fra Angelico was called John Faesulanus or Giovanni da Fiesole. The world bestowed the title Fra Angelico upon him as a tribute to his religious art and his religious virtues.

He was born circa 1387, near Vicchio di Mugello, Italy, where he showed artistic ability and piety at an early age. In 1407, Fra Angelico entered the Order of Preachers, the Dominicans, at Fiesole. For a time he was assigned to San Marco Monastery, in Florence. He spent his time providing that structure with the first of his magnificent paintings which provided a serene religious spirit while reflecting a classical influence that mirrored the Renaissance era in which he lived. In addition to his paintings in San Marco, he also performed his monastic life with remarkable virtue, being described by contemporaries as "angelic."

FRA ANGELICO
(D. 1455)
🌿
RELIGIOUS

Fra Angelico's art reflected an angelic approach. His figurines and scenes are mantled in exquisite lights, radiant with religious feelings. His early training in miniatures and illumination provided Fra Angelico with a remarkable ability to adorn his paintings with decorative splendor as well, making them unique.

The painter Fra Angelico

Fra Angelico and his brother had to leave Florence during a political struggle because they were loyal to the pope. They fled again later because of a terrible epidemic, going to Cortona and then to Fiesole. He remained there for sixteen years until he was invited to Florence and finally, in 1445, to Rome.

Pope Eugenius IV (r. 1431-1447) asked Fra Angelico to paint frescoes for him, and he also served Pope Nicholas V (r. 1447-1455). It is reported that Pope Eugenius also offered Fra Angelico the office of archbishop of Florence, an honor that Fra Angelico declined out of humility. The list of masterpieces provided by Fra Angelico is a long one filled with intricacy, beauty, and a masterful display of pious interpretation of the spiritual life. Fra Angelico died at La Minerva Friary in Rome on February 18, 1455. He was buried in Santa Maria Church in the Eternal City.

Pope John Paul II beatified Fra Angelico on October 3, 1982, declaring him patron of Catholic artists in 1984. Also honored was the profound spirituality evident in Fra Angelico's masterpieces mirroring his religious life and his interior union with Christ.

Frances Aldea Araujo ❦ See Martyrs of Madrid.

Foundress of the Sisters of Charity

This blessed might well become the patroness of the senior citizens of the modern world as she stands as a model of elderly accomplishments and courage. Remarkably, Frances Anne Carbonell founded a religious congregation at the age of seventy, after a life of dedication and resignation. Delays, tribulations, and disappointments were threads in the fabric of her life, but she used them to gain strength and to endure until she achieved what she believed to be God's Will.

FRANCES ANNE CARBONELL

(D. 1855)

FOUNDRESS

Frances was born in Senecelles, Majorca, Balearic Islands, Spain, on June 1, 1781. Her family was well off, and she was raised piously and devoutly. Frances received the grace of a religious vocation early in life and wanted to enter a convent, but her family refused permission for such a sacrifice. She accepted the refusal with grace and became a religious in spirit, translating her everyday life into acts of love. Her mother and siblings died while she was still young, and in 1821, her father passed away as well. Frances was alone and yet in union in Christ.

She remained in her home, praying, fasting, and caring for the sick and the poor. Her fellow parishioners and others recognized her pious nature, and people started coming to her for advice, because she was prudent and wise. Some called her "the Saint of Senecelles."

At age seventy, Frances used her own home and financial resources to found the Sisters of Charity. On December 7, 1851, she and two companions made their vows. These sisters cared for the sick and poor, taught children and adults, and organized school programs. When she died on February 27, 1855, the entire region was plunged into grief. Frances was declared Venerable in 1983.

Pope John Paul II beatified Frances on October 1, 1989, declaring:

"Throughout her life Francisca-Ana obeyed God's Will — a divine will that was sometimes difficult to discern . . . a life full of uncertainty, but a life in which there was no obstacle to serving God in everything. . . ."

Founder of the Congregation "La Annunciata"

Harsh times often spur renewal among people, and God provides them with eloquent defenders of the faith to lead them. Blessed Francis Coll found his future placed in jeopardy by the political turmoil of his time, but he also discovered that the enormous suffering among the faithful was a call for an eloquent defense of the Church's teachings. His response to that call was loyalty, honor, and unceasing labor.

FRANCIS COLL

(D. 1875)

FOUNDER

He was born on May 18, 1812, in Gombeny, in the Catalan Pyrenees of Spain. His father, Peter, died when Francis was only four, leaving a widow and ten children in dire straits. Francis' mother raised him devoutly, and he was confirmed in 1818. Four years later he entered the seminary at Vichy, France, earning his own way by teaching catechism and grammar to local children. One of Francis' classmates was St. Anthony Claret. In 1830, Francis entered the Dominicans at Vichy, but the monastic Orders were suppressed, and he had to study for the priesthood under great stress. He was ordained on March 28, 1836, in his original seminary.

Francis was assigned to the parish of Arles, and in 1839, was sent to Moyá. The area had been devastated by war, and the local people were starving. Francis aided them with charitable programs until 1849. He had maintained his religious life scrupulously, even though he could not reside in a monastery. In 1846, Francis willingly aided St. Anthony Claret in forming a new priestly group called "the Apostolic Fraternity."

He also became the director of the Third Order of Vichy, and in 1850 he opened the former Dominican monastery and began preaching throughout the Catalan region. When cholera struck the area four years later, Francis cared for all of the victims. He saw the response to his catechetical and preaching efforts, and in August, 1856, started a teaching branch of the Third Order of St. Dominic, calling the congregation "La Annunciata." By the time Francis died, "La Annunciata" had fifty houses and more than three hundred sisters.

In 1872, the Dominicans were able to return to Spain, as part of the Order, under the direction of the master general. It was discovered then that Francis had carefully nurtured all of the Dominican communities and institutions during the suppression, maintaining the Order even under assault.

On December 2, 1869, Francis was struck blind while preaching at Sallent. He endured great pain and suffering until his death on April 2, 1875, but he bore his last trials with calm and resolve. Francis' remains were enshrined in the motherhouse of the Dominican Sisters of "La Annunciata."

Pope John Paul II beatified Francis on April 29, 1979. During the beatification celebrations, Francis was praised as an apostolic preacher whose popular missions spurred Marian devotions and regenerated the faith. The spirit of Francis has endured more than one hundred years.

Founder of the Sisters of Our Lady of Suffrage and St. Zita

Really great souls rejoice in progress in the world, never forgetting that the earth is truly the Lord's own creation. A member of the scientific world of his era, Blessed Francis Fa'a di Bruno combined this sort of faith with scholarship. Called "a prophet of his time," he was not only the founder of a religious congregation but one of the leading mathematicians and astronomers of his era.

FRANCIS FA'A DI BRUNO

(D. 1876)

SCHOLAR

Francis was born in Alessandria, Italy, on March 29, 1825, the son of the Marquis Louis Fa'a di Bruno and his wife, Caroline. Francis was the youngest of twelve children.

He was educated in Alessandria and elsewhere in Italy, and at age sixteen entered the armed forces of Piedmont, reaching the rank of captain. In 1849, Francis was assigned to Paris, where he studied at the Sorbonne and earned his doctorate in mathematics and in astronomy. He also became a member of the St. Vincent de Paul Society. Francis resigned his commission as a result of his academic interests and studied under the leading mathematicians and astronomy leaders of his age.

He returned to Turin, Italy, and became a professor at the university in that city. In honor of his great knowledge and dedication, Francis received the degree of doctor of science from the universities of Paris and Turin. He wrote more than forty articles for American and European journals as well as treatises and studies, and his writings are included in the Catalogue of Scientific Papers of the Royal Society in London. Francis also wrote ascetical studies, sacred melodies, and invented scientific apparatuses.

But Francis' focus was on charitable works in Turin, and he showed special concerned for the well-being and safety of women and young girls. Francis established schools, retirement homes, and other charitable institutions, and in 1868, he founded the Sisters of Our Lady of Suffrage and of St. Zita to aid in his ministry.

Francis accomplished all this as a dedicated layman. He received ordination to the priesthood in Turin only in 1876, having completed his seminary studies while conducting the myriad activities of his apostolates. Francis died in Turin on March 27, 1888.

Pope John Paul II beatified Francis on September 25, 1988, calling him *"a prophet in the midst of the people of God."* The Holy Father praised Francis for knowing how *"to find positive responses to the needs of his time."* Pope John Paul II also said that Francis was *"a giant of faith and charity."*

Jesuit Laybrother

A simple doorkeeper, called "Brother Courtesy" by his contemporaries, has left a legacy of humble service and true Catholic Faith to this generation. "Brother Courtesy" was a Jesuit laybrother, named Francis Garate, and he lived only to praise God.

Francis was born on February 3, 1857, in a farming community called Azpeitia, near the Loyola castle, in Spain. The second of eleven children, Francis worked on his family farm and matured in the faith in a region of Spain attuned to Divine Providence. When he was fourteen, Francis went to Orduna, where he was employed as a house servant in the Jesuit College of Nuestra Señora de la Antigua. After three years of service,

FRANCIS GARATE

(D. 1929)

RELIGIOUS

Francis asked to be accepted by the Society of Jesus. The Jesuits had been expelled from Spain by that time, so Francis entered the novitiate at Poyanne in southern France. He made his first vows on February 2, 1876. The following year he was assigned to the College of Santiago Apostolo a La Guardia (Pontevedra). Francis was named infirmarian there, and he cared for the sick for a decade, serving in the sacristy as well.

In August, 1887, Francis made his final vows and was assigned to Duesto Bilbao soon after. There he became a porter, or doorkeeper, at the university. Francis would remain in this post humbly and devoutly until his death. "Brother Courtesy," as he was called, brought a gentle concern to his day-to-day routines. He was meek and charming, caring for one and all with a quiet joy that was quite contagious and calming. Francis died in Duesto Bilbao on September 9, 1929.

Pope John Paul II beatified Francis on October 6, 1985. During the celebration, this saintly brother was honored as a religious of perfection who chose the way of humble service that confounds each new age and brings aware souls to Christ.

Missionary to Quebec and First Bishop of Canada

The opening of the New World to Europeans also brought the faith to the American continent. One of the most important Catholic organizations of the time was the Paris Foreign Missionary Society. The honor of the faithful missionaries and martyrs of this society includes a great luminary, Francis de Montmorency Laval, the first bishop of Quebec, Canada, also called François of Quebec, was "a bishop according to God's Heart."

Francis de Montmorency Laval was born in Montigny-sur-Avre, France, on April 30, 1623, the son of Hughes de Laval and Michelle de Péricard. They were members of a distinguished family whose ancestor baptized St. Clovis.

FRANCIS DE MONTMORENCY LAVAL

(D. 1708)

MISSIONARY

After studying with the Jesuits at La Flèche, Francis received the position of canon at age twelve. He entered the college of Clermont in Paris intending to become a priest, but he received the family estate and titles in 1645 when his two older brothers died. In 1647, Francis was ordained and appointed archdeacon of Evreux, and made journeys of visitation throughout the area. He was appointed vicar apostolic of Tongkin (modern Vietnam), in the Paris Foreign Mission Society at age thirty, but never took up residence there because of the political and geographical conditions.

In 1654, Francis resigned his position and spent four years at the hermitage in Caen. Pope Alexander VII (r. 1655-1667) appointed Francis vicar apostolic of New France in 1658, and on December 8 of that year, Francis was consecrated a bishop. Shortly thereafter he set sail for Canada, reaching Quebec on June 16, 1659.

When he arrived in Canada he discovered a frontier diocese in need of organization and stability. He was responsible for all of North America except for the British-held lands of New England and the Spanish settlements. Actually, Francis said that his sole mission was to be "a bishop according to God's Heart." Contemporaries echoed that spiritual mission, saying about Francis:

"His heart is always with us." He certainly was a staunch patron of missionaries who went from Quebec to their far-flung posts.

Francis promoted missions and fought against the rampant liquor trade with the local Indian tribes. He erected a cathedral dedicated to the Immaculate Conception and restored the shrine of St. Anne at Beaupré to foster devotion. Francis also started the Catholic school system in Canada, all the while revered as a man of prayer and mortification. In 1684, Francis retired to the seminary that he had founded. He came out of retirement in 1701 and 1705 when disastrous fires engulfed the seminary. He died in Quebec on May 6, 1708.

Pope John Paul II beatified Francis on June 22, 1980, praising this episcopal pioneer of the New World as a priest and prelate who gave everything to see the Church thrive and to nurture the inhabitants of towns and wildernesses in the faith.

Founder and Mystic Miracle Worker

There have been few more dedicated "sons" of Holy Mother Church than Francis Palau y Quer, the Carmelite missionary and founder. He said of the Church: "On the day I was ordained to the priesthood I was consecrated through ordination to your service . . . I am yours with all that I do, all that I am and possess."

Francis Palau y Quer was born in Aytona (Lérida), Spain, on December 29, 1812, to a poor family. Raised devoutly and receiving the grace of a religious vocation, Francis started his four years of seminary in 1828, at Lérida. He became a Carmelite in Barcelona and was professed on November 15, 1833, and ordained a priest on April 2, 1836.

FRANCIS PALAU Y QUER

(D. 1872)

FOUNDER

When the Spanish political situation threatened the Catholic religious institutions, Francis went to France and labored there in exile from 1840 to 1851. He returned to Spain in 1852 and founded the "School of Virtue," an organization for catechetical instruction. Falsely accused of fomenting labor strikes, Francis was arrested and confined to the island of Ibiza from 1854 until 1860. During this exile, Francis experienced a mystical union.

Returning to Spain, Francis founded the Teresian Carmelite Missionary Sisters and a community of brothers that later became part of the Carmelite Order. Francis labored to make possible institutions that would carry the

Carmelite spirit into a troubled world, responding to God's Will and to the needs of men and women facing modern life.

He was a miracle worker and an exorcist of considerable fame in his own age. He served as a consultor at Vatican Council I in Rome and inspired many with his holiness and generosity. When Francis died in Tarragona, on March 20, 1872, Spain mourned his passing.

Pope John Paul II beatified Francis Palau y Quer on April 24, 1988, declaring that this *"Discalced Carmelite made his priestly life a generous offering to the Church, the flock of Christ."* The Holy Father said also: *"However, the most cherished work of Father Palau was the foundation of the Carmelite missionaries . . . . His spiritual daughters — the Carmelite Missionary Sisters and the Teresian Missionary Carmelites — flesh out and continue in the Church the spirit of that apostle."*

Founder of the Sisters of Perpetual Adoration of the Blessed Sacrament

The family has long been revered as the cradle of vocations and the nesting place of the saints. Francis Spinelli, a religious founder and an apostle of the Blessed Sacrament, put into his adult life the virtues and graces gained from his family as a child.

He was born in Milan, Italy, on April 14, 1853, and was baptized the following day in the basilica of St. Ambrose. His family moved to Cremona when he was young, and he was raised in Vergo, in the diocese of Bergamo, where the family spent the summer months.

FRANCIS SPINELLI

(D. 1909)

PRIEST

Francis suffered from a severe spinal problem as a young child but was cured of the condition in 1871, in Vergo. There he also accompanied his mother on her visits to the poor of the region. She trained him in Marian and eucharistic devotion as well. His mother also taught him the virtues of a priestly vocation, and in his teens he entered the seminary. An uncle, Father Peter Cagliaroli, and a friend, Blessed Luigi Palazzolo, also served as mentors for Francis, who completed his studies and was ordained at age twenty-two.

Francis was assigned to help his uncle and Blessed Luigi until December, 1875, when he had a revelation in the St. Mary Major Basilica in Rome. As a result of this experience Francis knew that he was being asked to found a religious congregation of women dedicated to adoring Christ in the Eucharist. In 1882, with Blessed Gertrude Comensoli, Francis started the Sisters of Perpetual Adoration of the Blessed Sacrament. Francis suffered many trials and problems because of this founding but endured despite pain and illness, until his death in Cremona on February 6, 1913.

Pope John Paul II beatified Francis on June 21, 1992, in Caravaggio, Italy, declaring: *"The life of the Servant of God, whom today I have been able to number among the choirs of the Church's blessed, assumes a prophetic importance in the holy mystery of the Eucharist . . . Franceso Spinelli, who lived 'to love Jesus in the Eucharist and to make him loved.' "* The Holy Father added: *"The Church offers him as a model of an authentic apostle especially to you the priests whom Providence calls to be stewards of the mysteries of salvation."*

Foundress of the Sister Oblates of St. Francis de Sales in Troyes

Desiring always to "disappear into Christ," is a hallmark of many friends of God. Francisca Salesia Aviat was one of these hidden souls in Christ's love.

A foundress born in Sezanne, France, on September 16, 1844, Francisca was baptized Leonia. Raised in a Catholic family, Francisca saw the problems of her own era and desired to promote the well-being of French working girls, who were exploited and endangered by many factions of society. Francisca worked among the girls and then founded the Sister Oblates of St. Francis de Sales in Troyes, taking vows in 1871. Father Louis Brisson aided Francisca in this great work, knowing the pressing need for such an apostolate. Francisca, a spiritual daughter of St. Francis de Sales, adopted the Salesian rule for her congregation.

FRANCISCA SALESIA AVIAT

(D. 1914)

EDUCATOR

She opened homes and schools in France and watched her Sister Oblates expand their missions to meet the needs of many areas. The Sister Oblates of St. Francis de Sales arrived in the United States in 1952. They also conducted retreats as part of their apostolate.

Francisca had to leave France in 1903 because of anti-religious legislation. She started again in Perugia, Italy, and directed her sisters from there. She drafted the congregation's constitution and saw it approved by Pope St. Pius X (r. 1903-1914) in 1911. Francisca died in Perugia on January 10, 1914.

Pope John Paul II beatified Francisca on September 27, 1992, declaring that she *"dedicated her life to educating young working women . . . ."* The Holy Father added: *"Union with the redemptive sacrifice of Christ by the daily practice of self denial was Mother Françoise's central orientation throughout her life. Her sole desire to be, as she said, 'God's little instrument.' "*

Founder of the Albertines

The early years of Blessed Frederick Albert's life taught him that endurance, loyalty, and faith were the foundations of a Christian vocation. This blessed faced economic and social trials almost unceasingly; nevertheless, he labored heroically until he achieved all that God asked from him for the world and for the honor and glory of the Church.

FREDERICK
ALBERT

(D. 1876)

FOUNDER

Frederick was born in Turin, Italy, on October 16, 1820, and the normal opportunities of life did not come knocking regularly. Frederick worked and saved, learning all that he could through trials and patience in the face of economic adversity. He had a vocation to the priesthood but could not attend seminary because of the lack of support and financial means. As an adult he took the required exams for the candidate, passed, was ordained, and brought a wealth of wisdom and basic common sense to his ministry.

Frederick served in various diocesan parishes and gained respect as a concerned pastor who cared for his people and their day-to-day problems. He also proved a remarkable counselor for the priests of the region. His years of trials gave him an insight into souls and their aspirations.

Frederick also understood the needs of his own age and gathered dedicated young women to conduct charitable programs to ease the suffering of the faithful. He founded the Vincentian Sisters of Mary Immaculate, also called the "Albertines," in order to complete his vision of service. Frederick Albert guided this congregation until his death in Lanzo Torinese, Italy, on September 30, 1876.

Pope John Paul II beatified Frederick on September 30, 1984, declaring: *"His spirit of faith, his unconditional obedience to the Pope and his bishop, and his priestly charity made him an element of balance among the members of the priesthood and a zealous pastor, particularly attentive to youth and the poor."*

Almighty God sometimes leads generous souls to the far corners of the earth. They do not have a permanent roof over their heads, and they are not granted the gift of being consoled by the success of their various apostolates.

FREDERICK JANSOONE

(D. 1916)

MISSIONARY

Frederick Jansoone was just such a wanderer for Christ, serving as a Franciscan emissary to those in need.

Frederick was born in the small village of Ghyvelde, near Lille, France, on November 19, 1838. His family was not financially secure, and his father died young. Frederick had entered the seminary while his father was alive, and this untimely death led to his withdrawal from studies for the priesthood. He simply had to give up his personal desires in order to support his mother. When she died, Frederick applied to the Friars Minor and was professed as a Franciscan on July 18, 1865. He was ordained a priest on August 17, 1870.

He served as a chaplain in the military and spent twelve years in the Holy Land, where he assisted the Church in various capacities. In 1888, Frederick was sent to Canada, and there he labored at the shrine of Our Lady of Cap-de-la-Madeleine. He was so recollected and holy that people flocked to him, knowing that he had wandered through so many regions of the world for Christ. He also demonstrated a profound spiritual life. Contemplative in nature but serving as the foundation for his ministry zeal, Frederick died in Montreal, Canada, on August 4, 1916.

Pope John Paul II beatified Frederick on September 25, 1988, announcing: " '*A true son of St. Francis, Father Frederic gives us the example of contemplative prayer which is able to embrace the works of creation, the events of daily life, and encounters with each person. May we receive as simply as he the Spirit which the Lord bestows on his people (cf. Num 11:29)!" "Good Father Frederic" shows us that the spirit of contemplation, far from inhibiting apostolic zeal, strengthens it. Close to God, he is also close to people. In the Holy Land and in Canada he never ceases to form those who listen to him to commit themselves to the* vita evangelica *along the ways traced by the Secular Franciscan Order, and especially in the very concrete apostolate of family and professional life. Attentive and brotherly towardsthe little ones "because (they) belong to Christ" (cf. Mt 9:41), Father Frederic taught his contemporaries to be consistent and ardent witnesses of the Gospel. May his glorification by the Church, contribute to arouse in the Order of Saint Francis and in the Church a renewed burst of holiness and apostolic zeal!*

Founder of the Society of St. Vincent de Paul

As charitable organizations come and go in the world, modern men and women learn to depend on tried and true associations that guarantee donations given will reach the people for whom they are intended. The Society of St. Vincent de Paul is one of those enduring, trusted organizations that functions only to extend the redemptive mercy of Christ to those less fortunate. St. Vincent de Paul, the wondrous holy man of France, stands as a symbol of the society, but the founding and the core values of that remarkable organization can be traced to Frederick Ozanam, who started the Conference of Charity of St. Vincent, the original society.

FREDERICK OZANAM

(D. 1853)

LAYMAN

Frederick was born in Milan, Italy, on April 23, 1813. While a student in Paris, he founded his charitable project, a society that was destined to serve men and women in countries throughout the world. Antonio Frederick Ozanam was a ferocious defender of the faith. At eighteen he wrote a treatise, "Reflections on the Doctrine of Saint Simon" which was well received. After a period of spiritual aridity and doubt, Frederick promised God "to devote my life to the services of truth which had given me peace," and he kept his vow for his remaining years. In 1836, Frederick left Paris only to return two years later to defend his thesis on Dante for a doctorate in letters. He was given his doctorate and the chair of commercial law at Lyons. He also substituted for a judge at the Sorbonne, becoming a full-tenured judge there in 1844.

Frederick was awarded the Grand Prize Gobert two years in a row in Paris. He had to retire to Italy because of ill health, but died in Marseilles on September 8, 1853. His Society of St. Vincent de Paul was founded with seven companions when he was twenty. He said that he founded the society to "insure my faith by works of charity." His literary efforts on defense of the faith display a brilliant intellect, eloquence, and profound spiritual insight.

Pope John Paul II beatified Frederick Ozanam in Paris on August 22, 1997, during the celebrations of World Youth Day. The Holy Father was joined by French bishops at Notre Dame Cathedral for the ceremony, where Frederick's zeal and spiritual maturity were praised.

Gabriel Pergaud ❦ See Martyrs of La Rochelle.

Founder of the Confraternity of the Holy Face

There are individuals in the world who appear as refreshing oases of charity and kindness in the wilderness of the world, blessing all who come into contact with them. Gaetano Catanoso, the priest founder and apostle of the Holy Face, was a human being transformed in this fashion by love.

Born in Chorio di San Lorenzo, Reggio Calabria, Italy, on February 14, 1879, Gaetano was the son of land owners who educated him in the faith and fostered his vocation. Gaetano entered the local seminary and was ordained a priest in 1902.

Serving as a pastor, he promoted devotion to the Holy Face as a reparation for modern sinfulness, establishing the Confraternity of the Holy Face. In 1920, he started the Holy Face Bulletin and promoted the Poor Clerics Association to sponsor vocations. In 1921, Gaetano became parish priest of Santa Maria de la Candelaria, in Reggio Calabria, and he revived the entire region, enlisting "flying squads" of priests who went into individual communities to promote the faith. Gaetano was a confessor to religious institutions and prisons. He also served as a hospital chaplain and spiritual director of the archepiscopal seminary.

GAETANO CATANOSO

(D. 1963)

PRIEST

He founded the Congregation of the Daughters of St. Veronica, Missionaries of the Holy Face, to aid in his apostolate, designing this congregation as a community devoted to prayer and reparation, to worship, and to catechesis programs. Gaetano opened the first convent in Reparo, and the first sisters received their habits in 1935. The congregation received diocesan approval in 1958.

Gaetano spent most of his life as "a victim of love" to the Sacred Heart of Jesus, offering himself in 1929. This hidden spiritual apostolate prompted his endless charitable works. Gaetano died on April 4, 1963.

Pope John Paul II beatified Gaetano on May 4, 1997, and at the ceremony he was honored as a victim of expiation for sins and as a true image of the Good Shepherd. Gaetano's devotion to the Holy Face transformed him during his lifetime. The Holy Father declared: *". . . he worked tirelessly for the good of the flock entrusted to him by the Lord."*

Gaspar Stangassinger, a remarkably handsome and affable young man, displayed the virtue of stability throughout his life. He was not inflexible, not bound by rigid codes, but compelled by his love of Christ and the Church that led him to spiritual perfection.

GASPAR (KASPAR) STANGASSINGER

(D. 1899)

RELIGIOUS

Blessed Gaspar was born in Berchtesgaden, Germany, on January 12, 1871, one of sixteen children born to a well-to-do farmer who owned a local quarry. The family was devout and well-respected. Gaspar was raised in the faith and received the grace of a religious vocation at a young age. In 1871, having attended local schools, he went to Freising to continue his studies, and in 1884 he entered the minor seminary. He entered the major seminary in 1890.

His father opposed any thought of a religious vocation, but Gaspar entered the Redemptorists in 1892 and was ordained three years later. Displaying both a mature spirituality and stability, he was named the assistant director of the Redemptorist Juniorate in Durnsberg. There he taught and counseled the young men enrolled in the Juniorate, gaining many graces and serving as a model religious for the entire congregation.

On the night of September 22, 1899, Gaspar woke up in the middle of the night in severe pain. He was diagnosed as a suffering from acute appendicitis, but peritonitis developed as well, draining his life away. Gaspar died on September 26 at Gars am Inn at the age of twenty-eight. He was declared Venerable in 1986.

Pope John Paul II beatified Gaspar on April 24, 1988, declaring: *"Shaped by the deep religious spirit of his family and called very early to the priesthood, his life was wholly centered on God."* The Holy Father added: *"He did not seek the extraordinary, but wanted 'to do what the day demanded.' "*

GENNARO MARIA SARNELLI

(D. 1744)

FOUNDER

Co-Founder of the Redemptorists

St. Alphonsus Ligouri, the founder of the Congregation of the Most Holy Redeemer, burned with the charity of Christ while he lived, drawing many to his apostolate. One of these founding pioneers who aided St.

Alphonsus was Gennaro (Januarius) Maria Sarnelli, who burned with the same ardor for Christ.

The son of Baron Angelo Sarnelli of Ciorani in Naples, Gennaro was born on September 12, 1702, and was raised in an aristocratic environment. The baron insisted that Januarius study the law and thus opposed his son's desire to enter the religious life. Obedient to his father's wishes, Gennaro became a lawyer and achieved success in that field before finally refusing his father's pleas and entering the seminary in 1728. Four years later, on July 8, 1732, he was ordained a priest. Gennaro aided St. Alphonsus in founding the Redemptorists and worked with the saint at Salerno until 1735 when his health demanded his return to Naples for recuperation. Praying and keeping the faith, Gennaro recovered and started a crusade in 1744 against the immorality of his own era.

Gennaro was a prolific writer, and his crusade was highly successful. He also demonstrated a remarkable ability to teach others of the efficacy of daily meditation. His teachings on meditation were endorsed and indulgenced by Pope Benedict XIV (r. 1740-1758) on December 16, 1746.

St. Alphonsus was with Gennaro when he died in Naples on June 30, 1744. He testified that Gennaro' countenance "suddenly became beautiful" and that a sweet aroma remained with his body, which was laid to rest in the Redemptorist church in Naples.

Pope John Paul II beatified James on May 12, 1996, declaring: *"This generous priest, a treasure of the Southern clergy, founder of the Salesian Sisters of the Sacred Hearts, who are primarily involved in the education of deaf-mutes, is held up today for the veneration of the universal Church, so that by following his example all the faithful can witness to the Gospel of charity in our times, especially by caring for the most needy. . . .*

"His human and religious life, like that of St. Alphonsus Maria de Liguori, of whom he was a friend and collaborator, was particularly expressed in a remarkable sensitivity to the poor, whom he approached and accepted in the light of their reality as children of God.

"His evangelizing activity was marked by a great dynamism. He was able to reconcile missionary involvement with his activities as a writer and with the equally demanding ministry of spiritual counselor and guide. Although he followed the cultural patterns of his day, the new blessed never neglected to seek fresh forms of evangelization to respond to new challenges. For this reason, although he lived in a historical period which in many ways very different from our own, Gennaro Maria Sarnelli can be held up to the Christian community today, on the threshold of the new millennium, as an example of an apostle who was open to accepting every useful innovation for a more penetrating proclamation of the eternal message of salvation."

Foundress of the Sisters of the Sacred Heart of Jesus and the Holy Angels

In an age in which health, youth, and beauty are extolled endlessly, certain individuals stand as contradictions and as symbols of the human spirit. Blessed Genoveva Torres Morales is more than a contradiction to modern aspirations. Her life confounds those who seek comfort in physical or material assets.

GENOVEVA TORRES MORALES

(D. 1956)

FOUNDRESS

Genoveva was born in Almenara, Castile, Spain, on January 3, 1870, the youngest of six children of a laborer family of the region. By the time she was eight years old, Genoveva had lost both her parents and four of her brothers and sisters. At age thirteen her left leg was amputated at the thigh, forcing her to endure pain and the continual use of crutches.

By 1885, Genoveva lived at the Mercy Home conducted by the Carmelites of Charity, sewing to aid in her support and maturing in her spiritual life. Drawn to the religious life, Genoveva asked to enter the Carmelites of Charity, but her physical problems served as obstacles.

Genoveva left Mercy Home and joined two other women who supported themselves by their own skills. In 1911, Canon Barbarrós recommended that Genoveva and her companions start a religious congregation dedicated to serving elderly women in their working class. Genoveva opened the first house of the Sisters of the Sacred Heart of Jesus and the Holy Angels in Valencia. Also called the "Angelicas," the members of the congregation received approval for their labors in 1953 from Pope Pius XII. Other foundations were established in Barcelona, Bilboa, Madrid, Pamplona, Santander, and Saragossa. Genoveva directed the work and ministry until her death on January 5, 1956.

Pope John Paul II beatified Genoveva on June 29, 1995, announcing:

" 'Have no fear . . .' we heard in the first reading of the Liturgy of the Word, 'For it is I who have made you a fortified city, a pillar of iron, a wall of brass . . . I am with you to deliver you' (Jer 1:17-19). He promised the prophet special divine help to enable him to face obstacles so that he would be able to carry out God's plan. We see these words fulfilled in the new Blessed Genoveva Torres Morales, who showed heroic strength in both her human activities and in her apostolic labors. Having suffered the amputation of a leg when she was young, she always had to walk with crutches but this did not prevent her from discerning and firmly accomplishing the Lord's Will. A woman of humble origin and background, she possessed the knowledge of divine love, acquired through her intense devotion to the Sacred Heart of Jesus Christ. She used to say: 'Love conquers all.' This love led her to devote her life to caring for retired *women, to remedy the loneliness and deprivation in which many of them lived,[1] looking after them materially and spiritually in a true home, beside them like an 'Angel in solitude.' To this end she founded in Valencia the Institute of the Sisters of the Sacred Heart of Jesus and the Holy Angels. Today her work continues to be of great significance, since loneliness and neglect, with the consequent danger they bring, are among the most distressing evils of every age. Blessed Genoveva Torres sought to deal with them and we ask her to continue to inspire generous souls who, faithful to the charism she received from the Spirit, may strive to follow her example and continue her work."*

George Haydock See Martyrs of England, Scotland, and Wales.

Founder of the Sisters of the Immaculate Conception

This Marianist prelate was a faithful son of Holy Mother Church, and he was a victim soul who achieved extraordinary heights of suffering in patient resignation. Sometimes called Georges Matulewicz, George Matulaitis endured all things for the salvation of souls.

George was born in Lugine, Lithuania, on April 13, 1871, the youngest of eight children in a family of farmers. Both his parents died when he was eleven, and at age fifteen, George was diagnosed with tuberculosis of the bone, a disease that would trouble him all of his life.

GEORGE MATULAITIS (MATULEWICZ)

(D. 1927)

VICTIM SOUL

He was educated by the Marianists at Mariampole, Lithuania, and was sent to the seminaries of Kielce and Warsaw, in Poland. He also attended the Ecclesiastical Academy of St. Petersburg, Russia, and the University of Fribourg, in Switzerland. After earning a doctorate, George was ordained a priest in St. Petersburg in 1898.

When he returned to Warsaw, George founded orphanages and organized charitable programs for people of all faiths. He became ill in 1905, and was near death when a community of sisters brought a doctor to his side. These sisters had been driven out of their convents by occupying forces but were operating underground missions. They sheltered George until he recovered. In return, George made a vow to honor the Blessed Virgin Mary in thanksgiving.

In 1907, George became a professor at the Ecclesiastical Academy in St. Petersburg and there he learned of the oppression inflicted upon the Marianists. He became a Marianist as a result and adopted the constitution of the congregation in order to revive it. In 1910, he moved to Fribourg and started rebuilding, having more than 250 members when he died. George also reclaimed abandoned or confiscated Marianist houses. He arrived in the United States in 1913 to open a house in Chicago.

Five years later he founded the Sisters of the Immaculate Conception, and in 1924 the Servants of Jesus in the Eucharist. George was appointed bishop of Vilna, Lithuania in 1918, and in 1925 he became an archbishop and apostolic visitor, appointed by Pope Pius XI (r. 1922-1939) to Lithuania. He urged the Marianists to sacrifice themselves for Christ as he revived the congregation. Pope Pius XI called George "a truly holy man," and "a man of God." George died in Kaunas, on January 27, 1927, after undergoing surgery for his tuberculosis.

Pope John Paul II beatified George on June 28, 1987, and at this ceremony the courage and honor of this blessed was extolled. He was praised as a prelate and religious who traveled the royal way of the Cross with unstinting fidelity.

Co-Worker of Blessed Francis Spinelli

The ancient sages used to speak of humility working its way through life the way a deep river wears away craggy obstacles in order to bring fruition to the fields. Jesus, the Lamb of God, beseeched his followers to learn his meekness and humility of heart. Gertrude Catarina Comensoli, also revered as Geltrude, was a daughter of Christian humility. Yet she was not a timid creature who allowed events to keep her from performing the Will of God or from her destiny. She also found a staunch ally in her earthly achievements, Blessed Francis Spinelli, who loved Christ in the Eucharist and labored to make him loved.

GERTRUDE CATARINA COMENSOLI

(D. 1903)

FOUNDRESS

Gertrude was born in Biennio, Brescia, Italy, on January 18, 1847, the fifth of ten children of a poor local family. She was baptized Catherine, and as a child she was introduced to the Holy Eucharist. Gertrude learned quickly to imitate her parents' reverence. She also received the grace of a religious vocation and entered the Sisters of Charity, the Maria Bambina Sisters, but had to leave that convent because of ill health.

Turning to a secular institute called the Company of Angela Merici, Gertrude worked and taught catechism. She then served for more than a decade as a companion to a countess. In 1879, Gertrude met Blessed Francis Spinelli, and together they founded, in Bergamo, the Sisters of the Blessed Sacrament, a congregation devoted to education and to adoration. Gertrude's sister Bartolomea joined the community also, and six houses were opened by 1881.

Differences in recognition of the apostolate led Gertrude and her sisters to move to Lodi, Italy. They returned to Bergamo the following year, and Gertrude expanded the congregation's ministries. She imbued her sisters with love for the Blessed Sacrament and for humble service to the Church. Gertrude died on February 18, 1903, in Bergamo. She was made Venerable by Pope John XXIII (r. 1958-1963).

Pope John Paul II beatified Gertrude on October 1, 1989, declaring: *"Once again it is the example of the poor and humble Christ, contemplated especially in the eucharistic mystery, which guides the commitment of Gertrude Comensoli on the difficult spiritual journey and the distressing events of the foundation of the Blessed Sacrament Sisters."*

Giovanni Piamarta 🌿 **See John Piamarta.**

Italian Apostle of Faith

A sense of the Church distinguishes this new blessed, a commitment to the faith and as a professional Franciscan tertiary and layman to spread the teachings of Christ. Giuseppe Tovini, a son of the Brescia region of Italy, was also known and respected by Pope Paul VI, a fellow Brescian.

GIUSEPPE (JOSEPH) TOVINI

(D. 1897)

🌿

LAY RELIGIOUS

Giuseppe was born on March 14, 1841, in Cividate Camuno, near Brescia. The eldest of seven children in a poor family, he was sponsored by his uncle, Father Giambattista Malaguzzi, and so was able to attend a boys' school for the poor in Verona. He subsequently finished school and went on to law school, obtaining his degree at the University of Pavia in 1865. He found employment in a law office as a notary, continuing to support his younger brothers and sisters who were left in his care when their parents died young. Aside from his work as a notary and as an attorney, Giuseppe was appointed vice rector and professor at the municipal college of Lovere, posts which required great sensitivity and spiritual discernment. Joseph displayed intense spiritual devotion and was noted for his practice of starting and ending each session of classes with prayers.

In 1867 he moved to Brescia, where he entered the law office of Mr. Corbolani. From 1871 to 1874 he served as the mayor of Cividate and brought many improvements to the area, including the founding of the Banca di Vallecamonica in Breno. In 1875 he married Emilia Corbolani, his former employer's daughter. They had ten children, three of whom entered the religious life, including one who became a Jesuit. Two years after his marriage, Giuseppe joined the Catholic Movement of Brescia and helped found the daily newspaper *Il Cittadino di Brescia*. This paper was edited by Giorgio Montini, the father of the future pontiff, Paul VI.

In 1878, Giuseppe aided in the formation of the diocesan committee of the *Opera dei Congressi*, a Catholic program designed to protect the faithful from the anticlerical attitudes of the era. One year later he was elected provincial councilor for Pisogne, becoming the provincial councilor for Brescia in 1882. Giuseppe understood the Church's essential role in aiding the poor of the region and founded banks in Brescia and Milan to assist the destitute. He also opened Catholic workers' societies and established a school, a college, and education programs, declaring that such institutions were "mission fields."

Giuseppe was always plagued by poor health, despite his arduous labors. He died in Brescia on January 16, 1897. Pope Paul II beatified Giuseppe in Brescia on September 20, 1998, declaring:

"Giuseppe Tovini, this lay Christian whom I had the joy of proclaiming blessed today, stands before us and speaks to us with the example of his life, a life totally dedicated to the defense and promotion of the moral and spiritual values indispensable for renewing society. He was able to combine his vocation as husband and father of a family with his commitment to many Catholic initiatives. During the hard struggles undertaken out of fidelity to the Gospel in the difficult political and social context of his time, he had recourse to the intercession of Mary, whom he had learned to venerate since childhood. To her motherly heart, he commended the problems of teachers, workers, and young people; it was she who inspired him in fulfilling his duties as a father; he was always confident in her during illness and in the many moments of trial. Today, the new blessed invites us as well to turn our gaze to the tender Mother of Divine Grace, to draw from her the necessary strength to follow Christ in every circumstance.

"Blessed Giuseppe Tovini was certainly a great witness of the Gospel incarnated in Italy's social and economic history in the last century. He is resplendent for his generous efforts to improve society. Between Tovini and Giovanni Battista Montini [Pope Paul VI] there is — as a matter of fact — a close, profound spiritual and mental bond.

"In fact, the pontiff himself wrote of Tovini: 'The impression he left on those I first knew and esteemed was so vivid and so real that I frequently heard comments and praise of his extraordinary personality and his many varied activities; astonished, I heard admiring expressions of his virtue and sorrowful regrets at his early death' (Preface by Giovanni Battista Montini to the biography of Giuseppe Tovini by Father Antonio Cistellini in 1953, p.1). Fervent, honest, active in social and political life, Giuseppe Tovini proclaimed the Christian message, always in fidelity to the guidance of the Church's Magisterium. His constant concern was to defend the faith, convinced that — as he said at a congress — 'without faith our children will never be rich; with faith they will never be poor.'"

Patroness of Families

The family remains the bulwark against "the new barbarism" predicted by sages of the past, and Blessed Giuseppina (Josephine) Garbriella Bonino demonstrates this adage in her life. She taught family values, in both material and spiritual arenas of life, and she perfected herself in this apostolate.

Giuseppina was born in Savigliano, Italy, on September 5, 1843, and was raised in a pious family. At age twelve she lived in Turin, where she advanced her spiritual life and took a vow of chastity at age eighteen. In 1869, Giuseppina returned to Savigliano to care for her father, who suffered from a terminal illness. In 1871, she underwent back surgery and journeyed to Lourdes to give thanks to the Blessed Virgin Mary. At Lourdes, Giuseppina was inspired to care for the poor, and upon returning home she began caring for orphans.

Wanting to be a contemplative, Giuseppina entered the cloister on two occasions but knew that this form of religious

GIUSEPPINA (JOSEPHINE) GABRIELLA BONINO

(D. 1906)

FOUNDRESS

life was not for her. Upon the advice of her spiritual director, she founded a congregation, the Sisters of the Holy Family, whose members cared for orphans, the elderly sick, and the poor. Giuseppina became superior in April, 1881, and remained in this post until her death. She guided her spiritual daughters and opened four other houses of the congregation. Giuseppina died in Savona, as she had predicted, on February 8, 1906.

Pope John Paul II beatified Josephine on May 7, 1995, announcing:

"The love of Christ, the Good Shepherd also found a unique expression in the life of Giuseppina Gabriella Bonino, foundress of the Sisters of the Holy Family of Saigliano. Her charism was family love, learned and practiced above all while living with her parents until adulthood and then by following the Lord's call in consecrated life. From the family as the domestic church to the religious community as the spiritual family: this is summary of her humble journey, hidden but of incalculable value, that of the family, the environment of extraordinary love in ordinary things.

"Giuseppina Gabriella, an exemplary daughter — she took care of her father and mother until their death — became a mother to numerous infants and children with no family. The message of her life, extended in the institute, remains most timely for today's society: every person who comes into the world hungers for love more than bread, and has a right to a family. The Christian community is called to respond to the situations of need which are inevitable."

The world mourns in a unique fashion when the very young are taken in death. Such deaths, called "out of season," deprive humanity in distinct ways. So it was with the passing of Grimoaldo Santamaria, though he had no fears or regrets. He was going home to the Father. A Passionist and a true son of Mary, Grimoaldo served, loved, and entered eternity.

GRIMOALDO SANTAMARIA

(D. 1902)

RELIGIOUS

Grimoaldo was born in Pontecorvo (Frosinone), Italy, on May 4, 1883, the eldest of five children. He was baptized Ferdinand and consecrated to the Blessed Virgin Mary; he also displayed a remarkable capacity for prayer and recollection at an early age. Grimoaldo entered the Congregation of the Passion at Santa Maria di Pugliano, the Passionists, and made his first vows on March 6, 1900, receiving the name Grimoaldo. He started his seminary training at Santa Maria di Corniano, near Ceccano, and was revered for his purity and devotion to the Blessed Mother. As a Marian apostle, he inspired everyone he met and demonstrated total reliance upon the Providence of God.

He was not destined for the priesthood. Grimoaldo fell ill in the seminary with acute meningitis and did not respond to medical care. He died on November 18, 1902, edifying all who came into contact with him during his final days on earth. Grimoaldo died a model of Marian devotion. As he passed from the world, he repeated the words: "God's Will be done."

Pope John Paul II beatified Grimoaldo on January 29, 1995, declaring: *"His biographers describe him as joyful even amid humiliations, contradictions, and difficulties in his studies. His companions noted that although Grimoaldo did nothing different from them, he did it with an extraordinary and growing intensity of love. Young people today and in the future can see in him a model of simple and generous spirituality, firmly rooted in Christ's paschal mystery."*

GUIDO MARIA CONFORTI

(D. 1931)

MISSIONARY

Archbishop and Founder

The days of the great missionaries are not gone from the world. They are not dim memories, wreathed in the past and woven into legends, and the beatification of Guido Maria Conforti attests to this truth. Following the example of St. Francis Xavier, Guido became a modern missionary pioneer, a founder, and the archbishop of Parma, Italy.

He was born on March 30, 1865, at Casalora di Ravadese, Italy, the son of Rinaldo and Antonia Conforti. At the age of seven he entered the Christian Brothers' school in Parma, and each day visited a crucifix to pray and to receive divine guidance. Guido began to read about St. Francis Xavier, and soon wanted a missionary life. Despite parental opposition, he entered the seminary in Parma at age eighteen, beginning his apostolate.

A mysterious illness threatened Guido's ordination, but he was healed at a shrine dedicated to the Blessed Mother. He was thus ordained on September 22, 1888, and worked in diocesan positions until December 3, 1895, the feast of St. Francis Xavier. On that day he founded a seminary for the training of missionaries. Three years later on that same date he founded the Congregation of St. Xavier for Foreign Missions.

Guido sent out two missionaries to China the following year, and he founded a mission aid society to assist the Xaverians overseas. At the time, he was also serving as assistant rector of the diocesan seminary, vicar of priests, and director of the Propagation of the Faith. On June 11, 1902, he made his vows with the Xaverians and began an almost endless series of visits and renewal programs. Four more missionaries were sent to China, and in 1912, the first Xaverian bishop of the missions was consecrated.

In September 1907, Guido was appointed archbishop of Parma, being consecrated on November 12. He became the "shepherd of two flocks" — the people of his archdiocese and his missionaries, hundreds of miles across the sea. In August, 1918, he became president of the Union of Italian Missionaries, and he witnessed the Holy See's approval of the congregation's constitution in 1920 as the missions thrived. Guido visited China in the Fall of 1928, returning by train across the wilds of Siberia.

The Xaverians spread to Asia, Africa, Brazil, Japan, the Philippines, Taiwan, Mexico, Spain, and the United States. The missionaries conduct parishes, hospitals, leprosariums, orphanages, schools, and colleges. Guido, having carefully guided the congregation as he guarded the faithful of Parma, died on November 5, 1931. Pope John Paul II beatified him on March 17, 1996, announcing:

"Called to be Pastor of a portion of God's people in an area where a disturbing rejection of the faith was occurring, Guido Maria Conforti discovered in the way of the mission ad gentes *a providential journey by which 'he could cause a new current of divine life to flow into the souls of believers, increasing in them the fire of great missionary zeal. . . .' But what was the source from which his tireless zeal and total dedication to the mission* ad gentes *drew strength? It was Christ's Cross, a source of inexhaustible love in those who give themselves to their brothers and sisters, near and far. Thus, this new blessed was a shining example of priestly spirituality, always motivated by living faith and indomitable missionary spirit. A model of genuine pastoral charity who knew how to invite believers to open their hearts to those who were distant without forgetting the needs of local communities, so that Christ, redeemer of man, might be proclaimed to all."*

Gulielmus Repin ❦ See **Martyrs of France**.

Founder of the Rogationist Fathers and the Daughters of Divine Zeal

This blessed, Hannibal Maria di Francia, was a soul of discernment, a human being who recognized that priests must serve "after the heart of God." This realization changed his life and led him to spiritual perfection as the founder of the Rogationist Fathers and Daughters of Divine Zeal.

Hannibal was born in Messina, Sicily, on July 5, 1851, during a politically turbulent era. When Hannibal was nine years old, Garibaldi's revolutionary troops controlled Sicily, preaching anti-Catholic and anarchical ideals. Hannibal fell under the influence of these sentiments and scoffed at the faith.

HANNIBAL MARIA DI FRANCIA

(D. 1927)

FOUNDER

As an adult, however, he experienced a sudden conversion and a call to the priesthood. He described the call as "unexpected," but it changed forever the direction of his life. He took his natural enthusiasms and energies and focused on the miserable economic conditions in Messina. Ordained a priest in 1878 after seminary studies, Hannibal labored in the poorest districts of Messina.

He met Melanie Calvat, the Mystic of La Salette, while working, and she inspired him to found the Rogation Fathers of the Heart of Jesus and the Daughters of Divine Zeal. The new religious were trained to care for the poor, sick, abandoned, and needy. They now work in Brazil, Argentina, Australia, Italy, Spain, Rwanda, the Philippines, and the United States.

Hannibal also erected a shrine dedicated to prayers for vocations. He died in Messina on June 1, 1927, mourned by thousands who had been inspired by his charity.

Pope John Paul II beatified Hannibal on October 7, 1990, declaring: *"The multitude of people who had not yet been reached by the Gospel and the insufficient number of evangelizers tormented his heart as an evangelizer and a priest. For that reason he founded two religious families: the 'Rogationists' and the Daughters of Divine Zeal and he fostered numerous initiatives to spread among the faithful the awareness of the need to pray ceaselessly for vocations.*

"He himself deeply loved his priesthood: he lived it with consistency, he exalted its greatness before the People of God. He often repeated that the Church, in order to carry out her mission, need, 'many holy' priests, 'after the heart of God.' He felt that that was an essential problem and insisted that prayer and

spiritual formation be primary in priests' preparations; if not, he wrote, 'all the efforts of Bishops and seminary rectors can be reduced to an artificial cultivation of priests. . . .' For him every real vocation is the fruit of grace and of prayer even before the cultural and organizational initiatives, which are also necessary, go into effect." The Holy Father added: *"He himself deeply loved his priesthood; he lived it with consistency, he exalted its greatness before the People of God."*

Founder of the Felicians

The faithful of Poland stand as insignias of courage, endurance, and loyalty through the long centuries of time. Blessed Honorat a Biala (Kozminski) joins the ranks of honored Polish confessors as an apostle and a Franciscan founder. His elevation to the altars of the Church provides yet another model of valor in the service of Christ.

HONORAT A BIALA (KOZMINSKI)

(D. 1916)

FOUNDER

Honorat was born Florence Wenceslaus John Kozminski in Biala, Poland, on October 16, 1829, the second of four children of an architect and his wife. From a devout, rather wealthy family, Honorat attended the Fine Arts School in Warsaw, but when his father died in 1845, the young man turned against his religion. In 1846, Honorat was accused falsely by the Russian occupiers of Poland and was imprisoned on a charge of treason. He endured illness and spiritual torments before his release in 1847, in the process having regained his faith in full.

Honorat became a Capuchin Franciscan in December, 1848, receiving his name in religion. He was ordained four years later on December 8, 1852, and started his ministry by writing and serving as a spiritual director. Honorat was revered in Warsaw, where he preached against the factions threatening the Church. Founding "Circles of the Living Rosary," he helped to revive the faith and bring the people back to prayer and frequent communion.

With Angela Truszkowska, Honorat founded the Sisters of St. Felix of Cantalice in November 1855, which was dedicated to charitable missions. The Felician Sisters were suppressed by the Russians in 1864 and transferred their motherhouse to Krakow, Poland. Honorat also founded the Sister Servants of Mary Immaculate in 1878. During the Russian period of suppression, Honorat moved to Zakroczym, where he was kept under house arrest in a local monastery but still managed to give great consolation to the people. He promoted the Third Order of St. Francis, using the rules and the spirit of this form of lay dedication to strengthen the faith in a time of severe trial.

In 1892, Honorat had to move to Nowe Miasto, where he was able to continue his ministry as a confessor and spiritual director under Russian control. In 1895, he was appointed commissary of the Capuchin Franciscans in Poland. Honorat died after a painful illness in Nowe Miasto on December 16, 1916.

Pope John Paul II beatified Honoratus on October 16, 1988, saying: *"He was a man of constant prayer, especially of adoration of the Blessed Sacrament, immersed in God and at the same time open to earthly reality. An eyewitness account said that 'he always walked with God.' "* The Holy Father added: *"He shows us how to read the signs of the times, how to persevere according to God's Will, and work in difficult times."*

Master General of the Dominican Order

A blessed who could serve as a model of wisdom and discernment for this modern age, Hyacinthe Marie Cormier was the seventy-sixth Master General of the Dominicans, a counselor to Pope St. Pius X, and a man who brought intellectual honesty and compelling moral judgments to all facets of his life and vocation.

HYACINTHE MARIE CORMIER

(D. 1916)

RELIGIOUS

He was born in Orléans, France, on December 8, 1832, baptized Henry Marie. Raised devoutly, he displayed a brilliant intellect and a disciplined piety that brought him to the attention of many. He was well prepared to pursue a brilliant career, but he chose to give his life to Christ, entering the venerable Dominican Order in 1856. Completing his seminary training, Hyacinthe was ordained and then given the task of restoring the Order in the provinces of Lyons and Toulouse.

Hyacinthe served as a professor of theology, demonstrating a firm grasp of the faith and a winning approach in the classroom. He was elected prior and then provincial superior for four separate terms. Hyacinthe drew on historical perspectives of the religious life to counterbalance the turbulent demands of his own era. He was a religious who practiced strict observances of the rules of his Order, tolerating no laxity in his own response to events or needs. In 1891, Hyacinthe was appointed aide to the Master General of the Order, and then Procurator General in 1896.

In May, 1904, Hyacinthe became the seventy-sixth Master General of the Dominicans. Pious and a strict observer of the Dominican religious spirit, he promoted academic studies in the Order. In 1910, he founded the Angelicum in Rome, where he was a close friend and aide to Pope St. Pius X. Hyacinthe not only broadened the apostolic scope of the Dominicans but deepened the spiritual and intellectual foundations as well. His Cause was opened in 1935.

Pope John Paul II beatified Hyacinthe on November 20, 1994, declaring:

"Truth is not an abstract notion. For us it is one person, the person of Christ, King of the universe. In his life, Father Cormier never ceased to live the truth and he passed it on to all his Dominican brothers with humility and perseverance. Did he not combine truth with charity in his motto, Caritas veritatis? *Indeed, the founder of the Angelicum University reminds us that God requires us to use the faculties of our spirit, a reflection of his own, to glorify him."*

Benedictine Foe of Fascism

During World War II, a diminutive Italian prince of the Church, Ildephonse Schuster, was one of the rare individuals who rose up to oppose Fascism and its inherent evils. He did not flee for safety when Mussolini took over Italy, and in time he became the famous enemy of the Italian Fascists. As the Benedictine cardinal archbishop of Milan, Ildephonse could strike fear into the hearts of the godless because he spoke as a prince of the Church.

ILDEPHONSE (ALFREDO) SCHUSTER

(D. 1954)

CARDINAL

Ildephonse was born in Rome on January 18, 1880, of German descent. Always known for his intense prayer life, he entered the Benedictines and strictly observed the Order's spiritual practices. He served in many capacities, displaying holiness and a firm faith.

In 1929, Ildephonse, recognized for his holiness and qualities of leadership, was consecrated the archbishop of Milan. The Holy See also named him a cardinal. Italy was in the grip of Fascism when Ildephonse governed Milan. As Mussolini and his confederates tightened their hold on the nation, Ildephonse studied that political system carefully. He made no protests in the early stages, seeing the advances and unity brought to all areas of Italian life. The rampant brutality of Mussolini's government, and the rise of the Nazis, alerted Ildephonse to the coming threat. He soon wasted no time in denouncing Fascism as a "heresy," an act that put him in considerable danger.

Small in stature, Ildephonse became a powerful presence in Italy. His sermons and his announcements clearly proclaimed him to be a foe of Fascism. Some in the government even suspected Ildephonse of wanting to overthrow Fascism and began campaigns that smeared his reputation and disgraced him publicly. As the war continued and Italians began to endure the results of Allied military power, the Fascists tried to silence Ildephonse, but he would not surrender his principles. He lived through the last terrible stages of the war, leading the Milanese people and trying to ease their burdens. Ildephonse died in Venegono, Italy, on August 30, 1954, having survived World War II and its horrors. Just before his death, Ildephonse told his seminarians: "You want something to remember me by. . . . All I can give you is an invitation to holiness."

Pope John Paul II beatified Ildephonse on May 12, 1996, observing:

"Love for Christ, expressed in tireless service to the Church, was the heart of the spirituality and apostolic activity of . . . Schuster, for many years the indefatigable pastor of the Archdiocese of Milan. 'A man of prayer, study, and action,' as he was described by Archbishop Giovanni Montini in the speech he gave on entering the Archdiocese, 'he had no other concern than the spiritual salvation of his people (Rivista diocesana Milanese, *January 1955, 9). His pastoral ministry was motivated by the spirit of prayer and contemplation proper to the Benedictine tradition. His monastic spirituality, nourished by daily meditation on Sacred Scripture, thus expanded into active collaboration with the Holy See and into his generous service to the Ambrosian community, 'edified and consoled by him until the very end by the regular, devoted celebration of the sacred mysteries and by the example of a clear and consistent life' (Ambrosian Missal, Preface of the Memorial)."*

Innocencio Canoura Arnau ❦ **See Martyrs of Asturias (Turon).**

Martyred Layman of the Congo

The Blessed Virgin Mother of God has been served by many stalwart champions over the centuries. Poets have sung her praises, and the artists of the world have portrayed her with piety and skill. There is, however, a unique and remarkable champion of Mary just now appearing before the world. Isidore Bakanja was a native of the Belgian Congo, and threats and mortal whippings did not compel him to abandon his devotion to Our Lady. He was martyred for wearing the Blessed Virgin's scapular.

ISIDORE BAKANJA

(D. 1909)

MARTYR

Born in the tribal lands of the Boangi, circa 1885, Isidore was educated by Christian missionaries in Mbandaka (Coquilhatville). There he worked as a mason, and there he was baptized on May 6, 1906.

Isidore was graced with a remarkable faith and with heroic devotion to the Blessed Mother. He learned his catechism and began to make converts among his own people while working for a kindly white colonist. When that colonist moved to the settlement of Ikile, Isidore followed him. In Ikile, however, he found himself in the hands of an atheistic, hateful white supervisor named

Longage. This supervisor had a particular prejudice against the rosary and scapular. He warned Isidore to put such devotions aside.

When Isidore remained loyal to the Blessed Virgin and wore the scapular, Longage beat him without mercy. Isidore was brutally scourged and dragged in chains to a rubber-processing room where he was left for dead. An inspector for the colonist's company found Isidore and cared for him at a nearby plantation. Isidore could not recover from the internal and external wounds inflicted upon him, and he spent days in pain as a result. He died as a child of Mary at Busirá on August 15, 1909, having publicly forgiven his murderer.

Pope John Paul II beatified Isidore on April 24, 1994, proclaiming:

Isidore Bakanja

from Faces of Holiness

"You were a man of heroic faith, Isidore Bakanja, young layman of Zaire. As a baptized person, called to spread the Good news, you shared your faith and witness to Christ with such conviction that to your companions you seemed one of those valiant lay faithful, the catechists. Yes, Blessed Isidore, absolutely faithful to your baptismal promises, you were a true catechist, toiling generously for 'the Church in Africa and for her evangelizing mission.' "

Passionist and Lay Brother

A Passionist lay brother, Blessed Isidore de Loor was one of those rare people who risk everything in the name of God. A model of suffering, he was a man who used pain as a ladder of perfection.

Isidore was born in Vrasene, Belgium, on April 18, 1881, the oldest of three children. The family attended daily Mass, and Isidore was raised with prayers and deep religious values. He attended school, but only for six years, as his family needed him in the labor force. Isidore received the grace of a religious vocation, and at the age of twenty-six he entered the Passionists as a lay brother, making Christ Crucified the center of his religious life. He was called Isidore of St. Joseph.

ISIDORE OF ST. JOSEPH DE LOOR

(D. 1916)

VICTIM SOUL

Isidore was drawn to prayer and solitude as a Passionist, strictly observing the customs of his monastic vocation and accepting all things as the Will of God. In 1914, he became the porter, or door keeper, at the monastery of Kortrijk. When the military destruction of World War I threatened the monastery, the monks evacuated. Isidore remained behind as a voluntary custodian. He endured the loneliness and military threats with calm, knowing he was fulfilling his obligations. Isidore was able to welcome his fellow Passionists when they returned.

He then suffered from a painful cancer that developed in his right eye. That eye had to be surgically removed, and Isidore endured the medical treatment with patience and calm, inspiring all who cared for him. In 1916, it was learned that the cancer had spread to his intestines. Isidore collapsed and was confined to his bed. There he prayed, asking forgiveness from his fellow Passionists for his faults. He died at Kortrijk Monastery on October 6, 1916, and miracles were reported immediately at his tomb.

Pope John Paul II beatified him on September 30, 1984, announcing: *"In Blessed Isidore de Loor it is given to us to contemplate above all the face of the suffering Christ, in whom the infinite love of God is revealed."* The Holy Father said also: *"The new blessed . . . is surely a fascinating and providential example for our era (taken up with freedom which is sometimes quite equivocal), of a growing conformity to the Will of the heavenly Father in following Christ Jesus."*

Jacob Hilarius Barbal **See James Hilarius Barbal**.

Founder and Patron of the Poor

Love was the healing virtue that emanated from the life and labors of Blessed Jacob Cusmano. The defender of the needy and suffering, Jacob understood their plight, and he invented new ways of attracting the attention of the world to the needs of many in society. He was born in Palermo, Italy, on March 15, 1834, in an uneasy time, and he was raised in the faith and alert to conditions in the city. Both impelled him to combine a medical and priestly career to benefit the sick and the wanting of the area.

JACOB (GIACOMO) CUSMANO

(D. 1888)

FOUNDER

Ordained and certified as a medical doctor, Jacob started his ministry by opening a "House for the Poor" in Palermo. Anyone in need could come to Jacob for medical care and for necessary material goods. To support this endeavor, Jacob also started the "Morsel for the Poor" Association, an organization that awakened the people of Palermo to the needs of those in their midst.

If they needed yet another symbol of charity, Jacob stood before the people seeking aid for those in prison. He did not live in a good district himself, and he did not use salaries or benefits to make himself comfortable. Jacob even begged in the streets of the city for the poor. He collected food, clothing, and other necessities and distributed to the indigent people who gathered around him.

When others came to join in this charitable labor, Jacob founded the Missionary Servants of the Poor and the Sister Servants of the Poor. The rule of both congregations was Christ-centered and based on the practice of the presence of God in all things. Jacob provided the ultimate example of such union with Christ when an epidemic of cholera struck Palermo in 1888. He did not spare himself but remained on duty throughout the epidemic, bringing whatever medical aid possible to victims and comforting all. This epidemic drained the last of Jacob's energies. He died on March 14, 1888, at age fifty-four, and all of Palermo went into mourning.

Pope John Paul II beatified Jacob on October 30, 1983, declaring: *"To heal the wounds of poverty and misery which were afflicting such a large part of the population because of recurring famines and epidemics, but also because of social inequality, he chose the way of charity; love for God which was translated into effective love for his brethren and into the gift of himself to the most needy and suffering in a service pushed to the point of heroic sacrifice."* The Holy Father addressed Jacob as the *"Servant of the Poor."*

Marianist Defender of the Faith

This blessed was a daring enemy of the Nazis in Austria, a singular badge of honor in World War II that was worn with peril and valor. A Marianist martyr, Jacob Gapp was also a champion of the Catholic press; a visionary who understood the emerging roles of the secular media in human affairs. The Gestapo — the dread secret police of the Nazis — hunted him down as an enemy.

JACOB GAPP

(D. 1943)

MARTYR

Jacob was born in Wattens, Austria, on July 26, 1897, the seventh child of Martin Gapp and Antonia Wach. He was educated locally and then by the Franciscans in Hall, an Austrian Tirolean town. Called to military service in May, 1915, he was wounded and received a medal after serving a period as a prisoner of war until 1919.

Returning from the war, Jacob entered the Marianist novitiate at Greisinghall, where he made his first vows in 1921. He was assigned to the Marian Institute at Graz, where he labored for four years. Jacob made his profession at Antony, France, on August 27, 1925, and entered the seminary. He was ordained at Fribourg on April 5, 1930, and sent to Graz.

While working for eight years in that area of Austria in the Marianist houses, Jacob displayed personal asceticism and charity for the destitute. The Nazis were coming into power in Germany, and Jacob began to warn the faithful about the incompatibility between Nazism and the Church. Not surprisingly, his outspoken opposition forced Jacob to flee Graz, and he was sent home by his own superior for his safety.

In October 1938 the Gestapo forbade Jacob from teaching religion. In December 1938 he denounced the Nazis from the pulpit and was advised to leave the country. He escaped to Bordeaux, France, and then in May, 1939, he went to Spain to labor in San Sebastián, Cadiz, and Valencia. However, the Gestapo lured him to France where he was arrested on November 9, 1942, and was taken to Berlin. All attempts to save him were denied since the Nazis feared him as a martyr.

Jacob was executed at the Platzensee Prison in Berlin at 7:08 p.m., by guillotine, on August 13, 1943. His remains were given to the Anatomical Biological Institute at the University of Berlin for anatomical racial purity studies by Nazi scientists.

Pope John Paul II beatified Jacob on November 24, 1996, proclaiming:

"Father Jacob Gapp gave his witness with the power of the courageous word and the deep convictions that between the pagan ideology of National Socialism and Christianity there could be no compromise. In this clash he rightly saw an apocalyptic battle. He knew where he had to stand and for this reason he was condemned to death."

Norbertine Priest

Many veterans carry permanent insignias of their suffering — scars and disabilities that remain with them for life. Jacob Kern, the Norbertine priest beatified by Pope John Paul II, was a wounded veteran of World War I, and his injuries were graces of perfection in his priestly ministry.

JACOB KERN

(D. 1924)

RELIGIOUS

Jacob was born in Vienna, Austria, on April 11, 1897, and was baptized Franz Alexander. One of three children in the family, Jacob entered the minor seminary at Hollabrunn at age eleven. Before he could complete his studies he was drafted into military service and sent to Völklabruck for officer training. In 1916, Jacob was assigned to the Italian front. He was wounded on September 11 and evacuated to Salzburg to recuperate.

Jacob returned to Vienna after recovering, but he was recalled to military service and served until the end of the war. Returning to his seminary studies,

Jacob entered the Premonstratensian Abbey of Geras, taking the place of a Norbertine who had left the monastery previously. Jacob entered the novitiate in 1920, receiving his religious name, and was ordained on July 23, 1922, in St. Stephen's Cathedral.

Jacob served in Geras Abbey in lower Austria, near the Czech border, and he was zealous, despite increasing pain. His wounds developed severe complications, and he had to have several ribs removed — the operation was performed without anesthetic because of his weakened condition. Jacob did not complain and apologized to the surgeon for being such a problem.

As he recuperated in Geras, Jacob seemed to gain strength and was scheduled for his solemn profession on October 20, 1924. He was scheduled for surgery that same day. Jacob predicted that his solemn profession would be in heaven. He died on October 20 during the operation. His remains were interred in Geras Abbey.

Pope John Paul II beatified Jacob in Heldenplastz, "Heroes' Square," in Vienna, Austria, on June 21, 1998, announcing: *"Blessed Jacob Kern stands before us as a witness fidelity to the priesthood. At the beginning it was a childhood desire that he expressed in imitating the priest at the altar. Later, this desire matured. The purification of pain revealed the profound meaning of his priestly vocation: to unite his own life with the sacrifice of Christ on the Cross and to offer it vicariously for the salvation of others."*

Patron of Slaves

Jacob Desiré Laval, the first blessed of the Congregation of the Holy Spirit and Immaculate Heart of Mary, was called to Mauritius, in 1861, and there he was revered by his co-missionaries as the one "who is a saint and who always says that he does nothing."

Jacob was born in Croth, France, on September 18, 1803. He spent his childhood watching his mother care for the needy of the region and learning about the priesthood from a pious uncle. Educated in local schools and then at Evreux, he studied at Stanislaus College, earning a medical degree in 1830. Though Jacob started his medical practice in St. André and St. Ivry-la-Bataille, he longed to serve in the missions. He gave up his practice and entered the seminary of St. Sulpice, where he was ordained a priest in 1838.

JACOB DESIRÉ LAVAL

(D. 1864)

❦

RELIGIOUS

Three years later, Jacob entered the Congregation of the Immaculate Heart of Mary, which had joined with the Congregation of the Holy Ghost. He was sent to Mauritius on September 14, 1861, to a parish of 80,000 souls, serving there for 26 years. Jacob converted

67,000 former slaves, and he instituted agricultural and sanitation reforms. He brought unique medical and scientific procedures and training to his missionary labors. In the Mauretian environment, Jacob was able to establish many sanitation and health standards to protect the people, especially the poor at the mercy of diseases and natural disasters in the region. He was tireless in his efforts to serve their spiritual and physical needs. Exhausted by his more than a quarter of a century of mission work, Jacob died on September 9, 1864, in Port Louis. He was mourned by people of all faiths. Jacob's Cause was opened in 1918.

Pope John Paul II beatified Jacob on April 29, 1979, stating that this missionary brought a true Christian dimension to his labors. As Jacob settled into his mission, the Holy Father declared: *"He has no overall plan, he has no theory about the apostolate. . . . He has all the kindness of a father, all the pity of a pastor, for these poor people. One by one they come towards him. He receives them with respect, sweetness, and cordiality."*

Martyr of the Spanish Civil War

James Hilarius Barbel, a victim of the Spanish Civil War, is a crown of the Christian Brothers and the Church because he radiated joy and resolve and endured suffering with patience and docility. He was born Emmanuel Barbal Cosan on January 2, 1898, in Enviny, in northern Spain. Serious by nature and powerful in build and in character, James was only twelve when he entered a minor seminary. When he developed hearing problems he was advised to return home, but in 1917 he applied to and was accepted as a novice at the Brothers' Institute in Irun, France. He taught school for sixteen years until his hearing problems forced him to stop. He then performed garden labors at San José, Tarragona.

JAMES HILARIUS BARBAL (COSAN)

(D. 1937)

MARTYR

In July, 1936, James was at Mollerosa, Spain, when he was arrested by anticlerical forces of the civil war as he sat writing a letter to his family. The following December, he was sent to a prison ship at Tarragona, where he joined several other brothers. The conditions of such prison ships were terrible, and the brothers suffered a great deal.

James was given a summary trial, at which time he openly declared his religious status. He was brought to the Mount of Olives on July 28, 1937, where he was executed. His last words were: "To die for Christ, my young friends, is to live." The firing squad aimed two volleys at James, but he was not harmed. The young soldiers fled in panic, and the commander had to kill James himself.

Pope John Paul II beatified James as a martyr of the Christian Brothers on April 29, 1990, praising the heroic calm and resolve displayed throughout his martyrdom. James was declared a true martyr, worthy of the palm of victory.

Jeanne Jugan ❧ See Marie of the Cross Jugan.

Romanian Franciscan and Marian Healer

In the modern efforts to bring about Church unity, several blesseds can serve as inspirations and guides. Jeremiah of Valachia Kostistk is one such blessed, and he stands as the historical symbol of the bridge between East and West. Though he lived centuries ago, this blessed Romanian-born Franciscan epitomizes the spirit of Christ for all ages.

JEREMIAH OF VALACHIA KOSTISTK

(D. 1625)

RELIGIOUS

He was born in Zaro, Romania, on June 29, 1556, and sought a religious vocation as a Franciscan. Jeremiah's homeland had long been a Franciscan mission territory, and the people revered the spirit of St. Francis. Jeremiah set out on his religious life and arrived in Italy, where he startled Naples and surrounding regions with his selfless imitation of Christ. He was devoted to Christ Crucified and to the Holy Eucharist, and Jeremiah had a special devotion to the Blessed Virgin.

He demonstrated that such faith has no borders, no national traditions.

The sick and the abandoned were the focus of Jeremiah's apostolate, but his reputation for wise counsel attracted people from all walks of life, and patients clamored for his attention. Bishops, nobles, and others tolerated no other caregivers when they needed medical care. Jeremiah's union with Christ provided the source of his self-sacrificing, and he radiated calm and comfort. This holy Romanian friar took a chill while visiting just such patients in March, 1625. He became very ill as a result and died on March 5, in Naples.

Pope John Paul II beatified Jeremiah on October 30, 1983, declaring: *"The glorification of this faithful Servant of the Lord, after three centuries of mysterious concealment, is reserved to our time, marked by the search for ecumenism and solidarity among peoples on an international level."* The Holy Father added: *". . . Jeremiah a Valachia is the first Romanian to ascend officially to the honors of the altar."*

Jesús Hita ❧ See Martyrs of the Marianist Congregation.

Doctor and Heroine of Motherhood

The most beautiful image bequeathed from century to century in human endeavor is that of the Madonna and Child. Almost every culture on earth responds to this symbol of the renewal of life, and the representation stirs the heart and mind. Blessed Joanna Beretta Molla of Brazil is a modern Madonna, and her maternal solicitude, her sacrifice in honor of life, has inspired a new generation of the faithful.

JOANNA BERETTA MOLLA

(D. 1962)

LAY RELIGIOUS

She was born on October 4, 1922, in Magenta, Brazil the tenth of thirteen children. Raised devoutly, Joanna earned degrees in medicine and surgery in 1949 and opened a clinic in Mesero, near Magenta. In 1952, she began specializing in pediatrics at the university of Milan. Married to Peter Molla in 1955, Joanna had three children and continued her medical and charitable labors. In 1961, just when she learned that she was to become a mother again, Joanna was diagnosed with a fibrous tumor in her ovary and was advised to undergo an operation that would kill her unborn child. Another procedure could be performed, but Joanna's life would be in grave danger. Joanna asked the surgeon to do whatever was necessary to save her child. That child, a daughter baptized Emmanuela, was born on April 28, 1962, in Magenta. Though the surgery performed at the end of her second month of pregnancy had been successful, Joanna died from complications after giving birth. Throughout her final sufferings, she praised God and remained serene in the faith.

Pope John Paul II beatified Joanna on April 24, 1994. In September 1997, the Holy Father heard Emmanuela thank her mother for giving her the gift of life twice; at conception and when she delayed treatment to ensure her daughter's birth. The Holy father stated: *"She had the grace of a united family, rich in faith and love. She was a happy mother,*

from *Faces of Holiness*

Joanna Beretta Molla

but a great trial lay in store for her in the course of her fourth pregnancy. In the dramatic choice between saving her own life or that of the baby she bore in her womb, she did not hesitate to sacrifice herself. What a heroic witness she gave, a true song of life, in sharp contrast to a certain mentality widespread today!"

Founder of the Congregation of the Poor Daughter of St. Cajetan

The Church has long considered the local parishes the front line of the Church, the cradle of the faith. This blessed, John Maria Boccardo, called the parish the true "mission land," and he spent his energies in imitating Christ as the Good Shepherd.

John Maria was born in Tertona di Moncalieri (Turin), Italy, in 1848. Raised in a pious family of the faith, he studied for the priesthood and was ordained in Turin in 1871. He was appointed assistant and then spiritual director of the seminaries in Chieri and Turin. In 1882, John Maria was made a parish priest at Pancalieri, where he would remain for the rest of his life.

JOHN MARIA BOCCARDO

(D. 1913)

PRIEST

He entered the pastoral ministry as a victim for the good of his parishioners, and within two years proved himself valiant and charitable. He cared for the sick throughout an epidemic, and when it was over, he started an apostolate to aid the abandoned aged, the orphaned, and the homeless. John Maria opened the Hospice of Charity and founded the Congregation of the Poor Daughter of St. Cajetan, which spread rapidly in Italy. He served as the "good father" of the faithful while practicing penances until his death on December 30, 1913.

Pope John Paul II beatified John Maria on May 24, 1998, in Turin's Piazza Vittorio, stating that the new blessed *"was a man of deep spirituality and, at the same time, a dynamic apostle, a promoter of religious life and the laity, ever attentive to discerning the signs of the times."*

Patron of the Poor

John Calabria was a man who said little, made no good-will tours, and sought only enough hours in a day to complete the work at hand. He desired no honors, no fame, no spotlight. Christ was his reward.

John was born on October 8, 1873, in an attic room in Verona, Italy. His family was almost desti-

JOHN CALABRIA

(D. 1954)

EDUCATOR

tute but faithful. John's father died when he was twelve, making it necessary for him to get employment as an errand boy. He received the grace of a religious vocation as he matured and he entered the seminary, living on meager amounts of food to survive. This education was interrupted by a two-year military tour of duty which placed John in service at the military hospital of the city. During this period of mandatory service, John founded a charitable union for the assistance of the sick poor. He also volunteered to care for typhus victims, and he suffered an attack of the disease as a result.

When able to returning to the seminary, John completed his studies and was ordained a priest by Cardinal Bacilieri of Verona on August 11, 1901. He was then assigned to parishes, where he began charitable programs for soldiers and chimney sweeps. On November 26, 1907, John founded the Casa Buoni Fanciulli, a home for orphaned or abandoned boys. He educated and trained the boys but also founded programs and facilities for the elderly and ill.

As his coworkers and aides grew in number, John began a religious congregation, the Poor Servants of Divine Providence, dedicated to the care of the most desperate of God's beings. The congregation of the Poor Women Servants of the Divine Providence brought dedicated young women to the cause as well. John also founded a lay institute, the Family of External Brothers, hoping to have an impact upon the secular life of Verona.

John was a devout promoter of Christian unity and wrote to many people to advance this union. One of his faithful correspondents in this concern was the English writer C.S. Lewis. John suffered physical and spiritual trials but accepted all with grace, dying on December 4, 1954, and his remains were placed in the congregation's motherhouse in Verona. He had taught a simple but sure lesson, saying: "it is no longer the time for compromises! We, Christians, must be strictly dedicated to holiness. . . ." He was declared Venerable in 1986.

Pope John Paul II beatified John on April 17, 1988, in Verona, Italy, with Blessed Joseph Nascimeni. At the ceremony in Bentgodi Stadium, the Holy Father praised John as a *"Saint of our time,"* extoling his unfailing courage in addressing the needs evident in his own region.

Theologian and Philosopher

JOHN DUNS SCOTUS

(D. 1308)

PHILOSOPHER

John Duns Scotus — or John of Duns, the Scot — was "the minstrel of the Incarnate Word," the "Herald of the Blessed Virgin," a defender of the Immaculate Conception and one of the leading Franciscan theologians and philosophers of his time. His teachings have endured through the centuries, and his saintliness has inspired new generations of the faithful.

He was born in Duns, near

Roxburgh, Scotland, circa 1266. About 1280, he entered the Franciscan Order and studied theology at Oxford under the brilliant William de Ware. Ordained in 1291, he also studied in Paris. He then taught at Oxford, Paris, and Cologne, but he was exiled by King Philip IV the Fair of France, who was in a dispute with Pope Boniface VIII (r. 1294-1303). John went to Cologne and lived there until his death.

John's school of philosophical thought was called Scotism, and it had an impact on the Franciscans and others in the Middle Ages. His commentaries on the *Sentences* of Peter Lombard were followed by his *Oxford Work* (*Opus Oxontense*), and by his *Parisian Papers (Reportatio Parisiensia)*. John also produced commentaries on Aristotle and a work called *Selected Questions (Questiones Quodlibetales)*.

John is called the "Subtle Doctor," and he affirmed the Augustinian tenet while using new techniques of philosophy. He included Aristotelian tenets, and the use of deduction and mathematics. He held that theology was not a scientific study in the strictest sense but one also based upon revelation and authority. He viewed theology as a practical science because it pursues a practical end: the possession of God. Above all, John was a truly holy man who gave Europe's faithful new insights into the mysteries of God and the Church.

John Duns Scotus is revered as a genuine Scholastic scholar and as a profound intellect, although he criticized many of the theologians of his era. He also advocated the doctrine of the Immaculate Conception, being the first theologian of note to proclaim this teaching. The Scotist School, chiefly among Franciscans, resulted from John's teachings, even though he died comparatively young. He is recorded as dying in Cologne on November 8, 1308.

Pope John Paul II beatified John Duns Scotus on March 20, 1993, giving praise to his philosophical genius and his abiding Franciscan spirituality.

John Faesulanus ❦ See Fra Angelico.

Martyred Australian Missionary

A member of the famed Pontifical Institute for Foreign Missions, John Baptist Mazzucconi offered his life in the Australian regions, and is the martyr of Woodlark Island. He was born in Rancio di Lecco, near Milan, Italy, on March 1, 1826, the ninth of twelve children born to Giacomo and Anna Maria Scuri Mazzucconi.

Educated in local schools, John received the grace of a reli-

JOHN BAPTIST MAZZUCCONI

(D. 1855)

MARTYR

gious vocation and entered the seminary at Monza. He studied as well in Milan, and was ordained on May 25, 1850. A charter member of the Pontifical Institute for Foreign Missions, John became a missionary priest, setting sail for Sidney, Australia, in March, 1852. He was assigned to the islands of Woodlark and Rook, where he hoped to begin his priestly labors.

The natives on these islands did not welcome Europeans or missionaries, and rebuffed all attempts at meetings or understanding. The native anger at the European intrusions did not abate, as new incidents fueled resentments. Two years after making their attempts, the missionaries, including John, had to leave the islands, returning to Sidney in January, 1855. John was very ill, but he recovered in Sidney.

On August 18, 1855, John boarded the schooner *Gazelle*, planning to rejoin his fellow missionaries, whom he believed had regrouped. The missionaries of the Woodlark and Rook stations had decided to abandon these posts, but John had not received word of this official determination. On September 7, 1855, he arrived in Woodlark Bay but ran aground on the coral reef. Natives in canoes came out to greet him, and one, named Avicoar, used a hatchet to kill John. The entire ship was then boarded and a general slaughter took place.

Eight months later, Father Timoleone Raimondi, who would become the bishop of Hong Kong in time, led an expedition to find the schooner. The expedition succeeded in discovering the truth about the martyrdom.

Pope John Paul II beatified John on February 19, 1984, as the first martyr of the Pontifical Institute for Foreign Missions. John was praised for his angelic purity and generosity, virtues that led him fearlessly across the world with the Good News of Christ.

Founder of the Congregation of the Holy Family

A leader in the twentieth century in Italy, John Piamarta understood that the world had entered into a struggle with ignorance and disillusionment. He spent his own energies on founding the Congregation of the Holy Family and the Humble Servants of the Lord to serve the needs of the young in his own region.

JOHN (GIOVANNI) PIAMARTA

(D. 1913)

REFORMER

John (Giovanni) was born on November 26, 1841, in Brescia, Italy, to a poor but devout family. He was educated in local schools and entered the seminary in 1860. Five years later he was ordained a priest for Brescia and his concerns quickly focused on the needs of the young in the region. John labored among them and started an institution for the children of local workers, knowing that such young ones often became ill because of the poverty rampant in their neighborhoods. He also cared for young men in Brescia, establishing the Institute Artigianelli with Monsignor Peter Capretti. The institute trained young men in professional skills and in Christian ideals. John built houses and workshops for more than one hundred Brescian youths, offering them spiritual and educational opportunities. An agricultural colony that he provided introduced new farming techniques into the region and prompted a rejuvenation of the local farming harvests and management systems.

In 1902, John realized that a religious congregation was needed to carry on his apostolate. He founded the Congregation of the Holy Family. With his mother, John also founded the Humble Servants of the Lord for women. The members of these congregations engaged in rural and urban apostolates, designed to strengthen families and to offer the faith to young and old alike. John died at Remedello on April 25, 1913, surrounded by members of his congregation. He was mourned by thousands of Brescians, who revered him as the defender of the poor and the innocent.

Pope John Paul II beatified John on October 12, 1997. In speaking of Giovanni Piamarta, the Holy Father declared: *"How many, thanks to his pastoral activities, were able to start out joyfully in life, having learned a skill and, above all, having encountered Jesus and his message of salvation! . . . Where did this extraordinary man of God find the energy for all his numerous activities? The answer is clear: assiduous and fervent prayer was the source of his tireless apostolic zeal and beneficial influence which he exercised on everyone he approached. He himself said, as the accounts of his contemporaries recall: 'With prayer one is strengthened by the strength of God himself . . .* Omnia possum.' "

Founder of the Congregation of the Missionaries of St. Charles

One of the truly saintly bishops of Italy, John Baptist Sacalabrini was hailed as the "Apostle of the Catechism" by Pope Pius IX, and was revered for his vision of the apostolate of modern religious. His missionary congregation and secular institute were imbued with John's faith.

He was born in Fino Mornasco, Italy, on July 8, 1839. One of eight children, John entered the seminary and was ordained at Como on May 30, 1863. He served as a professor and rector of St. Abundius Seminary, and was consecrated the bishop of Piacenza on January 30, 1876.

John was a model bishop, visiting every parish in Piacenza and celebrating three synods de-

JOHN BAPTIST SCALABRINI

(D. 1905)

BISHOP

signed to bring about renewal programs and the restoration of doctrine. He was a great defender of the poor and helpless — during a cholera epidemic, John sold all that he possessed to buy the food and medical supplies that saved hundreds of human lives.

John also had great concern for migrants, as he witnessed the great tides of immigrants in his own era. On November 28, 1887, John founded the Congregation of the Missionaries of St. Charles, called the Scalabrinis. He convinced Mother Cabrini to go to America to care for Italian immigrants in the New World. In 1895, John founded the Missionary Sisters of St. Charles for migrants, and he started a secular institute, the Scalabrinian Lay Missionary Women. All of these institutes were designed to aid the great masses of human beings on the move across the world.

John had a special devotion to the Holy Eucharist and to the Blessed Virgin Mary. He died on the feast of the Ascension, June 1, 1905. John's last words were: "Lord, I am ready. Let us go."

Pope John Paul II beatified John on November 9, 1997. *"The universal call to holiness was constantly felt and personally lived by John Baptist Scalabrini. He loved to say over and over: 'Would that I could sanctify myself and all the souls entrusted to me!' Striving for holiness and proposing it to everyone he met was always his first concern . . . . Pope Pius IX called him the 'Apostle of the Catechism' because of his efforts to promote the systematic teaching of the Church's doctrine to children and adults in every parish."*

Bishop of Trento

An aristocrat and a prelate of the profound charity of Christ, John Tschiderer von Gleifheim stands as a model bishop for the modern world. He was born into a high-ranking noble family at Bolzano, Italy, on April 15, 1777.

JOHN TSCHIDERER VON (ZU) GLEIFHEIM

(D. 1860)

BISHOP

Raised devoutly in a family well-connected to the outstanding churchmen of the time, John decided upon a priestly vocation. He entered seminary training and was ordained on July 27, 1800, by the bishop of Trento, Emmanuel Count Von Thul. John began his priestly ministry in the diocese and then was sent to Rome to earn his doctorate in moral and pastoral theology. He returned to the seminary to serve as a professor.

In 1810, John was made pastor at Sarnthal, and went to Meran nine years later. In 1826, he was a cathedral canon and pro-vicar of the diocese, so honored by Prince-Bishop Luschin. He demonstrated such holiness that in 1832 he was nominated a bishop by Prince-Bishop Galura of

Brixen, and in 1834 was nominated by Emperor Francis I (r. 1804-1835) as bishop of Trento. John was consecrated on May 15, 1835. In that role, John was revered for his virtue, gentleness, and charity.

He built churches, libraries, and charitable institutions with his own personal fortune. John literally gave away all that he possessed to the sick and the poor. He also distinguished himself by serving victims of two cholera epidemics in his area. He left his property to the seminary, now called the *Joanneum*, and he bequeathed a legacy to a school for the deaf and dumb. He died in Trento on December 3, 1860.

Pope John Paul II beatified John on April 30, 1995, in Trento, praising his episcopal zeal and apostolic labors of this scholarly holy man. Thousands of the faithful rejoiced at his beatification.

Founder of Opus Dei

A remarkable modern priest who "set forth the call to holiness," Josemaria Escrivá de Balaguer was the founder of Opus Dei, the international institute and personal prelature of the Holy See that seeks to transform today's society. He was also the symbol of the "sanctification of ordinary work" for thousands of Catholics in the world. Opus Dei functions in the world as a facet of illumined lay dedication.

JOSEMARIA ESCRIVÁ DE BALAGUER

(D. 1975)

PRIEST

Josemaria was born in Barbastro, Spain, on January 9, 1902, but moved with his family to Logroño when he was thirteen. He studied at the seminary at Logroño and completed his training for the priesthood at the Pontifical University of Saragossa. Ordained on March 28, 1925, he began serving as superior of the seminary at the age of twenty.

After ordination, Josemaria moved to Madrid, where he completed his civil law doctorate and started laboring for the poor and the sick. On October 2, 1921, he received an inspiration to start Opus Dei (Latin for "Work of God") This society was designed to promote holiness among individuals in the world. Josemaria also received inspiration to take Opus Dei to women as well as to men.

He risked his life during the Spanish Civil War and was forced to hide from authorities, eventually escaping to Andorra. He also aided General Francisco, and at the war's end, he began giving retreats and restoring Opus Dei. On February 14, 1943, Josemaria also founded the Priestly Society of the Holy Cross. He took up residence in Rome in 1946, receiving pontifical approval. All the while he lived his motto: " to hide and disappear so that only Jesus may shine." Opus Dei spread across the world, and Josemaria became a consultor to the Holy See under Pope Pius XII (r. 1939-1958).

The evangelization spread to Portugal, England, France, Ireland, Mexico, Australia, New Zealand, and South America, as well as to the United States. In time, Opus Dei owned publishing houses and radio stations dedicated to the use of modern media techniques in serving the Church. Josemaria sought the protection of a "personal prelature" for Opus Dei, a status that would place members under the pope, secured from the supervision of local bishops. Pope John Paul II granted this status to Opus Dei in 1983.

On June 26, 1975, Josemaria died of a heart attack at Opus Dei headquarters in Rome, the Villa Trevere, and his remains were enshrined in the prelatic church of Opus Dei in Rome. When he died, Josemaria left more than 60,000 members of Opus Dei in 80 countries and 1,000 priests dedicated to the Opus Dei apostolate.

Pope John Paul II beatified Josemaria on May 17, 1992, declaring: *"His fidelity allowed the Holy Spirit to lead him to the heights of personal union with God, which resulted in an extraordinarily fruitful apostolate . . . which Josemaria attributed entirely to the divine goodness, always considering himself an 'inept and deaf instrument,' giving proof of an extraordinary humility. . . ."*

Founder of the Christian Mercy Program

Called the Apostle of Charity, the new blessed, José Maria, stands as a symbol of the enduring faith and loyalty of the Catholics of Mexico. José understood the needs of the people, and he respected the unending courage displayed by the Catholic-Mexican people. He was a member of an upper-class family and educated by tutors and in private schools. José demonstrated an intellectual brilliance early in life.

JOSÉ MARIA DE YERMO Y PARRES

(D. 1904)

FOUNDER

In 1867, José became a member of the Congregation of the Missions and was sent to Paris to continue his theological education. Upon returning to Mexico, he left his religious community and prepared for the diocesan priesthood and in 1879, was ordained for the diocese of León in Mexico. There he aided the diocesan curia and was active in academic concerns. However, his health failed, and he was assigned as a chaplain for two missions just outside of León. When he discovered the state of poverty in the area, José's life was changed forever.

In December 1885, José opened the Sacred Heart Hospice and founded the Congregation of the Servants of the Sacred Heart of Jesus and the Poor.

These missionary women served the destitute and aided him in his ministry. Four years later, José went to Puebla, where he started the apostolate of Christian Mercy, a program to free women from prostitution. The Christian Mercy program provided many such women with education and training until it was suppressed by the Mexican government in 1928. José worked unceasingly in Puebla de los Angeles until his death.

Pope John Paul II beatified José Maria at the Basilica of Our Lady of Guadalupe in Mexico City on May 6, 1990, declaring: *"Father José Maria — the Apostle of Charity, as his contemporaries called him — combined love of God with love of neighbor, the synthesis of evangelical perfection, with a great devotion to the Heart of Jesus and with special love for the poor. His burning zeal for God's glory led him also to desire that all be truly missionaries."*

Founder of the Consolata Society for Foreign Missions

A founder and priest, Joseph Allamano burned with pastoral zeal and missionary visions that bequeathed to the world the great Consolata Congregations. His mission field was the entire world, where his disciples have raised the banner of Christ and the Church.

Joseph was born in Castelnuovo d'Asti, Italy, on January 21, 1851, the fourth child of Joseph and Marianna Cafasso Allamano. Educated at Valdocco, the institute operated by John Bosco's Congregation, Joseph entered the diocesan seminary at Turin. His education was difficult, as Joseph suffered from hemoptysis (coughing up blood) continually. He was ordained on September 20, 1872, in the Turin Cathedral, and he became a canon there. Joseph also restored the sanctuary and convent of the Consolata, succeeding his uncle, St. Joseph Cafasso, as head of this ecclesiastical house in 1880.

JOSEPH ALLAMANO

(D. 1926)

PRIEST

The hallmark of his priestly life, however, was his concern about the missions. To this end he founded the Consolata Missionary Fathers, which were approved by Rome on January 29, 1901. In 1902, two mission priests were sent to Zanzibar, where they baptized the king and opened twelve mission stations. The congregation labored in Africa and in North and South America, conducting hospitals, dispensaries, schools, and seminaries. It is also called the Consolata Society for Foreign Missions.

In 1910, Pope St. Pius X (r. 1903-1914) asked Joseph to found the Consolata Mission Sisters. The rule for this congregation was approved on January 29, 1910. Both congregations are devoted to Our Lady of Consolation, and both are concerned with the missionary identity of the Church.

Joseph served the needs of his societies until his death in Turin on February 16, 1926. He tried to continue celebrating Mass until the end, and his death was so peaceful that it was almost unnoticed by those in attendance. He was buried in the Turin cemetery, but his remains were transferred to the Consolata motherhouse.

Pope John Paul II beatified Joseph on October 7, 1990. The Holy Father stated: *"Rooted in him was the deep conviction that 'the priest is above all a man of charity, destined to the greatest possible good, to sanctify others by word and example, with holiness and knowledge."* The Holy Father added, *". . . he reminds us that in order to stay faithful to our Christian vocation we must know how to share the gifts we received from God. . . ."*

Jesuit Missionary

A missionary priest who was protected by the creatures of the jungles of Brazil, Joseph de Anchieta is hailed as the Jesuit Apostle of Brazil. He was also a thaumaturgist and a friend of animals and wild birds. Related to St. Ignatius of Loyola, he was united to Christ in his priesthood.

Joseph was born in San Cristobal de la Laguna, Spain, on March 19, 1534.

JOSEPH DE ANCHIETA

(D. 1597)

MISSIONARY

At age eighteen, Joseph consecrated himself to the Blessed Virgin and he entered the Jesuits at Coimbra, Portugal, on May 1, 1551. He was sent to Brazil two years later, going to the mission at Quisininga. Joseph would spend forty-four years in Brazil, founding missions, including Sao Paulo de Piratininga.

After ordination, Joseph learned the native languages and wrote catechisms. In 1567, he was appointed superior of the Jesuit province of Brazil, and a decade later he became the Jesuit provincial of Brazil. He was a thaumaturgist, healing many, and animals and birds came at his call. Witnesses claim that a wall of water rose around him when he prayed in the wilderness. While serving as a hostage for the Tamuins during negotiations with that native people, Joseph composed a 5,000-verse poem in his mind, remembering it months later in order to commit it to paper. He was able to suppress cannibalism and other pagan customs among the tribes because of the reverence he inspired.

Brilliant and scholarly, Joseph began a classical school, teaching Latin in Brazil's missions. This was the first such institute in the New World. Discovering that dramas and plays caught the attention of the local population, he taught actors to perform and staged doctrinal plays to educate his audiences. He continued to heal those who came to him and made his way through the perilous jungles without fear. Joseph died at Reritiba, Brazil, on June 9, 1597. The local tribes came in vast numbers to honor his passing, and the local bishop who preached at his funeral called him a first-ranked missionary.

Pope John Paul II designated Joseph *"this great son of Ignatius"* at his beatification on June 22, 1980, praising his gifts and his pioneering missionary work as well as the profound spiritual union that sustained his mission labors for so many decades.

Founder of the Little Daughters of St. Joseph

Recognizing the Kingdom of God in all aspects of modern society, Joseph Baldo combined the active and contemplative apostolates. The founder of the Little Daughters of St. Joseph, he was also a tireless devotee of Christ in the Eucharist, teaching that this age would not find rest until Christ reigned supreme.

Joseph was born in Puegnago, near Brescia, Italy, on February 19, 1843, the son of Angelo and Hippolita Casa Baldo. The farming family was extremely devout, and Joseph received the grace of a religious vocation. When he was sixteen he entered the seminary at Verona and was ordained on August 15, 1865. This ordination took place with a papal indult, because he was only twenty-two.

JOSEPH (GIUSEPPE) BALDO

(D. 1915)

FOUNDER

Joseph served as a curate in parishes after his ordination but was recalled to the seminary as vice-rector. He wrote books on prayers, sermons, and seminary training, and he taught at the seminary for over a decade. He then asked for a pastoral assignment, and in 1877, became parish priest at Ronco all 'Adige. Anticlerical freemasons threatened him from the first day, but Joseph stood up to them and started his ministry in charitable programs.

He founded schools for adults, a Workers' Mutual Assistance Society, a nursery, elementary schools, and a rural savings bank. Joseph also started the Servants of Charity of Our Lady of Succor to conduct home visits and care for the sick. A hospital opened by Joseph in 1888 was followed by the founding of a nursing congregation, the Little Daughters of St. Joseph, in 1894.

Joseph also established an Association of Christian Mothers, a Confraternity of the Blessed Sacrament, and a Society of the Forty Hours. He suffered from an illness for almost two years at the end of his life, happy to have pain that would cleanse his human weaknesses. Joseph died at Ronco all 'Adige on October 24, 1915, and his remains were enshrined in the chapel of his congregation in 1950.

Pope John Paul II beatified Joseph on October 31, 1989, announcing that from the first day as a parish priest, Joseph told his parishioners: *"I am your parish priest. Yours — that is, totally yours."* The Holy Father urged the faithful to *"confidently invoke Blessed Joseph Baldo, who shines in the glory of the elect, in order to imitate his example of faith, charity, and holiness."*

Patron of Evangelic Charity

Called a model of evangelical charity, Joseph Benedetto Dusmet was a Benedictine Cardinal of remarkable energy and discernment. He also promoted scholarship motivated by intense concern for the needs of others, serving as the inspiration and guide for his Order. Joseph was born in Palermo, Sicily, on August 15, 1818. Drawn to the religious life, he entered the Benedictine Order at St. Martino della Scale Monastery. After completing his studies, Joseph was professed in 1840 and was ordained a priest in 1842.

JOSEPH (GIUSEPPE) BENEDETTO DUSMET

(D. 1894)

CARDINAL

He served the Order in various capacities, displaying his unfailing loyalty and faith as political and social upheaval racked the area. In 1858, Joseph was elected the abbot of St. Nicoló de Arenis Monastery in Catania and was named the archbishop of Catania in 1867. Joseph would spend the next twenty-seven years giving his money, time, and energies to the people of the region. He beggared himself to the point that when he died there were no good linens in his residence to wrap his remains.

Earthquakes, volcanic eruptions, and outbreaks of cholera brought Joseph into the streets of the city to care for victims. He also established the Confederation of the Benedictine Order and served Pope Leo XIII (r. 1878-1903) in re-establishing the International College of Sant'Anselmo on the Via Aventina in Rome. Joseph was elevated to the rank of Cardinal in 1888. He died in Catania on April 4, 1894.

Pope John Paul II beatified Joseph Cardinal Dusmet on September 25, 1988, proclaiming: *"He gave that example of evangelic charity in times which were particularly difficult for the life of the Church. . . ."* The Holy Father praised Joseph also for his total generosity, saying: *". . . he literally stripped himself of everything in order to put on poverty, whose humble servant he was."*

Oblate Missionary

A pioneering Oblate missionary of Africa, Joseph Gérard was called the "Friend of the Africans." Pope John Paul II prayed at Joseph's tomb and beatified him in Maseru, in Lesotho, the arena of his missionary labors, where he became a beloved figure among the local populations of African peoples.

Joseph was born at Bouxières-aux-Chênes, France, on March 12, 1831, the son of Jean and Ursula Stofflet Gérard. Joseph aided his farm parents as a shepherd and then was allowed to study at Pont-á-Mousson. He entered the Nancy seminary on Easter Sunday, 1851, and then joined the Oblates of Mary Immaculate and completed his studies at Marseilles.

JOSEPH GÉRARD

(D. 1914)

❦

MISSIONARY

Joseph was ordained in Natal, South Africa, in February, 1854, and began his missionary labors in the field. His first assignment to the Zulu tribe was not successful, and Joseph went to the Basotho mission in 1862, determined to serve the tribes of the area faithfully. There he met Moshesh, the "Lion of the Mountain," the chief of Basutoland. Joseph took up residence in a tent in a valley and went from village to village to care for the sick. He baptized his first converts in 1865. By 1875 he had five hundred converts in his Mission of the Mother of God, winning them with his holiness and devotion.

The following year, Joseph went to St. Monica's mission. He labored there alone, celebrating his golden anniversary as a priest there in 1894, and continued his work at St. Monica's until 1897. He was beloved by all of the Africans of the region, as his solitary mission continued decade after decade in all seasons and all weather. His eyesight was weakening, and by May, 1914, he could no longer use his legs. Joseph offered his last Mass on May 24. On May 29, at Roma, Lesotho, he simply crossed himself and died. When word of his death spread, officials of the regional tribes, including Moshesh, the "Lion of the Mountain," gathered to lay him to rest as the "Friend of the Africans." People of all faiths profoundly mourned his passing.

Pope John Paul II beatified Joseph on September 15, 1988, announcing that he was *"a servant of reconciliation and peace."* The Holy Father described Joseph as *"a missionary eager to understand souls."*

Founder of the Congregation of the Sons of the Holy Family

This blessed bore the five wounds of Christ's Passion, which he called "the Lord's mercies." This physical suffering, however, did not limit his apostolate, which was focused on the modern family. Joseph Manyanet y Vives had a singular devotion to the Holy Face of Jesus and to the Holy Family, and he mirrored Christ in all of his ministries.

JOSEPH MANYANET Y VIVES

(D. 1901)

❦

STIGMATIC

He was born in Catalonia, Spain, on January 7, 1833, the son of Antonia and Bonaventura Manyanet y Vives, the ninth child of a devout family. Before he was two, Joseph's father died, and a priest, Valentino Lledos, became his guardian. Joseph was raised piously and entered the seminary at Lleida and then at La Seu d'Urgell, where he was ordained on April 9, 1859. He then labored in d'Urgell for twelve years and was much praised by Bishop Joseph Caixal.

Having devotion to the Holy Family, Jesus, Mary, and Joseph, he saw the dangers facing families in his own era and decided to found two congregation to foster Christian family formation. The Congregation of the Sons of the Holy Family was started by Joseph in 1864, in Tromp, Lerida, and the Missionary Daughters of the Holy Family of Nazareth opened ten years later. Members of Joseph's congregation reached the United States in 1920 continuing the labors of the fostering centers and schools. The motherhouse is in Barcelona.

Joseph maintained his dedication to the Holy Face of Jesus and spread his spiritual devotion through pamphlets and the magazine *The Holy Family*. He also erected the Expiatory Temple of the Holy Family in Barcelona, Spain. He went everywhere to spread the devotion, to Lourdes, France, and to Loreto, in Italy. He was suffering ill health and experiencing physical problems from the infirmity caused by the stigmatic wounds. Joseph died in San Andres de Palomar, Barcelona, on December 17, 1901, saying: "Jesus, Mary, and Joseph, may I breath forth my soul in peace with you."

Pope John Paul II beatified him on November 25, 1984, declaring: "... *the new blessed looked with foresightedness at the examples of Nazarene sanctity which the Holy Family teaches. From here was born his apostolic commitment to try to bring that message to the world and to make every home a Nazareth."*

Founder of the Oblates of St. Joseph

Called a "gem among bishops" by Pope Leo XIII (1878-1903), Blessed Joseph Marello is a luminary of Asti, Italy. The founder of a religious congregation, he was a truly holy individual, dedicated to his role as a shepherd of the faithful. Loyal and undeterred by opposition, Joseph understood his episcopal role in a difficult era.

Joseph was born in Turin, Italy, on December 26, 1844, the son of Vincenzo and Anna Maria Marello. Anna Maria died very young, and the family moved to Santi Martino Alfieri, where Joseph was raised. At age twelve he entered the seminary, desiring a priestly vocation and a life of true service. He suffered a bout of typhus in 1863, and vowed to complete his studies if he regained his health. He did recuperate, and he attributed this renewal of his physical well-being to Our Lady of Consolation. Joseph completed his studies and was ordained on September 19, 1868.

JOSEPH (GIUSEPPE) MARELLO

(D. 1895)

BISHOP

He was made a secretary to Bishop Carlo Savio of Asti and served in this capacity for thirteen years. Joseph accompanied his bishop to the First Vatican Council (1869-1870).

During this part of his ministry, he took over a retirement home to save it from financial ruin. He also served as a spiritual director and taught catechism. In 1878, Joseph founded the Oblates of St. Joseph, a religious community of priests and brothers, designed to assist bishops and clergy in evangelization. The members of the congregation arrived in the United States in 1929.

On February 17, 1889, Joseph was consecrated the bishop of Asti. He worked untiringly there for the young and the abandoned. In his beatification, Pope John Paul II described Joseph as a model Pastor of the People of God. He suffered even as he performed such charitable labors. Another religious congregation spread slanderous lies about him; lies that were exposed in time but caused him much humiliation. This abuse did not prevent him from laboring for the people, and in time he was cleared of all charges. Joseph visited every parish in his diocese and wrote six pastoral letters for the faithful. In May, 1895, Joseph went to Savona, to take part in the celebration of the third centennial of St. Philip Neri. There he suffered a cerebral hemorrhage and died on May 30 in the bishop's residence.

Pope John Paul II beatified Joseph on September 26, 1993, in the Campo del Palio of Asti, announcing: *"Bishop Joseph Marello, founder of the Oblates of St. Joseph, whom today I have the joy of declaring blessed, has a place in the marvelous history of religious vitality and holiness (in Asti). . . . Today we are paying homage to this Pastor who worked so hard in the Lord's vineyard."*

Founder of the Little Sisters of the Holy Family

A pastor who understood the needs of the faithful, on both the spiritual and the material levels of life, Blessed Joseph Nascimbeni moved heaven and earth to serve the souls entrusted to his care, bringing a renewed religious awareness to the rural areas and inspiring dedication and faithful service.

JOSEPH (GIUSEPPE) NASCIMBENI

(D. 1922)

FOUNDER

Joseph was born in Torri del Benaco, Italy, on March 22, 1851, and was baptized the same day. The son of Antonio and Amidaea Sartori Nascimbeni, Joseph was raised devoutly, and desiring a religious vocation, he entered the seminary at Verona where he completed his training and was ordained on March 19, 1874. He was then assigned to the village of San Pietro di Lavagno where he served as pastor and schoolmaster.

In 1877, Joseph was assigned to Casteletto di Brenzone, and served as a curate and assisted in the school. In 1884, he became the pastor, a ministry he would conduct for almost four decades. The village had a population of only ninety, but Joseph poured out his charity and priestly care to aid them in their changing world.

On November 4, 1892, Joseph founded the Little Sisters of the Holy Family with Mother Maria Mantovani. Dedicated to charitable works, the congregation spread rapidly, and Joseph saw more than a thousand sisters in his foundation before he died. He directed the congregation and continued his ministry, displaying an acute awareness of the dangers of the modern era and their devastating effects on the family and young people. Joseph founded this congregation because of the needs of the region and because he could attract no other sisters to aid his ministry. He was honored by Pope St. Pius X in 1911 (r. 1903-1914). Made a protonotary apostolic, Joseph accepted the honor but would not allow anyone to call him Monsignor.

On December 31, 1916, Joseph suffered a stroke and was left partially paralyzed. He did not stop his labors, and he bore all things with patience. He died at Casteletto del Garda on January 22 (or 21), 1922.

Pope John Paul II beatified Joseph in Verona, Italy, on April, 17, 1988. At the ceremony, the Holy Father praised Joseph as a symbol of Christ, the Good Shepherd, and as a pastor of consummate charity and virtue.

Founder of the Servants of the Most Sacred Heart of Jesus

Called the "Shepherd of Souls," Blessed Joseph Sebastian Pelczar endured great suffering to care for the people of his diocese. The horrors of World War I did not dim his vision of service to those in need, and the invasion of the Russians did not dampen his ardor for charity.

He was born in Korczyna, Poland, on January 17, 1842, and was raised devoutly in a troubled era. Becoming a priest and distinguishing himself as a pastor, Joseph was named titular bishop of Meletopolis on February 20, 1899, and was consecrated the bishop of Przemysl on January 13, 1901. He demonstrated zeal as the bishop of the diocese, and with his people faced the ravages and onslaughts of the military forces of World War I.

Joseph founded the Servants of the Most Sacred Heart of Jesus in 1894. Dedicated to domestic work, the congregation arrived in the United States in 1959. The members of the congregation were imbued

JOSEPH SEBASTIAN PELCZAR

(D. 1924)

BISHOP

with Joseph's spirit of charity and care, seeing this "Shepherd of Souls" as a true model of their endeavors.

The Russians entered Przemysl in March, 1915, burning more than a hundred churches and taking priests prisoner. Joseph led his clergy, nuns, and people in aiding the wounded and oppressed. He opened hospitals, clinics, and way stations, exposing himself to the enemy and to epidemics raging in the city. Joseph and his diocese survived the war and the invasions and began the great task of rebuilding. His memory is revered as a particularly saving grace in a dreadful crisis. Joseph died in Przemysl on March 28, 1924.

Pope John Paul II beatified Joseph on June 2, 1991, in Reszów, Poland, proclaiming: *"The Church which is now on a pilgrimage across this sub-Carpathian land, is kept alive by her hope for the kingdom of heaven. And today she has an exceptional reason to rejoice when the beatification of Josef Sebastian Pelczar renews and strengthens this hope in all."* The Holy Father added: *"Here is the man who did the will of the father."*

Patron of the Needy

Revered as the "Apostle of Madrid," Blessed Joseph Rubio y Peralta was the pastor of the poor of his time. A member of the Society of Jesus, he was an advocate of the lay ministry and of total commitment to the service of the suffering and abandoned.

Joseph was born in Dalias, in Almeria Province, southern Spain, on July 22, 1864. He entered the seminary at age twelve and two years later was sent to Granada to study philosophy, theology, and canon law. Joseph earned his degrees and became a doctor of canon law in 1897, in Madrid.

JOSEPH MARIA RUBIO Y PERALTA

(D. 1922)

RELIGIOUS

Ordained a priest on September 24, 1887, Joseph studied and then served the archdiocese. He spent two years in Chinchon and was appointed pastor in Estromera. Joseph was recalled to Madrid to teach in the seminary and to serve as archdiocesan notary. He accepted all assignments and performed them well, but in his heart, he desired a vocation as a Jesuit. In 1906, Joseph entered the Society of Jesus in Granada. He returned as a professed Jesuit to Madrid in 1911, and his lasting apostolate began.

He was a preacher who could touch the hearts of the people of Madrid, and thousands came to him for confession and spiritual direction. Joseph's gift to them in return was the peace of Christ and true resolve. Joseph used the Ignatian Spiritual Exercises to form devout lay men and women in Spain's capital. He also went into the suburban areas of the city with lay helpers where they aided the needy and the sick.

Over a period of two decades, Joseph served as the one friend that the poor of the city could rely upon to remedy their suffering. His amiable kindness, and the gentle concerns that he demonstrated, opened the hearts of one and all. Joseph continued this apostolate until his death on May 2, 1929. Thousands mourned his passing.

Pope John Paul II beatified Joseph on October 6, 1985, with two other Jesuits. At the ceremony, Joseph was praised for his imitation of Christ and for his dedication — an apostolate that brought him face to face with pain and suffering each day of his life.

Indian Missionary

The Apostle of Ceylon (now Sri Lanka) and a priest of Goa, India, Blessed Joseph Vaz gave himself entirely to his priestly apostolate, winning the hearts of young and old, rich and poor, in the name of Christ.

Born in Goa, India, on April 21, 1651, and of the Konkani Brahmin caste, Joseph was raised a Christian. His family was pious and dedicated to the faith, educating Joseph in catechetical areas as well as in the academic fields. He learned Portuguese and Latin and then took pre-seminary courses at the Jesuit College and at the College of St. Thomas. He completed his studies, was ordained in 1676, and was sent to the Kanar mission for three years. From these beginnings came his unique ministry as a confessor and preacher.

JOSEPH VAZ

(D. 1711)

🔥

PRIEST

In 1686, he went to Ceylon to undertake the great apostolate that distinguished his life. Ceylon was under Dutch control at that time, and the Church was being persecuted by the colonial authorities. The arrival of Joseph marked a turning point in Ceylon. He worked in disguise, going from village to village to preach and to console the faithful. The Dutch arrested him after a time, and he was imprisoned in Kandy, the capital of a native independent state. The king ordered Joseph's release in 1699.

The Oratorian Fathers and other missionaries arrived soon after to aid Joseph in his labors. He was already revered by people of all faiths because of his holiness and genuine concern for one and all. Joseph combined the wisdom and elegance of his own people with the joy of Christ. He cared for the abandoned sick of the streets and jungles during a smallpox epidemic and opened a hospital for victims, earning respect from all denomination and races. When Ceylon was erected as a diocese, Joseph was the natural candidate for the episcopacy, but he declined the honor. His health was strained because of his constant labors, and in 1710, he was unable to leave his residence at Kandy. Joseph died there on January 16, 1711, honored as the Apostle of Ceylon. He was buried in the church that he built. In 1754, the church was destroyed, and his actual grave lost.

Pope John Paul II beatified Joseph on June 21, 1995, at Colomba, Sri Lanka, declaring that the new blessed combined the virtues of his own heritage with the radiance of Christ to serve the needs of his adopted people of Ceylon. As the Apostle of Ceylon, Joseph will forever be honored.

Carmelite Tertiary

This blessed laywoman, dedicated totally to God, attained great mystical heights and is honored for her Carmelite spirituality which prompted her to serve the young women of her area and to inspire religious vocations.

JOSEPHA NAVAL GIRBES

(D. 1893)

LAYWOMAN

Josepha Naval Girbes was a Third Order Carmelite who was born in Algemesi, near Valencia, Spain, on December 11, 1820. Her parish priest taught her catechism, and she was confirmed in 1828, receiving her First Communion a year later. After the death of her mother in 1833, Josepha took charge of the family residence. A vow of perpetual virginity, taken in 1838, allowed Josepha to perform her apostoloate in her home. She became a Third Order Carmelite, remaining in the world and working to prepare young women of her area for marriage or for convent life.

Josepha did excellent embroidery work, and she gave lessons in the art to young women. They came to study and discovered that Josepha was a learned mystic who could impart the beauty of the faith. Josepha taught catechism and led many followers in advanced stages of prayer. She also assisted the dying and displayed heroism in the cholera epidemic of 1885.

A true spiritual daughter of St. Teresa of Ávila and St. John of the Cross, Josepha was revered as a mystic who had achieved mystical union with God at age fifty-five. She was also honored for fostering many religious vocations in her contact with others. Josepha died in Algemesi on February 24, 1893, at the age of seventy-one, after serving as a quiet, humble personification of penance, prayer, and contemplation.

Pope John Paul II beatified Josepha on September 25, 1988, declaring: *"The Church sings a song of joy and praise to God for the beatification of Josepha Naval Girbes, a secular virgin who dedicated her life to the apostolate in her native town. . . ."* The Holy Father added: *"A special characteristic of Josepha is her condition as a member of the laity. She, whose disciples filled the cloistered convents, remained as an unmarried woman in the world. . . ."*

Canossian Sister

Called the *Madre Moretta* (the Black Mother), Josephina Bakhita was a former slave who became a Canossian Sister in Italy. She was born in the Sudan, in northeastern Africa, about 1870, and at the age of nine was stolen by slavers. The slave traders gave her the name *Bakhita,* meaning "the Lucky One." She escaped from these slavers only to be caught by another, who took her as a gift to his daughter in El Obeid. There she was treated well until she broke a vase. Then she was sold to a Turkish officer who sold her again in the market in Khartoum. She was bought by the Italian vice-counsel, who returned to Italy, taking Josephina with him. There she was given to a Signora Michieli in Genoa. She was sent to a convent by her new owner, to be educated in the school operated by the Daughters of Charity of Canossa. Josephina became a Christian on January 9, 1890, and was baptized by the cardinal patriarch. She refused to leave the convent after discovering her religious vocation, despite the demands of Signora Michieli, who claimed ownership. The cardinal patriarch and the king's procurator were called upon to mediate the matter, and they decided in favor of Josephina's vocation.

JOSEPHINA BAKHITA

(D. 1947)

RELIGIOUS

Josephina was welcomed into the Canossian convent, and she made her novitiate and took religious vows. Her holiness and devotion were demonstrated in her labors as a cook, gate keeper, and keeper of linens. It was obvious that God had brought Josephina out of Africa to glorify him among the Europeans. With this in mind, Josephina, the *Madre Moretta,* traveled throughout Italy to raise funds for the missions. She served as a Canossian for half a century, dying in Schio, Italy, on February 8, 1947, and was revered by the people of her adopted land. She has not been forgotten by the Sudanese either. Her portrait hangs in the cathedral at Khartoum.

Pope John Paul II beatified Josephina on May 17, 1992, in the presence of three hundred Canossian Sisters and pilgrims, many from the Sudan. The Holy Father declared: *"In our time, in which the unbridled race for power, money, and pleasure is the cause of so much distrust, violence, and loneliness, Sister Bakhita has been given to us once more by the Lord as a universal sister, so that she can reveal to us the secret of true happiness: the Beatitudes. . . . Here is a message of heroic goodness modeled on the goodness of the Heavenly Father."*

Foundress of the Daughters of St. Camillus

Families are sometimes torn apart by tragedies and losses, and the children of such families are forced to endure lives deprived of parents, brothers, and sisters. Blessed Josephine Vannini faced such a crisis in her young life, but inspired Catholic religious intervened and allowed her spiritual beauty to flower for the world.

JOSEPHINE VANNINI (ADELAIDES)

(D. 1911)

FOUNDRESS

She was born in Rome, Italy, on July 7, 1859, and was baptized Judith Adelaides, the daughter of Angelo and Annunziata Papi Vannini. Her sister was Ginlia, and her brother was Augusto. The family, devout and happy, faced tragedy between 1863 and 1866, when parents Angelo and Annunziata died. The children were separated, and Josephine was given to the care of the Daughters of Charity of St. Vincent de Paul. Inspired by these religious, Josephine wanted to enter the convent, a desire that she maintained steadfastly even when reunited with her brother and sister in 1880.

Josephine entered the Daughters of Charity but became ill and spent time in another convent recuperating. Her spiritual director, Father Luigi Tezza, suggested that she found a new congregation, and with the aid of her aunt, Anna Maria Papi, Josephine founded the Daughters of St. Camillus on February 2, 1892. The congregation was elevated to the status of having a cardinal protector, His Eminence Lucido Maria Parocchi, on January 24, 1894. Josephine became superior general, and she opened houses in Italy, France, Belgium, and Argentina. The Daughters of St. Camillus serve the poor and the infirm. Josephine died on February 23, 1911, in Rome, and her remains were interred in Rome and then in Grottaferrata.

Pope John Paul II beatified Josephine on October 16, 1994, declaring: *"To serve the suffering; this was the special charism of Josephine Vannini, foundress of the Congregation of the Daughters of St. Camillus. To belong totally to God, who is loved and honored in the needy, was her constant concern, expressed in a daily, boundless charity towards the infirm, in the footsteps of the great apostle of St. Camillus of Lellis."* The Holy Father added: *"How contemporary are her witness and message! Mother Vannini makes a strong appeal to today's young men and women who sometimes hesitate to make total and definitive commitments. She invites all who are called to the consecrated life to respond generously, as she does all who fulfill their vocation in family life: God has a plan of holiness for everyone."*

Witness of Our Lady of Guadalupe

This Mexican-born blessed was given the extraordinary grace of a vision of the Blessed Virgin Mary, revered over the centuries as Our Lady of Guadalupe. Juan Diego is the baptismal name given to Cuauhtlatohuac, an Aztec or Chichimec by birth. He was walking on a hill, now part of Mexico City, called Tepayac, on Saturday, December 9, 1531. There he heard music and saw a bright and beautiful light. Juan saw as well a beautiful woman in a striking garb, surrounded by golden rays.

JUAN DIEGO

(D. UNKNOWN)

VISIONARY

The woman spoke to him, directing him to have a church built on the hill in her honor. Juan, hearing her, went to Bishop Juan de Zumárraga, a Franciscan missionary prelate. The bishop received Juan but was unable to give his account of seeing the woman much credence, recommending that Juan speak to the woman again and ask for a sign. Juan, then fifty-five and a devout convert, readily agreed.

Juan's uncle, Bernardino, was ill with a fever, and he took care of the elderly man before seeking the miraculous vision again. Sensing that his uncle was about to die of the fever, Juan ran at dawn on Tuesday, December 12, to St. James Convent for a priest. The woman met him and asked why he had chosen this side route. Juan explained his uncle's condition, and was told by the woman that the uncle was cured.

The vision then identified herself as Our Lady of Guadalupe. She appeared as the Immaculate Conception, accompanied by the sun, moon, and the stars. When Juan asked for a sign for the bishop, Our Lady told him to go the nearby rocks and there gather the roses. Juan knew that such flowers were out of season, but he did what he was told and gathered the blossoms in the folds of his *tilma:* the long cloak made of *maguey* and worn by high ranking Aztecs in many eras. Our Lady told Juan to keep the roses hidden there until he could give them to Bishop Zumárraga.

At the bishop's residence, where he was again received by the prelate, Juan opened his *tilma,* and the roses fell onto the floor. The bishop and his attendants knelt suddenly, an act that startled Juan until he looked down and saw the image of Our Lady of Guadalupe, exactly as she had appeared to him, imprinted on his *tilma.* That image became a national treasure of Mexico instantly and then a holy object enshrined in Mexico City. Our Lady of Guadalupe's shrine draws thousands of pilgrims today.

Pope John Paul II beatified Juan Diego by confirming his cult on May 6, 1990, in Mexico City, announcing: *"At the dawn of Mexican evangelization,*

Blessed Juan Diego holds a place all by himself; according to tradition, his indigenous name was Cuauhtlatohuac, 'The Eagle Who Speaks.' ... His lovable figure is inseparable from the Guadalupe event, the miraculous maternal manifestation of the Mother of God. ..."

Juan Pedro 🌿 See Martyrs of the Marianist Congregation.

Father of the California Missions

One of the most famous missionaries in the history of the United States, the Franciscan, Junípero Serra, blazed a trail on the west coast and bequeathed a necklace of missions for modern Californians and all American faithful. He also inspired the Serra Club, the association dedicated to promoting vocations.

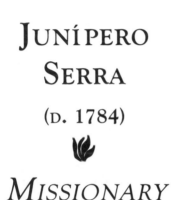

JUNÍPERO
SERRA
(D. 1784)
🌿
MISSIONARY

Junípero was born in Petra-Mallora, Majorca, on November 24, 1713. Raised devoutly, Junípero entered the Franciscans on September 14, 1730, displaying a remarkable brilliance even in his early years. He lectured on philosophy while a seminarian and then taught at the university of Palma. In 1749, Junípero taught at San Fernando College in Mexico. During his stay in Mexico, he seriously injured his leg and was lame for the rest of his life.

He asked to be sent to the Sierra Gorda Indian Mission and served there for nine years, writing a catechism in the Pamé language. He also preached missions and became popular in Mexico. In 1767, Junípero was appointed the superior of a group of fifteen Franciscans going to the missions in lower California. Two years later he went north, establishing San Fernando de Velicata and arriving in San Diego on July 1. Junípero founded the first of the California missions on July 15, 1769. Others followed: San Carlos (1770), San Antonio, San Gabriel (1771), San Luis Obispo (1772), San Francisco de Asis (1776), San Juan Capistrano (1776), Santa Clara (1777), San Buenaventura (1782), and Santa Barbara (1782).

Junípero is the Father of the California Missions and a remarkable spiritual figure in the opening eras of the New World. He confirmed more than five thousand native peoples of California, trying to provide safe havens and civilizing processes considered necessary at the time. Because his missionary foundations overshadow the other elements of his life, Junípero's brilliance and courage have been overlooked. He suffered many trials and severe physical pain throughout his ministry, but he never asked to be spared from his labors. Absolute confidence in the Providence of God was a hallmark of his vocation. Junípero died, exhausted and ill from his years of founding and preaching, at Monterey, California, on August 28, 1784.

Pope John Paul beatified Junípero on September 25, 1988, stating that this Franciscan *"sowed the seeds of Christian faith amid the mountainous changes wrought by the arrival of European settlers in the New World. . . . In fulfilling this ministry, Father Serra showed himself to be a true son of St. Francis. Today his example inspires in a particular was the many Serra Clubs around the world, the members of which do so much praiseworthy work in fostering vocations."*

Victim of Nazi Concentration Camp

German-Catholic priests, religious, and laypeople suffered at the hands of the Nazis during the era of World War II. These Germans would not surrender Catholic truths to the Nazis and were punished as a result. One of the martyrs of that era, Karl Leisner, went to Dachau concentration camp. But within this enclave of horror, he was ordained to the priesthood and celebrated a secret first Mass, despite his sufferings.

KARL LEISNER

(D. 1945)

RELIGIOUS

Karl (Carol) Leisner was born on February 28, 1915, in Rees, Germany, and was raised in the faith, showing an early interest in aiding Catholic young people. While a seminarian in Munster, Karl tried to teach catechism to the young, and the Nazis took him out of the seminary and forced him into six months of compulsive labor on agricultural settlements. The Gestapo also raided his home and confiscated his personal papers.

Karl was ordained a deacon by Bishop von Galen in 1939 and was then arrested. He was confined to Freiburg, Mannheim, and then Sachsenhausen for criticizing Adolph Hitler. On December 24, 1941, he was sent to Dachau. For three years he endured life in the camp. Then, on December 17, 1944, he was ordained in secret by the French bishop Gabriel Piquet, who had been admitted to Dachau with the help of local religious authorities. One week later, Karl was able to celebrate his first Mass.

On May 4, 1945, Dachau was taken by Allied forces, and Karl was released. He was so ill that he was placed in a sanitarium in Planegg, near Munich. He died there of tuberculosis on August 12, 1945.

Pope John Paul II beatified Karl on June 23, 1996, with his fellow German martyr, Bernard Lichtenberg, announcing: *"Christ is the Way. Bernard Lichtenberg and Karl Leisner bore witness to this at a time when many people*

*had lost their way and, because of opportunism or fear, had gone astray. Who-
ever observes the way of the two martyrs knows that their martyrdom was no
accidental stroke of misfortune along life's journey, but a final and inevitable
consequence of a life lived in following Christ.*

*"Even in their youth both of them set out on the way in which God had
called them and on which he wanted to accompany them. 'Christ, you have
called me. I say decisively and with conviction: here I am, send me' wrote Karl
Leisner at the beginning of his theological studies. He, who was very early to
recognize the anti-Christian nature of the ruling party, felt called, through his
desired service as a priest, to show people the way to God and to make no
concessions to the so-called 'popular world view.'"*

Mohawk Mystic of North America

The Lily of the Mohawks and a maiden and mystic of the American wilderness, Kateri Tekakwitha is one of the true holy of North America long before the United States came into existence. A soul chosen by God in the wilderness, Kateri stands as a consummate mystic and contemplative.

KATERI

TEKAKWITHA

(D. 1680)

MYSTIC

She was born at Ossernenon,
Auriesville, New York, circa 1656, the
daughter of a Mohawk warchief and
an Algonquin Christian woman, named
Kahenta. Kateri was orphaned at the
age of four when her parents died in
an epidemic of smallpox that left her
with a disfigured face and damaged
eyesight. An uncle took care of Kateri,
and she was treated kindly and raised
as a high-ranking Mohawk maiden by
the powerful older women of the tribe.
Her refusal of marriage offers, how-
ever, distressed her family and strained their relationships because Indian maid-
ens normally looked forward to the married state.

When a missionary, Father Jacques de Lamberville, arrived in Kateri's
village, she displayed unusual virtue and astounded him by asking for baptism.
Her open Catholic faith and contemplative nature added to the strain with her
people, and Kateri was subjected to abuse. To save her life, she fled to the
Christian community of Sault Sainte Marie near Montreal, four hundred miles
away, walking there under the protection of Christian Mohawk and Iroquois
warrior escorts.

In the safety of the Christian missions, Kateri flowered in prayer and in
holiness. She endured many trials, including a false accusation by a jealous
woman, but she remained steadfast in her devotion. She received her First Com-

munion on Christmas Day, 1677, and this union sped her mystical graces. Actually, Kateri was a mystery to her fellow Native Americans and to the missionaries who were trying to guide her toward perfection. She was so advanced spiritually that she stood as a contradiction to the wild lands and the primitive demands of the North American continent.

In 1679, Kateri took a private vow of chastity, dedicating herself to Christ. However, when she asked to become a nun, her request was answered with a gentle derision, as the concept of Native American vocations seemed totally alien to the Europeans.

Kateri died at Caughnawaga, Sault, Canada, on April 17, 1680. As she laid in state, her face glowed and all the blemishes disappeared. Two French trappers lovingly made her coffin, and word quickly spread: "the saint is dead." Kateri was declared venerable by Pope Pius XII (r. 1939-1958).

Pope John Paul II beatified Kateri on June 22, 1980, and at the ceremony she was recognized as a unique American who symbolized the flowering of the faith in the New World. Kateri was honored for her mystical graces, suffering, and loyalty to the Church on earth.

Missionary and Foundress of Xavier University in New Orleans

One of the wealthiest women in America, Blessed Katherine Marie Drexel offered her fortune, her life, and the total commitment of her heart for the benefit of others. Her apostolate confounded her own generation and set into action heroic religious dedication.

She was born in Philadelphia on November 26, 1858, the second daughter of Francis A. Drexel and Hannah, who died one month later. Francis married Emma M. Bouvier, who was Catholic and who raised Katherine and her sister in the faith. Katherine made her debut in Philadelphia Society in 1879, but was inclined toward the religious life. Her stepmother, Emma, died that same year, and Katherine's father died in 1901. As a result, Katherine and her sister each received an inheritance amounting to one thousand dollars a day.

In 1886, Katherine became ill and went to Germany to recover at a spa. While there, she recruited European priests and

KATHERINE MARIE DREXEL

(D. 1955)

FOUNDRESS

nuns for the American Indian missions, having recommended the establishment of a Catholic Bureau for such endeavors. When she had an audience with Pope Leo XIII (r. 1878-1903), Katherine was told to become a missionary. The following year she built schools in the Dakotas, Wyoming, Montana,

California, Oregon, and New Mexico.

In 1889, Katherine entered the Sisters of Mercy novitiate, receiving her habit on November 7 from Archbishop Ryan of Philadelphia. In 1891, Katherine professed her vows as the first member of the Sisters of the Blessed Sacrament for Indians and Colored People. She opened a novitiate, and by the end of the year, at Cornwall Heights near Philadelphia, there were twenty-one religious in the congregation. The first mission was St. Catherine's in Santa Fe, New Mexico. Other missions and schools followed, including Xavier University in New Orleans. The preliminary approval of the congregation was given by Pope St.

Blessed Katherine Drexel

Pius X (r. 1903-1914) in 1907. Katherine instituted a fourth vow in the congregation, beside those of poverty, chastity, and obedience. Katherine vowed "to be the mother and servant of the Indians and Negro races according to the rule of the Sisters of the Blessed Sacrament, and not to undertake any work which would lead to the neglect or abandonment of the Indian and Colored races." She also received prudent counsel on religious affairs from a contemporary, St. Francis Cabrini.

Elected superior general, Katherine continued to expand the scope of her congregation's labors. In 1912, while in New Mexico, she contracted typhoid fever and was forced to spend time recuperating. She recovered, and in 1915 founded Xavier University in New Orleans, the first U.S. Catholic institution of higher education for Blacks.

Katherine did not stop her many projects or the dispensing of her millions of inherited dollars until 1935, when a heart attack forced her to retire as superior. She went to the convent infirmary to pray and to mature in the contemplative life. She died on March 3, 1955, in Cornwell Heights.

Pope John Paul II beatified Katherine on November 20, 1988, calling her *"A woman of lively faith, deeply committed to the truth revealed by Christ, the truth she knew so well because she constantly listened to Christ's voice . . . in her life of exceptional apostolic service, God has shown forth the riches of his mercy and grace, and his power to achieve great things in human weakness. . . . In a remarkable way Blessed Katherine imitated Jesus. . . ."*

Martyred Chilean Teenager

A martyred virgin teenager of Chile, Blessed Laura Vicuña stands as a symbol of purity in the modern world and as an example for victims of injustice and cruelty tolerated in some cultures. She was born in Santiago, Chile, on April 5, 1891. Soon after, her father had to flee to the Andes Mountains because of political upheavals, taking Laura and her mother, Mercedes, into hazardous exile. He died when Laura was only three, and Mercedes became the mistress of a local *hacienda* (ranch), owner, one Manuel Mora.

LAURA VICUÑA

(D. 1904)

🔥

MARTYR

Laura attended the Salesian mission school at the age of eight with her sister, Julia. Even then Manuel would try to molest Laura when he was drunk. She made her First Communion when she was ten, already afraid of Mora because he was focusing his lewd desires on her. When she fought off his first assault, Mora refused to pay for her school tuition. The Salesian Sisters educated Laura for free, because of her piety and her courage.

On Easter Sunday, 1902, Laura was comforted by Bishop John Caglicro, as she offered her life to God for her mother's conversion. The following winter she became very ill, and Mercedes left Mora's *hacienda* in order to provide Laura with care and protection. They lived in Junion de los Andes, Argentina.

On January 14, 1904, Manuel Mora arrived on their doorstep to demand Laura's surrender to his lusts. When she refused him, he whipped and kicked her and then put her across her saddle to carry his to his *hacienda*. By this time the people of the area were watching him, so he threw Laura's unconscious body into the gutter and left. She lingered until January 22, 1904, when she died of severe internal injuries. Just before she died, Laura told her mother that she had given her young life to bring about a conversion in Mercedes. Laura's mother reformed and became a devout Catholic again.

Pope John Paul II beatified Laura on September 3, 1988, in Turin, Italy, calling her the *"Eucharistic flower of Junin de Los Andes, whose life was a poem of purity, sacrifice, and filial love."* The Holy Father expressed his hope that *"the tender figure of Blessed Laura, pure glory of Argentina and Chile, arouse a renewed spiritual commitment in those two great nations. . . ."*

Liberatus Weiss 🔥 **See Martyrs of Ethiopia.**

Passionist Priest and Thaumaturgist

Devoted to the Christ Child, Blessed Lorenzo Maria of St. Francis Xavier de Salvi was a Passionist missionary and thaumaturgist who healed the sick and wounded in the name of God. He was also a spiritual mentor who nurtured repentance and resolve among the faithful of his age.

LORENZO (LAWRENCE) SALVI

(D. 1856)

🔥

MISSIONARY

Lorenzo was born in Rome on October 30, 1782, the son of Antonio and Marianna Biondi Salvi. His father served as house steward for the Counts of Carpegna and raised Lorenzo devoutly. The young man was encouraged in the faith and had the honor of being confirmed by Cardinal Henry of York, the bishop of Frascati.

Lorenzo studied at the Jesuit Roman College, now the Gregorian, and entered the Passionists, taking religious vows on November 20, 1802. He was ordained a priest in Rome on December 29, 1805. As a Passionist — with the name Maria of St. Francis Xavier — he devoted himself to preaching, prayer, and study. He was also superior in various Passionist houses and a provincial consultor.

Lorenzo's consuming devotion was to the Infant Jesus. He carried the image of the Christ Child wherever he went, and he worked marvels through the image. People revered him as a holy man and as a special soul who cured the sick and wounded. His devotion to the Infant Redeemer was emulated by men and women of all classes, providing inspiration to thousands.

When Lorenzo died in Viterbo, in Capranica, on June 12, 1856, the faithful of the region mourned his passing. His remains were enshrined at Sant' Angelo di Vetralla, where they became a source of devotion and a pilgrimage destination.

Pope John Paul II beatified Lawrence on October 1, 1989, announcing: *"Blessed Lorenzo Salvi, a man of God, not only in intense prayer, but also in untiring dedication to the priestly ministry . . . Blessed Salvi succeeded in being a master of the spiritual life for many people who listened to him in his preaching, in the confessional, in spiritual direction."*

Model of Episcopacy

The fourth bishop of St. Hyacinthe, Canada, Blessed Louis Zephyrinus Moreau labored in the diocesan field of the Church in the New World. As a priest and a prelate, he transformed the normal duties of the episcopacy into sanctifying graces for Canada. A native of the New World, he understood the dimensions of needs and brought a heroism to his labors, serving one and all with tact and grace.

LOUIS ZEPHYRINUS MOREAU

(D. 1901)

BISHOP

Louis was born in Bécancour, Canada, on April 1, 1824, and he grew up in that richly Catholic community, receiving the grace of a religious vocation. He entered the local seminary, completed his studies, and was ordained. Louis was assigned to various ministries and was appointed secretary to the bishop of the diocese in 1852. He was named bishop of St. Hyacinthe and was consecrated on January 16, 1876.

Louis served St. Hyacinthe with remarkable charity and zeal. He dedicated the new cathedral, sponsored religious communities, and promoted education throughout the diocese. Louis founded a religious congregation dedicated to St. Joseph and a unique community — the Sisters of St. Hyacinthe, dedicated to helping priests and religious in their administrative burdens to release them for religious ministries. The sisters arrived in the United States in 1929. He also visited the parishes of the diocese and served as a loving, caring pastor. He died on May 24 in St. Hyacinthe.

Pope John Paul II beatified Louis on May 10, 1987, praising him as a pioneer of the Church in the New World and a model of episcopal charity.

Founder of the Brothers of Charity and the Sisters of St. Elizabeth

Also called Louis or Ludovico of Casoria, this blessed died on the eve of the twentieth century, in an era in which demands were being made on the Church to confront and eradicate many social ills. Louis Palmentieri was a Franciscan priest who set about founding institutions that would involve lay men and women in the apostolate of caring. Though he suffered crippling pain in the last decade of his life, he offered his physical ailments to God for graces and blessings on the charitable undertakings.

LOUIS PALMENTIERI

(D. 1885)

FRANCISCAN

Louis was born in Casoria, near

Naples, Italy, on March 11, 1814, and was baptized Archangelo Palmentieri. Raised in a devout family, he entered the Franciscans on July 1, 1832, and received the name Louis. Five years later, on June 4, 1837, he was ordained a priest and was assigned to teach philosophy, chemistry, and mathematics in the Naples Franciscan house. There he counseled students and came into contact with the secular world, which was overwhelmed with problems.

In 1847, while praying at the Church of St. Joseph in Naples, Louis had a profound mystical experience, one that he described as a "cleansing." He focused on the needs of the sick and poor as a result and responded to their needs by envisioning programs that would harness the energies of the laity. Louis started with small programs, but eventually he bought a villa on Naples' Capadimonte, where he founded a fraternity of Franciscans. He also established an infirmary for ailing Franciscans in his province.

Lay men and women who were Franciscan tertiaries came to aid Louis, and he founded the Brothers of Charity in 1859 and the Sisters of St. Elizabeth in 1862. The community members were called the *Bigi*, because of the color of the habits, *bigio,* or gray. With the aid of these religious, Louis opened a school for redeemed slaves from Africa, and members of his congregation arrived in the United States in 1919.

He suffered a terrible illness for ten years, even as he served the Franciscans and his congregations. Louis expanded his charitable works to Assisi, Florence, and Rome. He died in Naples on March 30, 1885, surrounded by his *Bigi* religious, and his Cause was opened within a year.

Pope John Paul II beatified Louis on April 18, 1993, and at this ceremony, Louis was revered for his Franciscan spirit of commitment and his generosity of soul. The Holy Father praised Louis as a true son of St. Francis of Assisi and as a luminary of the Order.

Foundress of the Oblates of the Sacred Heart of Jesus

LOUISA MONTAIGNAC DE CHAUVANCE

(D. 1885)

FOUNDRESS

Dedicated to the Sacred Heart and supported by a pious aunt who was inspired by her faith to start an apostolate to counteract the evils of the day, Blessed Louisa Montaignac de Chauvance devoted her life to the adoration of the Holy Eucharist and to the care of others.

Louisa was born on May 14, 1820, in Le-Havre-de-Grace, France, the daughter of a wealthy financier, Aimée, and his wife Anne de Ruffin Montaignac de Chauvance. Louisa was sent to a boarding school at age seven, and there she developed a profound devotion to the Sacred Heart of Jesus.

She was aided by an aunt at Mont Luçon when she started a group of women dedicated to restoring faith and ideals in France. This original group was formed in 1852. Louis felt drawn to the Carmelite cloister, but she made a private vow of chastity on September 8, 1843, dedicating herself to the Sacred Heart. Five years later she founded the Guild of the Tabernacle at Mont Luçon and opened an orphanage for the area.

She then founded the Oblates of the Sacred Heart of Jesus, dedicated to service and reparation, a congregation that received episcopal approbation on December 21, 1874. These sisters were dedicated to the particular ministry of giving of themselves "to renew society by their example and their holy lives." Louisa served as superior of the congregation, attracting many followers. She was elected Mother General on May 17, 1880, and she directed her sisters in operating orphanages, religious education, and in financing poorer parishes. The Oblates also conducted eucharistic adoration and retreats. She promoted devotion to the Sacred Heart and to the Holy Eucharist until her death. Louisa lived to see her congregation receive approbation from the Holy See. She died in Moulins on June 27, 1885.

Pope John Paul II beatified Louisa on November 4, 1990, declaring that Louis was *"a daughter of the Church, and a woman of the Church"* who understood that *"serving the Lord and serving the Church are the same thing."* The Holy Father added: *"Together, let us ask (her) to help us recognize the Love of the Heart of Jesus and ceaselessly remind people about it, as she was able to do so well during her entire life."*

Lucia Khambang ❦ See **Martyrs of Thailand**.

Founder of the Little Missionaries of Charity

Some holy men and women come upon the modern scene as comets of light, inspiring with love and awe all who have the privilege of seeing them at work. Blessed Luigi Orione, the beloved founder, missionary, and model of charity was just such a spectacular star of faith. He was born at Pontecurone, Italy, on June 23, 1872, and displayed a remarkable piety at a very young age. He entered the Franciscans at Voghera, but after experiencing a vision became ill and returned home. In October, 1886, Luigi went to St. John Bosco in Turin and was present at that saint's death. He was healed by St. John Bosco's corpse on funerary display.

Entering the seminary in Tortona, Luigi was ordained on April 13, 1895. While completing his studies, Luigi displayed concern for the poor and the aban-

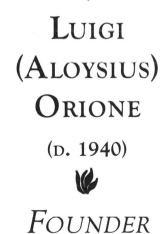

LUIGI (ALOYSIUS) ORIONE

(D. 1940)

❦

FOUNDER

doned. He opened San Luigi House at San Bernardino in 1893. Six years later, he founded the Hermits of Divine Providence and the Ladies of Divine Providence, as well as an orphanage in Rome. He was already displaying a gentle, contagious, joy of spirit and caring, one that would bring his many projects to fruition. Luigi was a true son of St. Bosco, and he carried the saint's legacy of charity to the world.

His patron was Pope St. Pius X (r. 1903-1914) in founding the Little Missionaries of Charity. Dedicated to the Blessed Virgin Mary, Luigi also erected a Marian shrine at Tortona. The local Catholics protected the shrine in a period of political unrest. The washerwomen and their allies halted any attempt by anti-Catholic forces to harm the holy structure.

Luigi did not remain at the headquarters of his congregation but went to new sites to personally give missions and to promote the faith. In 1921, he went to Brazil and in 1936, to Cardiff, Wales. Luigi visited the United States on two separate occasions, founding missions and charitable institutions and inspiring Americans with his Christian joy and concern for the suffering of the modern world. He died, exhausted by his labors, in San Remo, Italy, on March 12, 1940, mourned by thousands.

Pope John Paul II beatified Luigi on October 26, 1980, declaring that the new blessed was a giant among the apostles of charity, serving as an insignia of Christ in the modern world and the bearer of Christ's redemptive mercy. Luigi was hailed as Don Orione, a true spiritual son of St. John Bosco.

Founder and Apostle of Charity

The weak and abandoned of life have enjoyed few champions through the centuries, but Blessed Luigi Scrosoppi spent his every waking hour in the service of the defenseless. He also enlisted the aid of other dedicated individuals to carry this ministry into the world.

Luigi was born in Udine, Italy, on August 4, 1804. Receiving the grace of a vocation to the priesthood, he was ordained at age twenty-three. Luigi began his apostolate for the poor and the abandoned immediately, dedicating his priestly life to their welfare. He founded an institute of Providence for the formation of young women and the *Opere* program for deaf-mute girls. This blessed is also revered as Aloysius of Udine.

LUIGI (ALOYSIUS) SCROSOPPI OF UDINE

(D. 1884)

PRIEST

When young women came to aid Luigi in his ministry, he founded the Sisters of Divine Providence and placed the congregation under the patronage of St. Cajetan. Luigi also entered the Congregation of the Oratory of St. Philip Neri, and the Oratory served as a center for his labors. He taught love of Christ, loyalty to the pope and the Church, and total dedication to "the little ones," the vulnerable of society. Luigi spent his entire life aiding others, but his apostolate was founded upon his deep spirituality and his devotions. He also gave his family fortune to the poor. He died at Udine on April 3, 1884, mourned by the entire region.

Pope John Paul II beatified Luigi on October 4, 1981, declaring that Luigi and the other holy men and women honored that day, *trusted in the Lord, they invoked him, sure of his clemency and mercy. . . . At the summit of their thoughts above everything, they put charity. . . ."*

Salesian Martyr of China

This Salesian protomartyr and bishop was a defender of purity, even in the face of peril. With Blessed Callistus Caravario, Blessed Luigi Versiglia met his death with honor and with an extraordinary concern for others.

Luigi was born on June 5, 1873, at Oliva Gessi, Italy, and was a lively lad. Entering John Bosco's Oratory, he spent three years there. He then entered the Salesians in 1886, studying for the priesthood at the Gregorian in Rome. He received his doctorate in 1893 and became master of novices.

In 1905, Luigi was sent to the Salesian mission in China, serving as superior of six missionaries there. He opened a school for more than fifty pupils and fostered Gregorian chant. The 1910 revolution in China forced the Salesians to go to Hong Kong and then to Heung Shan, next to Macao. This was a particularly dangerous mission, as the region was in the control of pirates.

LUIGI (ALOYSIUS) VERSIGLIA

(D. 1930)

BISHOP

Luigi was consecrated a bishop on January 9, 1921, and headed the Macao missions. Upon arriving there in 1912, he established a Christian community and two leper colonies, and he traveled on foot, on water, and by horseback to reach mission outposts. On February 24, 1930, Luigi set out with Father Callisto Caravario on a mission voyage. The next day pirates boarded the ship, and the sainted bishop and his companion had to defend the young women sailing with them.

The women were not harmed because of his impassioned intervention, but Luigi and his companion were taken on shore by the pirates. When it became obvious that the pirates intended to kill them, Luigi pleaded for Father Callisto, saying: "I am an old man, kill me; but he is still young, spare him." The pirates ignored the pleas and shot them both on February 25, 1930, at Li

Thau Tsieu, China. Luigi's remains were enshrined in the cathedral at Lin Kong-How when they were recovered. The Communist Red Guards vandalized his tomb after the Communists gained control.

Pope John Paul II beatified Bishop Luigi with Callisto Caravario on May 15, 1983, announcing that the martyrs followed in the footsteps of Christ and the saints. *"The two martyrs' acts of supreme love finds find their broader significance in the framework of that evangelical ministry which the Church carries out on behalf of the great and noble Chinese people, beginning from the times of Father Matteo Ricci. In fact, in every age and in every place martyrdom is an offering of love for the brethren and especially for whose benefit the martyr offers himself. The blood of the two new blesseds is therefore is at the foundation of the Chinese Church, as the blood of Peter is at the foundation of the Church of Rome. We must therefore understand the witness of their love and their service as a sign of the profound harmony between the Gospel and the highest values of the culture and spirituality of China. In this witness, the sacrifice offered to God and the gift of self made to the people and to the Church of China cannot be separated.*

"Monsignor Versiglia and Don Caravario, following Christ's example, have perfectly embodied the ideal of the evangelical shepherd who is at once a 'lamb' (cf. Rev 7:17) 'who lays down his life for his flock' (Jn (10:11), the expression of the Father's mercy and tenderness but at the same time the lamb 'who sits on the throne' (Rev 7:17): victorious 'lion' (cf. Rev 5:5), courageous father for the cause of truth and justice, defender of the weak and the poor, victor over the evil of sin and death.

"Therefore today, little more then half a century from their slaughter, the message of the new blesseds is clear and relevant. When the Church proposes some life model for the faithful, it does so also consideration of the particular pastoral needs of the time in which such proclamations take place." (See also Callisto Caravario.)

Luis Batis ❧ **See Christopher Magallanes and Companions.**

Some souls are asked by God to give up the safe things, the familiar faces and even the countries of their births in order to accomplish his Will. Blessed Magdalena Catherine Morano made these sacrifices to insure that the charitable programs of St. John Bosco would flourish. She never looked back, never complained, but adapted herself to the needs around her.

MAGDALENA CATHERINE MORANO

(D. 1908)

RELIGIOUS

Magdalena Catherine was born on November 15, 1847, in Chieri, near Turin, Italy. When she was only eight, her father and an older sister died, making it necessary for Magdalena Catherine to find small jobs to aid the family finances. However, she did not neglect her education, and in 1866 earned a diploma as an elementary school instructor. For more than a decade, Magdalena Catherine taught in Montaldo, aiding as well the local parish catechetical program. She wanted to become a religious, but she had to wait until she had earned enough money to insure her mother's continued support.

In 1878, Magdalena Catherine entered the Daughters of Mary Help of Christians, founded by St. John Bosco and María Mazzarello. In 1881, Magdalena Catherine took her first vows and was assigned to Trecastagni, Catania, Sicily, to administer as institute for women. Accepting her new life with generosity and zeal, Magdalena Catherine remained in Sicily for a quarter of a century, founding new religious houses, and educational and catechetical programs. She established catechetical classes in all of the parishes of Catania. Magdalena Catherine labored faithfully until her death in Catania on March 26, 1908.

Pope John Paul II beatified Magdalena Catherine on November 5, 1994, in Catania, declaring:

"Beloved brothers and sisters, your ancient Church, which has recently celebrated her cathedral's 900th anniversary as a place of worship, is called by circumstances today to serve the city's rebirth, mobilizing the energies which the Lord constantly renews in her, through tireless activity at the service of good. Sister Magdalena Morano worked with precisely this in mind! She, the 'born teacher,' had come from Turin, the city of Don Bosco, with her outstanding pedagogical talent and her love for God and neighbor. On this island, Sister Magdalena carried out an intense and fruitful spiritual and educational activity for the benefit of your people. For long years she made

herself one of you, becoming the model of faithful service to God and to her brothers and sister. Look to her, beloved faithful, the better to carry out that apostolic and missionary project which all the members of the Church in Catania are striving to promote as they listen to the voice of the Spirit and concentrate their efforts on a diligent discernment of the 'signs of the times.'"

Martyr of Mauthhausen Concentration Camp

The martyrs of the era of World War II were remarkable men and women of valor. Some endured years of horror and pain, and others were killed in sudden violence. Blessed Marcel Callo endured several forms of martyrdom before dying, but he entered the arena of suffering with a willing heart, as he explained it, "as a missionary."

MARCEL
CALLO
(D. 1945)
❦
LAYMAN

Marcel was born on December 6, 1921, in Rennes, France, one of nine children, and was baptized two days later. Educated in local schools, he was apprenticed to a printer when he was almost thirteen. Marcel also belonged to the J.O.C., the Christian Worker's Youth organization and was conspicuous for his devout nature. He maintained his job, never missed attending the sacraments, and became engaged in August, 1942.

His happiness came in the midst of the conquest and occupation of France by the forces of the Third Reich, and, only after a few months of his engagement, the full weight of Nazi oppression reached Rennes. Marcel was forced to enter the Service of Obligatory Work, a program that transported young French men to Germany as slave labor. Marcel was assigned to a factory in Zella-Mehlis, Germany. He spent his time there organizing the Christian workers and rebuilding their morale under the dangerous and often inhumane conditions of forced labor. The diets and repressive labor schedules resulted in Marcel's physical collapse, but he forced himself to continue his work and his leadership. He even arranged for a French Mass, an act that brought him to the attention of the Gestapo, the dread Nazi secret police.

In April, 1944, Marcel was arrested for being "too Catholic" and sent to Mauthausen, the Gusen 2 concentration camp called "the hell of hells" by the few who survived. There he prayed and encouraged his fellow prisoners for the five months before his death from malnutrition and related conditions on March 19, 1945.

Pope John Paul II beatified Marcel on October 4, 1987, declaring:

"Yes, Marcel met the Cross. First, in France. Then torn from the affection

of his family and of a fiancée whom he loved tenderly and chastely — in Germany, where he re-launches the J.O.C. with some friends, several of whom also died witnesses of the Lord Jesus. Chased by the Gestapo, Marcel continued until the end. Like the Lord, he loved his own until the end and his entire life became eucharist. Having reached the eternal joy of God, he testifies that the Christian faith does not separate earth from heaven. Heaven is prepared on earth in justice and love. When one loves, one is already "blessed." Colonel Tibodo, who had seen thousands of prisoners die, was present on the morning of 19 March 1945; he testifies insistently and with emotion: Marcel had the appearance of a saint."

Blessed Marcel Callo

Marcellina Darowska **See Maria Marcellina Darowska.**

Founder of the Conceptionist Sisters of the Divine Heart

The obligation of the episcopal office cannot be overestimated in any era of human history, as the bishops of the Church serve as the guardians of the faith and the mentors of souls. To this end, countless bishops have dedicated their lives, enriching entire regions by their performance and zeal. Marcellus Spinola y Maestre was just such an inspired prelate, living by the motto "Either sanctity or death."

He was born on January 14, 1835, at Isla de Spinola, Spain, the son of Marquis Juan and Antonia Spinola y Maestre. Educated and raised piously, Marcellus was ordained a priest on March 21, 1864. He started his ministry by instituting charitable programs for the sick and abandoned, displaying the spirit of concern that would become the hallmark of his apostolate.

MARCELLUS SPINOLA Y MAESTRE

(D. 1906)

FOUNDER

Marcellus served as a pastor and then as a cathedral canon before becoming the auxiliary bishop of Seville in 1880, never ceasing his charitable endeavors. In 1885, he was made bishop of Caria, moving a year later to the diocese of Málaga. In 1896, Marcellus was consecrated the archbishop of Seville. He also began programs for young workers and educational institutions. He brought his concern for the poor and the sick to his new office. Prayerful and kindly, Marcellus recognized the need for a balanced in the Christian apostolate, and founded the Conceptionist Sisters of the Divine Heart. This is a congregation that combines the active and the contemplative life. He also started programs for young workers in Seville and promoted educational reforms in the archdiocese. Revered by his faithful and by the Holy See, Marcellus was designated as a cardinal. He died on January 19, 1906, before he could receive the honor in person.

Pope John Paul II beatified Marcellus on March 29, 1987, giving honor to this great episcopal leader of Spain and praising his charitable apostolate that led to the founding of his congregation of the active and contemplative ministries.

Dominican Nun

The spiritual journeys of the mystics are known to the faithful normally through their writings and recorded documents. Margaret Ebner, the "Mystic of Medingen," and a Dominican nun of Germany, was the first celebrated contemplative of that land to detail her graces and trials, thus providing a clear portrait of her soul for succeeding generations.

MARGARET EBNER

(D. 1351)

MYSTIC

She was born in Donauworth, Germany, about 1291, to a wealthy family and was given every advantage. She received the grace of a religious vocation, and she turned from comforts and privileges to become a nun. Margaret entered the Dominicans at María-Medingen, near Dillingen. She completed her novitiate training and was professed in 1306.

Six years later, Margaret became critically ill. Unable to continue her normal religious obligations, she was sent home by her superior to recover her health. Her illness lasted three years, and it took her seven years to regain her physical strength. During that decade of suffering, Margaret experienced profound spiritual gifts, including visions and revelations.

Her spiritual director, the remarkable priest Henry of Nordlingen, recognized the mystical nature of Margaret, and asked her to write of her experiences. He was away from Medingen at the time. From 1332 to 1351, she carried on an elaborate correspondence with her spiritual director, the first collection of this type in Germany. Margaret died at Medingen on June 20, 1351.

Pope John Paul II beatified Margaret on February 24, 1979, praising the devotions and endurance of the Mystic of Medingen, who was showered with many graces and persevered on a spiritual journey that led to union with Christ. Margaret was the first person beatified in the pontificate of Pope John Paul II.

Franciscan Tertiary

The mystics of this world normally live in convents or cloisters, hidden and dedicated to their religious commitments. Some such souls receive mystical gifts, and they are called upon to remain in the world, in the normal settings, where they endure unique trials. Marguerite Bays was a mystic and a stigmatic who lived in in the nineteenth century. She was not a member of a cloistered religious order, nor did she recite litanies in cloistered halls. Marguerite's convent was her own home, and she lived as a Third Order Franciscan, surrounded by everyday individuals who did not understand or appreciate her in many ways.

She was born at Siviriez (Pierroz), in Fribourg Canton, Switzerland, on September 8, 1815. Baptized the next day, she was raised in the faith, being confirmed in 1823 and making her First Communion at the age of eleven. Four

MARGUERITE (MARGARET) BAYS

(D. 1879)

VICTIM SOUL

years later Marguerite was apprenticed as a dressmaker. When her parents died in 1856 she ran the household, caring for her brother until he married. The introduction of her brother's wife into the house caused Marguerite considerable pain, as the woman appears to have disliked or even resented her. Marguerite maintained her spiritual life, despite the daily abuse. She continued to serve her parish as a catechist and joined to the Society for the Propagation of the Faith.

In 1853, Marguerite suffered cancer of the intestines but was miraculously cured on December 8, 1854. She then received the stigmata, the wounds of Christ, and experienced a deep mystical union. She was a true mystic, chosen as a victim soul and as a receptor of many graces. Many people came to see Marguerite and were inspired by her devotion and sufferings. Her remarkable spiritual advancement was evident, and she displayed courage, fidelity to the faith, and profound graces.

Marguerite had always asked to die on the feast of the Sacred Heart. She expired on June 27, 1879, the octave of the feast, and her funeral was celebrated with joy by the local Swiss, who celebrated because they had buried a saint.

Pope John Paul II beatified Marguerite on October 29, 1995, observing:

"The mission lived by Marguerite Bays is the mission incumbent upon all Christians. . . . Without leaving her country, she nevertheless kept her heart open to the dimensions of the universal Church and world."

Martyr for Purity

The mature Christian soul is not faced with day-to-day decisions about truth, virtue, or morality. These issues confront such souls, but they are not matters that have to be mulled over or debated because Christian doctrines chart a steady course and dictate a response that cannot be blurred by modern sophistry. The mature soul reacts to all things as a mirror of Christ, even in times of peril. Maria Clementine Annuarite Nengapete is a symbol of such maturity, and she is revered as the Martyr of Zaire, Africa.

MARIA CLEMENTINE ANUARITE NENGAPETE

(D. 1964)

MARTYR

Maria Clementine was born in Matali, Wamba, in Upper Zaire, on December 29, 1939. Her family was not Christian, but in time she and her mother and sister were attracted to the faith. They took instruction at their local mission and all three women were baptized in 1943.

Maria Clementine was devout from her earliest days as a convert, and she realized that she had received the grace of a religious vocation. With her mother's blessing, María Clementine entered the Holy Family Sisters at Bafwabaka at age fifteen. Completing her novitiate training and demonstrating spiritual maturity and generosity, she was professed in the religious life on August 5, 1959.

Maria Clementine continued to serve as a Holy Family Sister even as tragic consequences of political unrest engulfed her native land. On December 1, 1964, Maria Clementine was confronted by military troops led by a Colonel Olombe at Isiro. The colonel was attracted to Maria Clementine and made advances, which she rebuffed in the name of Jesus. Angered, the colonel demanded that Maria Clementine surrender to his desires. When she refused, the colonel killed her. She was instantly recognized as a martyr of purity in Zaire.

Pope John Paul II beatified Maria Clementine on August 5, 1985, in Zaire, Africa, praising the virginal purity of this blessed. Maria Clementine symbolizes the strength and courage of the Church in Africa. Her maturity of purpose and her devotedness to her Divine Spouse were honored in the joyful ceremonies.

from *Faces of Holiness*

Blessed Maria Clementine

Mystic of the Breviary

Called a "Mystic of the Breviary," Blessed María Angela Astorch was a Poor Clare Capuchin nun who evolved spiritually through prayer and liturgical celebrations that served as guideposts for her mystical union. This careful adherence to the liturgical life of the Church, and her own intellectual brilliance, allowed María Angela to mature in the spiritual realms and to serve as a teacher for other gifted souls.

MARÍA
ANGELA
ASTORCH
(D. 1665)

RELIGIOUS

She was born in Barcelona, Spain, on September 1, 1592, and was raised piously in the profound Spanish tradition. Entering the Poor Clare Capuchins in Barcelona, María made her novitiate and was professed. She demonstrated such religious perfection that she was made novice mistress, superior of the formation of professed nuns, and then abbess.

She came to the attention of many in Spain in this capacity because she was a brilliant woman who had studied ecclesiastical writers and sacred texts. Above all, María Angela had gained critical insight into the Divine Office — the Breviary or liturgical schedule of prayers and hymns recited daily in monasteries by priests and religious. Such prayers and hymns depict the unique spiritual adventures open to each human soul. María Angela used such knowledge to understand the individuals with whom she came in contact. She died in Murcia on December 2, 1665, mourned by all of the faithful of Spain.

Pope John Paul II beatified María Angela on May 23, 1982, declaring: *"From her we can learn to respect the ways of man and at the same time make men open to the ways of God."* The Holy Father said also: *". . . she was able to respect the individuality of each person, helping the one concerned 'to keep in step with God' which means something different for each one. In this way, her profound understanding did not become inert tolerance."*

Religious Catechist

Bearing trials and ills with a smiling face is not a widespread virtue in this or any other age. Embracing one's own death with joy is not something witnessed often, either. Blessed María Antonia Bandrés y Elósegui, a beautiful Spanish nun of the twenti-

MARÍA ANTONIA
BANDRÉS Y ELÓSEGUI
(D. 1919)

RELIGIOUS

eth century, thus came upon the world as both a surprise and a contradiction.

She was born in Tolosa (Guipúzcoa), Spain, on March 6, 1898, the second of fifteen children of Romón Bandrés and Teresa Elósegui. María Antonia was educated by the Daughters of Jesus, founded by Blessed Cándida María of Jesus. Throughout her childhood, María Antonia demonstrated intense charity, taking on labors seldom performed at the time.

She entered the Daughters of Jesus, as Blessed Cándida had predicted, on December 8, 1915, in Salamanca, and she was professed on May 31, three years later. Soon after, María Antonia became very ill. She displayed such serenity and joy, that people inside and outside of her community spoke of her often. María Antonia had declared: "How mistaken we are about life! This, yes, this is what dying means." María Antonia died on April 27, 1919, in Salamanca, singing the praises of Mary, Mother of Mercy.

Pope John Paul II beatified María Antonia on May 12, 1996, with Blessed Cándida María of Jesus Cipitria y Barriola. The Holy Father declared:

"One day Mother Cándida said to a student at her school in Tolosa, 'You will be a Daughter of Jesus.' The young girl was María Antonia Bandrés y Elósegui, who today is raised to the glory of the altars with her foundress. In love with Jesus, she enabled others to love him as well. As a catechist, an instructor of working people, missionary in her desire since she was already a religious, she spent her short life loving, serving, and sharing with others. United to Christ in her sickness, she left us an eloquent example of participation in the saving work of the Cross. The witness of life given by these two blesseds fills the Church with joy and should inspire their congregation, which has spread to many countries in Europe, America, and Asia, to follow their rich teachings, the model of their self-giving and their persevering fidelity to the charism received from the Spirit."

Carmelite Foundress

MARÍA OF JESUS CRUCIFIED BOUARDY

(D. 1878)

RELIGIOUS

In the modern controversies of the Middle East, the intensely fervent Catholic populations of many Arab lands are forgotten. The faithful of these nations have served the Church through the centuries and have revitalized the Catholic life in their areas through their sacrifices. Blessed María of Jesus Crucified Bouardy is one of these forgotten spiritual giants. Called the "Little Arab," she was a Carmelite foundress sometime known as María of Pau or Mariam.

María was born in Abelin, modern Israel, on January 5, 1846, one of thirteen children, and the only surviving offspring of the family. Orphaned at age three, María was adopted by a caring uncle and taken to Alexandria, Egypt, where she was trained as a domestic servant. Interiorly, she was being transformed by divine grace. María had her first vision at age thirteen.

She worked for a Muslim family and was treated kindly, but later was attacked by one of them when she refused to convert. María was miraculously cured of the wounds that she received from this brutal assault and went on to serve as a domestic. She worked for families in the cities of Alexandria, Jerusalem, and Beirut. Hired by the Nadjar family, María accompanied them to France, and there she discovered her own religious vocation. She entered the Carmelite monastery at Pau and made her novitiate.

In 1870, María was sent with other Carmelites to Mangalore, India, to start a new foundation. A year later she was professed as a lay sister, but her mystical experiences were beginning to appear in obvious ways. She bore the stigmata, levitated at prayer, and had visions. She was considered a prophetess by many, but she referred to herself as "the Little Nothing." The Carmelites sent her back to Pau, France, to ease her life, and she remained there until 1875.

In that year, María was sent to Bethlehem, Israel, to found a Carmel in that holy city. She also founded a Carmel in Nazareth. There she broke her arm, which became gangrenous. María died of the infection in Bethlehem on August 26, 1878.

Pope John Paul II beatified María on November 13, 1983, praising her fidelity, courage, and sacrifices, and asking her intercession for peace in her home region, where the Catholic Faith has long glorified God and has provided much needed charity and good.

Pioneer of Catholic Action

Life is a diverse combination of experience, the "times" or "seasons" of the Bible (Eccl 3:1), that bring joy and sorrow into the human heart. Blessed María Domenica Brun Barbantini endured many changes of roles in her own lifetime, and she discovered that such events led to wisdom and to union with God.

María Domenica was born in Lucca, Italy, on January 17, 1789. Educated in the faith, she married at age twenty-two but was widowed six months later, while expecting her first child. On the night that her husband died, María Domenica vowed to serve God alone for the rest

MARÍA DOMENICA BRUN BARBANTINI

(D. 1868)

FOUNDRESS

of her life. She gave birth to a son and carried on the family business while beginning an apostolate to the poor of the area.

María Domenica buried her son, who died after a brief illness at the age of eight. She continued her labors, and even before her son died she had formed the Pious Union of the Sisters of Charity to expand her apostolate. For a time, María Domenica resided in the local Visitandine convent, but in 1829, advised by Father Antonio Scalibrini, the Superior General of the order of St. Camillus, she founded a new congregation. The Sisters Servants of the Sick of St. Camillus, her congregation, received archdiocesan approval in 1841.

María Domenica was a pioneer in Catholic action in her era, introducing innovative programs to aid those in need. She died in Lucca on May 22, 1868.

Pope John Paul II beatified María Domenica on May 7, 1995, announcing:

"We rediscover the vigilant and caring image of the Good Shepherd in the newly Blessed Mother María Domenica Brun Barbantini, who, aware of having become "a new creature" in Christ's sacrifice, did not hesitate to respond to divine grace with a love expressed in daily service to her needy brothers and sisters. She bequeathed to her spiritual daughters a heritage and a mission which is very timely and precious. A practical Gospel love for the lowliest, the marginalized, the afflicted; a love expressed in acts of caring and Christian consolation, of generous dedication and tireless closeness to the sick and the suffering. The power and truth of the words of Jesus, who asked to be loved and served in the persons of his brothers and sisters who are hungry, thirsty, naked, strangers, sick and in prison, shine out in this apostolic and missionary task."

Missionary to Ecuador

The modern world is still blessed by missionaries who set sail toward uncertain futures in order to minister to those in need. In the last century, and even today, stalwart souls say goodbye to family and friends and brave the challenges of transplanting themselves for God. María Bernarda Butler was just such a soul.

MARÍA BERNARDA BUTLER

(D. 1924)

FOUNDRESS

She was born in Auw, Aargau, Switzerland, on May 28, 1848, the daughter of a local peasant family. Matured in the faith, María Bernarda entered the Franciscan convent of María Hilf in Altstätten, Switzerland, and was professed in 1869. She became novice mistress and then superior, serving until June, 1888, when she and six companions went to Portoviejo, Ecuador. In Chone, Ecuador, she founded the Franciscan Missionaries of Mary Help of Christians.

Forced to leave Ecuador because of difficulties, María Bernarda set out again with fifteen sisters and reached Bahia. They were then invited into Cartagena, Colombia, by Bishop Eugenio Biffi, who provided them with a wing of the women's hospital, *Obra Pie*. María Bernarda centralized her congregation there and founded houses in Colombia, Austria, and Brazil.

The congregation was dedicated to the spiritual and physical care of the poor and the sick. Devoted to the Holy Trinity and the Passion of Christ, María Bernarda chose the Blessed Virgin Mary as patroness of her religious community. She died at Cartagena, Spain, on May 19, 1924.

Pope John Paul II beaitified María Bernarda on October 29, 1995, announcing: *"As a perfect daughter of St. Francis of Assisi, she wished to serve God by serving her brothers and sisters. Her generosity was admirable. She radically detached herself from everything and risked her life for Christ, since her greatest wish was to proclaim the Lord to the ends of the earth."*

Patroness of Tuscany

Devotion to the Sacred Heart has served as the foundation of many saintly apostolates in the modern world. Christ Crucified has called men and women of generosity and daring to serve the abandoned and suffering, and the human condition has been enhanced because of their magnanimous response. María Margaret Caiani was one of the chosen laborers of Christ and the Sacred Heart.

MARÍA MARGARET CAIANI

(D. 1921)

FOUNDRESS

She was born in Poggio a Caiano, Italy, on November 2, 1863, the third child of Jacob and Luisa Caiani. Called Marianna Rosa by her family, María was devoted to prayer at a very young age. Her father died in 1884, and María had to work in the family shop until 1890, when her mother passed away. María was then free to respond to a religious vocation.

She and several other young women tried to enter several local convents but chose not to remain in any of them. Anxious to accomplish God's Will, they opened a school in Poggio a Caiano, and other young women joined them in their apostolate. This group became the Franciscan Minims of the Sacred Heart on September 15, 1902. In 1915, María Margaret was elected Superior General for life.

María Margaret's devotion to the Sacred Heart led her to serve the people of Tuscany with great generosity and care. Her congregation aided the elderly, military wounded, children, rural families, and the poor. She expanded the labors of her sisters to meet new needs, and in 1920 revised the congregation's constitution, aggregating the Minims to the Order of Friars Minor. María Margaret died on August 8, 1921, and was declared Venerable in 1986.

Pope John Paul II beatified her on April 23, 1989, declaring: *"Blessed María Margaret Caiani made an option for Christ Crucified, whom she loved in the symbol of his divine Heart. She loved him in the needy, the least, and the smallest."*

Carmelite Cloistered Nun

The Carmelite cloistered nuns raised to the altars of the Church during the pontificate of John Paul II are a remarkable group of women who demonstrate not only spiritual maturity in contemplation but intellectual prowess. These were not retiring, shy women but vibrant and dynamic individuals who had skills valuable to the Church and to the world. These nuns chose Carmel and a life of "being alone with the Alone," but they served humanity.

Blessed María Sagrario Cantarero is a fine example of the Carmelites

MARÍA SAGRARIO CANTARERO

(D. 1936)

MARTYR

being discovered by the modern faithful. She was born Elvira Moragas Cantarero in Lille, Spain, on January 8, 1881, the third child of Ricardo Moragas and Isabel Cantarero. Her father served as the pharmaceutical purveyor of the royal household, and in 1886 the family moved to Madrid. María Sagrario was given a good education, and she became the first woman of Spain to earn a degree in pharmacy.

When María Sagrario's father died, she continued his work, although she was drawn to the religious life. A younger brother was dependent upon her care, and her spiritual director told her to remain in the world for a time. She was in her early thirties when circumstances allowed her to enter the Carmel of St. Anne and St. Joseph in Madrid. On December 21, 1915, she received the name María Sagrario of St. Aloysius Gonzaga. María Sagrario was solemnly professed on January 6, 1920.

Seven years later, she was elected prioress, and then served three years as novice mistress. She was elected prioress for the second time in July, 1936, just as the Spanish Civil War crashed down upon the nation. The convent was attacked by the rebel forces, and Marie Sagrario had to lead the nuns to safe havens. On August 14, however, she was arrested with a companion by an armed unit of revolutionaries.

The secret police of the rebels questioned her about the "treasures" of the convent and the location of the other nuns, but she remained serenely silent. María Sagrario was taken to the Pradera of San Isidro on August 15, 1936, and there she was shot to death.

Pope John Paul II beatified María Sagrario on May 10, 1998, declaring that this blessed *"gave up everything to live for God alone in Christ Jesus."* The Holy Father added: *". . . she found the strength not to betray priests and friends of the community facing death with an integrity for her state as a Carmelite and to save others."*

Venezuelan Mother of the Abandoned

The Holy Eucharist has long been a fount of grace and strength for the holy. Many devout men and women have been able to commit themselves to extraordinary charitable activities because of the hours spent before the Holy Eucharist. Such devotion was a hallmark of the life of Blessed María of St. Joseph Alvarado Cardozo of Venezuela.

She was born in Choroní, Venezuela, on April 25, 1875, and was baptized Laura Evangelista. The faith was important to her family, and María of St. Joseph made her First Communion at age thirteen. She added to the occasion by making a private vow of consecration to Christ. In time, aided by her pastor, María of St. Joseph made a vow of perpetual virginity. This pastor, Father Vincente López Aveledo, stationed in Maracay, had founded a hospital, and María of St. Joseph performed charitable works there. During the smallpox epidemic of 1893, she demonstrated heroic endurance in caring for victims of the disease. María of St. Joseph was motivated throughout this ordeal by one desire, to seek Christ in sanctity.

MARÍA ALVARADO CARDOZO

(D. 1967)

FOUNDRESS

In 1901, aided by Father López Aveledo, María of St. Joseph founded the Augustinian Recollects of the Heart of Jesus, a congregation devoted to the care of the aged, orphans, and the sick. On September 13, 1903, she took her religious name, and she began her ministry, founding thirty-seven homes for the aged and orphans. Her daughters were taught: "Those rejected by everyone are ours; those no one wants to take are ours."

María of St. Joseph spent hours before the Holy Eucharist, and she made hosts to distribute freely to local parishes. She suffered a long illness and died on April 2, 1967, in Maracay, Venezuela. Pope John Paul II beatified María of St. Joseph on May 7, 1995, announcing:

"When she was a small child Blessed María Alvarado Cardozo discovered love for the Eucharist, in which she found the distinctive charism of her spirituality. She spent long hours of the day and night before the tabernacle. All her life she made with her own hands thousands of hosts in order to distribute them freely to priests. Her example is still followed by her daughters, who have offered the hosts for this Mass today. Her boundless love for Christ in the Eucha-

rist led her to dedicate herself to the service of the neediest in whom she saw the suffering Jesus. For this reason she founded in Maracay the Congregation of Augustinian Recollects of the Heart of Jesus, dedicated to the assistance of the elderly, orphans, and abandoned children. Charity, the virtue in which Mother María of St. Joseph most distinguished herself, led her to repeat constantly to her daughters: 'Those rejected by everyone are ours; those whom no one wants to take are ours.' Her deep piety, anchored in the Eucharist and in prayer, was enriched by a tender devotion to the Virgin Mary, whose name she took and whom she imitated, saying: 'I would like to live and die singing the Magnificat.' *The witness of this simple woman of our time invites everyone, especially the beloved sons and daughters of Venezuela, to live the Gospel faithfully."*

María Cecilia Cendoya Araquistain ❦ See Martyrs of the Visitation Order.

Foundress of the Servants of the Holy Trinity and the Poor

Standing firm in times of political unrest and military harassment is not something easily accomplished. The sight of armed units and the threat of punishment or death make most people turn aside or retreat. However, those compelled by charity and religious commitment do not fear such events or individuals so readily. They have a different perspective, a spiritual awareness that provides them with an uncanny or supernatural indifference to threats which allows them to perform their charitable labors in Christ's name.

MARÍA VICENTA OF ST. DOROTHY CHAVEZ OROZCO

(D. 1949)

❦

FOUNDRESS

Blessed María Vicenta of St. Dorothy Chavez Orozco was just such a soul of charity. The foundress of the Servants of the Holy Trinity and the Poor, she was born in Catija, Mexico, in the state of Michoacan, on February 6, 1867. The youngest of four children, María Vicenta was known for her devotion at an early age. In February, 1892, María Vicenta entered Holy Trinity Hospital, a small medical facility started by Father Augustin Beas in her neighborhood. While recovering from an illness, she received the grace of a vocation and a special calling to aid the sick. On July 10 of that year, she started caring for patients in the hospital. In 1895, María Vicenta took private vows with Catalina Velasco and Juana Martin del Campo. On May 12, 1905, she founded her congregation, the Servants of the Poor, renamed the Servants of the Holy Trinity and the Poor. María Vicenta became superior general in 1913, leading the congregation for three decades.

During the Mexican Revolution, María Vicenta and her sisters were in constant danger from anti-Catholic troops. She stayed in St. Vincent's Hospital in Zapotlán during its occupation by such forces in 1926 and endured vile insults and death threats until a commanding officer reprimanded his troops, praising her as a courageous model of charity. By 1942, María Vicenta had established seventeen new clinics, hospitals, and nurseries. She began to suffer eye problems that year but continued her labors until July 29, 1949, when she was no longer was able to attend chapel. Archbishop José Garibi Rivera, who became Mexico's first cardinal, was at María Vicenta's bedside celebrating Mass when she died — at the moment the Host was elevated. She died at Holy Trinity Hospital, in Guadalajara, on July 30, 1949.

Pope John Paul II beatified her on November 9, 1997, declaring her a member of charity and a symbol of the enduring Catholic Faith in the nation of Mexico.

Hospitaller Sister of Mercy

Blessed Maria Raffaella Cimatti was called "Mamma" by the wounded soldiers of World War II. Field Marshal Kesselring, commander of the German Army in Italy during the last stages of the war found her to be a compelling defender of the innocent. At age eighty-three, Maria Raffaella faced the German commander and saved her region from destruction.

Maria Raffaella was born on June 6, 1861, in Celle di Faenza, Ravenna, Italy, to a family of modest means. She had five brothers. Only two survived to adulthood, and they both became priests. Her father died in 1882, and Maria Raffaella educated her broth ers and served as a parish catechist. Her mother moved into the local rectory, and her brothers entered St. John Bosco's congregation, allowing Maria Raffaella to respond to her own call to the religious life. In 1889, she entered the Hospitaller Sisters of Mercy.

Two years later, Maria Raffaella made her religious profession, adding a vow of hospital-

MARIA RAFFAELLA CIMATTI

(D. 1945)

RELIGIOUS

ity. She was assigned as a pharmacist's assistant in Alatri and then in Frosinone. In 1921, Maria Raffaella became the superior in Forsinone and in 1928 took the same office in Alatri. She maintained that role until 1940, when she resigned as superior and asked to live as a simple religious.

In 1944, Maria Raffaella ministered to so many wounded soldiers that she became the favorite of hardened veterans who had survived the dangers of battle and now found solace in Maria's care. At age eighty-three, she labored night and day for the steady stream of wounded who were brought from the front.

Hearing word that Alatri would be bombed and reduced to rubble to stem the advance of the Allied troops, Maria Raffaella went to the German headquarters and registered her dismay to the supreme commander himself, Field Marshal Kesselring. Taken aback by the courage and the sincere concern of this venerable religious and possessed of a certain military chivalry, Kesselring accepted her demand and spared Alatri. Maria Raffaella died on June 23, 1945, in Alatri, and her Cause was opened in 1962.

Pope John Paul II beatified Maria Raffaella on May 12, 1996, declaring: " 'Blessed be God, because he has not . . . removed his steadfast love from me!' (Ps 65 [66]: 20). Divine Mercy is the key to interpreting the simple, profound spirituality of Maria Raffaella Cimatti, a religious of the Hospitaller Sisters of Mercy. Her activity was inspired by God's infinite mercy, of which the psalmist speaks, especially in her service to the poor and the suffering. This woman, who is raised to the honors of the altar today, spent herself in total consecration to God in silent daily service to the sick. She carried out her humble daily duties, as well the responsible tasks she was constantly required to fulfill, with a spirit of sacrifice and ever ready willingness, listening and accepting all those who came to her seeking advice or comfort."

Polish Educator

So many human aspirations have to be delayed or even sacrificed in this life because individuals have other obligations or lack the wherewithal to accomplish their goals readily. Almighty God, however, chooses particular souls for his Will, and he provides the means and the opportunities, sometimes after tedious delays. Blessed Maria Marcellina Darowska used such postponements and delays to mature and strengthen her faith, accepting all things as preparation for the task at hand.

She was born on January 16, 1827, in Szulaki, in the Ukraine. Her family was of Polish descent, named Kotowicz, and very devout. Prayerful, recollected,

MARIA MARCELLINA DAROWSKA

(D. 1911)

FOUNDRESS

and dutiful, Maria Marcellina hoped to enter the religious life. Her parents, however, did not promote this aspiration, and Marcellina could not go against their wishes. On his deathbed Maria Marcellina's father even made her promise that she would wed and raise a family. Accordingly, Maria Marcellina married a man named Karol Darowska in 1849. The couple had two children before Karol died, less than three years after their wedding. One child, a son, followed his father to the grave in 1853. Marcellina buried her son with his father and went to Rome, where she met Father Hieronim Kajsicwicz, who became her spiritual director. He was aware of her spiritual maturity and holiness, and he understood Maria Marcellina's religious vocation.

With the aid of her spiritual director, Maria Marcellina founded the Congregation of the Sisters of the Immaculate Conception of the Blessed Virgin Mary with Josephine Karska. Josephine died in 1860 after being stricken with typhus, and Maria Marcellina carried the burden of the new congregation alone.

In 1863, she brought her sisters to Jazlowicz, in the archdiocese of Lviv, Ukraine, where she opened a school for girls. This school proved instrumental in Maria Marcellina's ministry. With this institution she was able to influence young and old with the Church's doctrines of family life and a moral society. Countless women experienced a renewal in her schools. Maria Marcellina opened formation institutes, schools, and seven convents. She served for half a century, pioneering tuition-free schools. She died with her community at her bedside on January 5, 1911.

Pope John Paul II beatified Maria Marcellina on October 6, 1996, praised the new blessed as a valiant woman, and declared: *"She wanted to do everything so that truth, love and goodness would triumph in human life and transform the face of her beloved nation."*

Maria Teresa Fasce

(d. 1947)

Religious

Augustinian Nun

The saints have served through the centuries as insignias of holiness and perfection, instilling hope and courage in each new generation. The Italian blessed, Maria Teresa Fasce, an Augustinian nun who spent her life spreading devotion to St. Rita of Cascia, now rests beside her beloved patroness and shines as a new and radiant light of faith.

Maria Teresa was born on December 27, 1881, at Torriglia, near Genoa, Italy. In 1906, she entered the monastery of St. Rita in Casia, receiving the Augustinian habit the following year. She served as novice mistress and vicaress, and in 1920 was elected abbess for life.

Maria Teresa's special apostolate was the spread of devotion to St. Rita. Through her efforts, thousands visited the saint's basilica in Cascia. She also established an orphanage for girls, an Augustinian seminary, and St. Rita's Hospital, and sought ways in which to protect and nurture the abandoned, vulnerable, or needy of the region. During the war years, she faced the Nazis with determination and courage, denying them access to her convent and those in her care several times.

A woman of profound faith and trust, Maria Teresa suffered physically but kept silent and carried on her work. At her death, she expressed her faith exquisitely, declaring that she was not just leaving the world and her sisters but entering eternity with "faith, hope, and love." She died on January 18, 1947, and was laid to rest next to her beloved patroness, St. Rita.

Pope John Paul II beatified Maria Teresa on October 12, 1997, stating that Maria was one: *"Who lived in the constant contemplation of the mystery of Christ. . . . the Church holds her up today as a radiant example of the living synthesis between contemplative life and a humble witness of solidarity to men and women, especially to the poorest, the humble, the abandoned, and suffering."*

Maria Teresa Fasce

María Pilar Garcia **See Martyrs of Guadalajara.**

The "Strong Woman" of God

This blessed, Maria Theresa Gerhardinger, is a demonstration of the ability of one single person in the Church to make a difference. Maria Theresa was the foundress of the School Sisters of Notre Dame, a congregation now active in more than thirty-five countries of the world.

MARIA THERESA

OF JESUS

GERHARDINGER

(D. 1879)

FOUNDRESS

She was born in Stadtamhof, Germany, on June 20, 1797, the daughter of Frances and Willibald Gerhardinger, and she was baptized Caroline Elizabeth Frances. At age six, Maria Theresa entered a school conducted by the canonesses of Notre Dame. Napoleon's forces entered the area in 1809, and Maria Theresa continued her education without the canonesses, who were forced to leave. In 1812, she became a "royal teacher" at the King's School in Stadtamhof.

The death of her father in 1825 left Maria Theresa in the care of her mother, who came to live with her. On October 24, 1833, Maria Theresa, along with Maria Blass and Barbara Weinzierl, founded the School Sisters of Notre Dame with the aid of Bishop Michael Wittman. The congregation received episcopal sanction the following year. On November 16, 1835, Maria Theresa pronounced her vows in a chapel of St. Gall in Regensburg. A year later six novices entered the congregation.

Steadily building the congregation, Maria Theresa received a convent from King Louis Philippe (r. 1830-1848) in 1841. The motherhouse of the Notre Dame Sisters was thus erected in Munich. Two years later Maria Theresa's own mother died, and she suffered a severe illness. She recovered, and in 1847 sailed to America to start the new missions among the German immigrants. Baltimore became the first foundation. A second group of Notre Dame Sisters arrived in the United States in 1848, joined by yet another group the following year. Maria Theresa returned to Europe.

There she was superior general for life, receiving a decree from the Holy See in 1854. The congregation was also called the Poor School Sisters of Notre Dame at the time. She sent sisters to many lands and received awards for her aid to the wounded in the wars of the era. Maria Theresa also established a second motherhouse in Baltimore. She died in Munich on May 9, 1879, leaving more then 2,500 sisters and countless schools and missions. In Pope John Paul II beatified Maria Theresa of Jesus on November 17, 1985, and the pontiff stated:

"Maria Teresa of Jesus, a simple but determined and courageous religious, accomplished great things for mankind and the kingdom of God. In the founding of her order she showed herself a "strong woman" who did not shy away from sacrifice or difficulties of any kind in order to fulfill this work, which she always referred to as "God's work." Her order of teachers was a pioneering influence in the development of education in countless European countries and in America. The spiritual heritage of the new Blessed lives on today in some 7,500 School Sisters in Europe, North and Latin America, Asia, Oceania, and Africa. . . . May Blessed Mother Teresa of Jesus Gerhardinger continue to be a shining example and intercessor, not only for the sisters of her own congregation, but for all Christian educators as well."

María Gabriella de Hinojosa Naveros ❧ **See Martyrs of the Visitation Order.**

Albertine Servant of the Suffering

Chosen souls that emanate Christian charity attract others to the service of Christ and the needy of the world. The labors of St. Albert Chmielowski brought Maria Bernardina Jablonska to the religious life, and she became a spiritual daughter of this Apostle of Mercy in Poland.

MARIA BERNARDINA JABLONSKA

(D. 1940)

MYSTIC

Maria Bernardina was born in Pizuny, Poland, on August 5, 1878, and was raised in a devoutly religious family. Gifted spiritually and a contemplative, Maria resided in a hermitage for a time, and was called to a hidden apostolate of prayer and penance.

As she began to see the suffering around her, she followed the religious trail blazed by St. Albert Chmielowski in Poland. Drawn to his holiness, Maria Bernardina entered the Albertine Sisters, recently founded by the saint. She brought a spiritual insight and a profound awareness of human suffering to the convent. Her holiness and her abilities led to her election as superior, a role that she fulfilled with energy and prudence.

Her motto was simple: "To give, eternally to give." In the spirit of commitment and dedication, Maria Bernardina founded hospices for the sick and poor. She imbued her sisters with understanding that each human being shares in the suffering of everyone around them, and she pioneered charitable works to alleviate the needs of others. Maria Bernardina died in Krakow, Poland, on September 23, 1940.

Pope John Paul II beatified Maria Bernardina on June 6, 1997, at Zakopane, Poland, declaring: *"The Church places this devout religious before us today as an example. Her motto of life was the was the words: 'To give, eternally to give.' With her gaze fixed on Christ she followed him faithfully, imitating his love."*

Maria of the Cross Jugan ❦ **See Marie of the Cross Jugan.**

Martyr of the Nazis

Austrian Catholics, as their counterparts in Germany, protested the rise of Hitler and paid the ultimate price for their opposition to the Nazi menace. A Franciscan, Blessed Maria Restituta Kafka, was imprisoned for her defense of the crucifix, and she refused to deny her vocation to save her life.

MARIA RESTITUTA KAFKA

(D. 1943)

FRANCISCAN

She was born in Brno, now part of the Czech Republic, on May 10, 1894, baptized Helena. When her family moved to Vienna, Austria, Maria Restituta was raised in that great capital. She worked as a salesgirl and then entered nursing, which brought her into contact with the *Hartmannschwestern*, the Franciscan Sisters of Christian Charity. Maria Restituta entered that congregation in 1914, receiving her religious name.

A surgical nurse, Maria Restituta had served for two decades when the Nazis gained control of Austria. She was unrestrained in her opposition to the Nazis, calling upon the tradition that Viennese speak their minds. Maria Restituta even declared Hitler a "madman," and she retaliated against the Nazis by hanging a crucifix in every room of a new hospital wing.

When the Nazis demanded the removal of the crucifix, they also threatened Maria Restituta with dismissal. The hospital argued that they could not replace her, and the crucifixes remained on the walls. On October 28, 1942, Maria Restituta was arrested for plotting high treason against Hitler. Held as a prisoner for a time, she was offered her freedom if she would give up her religious life. She refused and was condemned to death. A petition for leniency reached the desk of Martin Bormann, one of the most powerful Nazis in the entire Third Reich. He replied merely that Maria Restituta should die to provide "effective intimidation" of those who might think about resisting.

While in prison and undergoing personal abuse, Maria Restituta distinguished herself by caring for other prisoners, including Communists, who later testified on her behalf. She was decapitated on March 30, 1943.

Pope John Paul II beatified Maria Restituta on June 21, 1998, in Vienna, announcing:

"Sister [Maria] Restituta Kafka was not yet an adult when she expressed her intention to enter the convent. . . . Because of her courage and fearlessness, she did not wish to be silent even in the face of the National Socialist regime. Challenging the political authority's prohibitions, Sister Restituta had crucifixes hung in all the hospital rooms. On Ash Wednesday, 1942, she was taken away by the Gestapo. In prison her 'Lent' began, which was to last more than a year and to end in execution. Her last words passed on to us were: 'I have lived for Christ; I want to die for Christ.' Looking at Blessed Sister Restituta, we can see to what heights of inner maturity a person can be led by the divine hand. She risked her life for her witness to the Cross. And she kept the Cross in her heart, bearing witness to it once again before being led to execution, when she asked the prison chaplain to 'make the Sign of the Cross on my forehead.' "

Foundress of the Good Shepherd Sisters in Poland

The apostolates of holy men and women in the modern world reflect the Christian tradition of mirroring Jesus to all humanity. These saints and blesseds labored to "disappear" into Christ, to become one with him, and to reflect his grace to those in need and to those hungering for spiritual truths. Knowing their own limitations as humans, the holy of the faith yearn to bring Christ to one and all, by radiating his mercy and love. Maria Karlowska followed this path of service during her life. The foundress of the Good Shepherd Sisters in Poland, she serves as a model of the imitation of Christ.

MARIA KARLOWSKA

(D. 1935)

MYSTIC

Maria was born in Kartowo, Poland, on September 4, 1865, and raised in a pious family and community. As a young woman, she developed a great devotion to the Sacred Heart of Jesus. Maria desired only to live for the Sacred Heart and to become a perfect instrument for Christ's mission in the world. She began to care for the poor and sick and concerned herself with young women in her region.

Out of this concern grew the Congregation of the Good Shepherd of the Divine Providence. Maria worked mainly in Plock, Pomerania, now considered part of Poland. Her motto was to make Christ "more visible than we ourselves." She lived to see her congregation expand and receive official approbation. Maria died in Pniewita, Poland, on March 24, 1935.

Pope John Paul II beatified Maria on June 6, 1997, at Zakopane, Poland, with Maria Bernardina Jablowska, stating that Maria Karlowska: *"worked as a true Samaritan among women suffering great material and moral deprivation. . . . Her devotion to the Savior's Sacred Heart bore fruit in a great love for people. . . . Thanks to this love she restored to many souls the light of Christ and helped them to regain their lost dignity."*

Apostle of the Divine Mercy

Trust in Divine Providence is a hallmark of many holy apostolates, in which the saints and blesseds dared all things because of their reliance upon the grace of God. Maria Faustina Kowalska stands as Poland's "Apostle of trust in God and his mercy."

MARIA
FAUSTINA
KOWALSKA

(D. 1938)

RELIGIOUS

She was born on August 25, 1905, in Glogowiec, Poland, the third child of a devout peasant family, and was baptized Helena in the parish church of Swinice, Warckie. María Faustina was pious and prayerful at an early age. She had only three years of formal education when went to live and work as a domestic in Aleksandrow, near Lodz, at age sixteen.

Even as a small child, Faustina reported seeing bright lights during her prayers at night, and this continued in Aleksandrow. One afternoon she stepped into the courtyard of her employers' home and saw it engulfed in flames. Her screams brought the mistress of the house, who didn't see flames, but did see Faustina faint. A doctor summoned by the family pronounced Faustina healthy, but Faustina resigned her position and went home. Upon her return, she announced to her parents that she desired a religious vocation. Her father refused to give his permission, even though he and Faustina's mother had long recognized an intense spirituality in their daughter.

Disheartened, Faustina took a second job as a domestic and tried to live like other girls her age. While at a dance with one of her sisters, Faustina experienced a vision of Christ suffering. This was all the prompting she needed. The next day Faustina packed her belongings and went to Warsaw. Within the year she was permitted to enter the Congregation of the Sisters of Our Lady of Mercy (1925), and served as a cook, gardener, and portess, or door-keeper, in the congregation's convents in Krakow, Plock, Poland, and Vilnius, Lithuania. Maria Faustina was kind and charitable, but throughout her life, few understood her profound spiritual interior graces. She experienced visions, prophecies, and an internal stigmata.

On the evening of February 22, 1931, Sister Faustina experienced a vision like none before. She saw Jesus, clothed in a white garment, with one hand raised in a blessing, the other touching his garment at his breast. From his breast emanated two rays — one red, the other pale. He told Faustina to " 'Paint an image according to the pattern you see, with the signature: Jesus, I trust in you.' "

Faustina was not a painter or an artist. After struggling to make herself believed, her spiritual director, Reverend Michael Sopocko, helped located an artist to do the painting, and the image of the Divine Mercy was displayed to the public for the first time on April 28, 1935. Devotion to the Divine Mercy continued to grow just as Faustina continued to grow in her union with Christ. Following the instructions of Father Sopocko, Faustina recorded her visions and prophecies in a diary, and these mystical writings have been translated into many languages. Faustina predicted the date of her own death from tuberculosis at age thirty-three — October 5, 1938.

Pope John Paul II beatified Maria Faustina on April 18, 1993, declaring: *"O Faustina, how extraordinary your life is! Precisely you, the poor and simple daughter of Mazovia, of the Polish people, were chosen by Christ to remind people of this great mystery of divine mercy!"*

María Engracia Lecuona Aramburu ❦ See Martyrs of the Visitation Order.

Co-Foundress of the Capuchins of the Divine Shepherdess

Sometimes pious works are started with vigor and dedication, only to be abandoned or left to the care of others. Individuals mean well but are not able always to complete what they begin in such earnest. If the pious work is the Will of God, he raises up the heroic souls to persevere and to accomplish the vision. María Anna Mogas Fontcuberta was the heroic

MARÍA ANNA MOGAS FONTCUBERTA

(D. 1886)

FOUNDRESS

soul chosen to guide and protect the Congregation of the Capuchins of the Divine Shepherdess.

María Anna was born in Corró de Vall, Grenollers, Spain, on January 13, 1827. Her father died when she was seven, and her mother died seven years later. María Anna was thus raised by an aunt in Barcelona. This aunt was devout and installed the faith and the practice of virtues in María Anna's daily life.

When María Anna matured in the world and in the spiritual life, she met Father Joseph Tous Soler, who was an exclaustrated Capuchin monk; a Franciscan who had been given permission to minister to people in the world. Two former cloistered Capuchin nuns were being directed by Father Soler, and they asked María Anna to assist them in founding a new congregation dedicated to the education of children. When María Anna agreed to help them, the Congregation of the Capuchins of the Divine Shepherdess was formed in 1850. Bishop Luciano Casadevail of Vich received the new community and gave them a school in Ripoli. María Anna was clothed in the habit and elected superior.

The first years were difficult ones, as the congregation lacked financial resources and commitment of the laity. The two former Capuchin nuns returned to the cloister, leaving María Anna to deal with the harsh realities of such an undertaking. She took the necessary academic tests to direct a school and began recruiting new members for the congregation.

María Anna followed the Franciscan spirit in her congregation, but her devotion to the Blessed Virgin Mary was instilled in her sisters as well. The congregation spread rapidly, and in time she went to Madrid, where she directed the congregation, which developed a second group in Barcelona. Her faith and generosity served the Church throughout Spain. María Anna died in Fuencarral, on July 3, 1886.

Pope John Paul II beatified María Anna on October 6, 1996, declaring Maria: *"knew how to respond generously to [God's intimate love for his children], and thus to yield abundant fruit. Renouncing a well-to-do social position, she forged, in union with the tabernacle and the cross, a spirituality inspired by the Heart of Christ."*

María Angela Olaizola Garagarza ❦ **See Martyrs of the Visitation Order.**

The Carmelite cloister has endured through the centuries as "the desert of souls," where men and women follow the pioneering contemplatives of the early Christian era in living penitential routines of continuing praise. Dating back to Mount Carmel and spanning the ages, Carmel calls a diverse number of individuals to the cloister, and some face dangers from political forces without shrinking from their commitments.

MARÍA MARAVAILLAS DE JESÚS PIDAL Y CHICO DE GUZMÁN

(D. 1974)

FOUNDRESS

María Maravaillas de Jesús Pidal y Chico de Guzmán was a Discalced Carmelite cloistered nun but she was also a pillar of strength in tumultuous times. She was born in Madrid, Spain, on November 4, 1891, the daughter of Luis Pidal y Mon, the marquis of Pidal, and his wife, Cristina Chico de Guzmán y Munoz. Luis was the Spanish ambassador to the Vatican at the time.

María Maravaillas was extremely devout at an early age, making a vow of chastity at age five. She matured in the faith and entered the Carmelite Monastery of El Escorial in 1920. Four years later, she and three other Carmelites founded a daughter convent in Cerro de los Angeles, and there made her solemn profession. In 1933, María Maravaillas founded another Carmel in Kottayam, India.

When the Spanish Civil War engulfed Spain in chaos and terror, María Maravaillas and her nuns found haven in an apartment in Madrid. The following year, 1937, she founded another Carmel in the Batuescas region of Salamanca. She also erected Carmels in Mancera de Abajo, Duruclo, Cabreira, Arenas de San Pedro, San Calixto, Aravaca, Talavera de la Reina, La Aldehuela, and Montemor-Torremolinas. María Maravaillas and was able to restore the damaged Carmel of the Escorial, establishing a community there when the Civil War ended. She combined all of these Carmels in an association of St. Teresa in 1972.

Throughout her life she demonstrated not only courage and practical wisdom, but the joy of her religious life. She said: "What happiness to die a Carmelite" as she died in the Carmel of Aldehuela on December 11, 1974.

Pope John Paul II beatified María Maravaillas, announcing that she was *"another shining example of holiness."* The Holy Father said also: *"A well-known person in her time, she was able to make the most of this fact to attract many souls to God. . . . She lived with heroic faith, formed in response to an austere vocation, by putting God at the center of her life."*

Maria Phon ✝ See Martyrs of Thailand.

María Poussepin ✝ See Marie Poussepin.

Heroine of Charity

One of the great hallmarks of the holiness of saints is their ability to labor quietly in their own ways for the faith by bringing hope and consolation even during the darkest and most dangerous times in history. Blessed María Rafols, called a *"Heroine of Charity"* by Pope John Paul II, lived in the Napoleonic Era, when cities and human aspirations were in ruins, all because of the ambitions of one man.

MARÍA RAFOLS

(D. 1853)

🌺

RELIGIOUS

She was born on November 5, 1781, in Villafranca del Penedés, to a simple family of modest means. Brilliant and gifted, María was sent to a boarding school in Barcelona. There she was noted for her life of solitude and prayer. When her education was completed, María joined a group of twelve women being trained by Father Juan Bonal for service in Our Lady of Grace Hospital in Saragossa. The ministry of the hospital was quite varied, as the staff cared for the sick, disabled, orphaned, and the mentally ill.

María demonstrated a profound spiritual marturity and was appointed superior at the age of twenty-three. Her youth was resented by hospital employees at first, but she earned their respect. During the occupation of Spain (1808-1813) by the forces of Napoleon Bonaparte, emperor of France, María labored in bombed ruins and had to beg for food and medicine. She even went to a French general in the nearby enemy camp, seeking his aid.

In 1825, María and her community took public vows. During the era of the Carlist Wars (the political upheaval that troubled Spain for years after the ending of the Napoleonic Wars), María was unjustly accused and imprisoned. When she was released, she retired to one of the foundling homes that she had opened. María died on August 30, 1853, in Saragossa.

Pope John Paul II beatified Maria on October 16, 1994, declaring:

"In Blessed María Rafols we contemplate God's action, which made a "Heroine of Charity" of the humble young girl who left her home in Villafranca del Penedés (Barcelona) and, in the company of a priest and eleven other young women, began a journey of service to the sick, by following Christ and, like him, giving her 'life a ransom for the many' (Mk 10:45). A contemplative in action: this is the style and message María Rafols leaves us. The silent hours of prayer in the chapel loft of Saragossa's Hospital of Grace, known as the Domus infirmorum urbis et orbis *[home for the sick of the city and the world], were*

continued in her generous service to all the defenseless collected there: the sick, the mentally ill, destitute women and children. Thus she showed that charity, true charity, has its origin in God, who is love (1 Jn 4:8). After spending the better part of her life in selfless, hidden service at the Foundling Home, where she poured out her love, self-denial and tenderness, she embraced the Cross and made her total surrender to the Lord, leaving to the Church, and especially to her daughters, the great teaching that charity never dies nor passes, the great lesson of a charity without borders, lived in the dedication of each day. All consecrated persons can see in her an expression of the perfection of charity to which they are called and to a deep experience of which the celebration of the present Synod Assembly seeks to contribute."

Patroness of Genoa

The "Little Way" of humility is a sure road to perfection for many souls. Overlooked by the prominent and the busy individuals of the world, such souls perform their simple tasks with heroic fidelity and spiritual splendor, unheralded and unsung. Blessed María Repetto, the "Holy Nun" of Genoa, Italy, was a soul involved in the "Little Way."

She was born in Voltaggio, in the northern region of Italy, on November 1, 1807, the oldest daughter of Giovanni Battista and his wife, Teresa Gozzola. She was raised by her family with a strong sense of duty, and she helped to form her eight brothers and sisters, fostering their religious vocations. Four of her sisters entered convents and a brother became a priest.

MARÍA REPETTO

(D. 1890)

RELIGIOUS

At age twenty-two, having served her family faithfully, María entered the Conservatory of Our Lady of Refuge. This religious institution was located in Genoa, and María was content to serve as an infirmarian, gate keeper, washerwoman, and general laborer of the community. She did not seek a loftier role, but her lowly status did not hide her holiness or her spiritual graces.

The people of Genoa recognized María's holiness very quickly, and the sick were brought to her for loving treatment. During the cholera epidemics of 1835 and 1854, María went to the aid of countess victims. She served these victims without fear and with extraordinary tenderness. The people of Genoa also recognized María's spiritual insight and her mystical awareness. They visited the Conservatory of Our Lady of Refuge every day, seeking María's counsel.

When María died on January 5, 1890, the entire city of Genoa went into profound mourning. Her remains were laid to rest in the chapel of the Conservatory.

Pope John Paul II beatified María on October 4, 1981, announcing: *"Right from her youth María Repetto learned and lived a great truth, which she has transmitted also to us: 'Jesus must be contemplated, loved and served in the poor, at all moments of our life.'"* The Holy Father added: *"To serve Christ's poor was a program of her Institute, a program which she carried out in fifty years of religious life, serving Jesus above all, growing in the perfection of love. . . ."*

María Anna Rivier 🌿 **See Marie Anna Rivier.**

Religious Reformer of the Bethlehemite Order

The holy city of Bethlehem remains a steady symbol of dedication, joy, and hope for the world. In Guatemala and in eighteen other nations that insignia has been refurbished by a remarkable religious congregation, and by Blessed María Encarnación of the Sacred Heart Rosal. This new blessed dedicated her life to the mystery of Bethlehem and to the way of perfection.

MARÍA ENCARNACIÓN ROSAL

(D. 1886)

FOUNDRESS

She was born on October 7, 1815, in Quetzaltenango, Guatemala, and was baptized Vicenta. Raised devoutly, María Encarnación received the grace of a religious vocation while young. By age fifteen she knew that she was called to be a nun and entered the Bethlehemites, a cloistered congregation founded in 1688 and a spiritual institution that was part of Blessed Peter Betancur's ministry.

In the Bethlehemite convent, María Encarnación found that laxities and distractions were tearing at the fabric of the cloister. She completed her novitiate training and took her vows, maturing in the spiritual life and attaining virtues. In 1855, she was elected prioress of the community and immediately set about revising the rules of the congregation. Opposed by those who preferred a less demanding way of life, María Encarnación founded a new Bethlehemite house in Quetzaltenango in 1861.

She had unique gifts of contemplation and a special devotion to the Sacred Heart of Jesus that she forged into her new community. She also practiced penance and reparation for the sins of the modern world. María Encarnación died in the odor of sanctity in Quetzaltenango (Tulcán) on August 24, 1886, joining the great Latin American friends of God.

Pope John Paul II beatified María Encarnación on May 4, 1997, declaring: *"Mother María Encarnación Rosal, the first women from Guatemala to be beatified, was chosen to continue the charism of Blessed Pedro de San Jose Betancur. . . . Giving up many things did not matter to her, as long as the essential was saved; as she said: 'May all be lost, except charity.'"*

Missionary of the Institute of Capuchin Sisters

Acts of kindness often go unnoticed by those involved in the lunatic race of business and events. Blessed María Francesca Rubatto's entire life revolved around charity, and in coming to the aid of one stricken individual, she changed her life forever and brought untold graces to the Church and to the world.

María Francesca was born in Carmagnola, Italy, on February 14, 1844, and was baptized Anna María. She lost her father when she was only four, and she was raised by her mother. María Francesca made a vow of virginity and refused any thoughts of marriage at an early age, despite her lay status. When she was nineteen, her mother died, and María Francesca moved to Turin, Italy, where she was welcomed by the noblewoman Marianna Scoffone.

MARÍA FRANCESCA OF JESUS RUBATTO

(D. 1904)

MISSIONARY

María Francesca began to teach catechism to the children of the city and to visit the sick and the poor. She continued this apostolate faithfully until 1882, when Marianna Scoffone died. María Francesca went to the Ligurian coastal region to rest and recuperate from her labors.

In Loano, just after attending Mass at the local Capuchin Franciscan church, María Francesca saw a young worker struck on the head by a stone from a convent under construction. She cleaned his wound and gave him two day's wages so that he could rest, and then went on her way. The story of the accident was repeated everywhere, and the group building the convent heard of her kindness. They asked María Francesca to enter their convent as spiritual guide, and a Capuchin Franciscan, Father Angelico Martini, convinced her to join the group a year later. Bishop Filipo Allegro named her superior of the group that became the Institute of the Capuchin Sisters of Mother Rubatto, and is now called the Capuchin Sisters of the Third Order of Loano.

In 1892, María Franciesca started missions in Montevideo, Uruguay, and in Argentina. She crossed the Atlantic ocean seven times and founded another mission in Alto Alegre with Capuchin missionaries and converts. María Francesca returned to Montevideo in 1904, intending a brief stay; however she remained in Montevideo for a year and died there on August 6, 1904. She was buried in Montevideo.

Pope John Paul II beatified María Francesca on October 10, 1993, declaring: "[Maria] *Francesca of Jesus . . . who made your life a constant service to the lowliest, witnessing to God's special love for the lowly and humble . . .*

faithfully following the footsteps of Francis, the lover of evangelical poverty, you learned not only to serve the poor, but to make yourself poor. . . ."

Silent Heroine for Church Unity

Church unity has become an imperative among many groups belonging to Christendom, as more and more followers of Christ understand the magnitude of forces arrayed against the Church. A Trappist nun, María Gabriella Sagheddu, is called "the Silent Heroine of Church Unity," one of several blesseds who sacrificed themselves that all might be one again in Christ.

MARÍA GABRIELLA SAGHEDDU

(D. 1939)

RELIGIOUS

She was born in Dorgali, Sardinia, on March 17, 1914, the daughter of a devout shepherd family in a region that bred strong-willed, resolute people of the faith. Willful and difficult as a child, María Gabriella lost her father at age three, a tragedy that had a tremendous impact on the financial and emotional stability of her family.

At age eighteen, María Gabriella experienced a profound and lasting spiritual conversion. She changed totally and began to explore the possibility of a religious vocation. At the age of twenty-one, she entered the Trappistine Monastery at Grottaferrata, now located in Viterbo, but once operating near Rome. There she made her novitiate and there she was professed in 1937.

Aware of the ongoing dissension in the Christian faith, María Gabriella offered her life for Church unity. In this heroic act, she displayed faith, courage, and hope. Pope John Paul II declared: *"This strong, little Trappistine nun . . . has taught that to foster the spiritual life and to promote great ideals, one must be prepared to pay the price personally."* María Gabriella understood the perils of modern society and the need for Christians to unite with the Holy See to achieve a true defense of the faith.

Soon after her sacrificial offer, María Gabriella was stricken physically and spiritually. She developed tuberculosis and was plagued with a profound spiritual dryness. She did not withdraw her pledge to suffer and to die for unity. All of this was endured in silence. The members of her own community remarked that María Gabriella served quietly and humbly, almost unnoticed in the daily monastic routines. Only her superiors knew of her offer and her sufferings. María Gabriella died on April 23, 1939, on the Sunday of the Good Shepherd. The Gospel proclaimed: "There will be one flock and one shepherd."

Pope John Paul II beatified María Gabriella on June 25, 1983, and the ceremony was attended by Anglicans, Lutherans, and Orthodox Church representatives. The Holy Father proclaimed her *"voluntary spiritual martyrdom"* at her beatification, which was held at St. Paul's Basilica Outside the Walls. The ceremony ended the Week of Prayers for Christian Unity. The Holy Father declared:

"Sister María Gabriella had never studied the problem of separation or the history of ecumenism, and, in fact, knew very little about it. She was simply dominated by the desire that all men might return to God and that his Kingdom might come in every heart. She had already offered her existence for this by embracing the humble and silent life of a Trappist nun with its daily renouncements and its long hours of hard work and prayer. 'As for my part, I feel that I have already given all that was in my power to give,' she had written very frankly to her spiritual father. Maybe it was exactly for this reason that God wanted to make her a visible sign of the total gift of self that is asked by every Christian. The explicit act of offering her life conformed her even more perfectly to Christ, the Lamb who immolated himself so that all might be one."

Member of the Congregation of St. Marcellina

The hidden sufferers of the world bring down graces that sustain the faithful and intone a wondrous hymn of praise at the Throne of God. In an age of "letting it all hang out" and rugged individuals concerned with their own comforts and rights, such truly hidden souls are precious and deserving of the world's reverence and awe. Blessed Maria Anna Sala, a member of the Congregation of St. Marcellina, was a victim of faith and love in silent suffering.

She was born in Brivio, Italy, on April 21, 1829, the fifth of eight children of Giovanni and Giovannina Sala. The family was devout and active in their local parish, and the children were raised in the faith. Maria Anna was sent to the Sisters of St. Marcellina to be educated. This convent school was in Vimercate.

MARIA ANNA SALA

(D. 1891)

VICTIM SOUL

Maria Anna, graced with many virtues and gifts, graduated from the convent with a teaching certificate and a religious vocation. She desired to enter the Sisters of St. Marcellina but faced a domestic crisis that forced her to delay her religious aspirations. Financial reverses and her mother's illness brought María Anna home to assume responsibilities in the household. She continued these labors until 1848, when circumstances again allowed her to go to the convent.

Maria Anna entered the Congregation of St. Marcellina and completed her novitiate, making her profession on September 13, 1852. As a member of the congregation, Maria Anna taught in the Marcellina schools in Cernusco, Chambéry,

Genoa, and Milan for four decades. In each convent school she served with humility, patience, and strict fidelity to the rules of her religious life.

In 1883, Maria Anna was diagnosed with malignant cancer of the throat. She continued her teaching even as the illness sapped her strength. The medical diagnosis did not alarm her, and Maria Anna asked to continue teaching, despite the growing cancer and the debilitating medical treatments. Silent about her suffering, Maria Anna taught until 1891, when she collapsed and was placed in the infirmary of the Milan Marcellina convent. She died on November 24, 1891, uncomplaining and joyous. In 1920, when her Cause was opened, the body of Maria Anna was exhumed. Her remains were found to be intact.

Pope John Paul II beatified Maria Anna on October 26, 1980, praising her silent suffering, her resolute following of Christ Crucified, and her spiritual maturity even in the most dire periods of pain and suffering.

Foundress of the Congregation of the Missionary Teaching Sisters of the Immaculate Conception

Some of the greatest saints of the Church demonstrated not only ardor and zeal but a remarkable amount of tenacity and common sense about life. Blessed María of Mount Carmel Sallés y Baranqueras was one of these practical individuals who said simply: "I want virtue, real virtue and learning; as for the rest, God will provide."

She was born in Vich, Spain, on April 9, 1848, the oldest child of José and

MARÍA OF MOUNT CARMEL SALLÉS Y BARANQUERAS

(D. 1911)

EDUCATOR

Francisca Baranqueras Sallés. María of Mount Carmel was baptized Carmen Francisca Rosa. She studied at the *La Enseñanza* school operated by the Company of Mary and received the grace of a religious vocation. After graduation, María of Mount Carmel started educating young women, using the Dominican spirit of combining the active life with contemplation. In order to achieve the apostolate, María of Mount Carmel founded the Congregation of the Missionary Teaching Sisters of the Immaculate Conception. The members of this congregation were trained to witness to the presence of Mary Immaculate in the secular world.

María of Mount Carmel founded thirteen schools and many convents. Her congregation went to Brazil in 1911, and then to Asia and Africa. The Conceptionists, as María of Mount Carmel's Sisters are called, continue to manifest the love of God for humanity through Mary. María of Mount Carmel died in Madrid on July 25, 1911, speaking lovingly of "our Immaculate Mother."

Pope John Paul II beatified María of Mount Carmel on March 15, 1998, declaring that she was *"a valiant woman,"* one who based her life and work on a *"Christocentric and Marian spirituality nourished by solid and sensible piety."*

Co-Foundress of the Servants of Jesus of Charity

Women who sacrifice themselves totally for the poor and sick stand as vibrant flames of love in the wilderness of today's world, and people of all faiths look upon their apostolates with reverence and respect. Blessed María Josefa of the Heart of Jesus Sancho de Guerra is just such a model of true caring. She taught her followers to seek the face of Christ in the suffering of the world.

María Josefa was born on September 7, 1842, in Vitoria, Spain, to a poor family. Raised devoutly and without material comforts, María Josefa was no stranger to the vicious circle of poverty and its devastating effects. In 1864, because of her piety and keen awareness, María Josefa entered the Servants of Mary, a new religious congregation that sent her into the poorest districts of Madrid. During the plague of 1865 she worked without rest, and she continued her labors until 1871.

MARÍA JOSEFA SANCHO DE GUERRA

(D. 1912)

FOUNDRESS

In 1871, María Josefa and two companions left the Servants of Mary to found a new congregation in Bilbao — the Servants of Jesus of Charity. While the congregation faced terrible financial problems in the beginning, María Josefa cared for the sick while other members worked diligently to raise funds. In time, the Servants of Jesus of Charity spread to other European countries, to Latin America, and Asia. María Josefa guided the congregation, despite her own intense sufferings. She died in Bilbao on March 20, 1912.

Pope John Paul II beatified María Josefa on September 27, 1992, declaring: *"Blessed María Josefa of the Heart of Jesus Sancho de Guerra incarnated the words of Christ . . . she founded the Servants of Jesus of Charity, entrusting to them the mission of finding the face of Christ in so many brothers and sisters, alone and sick, and soothing them with oil of fraternal love."*

Poor Clare Abbess and Religious of Perfection

Some perfected souls have an almost euphoric splendor radiating from their lives. St. Francis of Assisi emanated that aura while he performed his apostolate, forming the pattern of poverty and penance for St. Clare and their followers. The seraphic splendor of the Franciscan Order was glimpsed as well in the life of Maria Crucifixa Satellico, a Poor Clare cloistered nun.

MARIA CRUCIFIXA SATELLICO

(D. 1745)

RELIGIOUS

She was born Elisabeth Maria Satellico in Venice, Italy, on January 9, 1706, the daughter of Pietro and Lucia Mander Satellico. The family lived with a maternal uncle, a priest, who aided in Maria Crucifixa's spiritual formation. The child showed an innate ability for prayer, music, and singing and grew up desiring a religious vocation as a Poor Clare cloistered nun.

Accepted as a student of the Poor Clare Monastery of Ostra Vitere, Maria Crucifixa played the organ and directed the monastic music. In 1725, she received the Poor Clare habit and her religious name, and she was professed on May 19, 1726. The goal of perfection was the source of her religious life, and Maria Crucifixa was devoted to the Most Holy Trinity and the Holy Eucharist.

Elected abbess, Maria Crucifixa led by example and also became a patroness of the local poor. She died at age thirty-nine, on November 8, 1745, and was buried at the Church of St. Lucy in Ostra Vetere, revered as a woman of seraphic splendor. Pope John Paul II beatified Maria Crucifixa on October 10, 1993, declaring: *"The Church . . . salutes you . . . faithful daughter of Francis! You have configured your life to him who for love of humanity let himself be nailed to the Cross . . . and now you contemplate the glory of your Lord."*

Foundress of the Sisters of Mercy of the Holy Cross

MARIA THERESA SCHERER

(D. 1888)

FOUNDRESS

In the modern age, the Church has raised up spectacular souls capable of bridging the centuries of faith with the needs and methods of each new era. This blessed, Maria Theresa Scherer, was such a soul. She embraced all of the works of charity and became famous as "the Mother of the Poor."

She was born Anna Maria Catherine Scherer in Meggen, Switzerland, on October 31, 1825. When her father died in 1831, Maria Theresa was taken by two uncles to be raised as their ward. She was quick, bright, and exuberant, and she displayed her concern for the poor at an early age with a profound spiritual maturity. At age sixteen, Maria Theresa, seeing the need for dedicated laborers in the medical institutions of her era, started doing hospital work. She learned quickly, and she attracted companions who were eager to form a religious group dedicated to such a ministry. With four such companions, Maria Theresa founded the Sisters of Mercy of the Holy Cross on October 27, 1845, assisted by Father Theodosius Florentini of Altdorf. Maria Theresa had been working to form the congregation in Altdorf for about a year. The congregation was designed to incorporate two separate ministries, nursing and teaching.

Elected superior, Maria Theresa centered her activities in Ingenbok, opening a motherhouse there and attracting new religious aspirants. She had a simple but dynamic motto: "No work of Christian love of neighbor may be considered beyond the scope of this institute." With this motto, Maria Theresa was able to adapt her sisters to the compelling needs of the time and to make innovative apostolates to aid all who needed their care.

She quickly became known as the "Mother of the Poor," opening hospitals and schools for the handicapped and embracing the social apostolate for workers in the region. Her labors required a considerable amount of travel, which she endured despite severe physical sufferings. While on a visitation to her Rome house, Maria Theresa became very ill. She was taken to Ingenbohl, where she died on June 16, 1888. At the time of her death, her congregation had almost 1,700 sisters. A mission was opened in the United States in 1912.

Pope John Paul II beatified Maria Theresa on October 29, 1995, announcing: *"Maria Theresa Scherer fought the good fight. Through her life and work she reminds us of the essential place of the mystery of the Cross, by which God proclaims his love and grants salvation to the world . . . Maria Theresa remains an example for us. Her inner strength was a result of her spiritual life: she spent many hours before the Blessed Sacrament, where the Lord communicates his love to all who live in close relationships with him."*

Co-Foundress of the Sisters of the Sacred Heart of Jesus

The word *nobility* is used by the world to denote aristocratic rank in society, the privileged level of existence inherited by some families or clans. This word is also used to express a profound goodness, a valor, and a level of service freely given. Maria of the Sacred Heart Schinina was eminently entitled to both definitions of the

MARIA SCHININA

(D. 1910)

🌿

FOUNDRESS

word while she lived, and in death she is revered as a soul united to God.

Maria of the Sacred Heart was born in Ragusa, Sicily, on April 10, 1844, a member of an aristocratic family. Raised to the social status of her lineage, Maria had the rights and privileges of the nobility from birth. She also developed spiritual graces, being raised devoutly by her family.

At age sixteen, Maria saw Italy and her own region convulsed by the *Risorgimento* and the campaign for unification. Unlike many of her noble class, she was not able to turn away from the suffering caused by the war and by the resulting famine. She set about recruiting companions to aid prisoners of war and the tormented peasantry of her region. The nobles of Sicily were shocked and horrified to witness Maria's religious labors because such a ministry spanned the stiff divisions between the social classes. However, the archbishop of Syracuse came to her defense, and he aided her when she and five companions started the Sisters of the Sacred Heart of Jesus. They opened their doors to peasants and nobles, even to prisoners of war, who were despised by others.

No one in need was turned away by Maria. She provided a safe haven to Carmelites forced to flee their home convent because of political unrest. During a devastating earthquake, Maria opened her motherhouse to the refugees from Messina and Reggio di Calabria. All received food, medicine, and devoted care. There also, secular priests and religious came to learn the newest methods of conducting charitable labors, and she financed seminaries and study programs. Maria died in Ragusa on June 11, 1910, mourned by the nobles and the common people of the region as a true heroine of Christian love.

Pope John Paul II beatified Maria on November 14, 1990, saying: *"The spiritual journey of Blessed Maria Schinina of the Sacred Heart began with a deep penetration by God's love, which is expressed in the symbol of the Heart of Jesus; in order to respond to this love in her spirituality, she emphasized contemplation, adoration, and reparation."* The Holy Father added: *"Her charism remains ever alive and timely. . . ."*

Foundress of the Sisters of the holy Family of Nazareth

MARIA OF JESUS SIEDLISKA

(D. 1902)

FOUNDRESS

The Holy Family has long been a symbol of peace, dedication, and charity for the world. One Polish woman took that great insignia to represent unstinting service for those in need in the modern era. She was Blessed Maria of Jesus Siedliska, the foundress of the Sisters of the Holy Family of Nazareth and a defender of the rights of the poor and their children.

She was born in Rozkowa Wola, Poland, on November 12,

1842, and was baptized Francisca. The daughter of Adolph and Cecilia Morawska Siedliska, Maria of Jesus was quite frail as an infant, needing special care. Her mother also suffered a serious illness, and Maria of Jesus was educated by a tutor who saw in her intellectual brilliance and the wit and genuine warmth that would distinguish her throughout her life. During her mother's illness, Maria of Jesus began an intense devotion to Our Lady Czestochowa, a devotion that would become a hallmark of her holiness.

Maria of Jesus' confirmation in 1855, and her growing dedication, alarmed her parents, who took her on a long journey to France, Germany, and Switzerland to discourage her religious vocation. Maria's father finally agreed to her aspiration while on this sightseeing trip. She returned home and was aided by a Capuchin priest, Father Leander Lendzian, in starting her congregation in Rome in 1875. She became Mother Maria of Jesus the Good Shepherd. Concerned about neglected and abandoned children, Maria of Jesus began a series of charitable works and founded the Sisters of the Holy Family of Nazareth, taking the name María of Jesus the Good Shepherd. Pope Pius IX (r. 1846-1878) approved the congregation on October 1, 1873. The beautiful personality traits that Maria of Jesus possesses won many to her apostolate.

She located her motherhouse in Rome, but returned to Poland in 1881 to begin a foundation there. By 1884, Maria of Jesus was operating four convents in Poland, where her spirit took root. She opened a mission in the United States, and in 1895 began her apostolate in London, which was well-received. Maria of Jesus of the Good Shepherd died in Rome, on November 21, 1902.

Pope John Paul II beatified Maria of Jesus on April 23, 1989, declaring: *"Throughout her whole life she was able in a mature manner to combine prayer with the active apostolate, creating initiative with a concrete obedience to the Will of God in the Church. . . . The source of inspiration and reference point for her and her spiritual daughters was the model of the hidden life of the Holy Family of Nazareth."*

Foundress of the Holy Spirit Missionary Sisters

Almighty God elects some souls to a level of greatness that goes almost beyond human comprehension, asking them to bear trials and tribulations that would cripple the less inspired. Maria Helen Stollenwerk, a spiritual daughter of Blessed Arnold Janssen, was just such a chosen vessel of suffering and endurance.

She was born in Germany on November 28, 1852, and raised devoutly in an era of po-

MARIA HELEN STOLLENWERK

(D. 1852)

FOUNDRESS

litical unrest. Her childhood experiences made her particularly aware of the need for religious ministries in the world. Active in the Holy Child Association as a young woman, Maria Helen received the grace of a religious vocation in 1882. She journeyed to Steyl, in the Netherlands, where she was aided by Blessed Arnold Janssen in founding her religious congregation. Maria Helen started the Holy Spirit Missionary Sisters on December 8, 1889. She was made superior and set about recruiting new members and founding new houses. Her motto was: "To God, the honor; to my neighbor, the benefit, and to myself, the burden."

In 1896, the congregation was divided into two separate entities: the original missionary institute and a cloister. Maria Helen was directed to enter the cloister, thus having to relinquish her vision for the community and giving control of the congregation to others. Her suffering was intense, but she remained obedient and resigned as superior. Entering the cloister, she was obliged to undergo another novitiate and take a new religious name, "*Maria Virgo*." Maria Helen fulfilled all of her new obligations without complaint. One year later she became ill, and she died as a cloistered nun on February 3, 1900, in Steyl. Hidden, possessing no honor or title, Maria Helen died in saintly obedience.

Pope John Paul II beatified Maria Helen on May 7, 1995, announcing:

"If we think of Mother Maria Stollenwerk, we find ourselves before a great feminine personality and missionary pioneer, although she was not able to fulfill her greatest desire: to be send on mission herself. In brief, we can state that her whole life was a sign of her being touched by God. From her childhood the new blessed's life of prayer was inspired by the Pontifical Society of the Holy Childhood. She was particularly affected by the loss of those children who were deprived of the right to life. Through her meeting with Blessed Arnold Janssen, she believed she would be able to fulfill her dream of becoming a missionary sister. With him she eventually founded the Congregation of the Missionary Servants of the Holy Spirit. The congregation's name shows how much Mother Maria Stollenwerk had at heart the adoration of the Holy Spirit. The Holy Spirit inspired her to proclaim the Gospel, and, as St. Paul said, to become all things to all men (cf. 1 Cor 9:16-22). The new blessed saw the Holy Spirit as the driving force of missionary activity. Thanks to this basic attitude of trust in the power of God's Spirit and to the faith flowing from her eucharistic adoration and her constant closeness to the Lord by whom she felt sent, Mother Maria Stollenwerk could state: 'Only God can fill our hearts. He is too great and too vast to be understood by creatures.' "

Foundress of the Franciscan Missionary Sisters of Egypt

Modern travelers book passage on boats and planes to visit Egypt, where pyramids and ruins sit in splendor on the banks of the Nile. Despite political unrest in some eras, a steady stream of visitors has poured into Cairo through the decades. Few, however, arrived on the Nile to dedicate their lives to the people of that great metropolis. Maria Catherine Troiani went to Egypt to stay forever among the families of Cairo, arriving not as a tourist but as a pilgrim of the spirit.

MARIA CATHERINE OF ST. ROSE TROIANI

(D. 1887)

MISSIONARY

Maria Catherine was born in Giuliano, near Rome, Italy, on January 19, 1813. She was baptized Constanza and was educated in the faith and in the teaching profession. The Franciscan Sisters of Terentino educated Maria Catherine, and she received the grace of a religious vocation while in their care. She had a missionary spirit as well, and a remarkable love of Egypt and Palestine. These combined in Maria Catherine to lead her far from her native land to serve the young women of the Middle East.

Maria Catherine served as a teaching sister in the Franciscans for thirty years. She never surrendered her desire to aid the peoples of Egypt and Palestine, and when given permission to establish a school in Cairo, Egypt, she gathered companions and set sail without hesitation. Welcomed in Cairo, Maria Catherine saw her apostolate grow and realized that she had to form a new congregation to meet the need of her newly chosen mission. She received approval for such a congregation, calling the new group the Franciscan Missionary Sisters of Egypt.

These Franciscans educated young Egyptian and Palestinian women and opened charitable institutions to aid the poor. María Catherine died in the motherhouse in Cairo on May 6, 1887, mourned by Christians and Muslims, who respected her vision and her unsparing generosity in service.

Pope John Paul II beatified María Catherine on April 14, 1985, praising her vision and her courage in using the faith to span time and cultural differences for the benefit of the young and the needing.

María Angeles Valtierra ❧ See Martyrs of Guadalajara.

Foundress of the Daughters of the Sacred Heart in Mexico

Some pious works or holy apostolates depend not only upon the inspiration of their original founders but also upon the sustaining efforts of the staunch and courageous men and women who come after the initial stages. María of Jesus Sacramentado Venegas de la Torre was one of the stalwart individuals chosen by God to carry on the labors of union already formed in her native land, Mexico.

MARÍA OF JESUS SACRAMENTADO VENEGAS DE LA TORRE

(D. 1950)

FOUNDRESS

Born on September 8, 1868, in Jalisco, Mexico, she was raised devoutly by her family. Recollected and prayerful, she spent long hours in the parish church. She also joined the Children of Mary on December 8, 1898, receiving as well the grace of a religious vocation. Marie of Jesus entered the Sacred Heart of Jesus in Guadalajara on December 8, 1905.

This pious union was founded originally by Guadalupe Villaseñor de Perez Verdia, a noblewoman of Guadalajara. Canon Atenógenes Silva y Alvarez Tostado aided the noblewoman in this endeavor, as he was active in spreading devotion to the Sacred Heart of Jesus. When María of Jesus entered the community, she brought spiritual graces and a profound capability of leadership. These gifts were recognized, and under María of Jesus' discretion, the Daughters of the Sacred Heart received canonical recognition as a religious institute. She is thus called the foundress of the congregation.

The community conducted its ministry in the Sacred Heart Hospital of Guadalajara. María Jesus' holiness won the respect of many, and when she died on July 30, 1959, the entire region was plunged into mourning. Thousands came to María of Jesus' funeral. Her Cause was opened in 1978.

Pope John Paul II beatified María of Jesus on November 22, 1992, praising her role in the charitable projects undertaken and as a glory of Mexico and the faith.

María Inés Zudaire Galdeano ❦ **See Martyrs of the Visitation Order.**

Foundress of the Daughters of the Sacred Heart of Jesus

The last words of this blessed, concerning the crazed man who had inflicted mortal stab wounds upon her person, were: "I forgive him . . . for the Work." This "Work" was an apostolate of the Sacred Heart, a ministry of adoration and reparation. Marie of Jesus Deluil-Martiny imitated Christ's sacrifice in her own life and even in her death.

She was born in Marseilles, France, on May 28, 1841, and was baptized Marie of Jesus Deluil-Martiny. Educated at the Visitation Convent in Lyons, Marie was graced with a pious upbringing. She became a member of the Guard of Honor of the Sacred Heart of Jesus in the convent. This organization was designed to give praise and acts of reparation to the Sacred Heart, and the devotion inspired Marie of Jesus and brought her the

MARIE OF JESUS DELUIL-MARTINY

(D.1884)

FOUNDRESS

grace of a religious vocation. She visited St. John Vianney at Ars to discuss her religious vocation and the tragedies that had befallen her in losing her sisters and a brother.

With the aid of Father Colage, S.J., Marie of Jesus planned her new congregation, the Daughters of the Sacred Heart, designed to give praise to the Sacred Heart of Jesus, offering the community to the patronage of the Blessed Virgin Mary. In 1873, Cardinal Deschamps desired a center of reparation established in Belgium and was interested in her work. On June 20, of that year, Marie of Jesus and her companions received their habits. They were given final approbation for the rule on August 2, 1878.

Marie of Jesus erected her first house at Berschem, near Antwerp, Belgium, and erected a shrine to the Sacred Heart there as well. Establishing other convents, Marie of Jesus located the motherhouse in Rome, which received Vatican approbation on February 2, 1902, eighteen years after her death. She was killed by a crazed gardener in the La Servianne Convent, Marseilles, on February 27, 1884. Her remains were taken to the Basilica of the Sacred Heart in Berschem, and her Cause was opened in 1921.

Pope John Paul II beatified María on October 22, 1989, declaring:

"Marie of Jesus contemplated the Mother of the Savior at the foot of the Cross and present in the heart of the Church at its birth. The Virgin Mary was her true model. With Mary, the foundress of the Daughters of the Heart of Jesus prays and keeps watch so that God's children do not cease proclaiming to the wonders of his love. . . . At a very young age Marie was able to share with her neighbors her ardent desire to live in the Sacrifice of the Mass. When she founded

the Daughters of the Heart of Jesus, she put eucharistic adoration at the center of their religious life. Deeply understanding Christ's sacrifice, she wanted to unite themselves continually to the offering of the Blood of Christ to the Blessed Trinity."

Foundress of the Sisters of the Names of Jesus and Mary

In this age of preoccupation, the generous souls on earth stand not only as contradictions to the modern malaise but as beacons of Christian hope. Seeing such stalwart, faithful individuals, all believers can hope for the grace and the courage to ascend to true human greatness. A striking symbol of such ascent is Marie Rose Durocher, a soul who forgot herself in order to overcome countless adversities in the care of others. Against all odds, Marie Rose Durocher founded the Sisters of the Names of Jesus and Mary.

MARIE ROSE DUROCHER

(D. 1849)

EDUCATOR

She was born Eulalie or Melanie, on October 6, 1811, in Sainte-Antoine-sur-Richelieu, Canada, the daughter of Oliver Amable Durocher and his wife. The couple raised a large family of consecrated souls, imbuing their children with the faith.

Marie Rose was educated by the Notre Dame Sisters in Saint Denis and Montreal, Canada. At age eight she lost her mother and had to assume maternal responsibilities that matured her rapidly. She was never robust or strong, and this physical weakness kept her from being admitted to the religious congregations in Quebec. To aid in her recovery, Marie Rose went to Belseil, where her brother, Eusebius, was a parish priest. She served as her brother's housekeeper for thirteen years.

During this time, Marie Rose took care of sick priests and seminarians, establishing a sodality and operated the charitable programs of the parish. Marie Rose, a devout Marianist, encouraged others to dedicate themselves to the Blessed Virgin. As her work increased, she was aided by the Oblates of Mary Immaculate. Bishop Ignace Bourget also heard of her and asked Marie Rose to form a new teaching congregation.

On December 8, 1844, Marie Rose, Mother M. Agnes and Mother M. Madeleine took their vows as the Sisters of the Holy Names of Jesus and Mary and the congregation was founded in Longueuil. Marie Rose attracted many new members. Her contemporaries described her as lovable, light-hearted, and kindly. Marie Rose would live only six more years as a consecrated religious.

She founded convents and established schools, taking part in the Catholic renaissance of Canada at that time. Her congregation would eventually carry her spirit and vision to the United States, Brazil, Peru, Haiti, and Lesotho. Marie

Rose died on October 6, 1849, and was buried at the congregation's mother house in Outremont, Quebec, Canada.

Pope John Paul II beatified Marie Rose in Quebec on May 23, 1982, stating: *"Marie Rose Durocher acted with simplicity, prudence, humility, and serenity. She refused to be halted by her personal problems of health or the initial difficulties of her new-born work. Her secret lay in prayer and self-forgetfulness, which, according to her bishop, reached the point of real sanctity."*

Foundress of the Ursuline Sisters in Canada

When the New World was discovered, the Europeans arrived on its shores with varying ambitions and goals. Many came to conquer and exploit the new continent and its inhabitants, but others came to bring Christ's charity to all. Blessed Marie of the Incarnation Guyart, the foundress of the Ursuline Sisters in Quebec, Canada, was motivated by faith and generosity. In time she bridged the gap between the new settlers and the Native American populations, becoming the patroness of the Algonquin and Iroquois nations.

MARIE OF THE INCARNATION GUYART

(D. 1672)

FOUNDRESS

Marie of the Incarnation was born in Tours, France, on October 28, 1599. Married and widowed, Marie joined the Ursulines in Tours and then sailed for Canada with Madame de la Peltrie, a rich widow of Alençon. They arrived in Quebec on August 1, 1639, to found the oldest institution of learning for women in North America. Marie of the Incarnation's son, Dom Claude Martin, became a Benedictine and her biographer.

Called "Theresa of her time and of the New World," Marie of the Incarnation spent three years in the Lower Town, taking over a convent in 1642 that was given to the Ursulines by the company of New France. Their first pupils were Native Americans, and Marie of the Incarnation mastered Algonquin and Iroquois in order to provide her students with a catechism and a sacred history. Eventually she would compose dictionaries in both languages. When the convent was destroyed by fire in 1650, Marie saw a new one built upon the ashes of the old. Marie's friend Madame de la Peltrie died in 1671, leaving Marie of the Incarnation to continue her labors and her particular devotion to the Sacred Heart of Jesus. Blessed Bishop Francis de Montmorency-Laval approved the rule in 1681.

A devout, brilliant woman who guided the Ursulines through perilous times by combining a contemplative spirituality with acute administrative skills, Marie of the Incarnation died in Quebec on April 30, 1672. Her correspondence, some 12,000 letters, provides a valuable look at life in Quebec in the seventeenth century.

Pope John Paul II beatified Marie of the Incarnation on June 22, 1980, declaring that she had come to the New World from France but had completed her life in Quebec, attaining holiness and a record of service that elevated her to the honor roll of Canada's founding settlers. The Holy Father also praised Marie of the Incarnation's contemplative gifts, treasures that she put at the service of her fellow Canadians.

Foundress of the Daughters of the Cross

The saints and blessed of this world have followed Christ in unique and particular ways, drawn by faith and love. Some have walked on the bright path of the active apostolate, bringing the redemptive grace of Christ's love to those

MARIE THÉRÈSE HAZE

(D. 1876)

FOUNDRESS

in need. Some have traveled "the way of darkness," the interior, spiritual path of suffering that cleansed and perfected their spirits. Marie Thérèse Haze, the foundress of the Daughters of the Cross, cooperated with the grace of God in an active apostolate but experienced the way of interior suffering at the same time. She taught that "that a crushed heart becomes the throne of grace."

Marie Thérèse Haze was born in Liège, Belgium, on February 27, 1782. Her father was secretary to the local bishop and very devout, and the family life was happy: until the French Revolution brought its terrors. Marie Thérèse's father had to flee Liège, suffering a heart attack in the process, and he died separated from his family. Marie Thérèse 's mother raised her children alone, aided by her daughter's dedication and skills. Marie Thérèse even aided in financing her brother's university education. He did not live to pursue a career; Marie Thérèse 's mother died young as well.

Marie Thérèse was a master of the embroidery art. Through this creative skill she had supported her family, and she used her skill to provide her own income. While teaching young women that art of embroidery, Marie Thérèse also instructed them in the catechism, and her classes became popular. Soon she was joined by others and an apostolate began.

In 1833, Marie Thérèse founded the Daughters of the Cross, becoming Mother Marie Thérèse of the Sacred Heart of Jesus and dedicating her congregation to the service of the poor. The community spread throughout Europe, Asia, Africa, and America. Marie Thérèse Haze died on January 7, 1876, at the age of ninety-four.

Pope John Paul II beatified Marie Thérèse on April 21, 1991, declaring:

"In the humility of the Incarnation, in the generosity of the love which makes all of us 'children of God' (1 Jn 3:2), the Daughters of the Cross find an example for placing themselves in the service in the poorest of their neighbors. Blessed Marie Thérèse invites them to put into action the Gospel call to serve Christ in the person of the frailest and most suffering members of his Body. This basic inspiration follows that of Peter who proclaims, after the cure of the cripple, that healing comes from the Lord, who was crucified and is risen."

Co-Foundress of the Little Sisters of the Poor

The Little Sisters of the Poor have earned respect and reverence in many lands for their humble, unstinting care of the elderly, the abandoned, and the needy. While the generosity and fidelity of the members of this esteemed congregation are heralded, few understand the profound sacrifices endured by the foundress, Jeanne Jugan, Marie of the Cross. Pope John Paul II has introduced Marie of the Cross to the entire world, offering a life of humility, obedience, and imitation of Christ Crucified.

MARIE OF THE CROSS JUGAN

(D. 1879)

VICTIM SOUL

She was born on October 25, 1792, in Cancale, Brittany, France, and was baptized Jeanne. The sixth child of Joseph and Marie Jugan, she was little more than three when her father died at sea. Economic problems plagued the family, and the political unrest of the era added to their difficulties.

At age sixteen, Marie went to the estate of the Viscountess de la Choue to seek employment. This noble person recognized the spiritual graces of the young girl and befriended her in many ways. Marie served as a maid on the estate, but the viscountess taught her genteel manners and fostered Marie's virtues, especially that of charitable service. In time, the viscountess said goodbye to Marie and moved to Saint-Servan. Then twenty-five, Marie worked in a hospital and became a member of the Third Order of the Heart of the Admirable Mother.

In 1837, Marie and two companions, Françoise Albert and Virginie Tredaniel, founded the Little Sisters of the Poor. They were dedicated to the care of the aged, the abandoned, and the needy. Marie's work was so outstanding and well-received that she was eventually awarded medals from the French Academy and the Freemasons for her work, and she opened a second and a third foundation. By 1851, Marie had five houses and more than three hundred sisters. At her death there were 2,400 Little Sisters of the Poor.

Toward the end of her life, a priest named Le Pailleur gained control of the congregation. He abused Marie of the Cross severely, dismissing her as superior and keeping her hidden from the people of the region. She did not complain about this outrageous behavior, viewing all things as providing grace. She died in obscurity on August 29, 1879.

Pope John Paul II beatified Marie of the Cross on October 3, 1982, stating that this woman of the people had dedicated herself entirely and had endured great suffering with dignity and trust in God. Standing as a beatified of the faithful, Marie's vision of service continues in the modern world.

Hospitaller of Mercy

Some rare souls emanate resolve, courage, and love. Their presence encourages others to sacrifice and arduous labors, and their joy refreshes all who meet them. Blessed Marie Catherine Simon de Longpré was one of these rare souls. She is also revered as Marie Catherine of St. Augustine, and she inspired praise and even poetry in Canada, her adopted land.

MARIE CATHERINE SIMON DE LONGPRÉ

(D. 1668)

❧

RELIGIOUS

She was born in Saint-Sauveur le Vicomte, France, on May 13, 1632. Dedicated at an early age to the sick and the poor, Marie Catherine entered the Hospitallers of Mercy of St. Augustine, receiving the religious name of Marie Catherine of St. Augustine.

As a member of this religious congregation, Marie Catherine demonstrated heroic devotion to the sick entrusted to her care. She not only displayed medical skills but spiritual wisdom when called upon as a spiritual counselor. Many patients and medical officials came to rely on her practical knowledge and her vast font of spiritual devotion. She had many spiritual graces and a beautiful spirit that attracted people of all walks of life who learned to trust her judgment.

As word of her medical abilities and holiness spread, Marie Catherine was asked to sail from France to Quebec, where she served as a model for the evolving medical facilities and religious institutions. In a spirit of religious obedience, Marie Catherine arrived in the New World to aid others. She again impressed many with her wisdom and her skills. Her nursing experiences broadened the horizons of care in Quebec, bringing comfort to thousands.

Marie Catherine inspired many forms of praise, but she remained obedient to her religious rule and to her vocation. She died on May 8, in Quebec, mourned by the entire region.

Pope John Paul II beatified Marie Catherine on April 23, 1989, announcing: *"In the secret of her soul she received the gift of being ceaselessly present to God, to Christ the Redeemer. She lived in union with the Sacred Heart of Jesus and placed all her confidence in Mary."* The Holy Father also declared: *"A tireless apostle, she was generous in fulfilling her important responsibilities and infinitely capable and patient in lovingly caring for the sick. In the spiritual springtime of the first era of the Church in Canada, one can inscribe among the 'founders' Marie Catherine."*

Foundress of the Little Sisters of the Holy Family

Christ advised his followers to imitate him by being humble of heart, and generations of saints have patterned their lives and ministries in this image. A Canadian blessed, Marie-Leonie Paradis, embraced the "Little Way" in the modern era, but she went beyond the mere practice of humility in daily routines. Marie-Leonie brought countless dedicated women into a life of service, humble labor, and spiritual graces in order to serve God and the Church.

She was born Alodie Virginia Paradis on May 12, 1840, in Acadie (Sainte Marguerite de Blairfindie), a suburb of Montreal. At age thirteen, Marie-Leonie entered the Holy Cross Sisters at Saint-Laurent, where she received her religious name. She made her vows in 1857 and was sent later to St. Vincent's Orphanage in New York City.

In 1864, Marie-Leonie became directress of a group of sisters engaged in household management in Indiana. She had many volunteers for this work and asked permission to establish a new congregation, the Little Sisters of the Holy Family. Canonical erection of the congregation came on January 27, 1896. Marie-Leonie had remained a Holy Cross Sister, but became a "Little Sister" when the congregation was erected. Papal approval from Pope St. Pius X (r. 1904-1913) was announced in May 1, 1905.

MARIE-LEONIE PARADIS

(D. 1912)

FOUNDRESS

Serving the Holy Cross Sisters originally, Marie-Leonie's Little Sisters began keeping households in the apostolic delegation in Canada and in Washington, D.C. They also served in other episcopal residences and operated homes for retired priests. When Marie-Leonie died at Sherbrooke, Quebec, on May 3, 1912, there were more than six hundred sisters caring for clerical and episcopal households in Canada, the United States, and in Honduras. The vision that Marie-Leonie shared of service to priests and humble labors continues to inspire generous young women.

Pope John Paul II beatified Marie-Leonie at Montreal on September 11, 1984, stating that he rejoiced in beatifying Marie-Leonie in her homeland. The Holy Father declared further:

"Never doubting her call, she often asked: 'Lord, show me your ways,' so that she would know the concrete form of her service in the Church. She found and proposed to her spiritual daughters a special kind of commitment: the service of educational institutions, seminaries, and priests' homes. She never shied away from the various forms of manual labor which is the lot of so many people today and which held a special place in the Holy Family and in the life of Jesus of Nazareth himself. It is there that she saw the Will of God in her life. It was in carrying out these tasks that she found God . . . in the sacrifices which were required and which she offered in love, she experienced a profound joy and peace. She knew that she was one with Christ's fundamental attitude: he had 'come not to be served, but to serve.' She was filled with the greatness of the Eucharist and with the greatness of the priesthood at the service of the Eucharist. That is one of the secrets of her spiritual motivation."

from Faces of Holiness

Marie-Leonie Paradis

Foundress of the Dominican Sisters of Charity
of the Presentation of Tours

The image of Mother Teresa remains vibrant in this modern era, but in the eighteenth century there was another woman who embraced total poverty in order to serve the needy of her age. Her name was Marie Poussepin, and she founded a religious congregation dedicated to absolute poverty and the care of the most miserable. Her example as a Dominican inspired Blessed Hyacinthe Cormier, who was beatified with Marie.

MARIE
POUSSEPIN
(D. 1744)

FOUNDRESS

Marie was born at Dourdan, near Paris, France, on October 14, 1653, to a middle-class family that met financial reverses. At a very young age, Marie took charge of her father's stocking factory and kept the family and local workers secure. In this capacity, Marie also used innovative machines and new methods of training workers.

She was a Dominican tertiary, entering that Third Order in 1693, and she served in many other charitable programs.

Her desire to serve the poor prompted Marie to found a Dominican Fraternity in Sainville, France, and she started a school for girls. Twenty such communities were soon established in the area around Paris. From this beginning came the Dominican Sisters of Charity of the Presentation of Tours. The bishop of Chartres, however, demanded that all ties to the Dominicans be renounced by Marie, who had to comply, but the congregation was restored to its original spiritual base in the late nineteenth century and was recognized as Dominican in the twentieth century.

Charity was Marie's sole focus, and she made her entire life an offering of love, seeing Christ in all who came to her for aid. She was dedicated to the welfare of each parish, to the education of young people, and the service of the sick poor. Her congregation mirrored this virtue, and her sisters were trained to accept all labors as their religious commitment. Marie's congregation now serves in Burkina Faso, Iraq, Colombia, France, India, and Spain. There are four thousand spiritual daughters of Marie presently in the world. Her vision and her rule flourished after her death in Sainville, France on January 24, 1744.

Pope John Paul II beatified Marie on November 20, 1994, in Rome, declaring: *"The fire of love which Christ came to kindle on the earth would be doomed to being extinguished had not families the courage to keep it burning. During this year dedicated particularly to them, Marie Poussepin brings us a message of joy and hope: born into a family which raised her and which she supported, she is henceforth held up for our veneration as one of our sisters in humanity, a daughter of our humble and generous God, capable of understanding family problems and also of showing us where to seek their solution: in the love which springs from the heart of Christ, King of the universe."*

Wisdom is a rare commodity, even in this era of information, databases, and speedy news flashes. Few take the time to process the known into the philosophical realms called spiritual awareness or true wisdom. Marie-Louise Trichet

MARIE-LOUISE OF JESUS TRICHET

(D. 1759)

FOUNDRESS

founded her entire life on the concept of *sapientia*, or wisdom, and she started a religious congregation to restore that virtue to the world.

Marie-Louise was born in Poitiers, France, in 1684, to a devout Catholic family that remained loyal to the Church in perilous times. This spiritual daughter of St. Louis de Montfort was raised with a concern for others, a virtue that would frame the remarkable apostolate of her life.

In 1703, she founded a group of young women called *La Sagesse,* or "Wisdom." These young women aided the poor, the crippled, and the blind of their region. Persevering in the ministry, Marie-Louis came under the influence of

provided by the Daughters of Wisdom

Blessed Marie-Louise

St. Louis de Montfort, understanding the saint's vision of Catholic programs that would oppose the secularism and materialism of the age. Marie-Louise guided her companions and adopted a religious life for them, naming the group the Daughters of Wisdom. St. Louis de Montfort received Marie-Louise's vows and gave the habit to her and the other members of her new congregation. A young woman named Catherine Brunet joined Marie-Louise in 1712.

The Daughters of Wisdom opened a school in 1715 in La Rochelle. Dedicated to the Blessed Virgin Mary in all their ministries, the sisters won the respect of La Rochelle and began new foundations. Some Daughters of Wisdom were martyred during the French Revolution, the ultimate sacrifice for the faith.

The motherhouse of the Daughters of Wisdom was established at Saint-Laurent-sur-Sevre by Marie-Louise. When St. Louis de Montfort died, his remains were enshrined at the motherhouse by his spiritual daughters. Marie-Louise died on April 28, 1759, having founded thirty convents and institutions of charity. Marie-Louise's sisters arrived the United States in 1904.

Pope John Paul II beatified Marie-Louise on May 16, 1993, declaring: *"Marie-Louise of Jesus let herself be seized by Christ; she passionately sought the interior union of human wisdom with the eternal wisdom. The natural outcome of this bond of deep intimacy was an activity passionately devoted to the poorest of her contemporaries."*

Foundress of the Sisters of the Presentation of Mary

One of the many heroic blesseds was Marie Anna Rivier, who was called "the woman apostle" by Pope Pius IX (r. 1846-1878). Marie was the foundress of the Sisters of the Presentation of Mary, called the "White Ladies," born out of the French Revolution. She was born in Montpezat-sous-Bauzon, France, on December 19, 1768.

MARIE ANNA RIVIER

(D. 1838)

FOUNDRESS

Raised in the faith and trained to respond to life's inequalities with generosity and dedication, Marie was keenly aware of the sufferings of the needy in her region of France. As a child she had been crippled by a bad fall, and every day her mother had carried her to the local parish church where she prayed at the feet of Pietà for her child's recovery. For four years the mother carried her child and prayed, and the child learned to pray, believing with a child's faith "the Blessed Virgin will cure me." On September 18, 1774, Marie began to walk again.

The faith-filled child grew into a committed, faith-filled young woman, and by the time she was eighteen, Marie was devoted to caring for the abandoned children that she discovered near her home. As she continued these charitable labors, other young women came to her aid, and Marie realized that a religious congregation was needed to continue this work.

With the aid of Abbe Pontanier, Marie founded the Sisters of the Presentation of Mary in Montpezat-sous-Bauzon in 1796. The first novitiate of this congregation was opened in Theuyts, and there she trained the young volunteers who shared her ideals and devotion. This was also a time of revolutionary terror in France — priest were tracked down, religious activity was suspect, and executions were frequent. Marie, still frail and a small 4'3", secretly held

Sunday assemblies, prayer vigils, and rosaries. While cautious, Marie continued her efforts for the faith, opening forty-six schools in just eight years in the diocese of Viviers alone. In 1819 Marie established the motherhouse of the "White Ladies" at Bourg-Saint-Andéol.

Though the motherhouse was terribly poor, Marie taught that welcoming the most destitute is sacred. Her ideals attracted other faithful, and the Sisters of the Presentation of Mary continued to grow rapidly, operated schools, orphanages, and other charitable institutions. Some of the "White Ladies"

Blessed Marie Rivier

Photo courtesy of The Sisters of the Presentation of Mary

went to open missions in Canada, and the first foundation in the United States opened in Glens Falls, New York, in 1873. Marie died in the motherhouse of her congregation, revered by her spiritual daughters and many officials and laypersons, on February 3, 1838.

Pope John Paul II beatified Marie on May 23, 1982, announcing:

"So what is the secret of Marie Rivier's zeal? One is struck by her boldness, her tenacity, her expansive joy, her courage, 'which was enough to a thousand lives.' There were, however, many difficulties to discourage her: her childhood illness which lasted until she was healed on a feast of Our Lady, a lack of physical growth, a poor state of health throughout the seventy years of her life, the ignorance of religion that surrounded her. But her life demonstrates well the power of faith in a simple upright soul, which surrenders itself entirely to the grace of its baptism. She relied on God, who purified her through the Cross. She prayed intensely to Mary and with her presented herself before God in a state of adoration and offering. Her spirituality is solidly theological and clearly apostolic: 'Our vocation is Jesus Christ; we must fill ourselves with his spirit, so that his Kingdom may come, especially in the souls of children.'"

The vision experienced by one human being can be communicated over time and distances to inspire young souls of coming generations. The spiritual graces bestowed in such visions can set other souls on fire and bring about lasting religious fervor. Marthe Le Bouteiller was influenced by two women in her life, one a canonized saint, and she became a model of religious consecration.

MARTHE LE BOUTEILLER

(D. 1883)

RELIGIOUS

Marthe was born Aimée Le Bouteiller on December 2, 1816, the third of four children of André and Marie-Française of La Henriére (Percy), France. The family operated a small farm in La Manche province. André Le Bouteiller died in 1827, but the family survived financially. Marthe attended a local school operated by Sister Marie-Française Farcy in La Henriére, and there she received the grace of a religious vocation. "Sister Farcy" encouraged vocations among many young women in the area.

At age twenty-four, Marthe entered the Congregation of the Sisters of Saint-Sauveur-le-Vicomte, founded by St. Mary Magdalen Postel. She made her novitiate and profession and was assigned to work in the kitchens, storerooms, and gardens. Marthe would perform her convent duties in such menial arenas for four decades, becoming a model religious. Her piety and kindness became the hallmark of her convent life. She died, beloved by her community and the laity in Saint-Sauveur-le-Vicomte, on March 18, 1883.

Pope John Paul II beatified Marthe on November 4, 1990, announcing:

"May this new blessed help the young people of today and tomorrow find joy in giving themselves to the Lord in religious consecration! May she help them to grasp the primacy of the spiritual life in order to take part in the building up of the Church and perform fruitful activity in the service of mankind! On their life's journey our contemporaries need to see faces that show the true happiness which intimacy with God brings. Sister Marthe, a true Sister of Mercy, was able to let the love of God shine around her. The extreme simplicity of her life did not prevent the other sisters from recognizing her true spiritual authority. She bore fruit to the glory of the Father: 'by this is My Father glorified, that you bear much fruit and become My disciples' (Jn 15:8)."

Martin of St. Nicholas Lumbreras ❧ **See Martyrs of Japan.**

Martyrs of the Spanish Civil War

The Spanish Civil War claimed the lives of countless dedicated Catholic religious when the Communist-inspired revolutionaries unleashed a vicious anti-Catholic persecution. Two Spanish bishops and seven Christian Brothers were slain by the rebels and are revered as the

MARTYRS OF ALMERIA

(D. 1936)

MARTYRS

Martyrs of Almeria, Spain. The bishops cruelly slain were Diego Ventaja Milan of Almeria and Emmanuel (Manuel) Medina Olmos of Guadix. The martyred Christian Brothers were all arrested by the military forces of the Communist Popular Front of Almeria.

Five of the Christian Brothers were arrested in their classrooms by the revolutionary forces. The other two were hunted down by the Communists in the town. Abused and tormented by their captors, the Christian Brothers were confined to a series of holding areas; sacred places profaned and then used to keep religious in captivity. Physical and mental abuse was part of the revolutionary pattern of treatment, and the martyrs endured pain and indignities.

The bishops died first. On August 29 they were taken to an isolated place and shot. The next day, Brothers Edmigio Rodríguez, Amalio Mendoza, and Valerio Bernardo Martinez were also shot by the rebels. Their bodies were thrown into a well to avoid any public outcry. On September 8, Brothers Evencio Ricardo Uyarra and Teodomiro Joaquin Säiz Säiz were slain by the side of a road, and on September 12, Brothers Aurelio María Acebrón and José Cecilio Gonzalez were martyred in a similar manner.

Pope John Paul II beatified the Martyrs of Almeria on October 10, 1993, stating: *"All of them, faithful servants of the Lord, were like those messengers of the king, who according to what we heard in the Gospel were also 'mistreated and killed.' " (Mt. 22:6) The Holy Father added: "The Church hears these words of the martyrs. . . . She looks with veneration at their witness."*

MARTYRS OF ARMENIA

(D. 1895)

MARTYRS

Victims of the Turks

The constant wars in Europe and the Middle East have provided the Church with an honor roll of men and women who went to their deaths in the faith, generous to the end. Salvatore Lilli of Cappadocia, and his Franciscan companions, have been elevated to the rank of blessed as the Martyrs of Armenia.

Salvatore was born in Cappadocia-Aquila, Italy, on June 19, 1853, the son of Vincenzo and Annunziata Lilli. In 1870, he entered the Franciscans, making his religious vows on August 6, 1871. Two years later, he was sent to Bethlehem, Israel, where he studied for the priesthood in the Order's seminary. Salvatore was ordained in Bethlehem on April 6, 1878. He was then assigned to Jerusalem, where he labored in the mission for two years.

In 1880, Salvatore was sent to the Franciscan mission in Marasco, Armenia. He learned the language and the customs and brought his innovative style and spiritual insights to the people of the region, bettering their living conditions. In the process of preaching to the local populations, Salvatore erected schools, clinics, havens, and even entire villages set on prosperous methods of industry, hygiene, and the faith. In 1891, he became the hero of the region during a cholera epidemic. For more than six weeks, Salvatore labored unceasingly in treating the victims of the disease.

His missionary efforts were redirected in 1894, when he was assigned to the mission of Mujuk-Deresi, Armenia. The Islamic Turks occupied the region and took Salvatore and seven companions into custody. Tortured and ordered to abjure Christ and the faith, Salvatore and his fellow religious refused to deny the Church. They were martyred for their loyalty on November 22, 1895, in Mujuk-Dersi.

Pope John Paul II beatified Salvatore and the seven martyrs on October 3, 1982, declaring that their martyrdom was recognized by the faithful as the fruit of lifelong dedication and service to Christ and that the Church views their sacrifices with reverence.

Christian Brothers and Spanish Educators

The de la Salle Christian Brothers of Spain have bequeathed that nation and the Church a remarkable legacy of faith, courage, and loyalty. As martyrs of the Spansh Civil War, they are revered in the modern world and are designated as special groups of honored souls. Eight de la Salle Christian Brothers, with a Passionist priest companion, are called the Martyrs of Asturias (Turon), Spain.

The Communist-led rebel forces of Spain were in control of Asturias Province in the northwestern part of the country, in a mining town called Turon. On October 4, 1934, these rebels used heavy military force to vanquish opponents of the Second Republic. In Turon they put their anti-Catho-

MARTYRS OF ASTURIAS (TURON)

(D. 1934)

❦

MARTYRS

lic regime into place, destroying or profaning sacred structures and hunting down Catholic personnel. The Christian Brothers operated a school in Turon for the sons of local coal miners. Cyril Bertrand Tejedor and his fellow teachers defied the rebels by continuing instruction in religion and by urging attendance at Mass. They were not intimidated by threats.

On the First Friday of October, 1934, the local authorities entered the Christian Brothers residence and discovered Passionist Father Manuel Arnau (Inocencio de la Immaculada) preparing to celebrate Mass. He and the Christian Brothers were arrested, marched to a local cemetery, and shot. The martyrs were:

Cyril Bertrand Tejedor ♥ A Christian Brother, born José Sanz Tejedor, in Lerma, Spain, on March 20, 1888. He became a Christian Brother in 1907. Cyril taught in many schools of the congregation and served as superior in Santander in 1925. In 1933 he was sent to Turon, and he started this assignment by making a thirty-day retreat. An eyewitness to the execution of Cyril Bertrand and his companions stated that the martyrs heard their sentence calmly and walked to their doom with dignity and soft prayers.

Marciano José (Filomeno) Lopez ♥ Born in 1900 in Spain. He was assigned to Turon only six months before his martyrdom. He did not teach because he was deaf and had severe health problems.

Julian Alfredo (Vilfridio Fernández) Zapico ♥ A Christian Brother born in 1903. Julian was transferred to Turon only one month before his martyrdom. He was assigned to that troubled region because he was viewed as a religious with a firm resolve and character, one needed in such a crisis.

Victoriano Pio (Claudio Bernabé) Cano ♥ A Christian Brother who arrived in Turon only twenty days before his martyrdom. Born in 1905, he was honored for his brilliant musical abilities.

Benjamin Julian (Vicente Alonso) Andres ♥ A revered Christian Brother, born in 1908. He had been sent to Turon a year before his martyrdom because he had a sound sense of political matters. Benjamin was also beloved for his sense of joy and optimistic outlook on life.

Augusto Andres (Román Martin) Fernández ♥ A Christian Brother born in 1910. When his school was closed by anti-religious rebels, he was sent to Turon. Augustino taught in the coal mining town for about one year before being martyred.

Benito de Jesús (Hector Valdivieso) Sáez ♥ A Christian Brother born in Argentina in 1910. After becoming a religious, he was involved in Spain's Eucharistic Crusade and was recognized as a talented writer.

Aniceto Adolfo (Manuel Seco) Gutierrez ♥ Born in 1912, this Christian Brother was just twenty-two years old when he was martyred.

Innocencio Canoura Arnau ♥ A Passionist priest born in 1887, Father Arnau was a scholarly man who taught literature, philosophy, and theology. He was at the Christian Brothers' residence to hear the confessions of students in preparation for First Friday liturgies on October 5 when he was marched out with the Christian Brothers to be shot.

Pope John Paul II beatified the Martyrs of Asturias on April 29, 1990, declaring: *"In the eyes of their persecutors, they were guilty of having dedicated their lives to the human and Christian education of youth. . . ."* The Holy Father added: *"The Passionist priest met occasionally with the de la Salle Brothers. In that way God in his inscrutable providence wished to unite in martyrdom members of two congregations who worked in solidarity for the Church's one mission."* (See also Martyrs of the Passionists.)

Martyrs of Avrillé 🔥 **See Martyrs of France.**

Claretian Martyrs of the Spanish Civil War

The Congregation of the Missionary Sons of the Immaculate Heart of Mary, known as the Claretians, suffered greatly during the Spanish Civil War. Felipe de Jesus Munarriz and fifty companions, including nine ordained priests and forty-two Claretian seminarians, died when the Communist-led rebels decided to erase that congregation's history from the town of Barbastro, in northern Aragon, Spain.

MARTYRS OF BARBASTRO

(D. 1936)

MARTYRS

On Monday, July 20, 1936, rebel militia forces entered the Claretian house in Barbastro, arresting the entire seminary community. Father Felipe de Jesus Munarriz, the superior, was taken prisoner separately, and the members of the faculty were also arrested. Within two weeks of their arrest, Father Felipe and other Claretian faculty were taken to the local cemetery where they were shot to death, on August 2, 1936.

The seminarians were imprisoned in a theater with other religious. Abuse and filth served as tormenting agents, and prostitutes were brought to tempt them. Throughout their ordeal, the Claretians seminarians waited with faith and calm, leaving written testimonies of their courage and hope in Christ. They also forgave their tormentors publicly. Six senior religious were the first of this group to die. They were killed on the morning of August 12, calling out: *Viva Cristo Rey*, "Long live Christ the King." At midnight, twenty more died with the same religious fervor. On August 15, twenty more Claretians died, many of them celebrating the anniversary of their religious profession as they were martyred. Two other seminarians who had been hospitalized were killed three days later. Seven Claretians were spared because of their age; two Claretians from Argentina were exiled.

Pope John Paul II beatified the Claretian martyrs of Barbastro on October 25, 1992, honoring the profound faith and honor displayed by young and old alike during their frightful torment. The Holy Father declared: *"Since the ma-*

jority of them were young people and students of theology, their lives can be seen as a direct call to you, novices and seminarians, to recognize the lasting validity of an adequate formation and intense preparation based on a solid piety in fidelity to your vocation and your membership in the Church, serving her through your own congregation; in a life of abnegation in community; in perseverance and the witness of your own religious identity. Without all these prerequisites, our blessed would not have been able to receive the grace of martyrdom."

Martyrs of Daimiel ❦ See **Martyrs of the Passionist Congregation.**

Peter Ruiz de los Paños y Angel and Companions

As political and ideological tensions penetrated the various regions of Spain in the 1930's, a unique community arose to foster vocations and ministries. The Diocesan Worker Priests sponsored young seminarians and promoted apostolates that would strengthen the faith. The Communist-led revolutionaries of the Spanish Civil War thus singled out these priests as particular enemies of their atheist agenda.

MARTYRS OF THE DIOCESAN WORKER PRIESTS

(D. 1936)

MARTYRS

Peter Ruiz de los Paños y Angel was the director general of the Diocesan Worker Priests, and he and eight of the community's members were arrested by the revolutionary forces. Peter was born in Mora, Toledo, Spain, on September 18, 1881. Ordained a priest after seminary training, he served in the seminaries of Badajoz, Málaga, and Seville and then became the rector of the Plasencia College and the Spanish College of Rome. Peter also founded the Disciples of Jesus, a women's congregation dedicated to fostering vocations.

Peter was martyred on July 23, 1936, in Toledo, Spain, the victim of the revolutionary Communist forces. His eight companions were martyred at different times during the same year.

Pope John Paul II beatified the martyrs of the Diocesan Worker Priests on October 1, 1995, declaring that Peter and the Diocesan Worker Priests *were "the mature fruit of the Redeemer's paschal mystery."* The Holy Father added: *"Pedro Ruiz de los Paños further enriched the Church by founding the Disciples of Jesus, dedicated to the vocations apostolate. Today, these women religious deeply rejoice, together with the Church in Castille, Cataluña, and the community of Valencia, the native land of the new blesseds."*

George Haydock and Sixty-two Lay and Religious

The number of Catholics who went to their deaths during the most severe anti-Catholic periods in English history remains a glorious episode in the annals of devotion to the Catholic Faith. These devout men and women refused to deny the Church, and they were brutally and then cruelly slain. Some of the most promising young scholars of the land chose death before the dishonor of apostasy, thus confounding the Crown and its agents.

The Martyrs of England, Scotland, and Wales are commemorated as companions of George Haydock. Sixty-three of these martyrs were ordained Catholic priests. Twenty-two were laypeople from various social ranks and walks of life. These martyrs were arrested, tried, and executed particularly during the reign of Elizabeth I (r. 1558-1603) and

MARTYRS OF ENGLAND, SCOTLAND, AND WALES

(D. 1584-1679)

MARTYRS

Oliver Cromwell (r. 1653-1658), the Lord Protector, because they refused to accept statutes from these monarchs that denied the Catholic Church's role in their homeland.

Restrictions concerning the powers of the Church were inherent in declarations made concerning royal supremacy in England. The martyrs were following in the footsteps of Sts. Thomas More and John Fisher in refusing to deny the declarations of Catholic councils and the traditional beliefs of the Church. King Henry VIII (r. 1509-1547) enacted legislation to silence Catholic opposition, and Queen Elizabeth I continued the government's repression with a series of acts that made reconciliation to the Catholic Church a treasonable activity. Missionaries were thus condemned for their efforts at conversions and practicing the liturgies of the faith. Anyone caught harboring a Catholic priest came under the same treasonable charges.

George Haydock, singularly praised in this beatification, was born in 1556 at Cotton Hall, England, the son of Evan and Helen Haydock. He was sent to Douai, France, and then Rome, Italy, to be educated. George was ordained a priest on December 21, 1581, probably at Reims, France. He returned to England to begin a missionary apostolate but was arrested soon after and placed in the Tower of London. Kept in solitary confinement, George suffered from malaria, which he had contracted in Rome. In May 1583, George was given a certain freedom of movement and was able to administer the sacraments to his fellow prisoners.

On February 5, 1583, George was indicted with companions. On January 11, 1584, he was taken in a cart to his execution, all the while reciting the hymn

Te lucis ante terminum. Witnesses to the execution reported that he was hanged, drawn, and quartered, the usual method used to slay priests. He was still alive when disemboweled. Some of the better known martyred companions of George Haydock are as follows:

William Carter (d. 1584) ❦ A London Catholic bookseller imprisoned for printing "lewd" materials, the designation given to any books or pamphlets concerning the Catholic Faith. When his house was searched and other Catholic articles discovered, William was put to the rack. He spent eighteen months in prison, and his wife died alone. William was condemned to death and was able to confess to a priest. He was hanged, drawn, and quartered at Tyburn on January 11, 1584.

Hugh Grant and Marmaduke Bowes (d. 1585) ❦ Hugh was a Catholic missionary and layman who befriended Marmaduke Bowes and died with him at York, England. Hugh was born in Durham, and was sent to Reims, France, for seminary training. He was ordained in 1584. The following year he returned to his native land, where he was arrested immediately.

Marmaduke met Hugh before his arrest, and when Marmaduke heard that Hugh had been taken by the authorities, he went to York to intercede for him. Marmaduke was taken prisoner and tried with the missionary. Hugh and Marmaduke were martyred in York on November 26, 1585.

Alexander Crow (d. 1586/7) ❦ A priest trained at Douai seminary, he worked in northern England. He was born in Yorkshire and was in his twenties when he went to Douai, France, to study for the priesthood. Ordained in 1584, Alexander returned to England, centering his missionary apostolate in the north. He was arrested in Duffield and taken to York. There he was hanged, drawn, and quartered on November 30, 1586/7.

Nicholas Woodfen (d. 1586) ❦ A missionary priest who worked in England under the alias Devereux and may have actually been a Wheeler. He was born in Leominster, Hereforshsire, circa 1530. After studying at Reims, France, Nicholas was ordained a priest in 1581. He returned to England and labored among the lawyers of London until his arrest. Nicholas was hanged, drawn, and quartered on January 21, 1586.

William Pichard (d. 1587) ❦ A priest martyr who was exiled from England but returned to serve the faithful. He was born in Battle, Sussex, in 1557, and studied at Oxford. Trained at Reims, France, he was ordained at Laon in 1583. William returned to England, and was exiled, but returned to his homeland almost immediately. Arrested, he converted thirty prisoners while in captivity. He was hanged, drawn, and quartered by a cook, who acted clumsily while serving as a substitute executioner, on March 21, 1587, at Dorset.

Edmund Duke and Companions (d. 1590) ❦ Priests caught up in the English hysteria following the defeat of the Spanish Armada. Edmund landed at Tynemouth in 1589, arriving from Rome, Italy, with Fathers Richard Hill, John Hogg, and Richard Holiday. They labored until their arrest and then were imprisoned at Durham. They were hanged, drawn, and quartered on May 27, 1590.

Roger Thorpe and Thomas Watkinson (d. 1591) ❧ Robert was a priest, born in Yorkshire. He studied for the priesthood and was ordained at Reims, France, in 1585. He returned to England and was arrested in the home of Thomas Watkinson on the eve of Palm Sunday in 1591. They were taken to York, where they were martyred on May 31, 1591.

George Errington and William Gibson (d. 1596) ❧ Two English Catholic laymen, convicted on the charge of "persuading to popery." Devout Catholics, George and William were approached by a Protestant minister who claimed to desire to convert to the faith. The minister betrayed them to the authorities, and they were arrested. The martyrs were slain at York on November 29, 1596.

Peter Snow and Ralph Grimstow (d. 1598) ❧ Peter was a priest, ordained after studying at Douai, France. He returned to England in 1597 and labored there. Arrested in 1598, Peter was imprisoned, and Ralph went to his defense before the authorities. He was also tried for treason as a result. Peter and Ralph were martyred in York on June 15, 1598.

Christopher Wharton (d. 1600) ❧ He was offered a pardon and bribes to abjure Christ and the Church but chose martyrdom. Christopher was born in Middleton, West Riding, England, and was educated at Oxford. He converted to the faith, studied at Douai, France, and was ordained on March 31, 1584. Two years later he returned to England, but was soon arrested. Christopher was tried in York, refusing all offers of government officials. He was martyred in York on March 28, 1600.

The other martyrs in this group are: Francis Ingleby (1586), John Fingley (1586), Robert Bickerdike (1586), William Thomson (1586), John Sandys (1586), Richard Sargeant (1586), John Lowe (1586), Robert Dibdale (1586), John Adams (1586), Edmund Sykes (1587), Stephen Rowsham (1587), John Hambley (1587), George Douglas (1587), Richard Simpson (1588), Edward Burden (1588), Henry Webley (1588), William Lampley (1588), Nicholas Garlick (1588), Robert Ludlam (1588), Robert Sutton (1588), Richard (Lloyd) Flower (1588), William Spenser (1589), Robert Hardesty (1589), Thomas Belson (1589), Richard Yaxley (d. 1589), George Nichols (1589), Humphrey Pritchard (d. 1589), Nicholas Horner (1590), Alexander Blake (1590), George Beesley (1591), William Pike (1591), Mountford Scott (1591), Joseph Lambton (1592), Thomas Pormort (1592), William Davies (1593), Anthony Page (1593), Christopher Robinson (1597), John Bretton (1598), Edward Thwing (1600), Thomas Palaser (1600), John Talbot (1600), Robert Nutter (1600), John Norton (1600), Roger Filcock (1600), Thomas Hunt (1600), Thomas Sprott (1600), Robert Middleton (1601), Thurston Hunt (1601), Robert Grissold (1604), John Sugar (1604), Robert Drury (1607), Matthew Flathers (1608), Roger Cadwallador (1610), Thomas Atkinson (1616), Roger Wrenno (1616), John Thules (1616), William Southerne (1618), Thomas Bullaker (1642), Henry Heath (1643), Arthur Bell (1643), Edward Bamber (1646), John Woodcock (1646), Thomas Whittaker (1646), Nicholas Postage (1679), and Charles Meeham (1679).

Pope John Paul II beatified George and the martyrs on November 22,

1987, praising the courage and loyalty of these men of the British Isles, who confounded their oppressors by dying with honor and with joy. They were honored as following in the footsteps of the great English confessor who brought glory to the faith in that land.

Members of the Order of St. Francis

Some daring souls are asked to go half way around the world to carry the Gospel, the Good News of Christ, to those who sit in darkness. These souls respond with enthusiasm, despite the perils, most often imitating the zeal of the founders of their religious communities. Blesseds Liberatus Weiss, Michele Pio, and Samuel Marzorati, were Franciscans, imbued with the missionary visions of *Il Poverello*, St. Francis of Assisi.

MARTYRS OF ETHIOPIA

(D. 1716)

MARTYRS

Liberatus was born in Konnersreuth, Bavaria, Germany, on January 4, 1675. He entered the Franciscans of the Austrian Province of St. Bernardine in 1693 and was ordained to the priesthood in 1698.

Michele Pio was a Franciscan born near Pavia, Italy, and a missionary priest. Samuel Marzorati was also a Franciscan, born in Varese, Italy, in 1670. He entered the Order at Lugano, where he was ordained. Sent to Rome, Samuel studied medicine and surgery and went to Egypt in 1705. He intended to go to Ethiopia but reached the island of Socotra in March, 1706. For five years he labored in vain and then returned to Egypt in 1711.

At the same time, Liberatus and Michele tried to get to Ethiopia but were unable to reach their destination. They were then requested by the Congregation for the Propagation of the Faith to make another attempt. Liberatus, Michele, and Samuel formed a team and arrived in Gondor, Ethiopia, on July 20, 1712. They were received by Emperor Justos cordially, but he would not give them permission to identify themselves as Roman Catholics or to preach to the people.

The missionaries spent their time learning the language, and they converted a priest of the Ethiopian Church. The three Franciscans spent two years in isolation until Father Giacomo d'Oleggio joined them. Seeing the situation, Father Giacomo left Ethiopia bearing a letter to the Cardinal prefect of the Propagation and seeking reinforcement. The three others planned to leave if aid did not arrive.

The political situation deteriorated rapidly around them, however. Emperor Justos became ill, and the young son of the previous emperor was proclaimed the true heir to the throne. As part of this insurrection, the three Franciscans were arrested. On March 3, 1716, Liberatus, Michele, and Samuel were stoned to death at Abbo, Ethiopia.

Pope John Paul II beatified Liberatus and his companions on November 20, 1988, declaring: *"Deeply convinced that they were not the masters of what they possessed, the blessed martyrs understood that they were representatives and messengers of the gifts they received from Christ. They knew that they were sent by him to the people of Ethiopia."*

William Repin and Companions

The French Revolution, another demonstration of the horrors brought about by the atheist forces that singled out the Catholic Church for repression, claimed the lives of William Repin and his ninety-eight companions, who are also called the Martyrs of Avrillé. This group is composed of twelve priests, three women religious, and eighty-four lay men and women.

William Repin was born on August 26, 1709, in Thorace, France, and was raised in a devout and industrious family that imbued the lives of the children with the faith. Receiving the grace of a priestly vocation, William, sometimes called Gulielmus, entered the seminary of the diocese and was ordained a priest. His first assignment was the parish of Martigne-Brand. He labored there for half a century, becoming a part of the daily lives of the people of the region.

MARTYRS OF FRANCE

(D. 1792-1794)

MARTYRS

When the French Revolution swept across the land, William refused to accept the new ideology, which he recognized as pagan, vicious, and bent on destroying the Catholic Church. Accordingly, William refused to sign the oath of allegiance to the new Republic. He was arrested with other Catholics of the region on December 24, 1793. Taken prisoner also were priest brothers, John and René Lego, and Sisters Rosalie du Verdier de la Sorinire, María Anna Vaillot, and Odilla Baumgarten. They were guillotined on January 2, 1794, at Angers.

Other martyrs of this group of blesseds were slain near Avrillé on February 1, 1794. Twenty-four women, including a teacher and a woman surgeon as well as young Catholic girls were slain at Angers and Avrillé as part of the revolutionary campaign of terror. The bodies of the victims were not allowed to be viewed by the local citizens but were dumped into a mass grave at Avrillé. Word spread rapidly, and the site became a popular pilgrimage destination for the region. A memorial honoring the deaths was erected at Champs-des-Martyres.

Pope John Paul II beatified William Repin and his companions on February 19, 1984. At the ceremony, the Holy Father honored these who gave their lives for the faith. The martyrs were revered as coming from all walks of life, yet bound by Christ.

Christian Brothers

As the Christian Brothers laid down their lives in Spain for the faith, so did they refuse to abjure the Church during the terrors of the French Revolution. Solomon Leclerq (beatified in 1926) and his companions suffered particularly slow and cruel deaths. The Christian Brothers who died with Solomon in 1794 are honored now as martyrs of the French Revolution.

MARTYRS OF THE FRENCH REVOLUTION

(D. 1794)

MARTYRS

These Christian Brothers refused to agree to the Civil Constitution of the Clergy and were forced out of their schools and residences as a result. Solomon Leclerq was secretary to the Superior General. He was arrested on August 5, 1792, and was shot to death on September 2. Brother Léon Mopinot was sixty-eight years old and a teacher in Moulins. Arrested, he was imprisoned in several different rotting hulks of ships anchored in the harbor of Rochefort. Brother Léon died after two months in the hold of one of these ships. Brother Roger Faverge, who had been born in Orléans in 1745, suffered the same imprisonment and fell ill with typhus. Moved to an island in the harbor, he died there.

Brother Uldaric Guillaume was born in Fraisans in 1755. When his school in Nancy was closed, he taught his students secretly until his arrest. He lasted fifteen months and was buried on an island in the harbor of Rochefort. The horrors of the Christian Brothers' martyrdom were unimaginable, marking a hideous high point in the vicious methods used to try to eradicate Catholic teaching from the land. Pope John Paul II beatified the Christian Brothers martyrs on October 1, 1995. At the ceremony of beatification the martyrs were praised for their courageous offerings of self, despite their agonies and slow, cruel deaths. The loyalty of these martyrs was recognized as an insignia of their dedication to Christ and the Church.

MARTYRS OF GUADALAJARA

(D. 1936)

MARTYRS

Carmelite Cloistered Nuns

Women religious were not spared by the communist-led revolutionary forces of the Spanish Civil War. In some instances, cloisters and their religious communities were singled out and persecuted with a special ferocity. The Blessed Martyrs of Guadalajara were Carmelite cloistered nuns caught up in the violence. They include María Pilar of St. Francis Borgia, who was born Jacoba Martinez Garcia on December 30, 1877 in Tarazona (Zaragoza). She entered the Carmelite cloister at Guadalajara on October 12, 1898, taking vows the following year.

H.Teresa   H.Pilar   H.Angeles

from *Faces of Holiness*

Blessed Carmelites of Guadalajara

With her was María of the Angels of St. Joseph, who was born Marciana Valtierra Tordesillas on March 16, 1905 in Getafe, near Madrid. She entered the Carmel of Guadalajara on July 14, 1929. Teresa of the Child Jesus and St. John of the Cross, the third martyr, was born Eusebia Garcia y Garcia in Mochales on March 5, 1909. She entered the Guadalajara Carmel at age sixteen and made her first profession in 1926.

As the Communist militia groups ravaged sacred buildings and murdered religious, the Carmelites were forced to flee from their convent. They hoped to find places of refuge with devout Catholic families in the area, where they could remain hidden throughout the tragic period. These Carmelite Sisters did not find the haven they sought, as militia units of Communists were patrolling in the streets. They were confronted by one patrol while in the town. On July 24, 1936, María of the Angels was killed by gunfire. María Pilar received a mortal wound. Teresa of the Child Jesus was offered her freedom if she denied Christ, the Church, and the Carmel. She refused and was slain.

Pope John Paul II beatified the Carmelite Martyrs on March 29, 1987, announcing that these nuns exemplified the true spirit of Carmel, surrendering themselves in death as they had offered themselves to Christ in their religious lives.

"The three daughters of Carmel could have addressed these words to the Good Shepherd when the hour came for them to give their lives for their faith in the divine Bridegroom of their souls. Yes, 'I fear nothing,' not even death. Love is greater than death and 'you are with me.' You, the Bridegroom on the Cross! You, Christ, my strength! This following of the Master, which should bring us to imitate him even to giving up our lives for love of him, has been an almost constant call in early times and always, for Christians to give this supreme witness of love — martyrdom — before everyone, especially before their persecutors. . . . In this way we see that martyrdom — the ultimate witness in defense of the faith — is considered by the Church as a very eminent gift and as the supreme test of love, through which a Christian follows the very footsteps of Jesus, who freely accepted suffering and death for the salvation of the world."

The act of forgiveness is the ultimate crown of martyrdom. The ability and grace to pray for one's tormentors serves as the true mirroring of Christ. Forgiveness was an element in the martyrdoms of priests and religious in the

MARTYRS OF THE HOSPITALLERS OF ST. JOHN OF GOD

(D. 1936-1939)

MARTYRS

Spanish Civil War, and this gracious Christian attribute characterizes the deaths of Braulius María Corres Diaz de Cerio and his seventy companions of the Hospitallers of St. John of God, including Frederick Rubio Alvarez.

Braulius María and his companions died at the hands of the Communist-inspired revolutionary militias at different times in several locations in Spain. Some had come to Spain to train as Hospitallers, dedicated to the care of the sick and abandoned.

All died brutally, guilty only of being Catholics and devout religious. They stayed united spiritually throughout, inspired by the holiness of their founder and the community of life which had formed their souls. The martyred Hospitallers were:

Apostolic School of Talavera de la Reina (Toledo)

Federico Carlos Rubio Alvarez, Benavides (Léon), 73 years old; Primo Martínez de S. Vicente Castillo, San Román de Campezo (Alaya), 67 years old; Jerónimo Ochoa Urdangarin, Goñi (Navarre), 32 years old; Juan de la Cruz (Eloy) Delgado Pastor, Puebla de Alcocer (Badajoz) 22 years old.

Sanitarium San Juan de Dios, de Calafell (Tarragona)

Braulius María (Pablo) Corres Díaz de Cerio, Torralba de Río (Navarre), 39 years old; Julían (Miguel) Carrasquer Fos, Sueca (Valencia), 55 years old; Eusebio (Antonio) Forcades Ferraté, Reus (Tarragona), 60 years old; Constancio (Saturnino) Roca Huguet, Sant Sadurní d 'Anoia (Barcelona), 41 years old; Benito José Labré (Arsenio) Mañoso González, Lomoviejo (Valladolid), 57 years old; Vicente de Paúl Canelles Vives, Onda (Castellón), 42 years old; Tomás Urdanoz Aldaz, Echarri (Navarre), 33 years old; Rafael Flamarique Salinas, Mendívil (Navarre), 33 years old; Antonio Llauradó Parisi, Reus (Tarragona), 33 years old; Manuel López Orbara, Puente de la Reina (Navarre), 23 years old; Ignacio Tejero Molina, Monzalbarba (Zaragoza), 20 years old; Enrique Beltrán Llorca, Villareal (Castellón), 37 years old; Domingo Pitarch Gurrea, Villareal (Castellón), 27 years old; Antonio Sanchiz Silvestre, Villamarchante (Valencia), 26 years old; Manuel Jiménez Salado, Jerez de la Frontera (Cadiz), 29 years old.

Colombians

Rubén de Jesús López Aguilar, Concepción (Antioquia, Colombia), 28 years old; Arturo (Luis) Ayala Niño, (Paipa (Boyacá, Colombia), 27 years old; Juan Bta. (José) Velázquez Peláez, Jardin (Antioquia, Colombia), 27 years old; Eugenio (Alfanso, Antonio) Ramírez Salazar, La Ceja (Antioquia, Colombia), 23 years old; Esteban (Gabriel) Maya Gutiérrez, Pácora (Antioquia, Colombia), 29 years old; Melquíades (Ramón) Ramírez Zuloaga, Sonsón (Antioquia, Colombia), 27 years old; Gaspar (Luis, Modesto) Páez Perdomo, La Unión (Huila, Colombia), 23 years old.

Sanitarium San José, de Ciempozuelos (Madrid)

Flavio (Atilano) Argüeso González, Mazuecos, (Palencia), 58 years old; Francisco Arias Martín, Granada, 52 years old; Tobías (Francisco) Borrás Romeu, San Jorge (Castellón), 76 years old; Juan Jesús (Maríano) Ardradas Gonzalo, Conquezuela (Soria), 58 years old; Guillermo (Vicente) Llop Gayá, Villareal (Castellón), 56 years old; Clemente Díez Sahagún, Fuentes de Nava (Palencia), 75 years old; Lázaro (Juan María) Múgica Goiburu, Ideazábal (Guipúzcoa), 69 years old; Martiniano (Antonio) Meléndez Sánchez, (Málaga), 58 years old; Pedro María Alcalde Negredo, Ledesma (Soria), 58 years old; Julián Plazaola Artola, San Sebastián (Guipuzcoa), 21 years old; Hilario (Antonio) Delgado Vílchez, Cañar (Granada), 18 years old; Pedro de Alcántara Bernaltc Calzado, Moral de Calatrava (Ciudad Real), 26 years old; Juan Alcalde, Zuzones (Burgos), 25 years old; Isidoro Martínez Izquiero, Madrid, 18 years old; Angel Sastre Corporales, Vallaralbo del Vino (Zamora), 20 years old; Eduardo Bautista Jiménez, La Gineta (Albacete), 51 years old; José Mora Velasco, (Córdoba), 50 years old; José Ruiz Cuesta, Dílar (Granada), 29 years old; Diego de Cádiz (Santiago) García Molina, Moral de Calatrava (Ciudad Real), 44 years old; Román (Rafael) Touceda Fernández, Madrid, 32 years old; Miguel (Miguel Francisco) Ruedas Mejías, Motril (Granada), 34 years old; Arturo Donoso Murillo, Puebla de Alcocer (Badajoz), 19 years old; Jesús Gesta de Piquer, (Madrid), 21 years old; Antonio Martínez Gil-Leonis, Montellano (Seville), 20, years old.

Institute San José de Carabanchel Alto (Madrid)

Proceso (Joaquín) Ruiz Cascalcs, Bcniel (Murcia), 48 years old; Cristino (Miguel) Roca Huguet, Mollins de Rei (Barcelona), 37 years old; Eutimio (Nicolás) Aramendía García, Oteiza de la Solanna (Navarre), 57 years old; Canuto (José) Franco Gómez, Aljucer (Murcia), n.d.; Dositeo (Guillermo) Rubio Alonso, Madrigalejo (Burgos), 67 years old; Cesáreo (Maríano) Niño Pérez, Torregutiérrez, (Segovia), 58 years old; Benjamin (Alejandro) Cobos Celada, (Palencia), 48 years old; Carmelo (Isidro) Gil Arano, Tudela (Navarre), 57 years old; Cosme (Simón) Brun Arará, Santa Coloma de Farners (Girona), 41 years old; Cecilio (Enrique) López López, Fondón (Almeria), 35 years old; Rufino (Crescencio) Lasheras Aizcorbe, Arandigoyen (Navarre), 36 years old; Faustino (Antonio) Villanueva Igual, Sarrión (Teruel), 23 years old.

Hospital San Juan de Dios, de Barcelona, and the Sanitarium of Sant Boi de Llobregat (Barcelona)

Juan Bautista Egozcuezebál Aldaz, Nuin, (Navarre), 54 years old; Pedro de Alcántara (Lorenzo) Villanueva Larráyoz, (Navarre), 54 years old; Francisco Javier Ponsa Casallach, Moiá (Barcelona); Juan Antonio Burró Mas, Barcelona, 22 years old; Asisclo (Joaquín) Piña Piazuelo, Caspe (Zaragoza), 58 years old; Protasio (Antonio) Cubells Minguell, Coll de Nargó (Lleida), 56 years old.

Hospital San Rafael, de Madrid

Gonzalo Gonzalo Gonzalo, Conquezuela (Soria), 27 years old; Jacinto Hoyuelos González, Matarrepudio (Santander), 22 years old; Nicéro Salvador del Río, Villamorco, (Palencia), 23 years old.

Pope John Paul II beatified the martyred Hospitallers of St. John of God on October 25, 1992, declaring:

"Unanimous is the witness offered by the Brothers of St. John of God . . . who died giving glory to God and forgiving their assassins. At the moment of their martyrdom several of them repeated the words of Christ himself: 'Father, forgive them, they know not what they do' (Lk 23:24). All of them chose death rather than renounce their faith and their religious life. They went to their execution, rejoicing in the gift of martyrdom, of which they felt unworthy, despite fact that all of them, especially the young ones, had their hearts set on great apostolic ideals of proclaiming the Gospel to others; some of them by caring for the sick, and the others through the ministry of preaching as missionaries. The seven Hospitaller Brothers of Colombia deserve special mention, for they are the first sons of that land to be raised the honors of the altar. They were in Spain to finish their religious and professional formation when the Lord called them to give this witness of their faith. Today, in conjunction with the fifth centenary of the evangelization of America, we publicly acknowledge their martyrdom and present as the first fruits of the Colombian Church."

Dermot O'Hurley and Companions

MARTYRS OF IRELAND

(D. 1579-1654)

MARTYRS

Cruelty was the hallmark of the English persecution of Catholics in Ireland from 1579 to 1654, in which the archbishop of Cashel and sixteen Irish faithful were slain. These Irish Catholics died because they would not renounce the authority of the pope. The excommunication of Queen Elizabeth I (r. 1558-1603) by Pope St. Pius V in 1570 unleashed a new persecution in England, and an Irish uprising of nobles spurred the same reprisals in Ireland.

Other martyrs died from 1602-

1621, as the Irish refused to surrender the faith. The insurrection of 1641 brought even more persecutions, and the terrible era of Oliver Cromwell, Lord Protector of England (r. 1653-1658), claimed the last of these courageous followers of Christ. The martyrs of Ireland included:

Dermot O'Hurley (d. 1584) ❦ The son of William O'Hurley of Lickadoon, Ireland, he was educated as a Catholic in various European capitals and was revered as a brilliant and eloquent defender of the faith. Dermot taught at the Louvain, in Belgium, Reims, France, and Rome, Italy. He had a doctorate degree and was deemed courageous in his Catholicism.

In 1581, Pope Gregory XIII (r. 1572-1585) appointed Dermot the archbishop of Cashel, consecrating him on September 11 of that year. Dermot set sail to Ireland to assume his episcopal see but was arrested almost immediately by English authorities. The Irish nobles were in revolt against England at the time, and it was hoped that Dermot was privy to their plans and would be able to betray their military intentions.

In March 1584, the English resorted to hideous tortures to break Dermot's resolute silence. His legs were oiled and roasted over a fire, causing him excruciating pain. He refused to provide any information, and the torment continued day after day without any success.

Dermot was returned to his prison cell in a pitiful condition as a political storm broke over his torture. English jurists, horrified as details of his sufferings spread over the land, announced that there was no legal reasons for Dermot to endure imprisonment, let alone such hideous punishment. The jusrists were ignored by the crown authorities. Sometime in June, between the 19th and the 29th, Dermot, archbishop of Cashel, was hanged on St. Stephen's Green.

Patrick O'Healy, O.F.M. ❦ The Franciscan bishop of Mayo, Ireland, he was arrested and martyred with Conn O'Rourke on August 13, 1579. Bishop O'Healy's last sermon was a reassertion of papal authority, addressed to all who had gathered to watch his execution.

Conn O'Rourke, O.F.M. ❦ The Franciscan priest who died with Bishop O'Healy at Kilmallock. He gave his life to protest the English attempts to repress the Church in Ireland.

Matthew Lambert ❦ This martyr was a devout baker who was martyred at Wexford with several companions in July, 1581. He stated that he was not learned enough to comment on the problems between the pope and Queen Elizabeth I, but he believed in the teachings of the Church.

Robert Meyler ❦ A Catholic sailor, Robert professed the faith and died with Matthew Lambert at Wexford, in July, 1581.

Edward Cheevers ❦ Another Catholic sailor, Edward was arrested with Robert Meyler and Patrick Cavanagh and died at Wexford, in July, 1581.

Patrick Cavanagh ❦ The last sailor companion of Matthew Lambert, martyred in Wexford, July, 1581.

Margaret Ball ❦ This widowed housewife of Dublin was arrested for giving priests sanctuary in her home. She was turned over to the English by her apostate son and was thrown into Dublin Castle dungeon. Margaret died there from abuse and torment in 1584.

Maurice McKenraghty ❦ The chaplain of Lord Dermot who led a revolt against English tyranny in the south of Ireland, Maurice was arrested in 1585. He was given the opportunity to deny papal supremacy but refused and was martyred at Clonmel on April 20, 1585.

Dominic Collins, S.J. ❦ A Jesuit lay brother living at Youghal, Dominic was arrested and tortured by the English, who demanded that he divulge the plans of the Spanish to invade England. Dominic knew of no such plans, and he refused to deny the Holy See. He was hanged at Youghal on October 31, 1602.

Conor O'Devany, O.F.M. ❦ The Franciscan bishop of Down and Connor, Ireland, he was arrested with Patrick O'Loughbrain, O.F.M. The two were tortured and then martyred in Dublin on February 1, 1612, as part of the renewed English suppression of the era.

Patrick O'Loughbrain ❦ See Conor O'Devany, above.

Francis Taylor ❦ The was the son of a wealthy, landed family of Swords and a merchant of Dublin. In 1595, Francis became Lord Mayor. He was elected to Parliament but his victory was overturned, and he was thrown into prison. He was martyred for the faith on January 30, 1621, after seven years of imprisonment and torment.

Peter Higgins, O.P. ❦ A Dominican priest of Dublin, well-liked by people of all faiths, Peter was arrested in the furor of wild rumors following the Insurrection of 1641. Dublin was wracked by rumors that Protestants had been massacred in Ulster at the instigation of priests. Peter died in Dublin on March 23, 1642, innocent of any crime except his loyalty to the Church.

Terence Albert, O.P. ❦ The bishop of Emily, Ireland, this Dominican was captured by Ireton, Cromwell's son-in-law. Terence was visiting Limerick when Ireton's forces took the town. He was arrested and condemned for encouraging the Irish defense. Terence died in Limerick on October 31, 1651.

John Kearney, O.F.M. ❦ A Franciscan priest, John defied the ban on priests issued by Cromwell. He was arrested and hanged at Clonmel, County Tipperary, on March 11, 1653.

William Tirry, O.S.A. ❦ An Augustinian priest, this last martyr of the group was caught in his vestments and arrested in 1654. Standing on the scaffold, William urged the Irish to endure all things and to remain steadfast to the faith. He was martyred on May, 2, 1654.

Pope John Paul II beatified the Irish Martyrs on September 27, 1992, declaring: *"And how can we fail to sing the praises of seventeen Irish Martyrs being beatified today?"* The Holy Father added: *"We admire them for their personal courage. We thank them for the example of their fidelity which is more than an example: it is a heritage of the Irish people and a responsibility to be lived up to in every age. In a decisive hour, a whole people chose to stand firmly by its coventant with God: 'All the words which the Lord has spoken we will do' (Ex 24:3). Along with Saint Oliver Plunkett, the new Beati comprise but a small part of the host of Irish Martyrs of Penal Times. The religious and political turmoil through these witnesses lived was marked by grave intolerance on every side. Their victory lay precisely in going to death with no hatred in the hearts. They lived and died for love. Many of them publicly forgave all those who had contributed in any way to their martyrdom. The Martyrs significance for today lies in the fact that their testimony shattered the vain claim to live one's life or to build a model society without an integral vision of our human destiny, without reference to our eternal calling, without transcendence. The Martyrs exhort succeeding generations of Irish men and women: 'Fight the good fight of the faith; take hold of the eternal life to which you were called . . . keep the commandment unstained and free from reproach until the appearing of our Lord Jesus Christ' (1 Tim 6:12-14)."*

Augustinian Missionary Priests

Again and again Catholic missionaries attempted to penetrate the Japanese islands, a nation sealed by the Tokugawa Shogunate against all Christian or European influences. Despite the obvious perils, the missionaries tried to reach the suffering Christians of Japan, and they paid for apostolic zeal with their lives. Blesseds Martin of St. Nicholas Lumbreras and Melchior Sanchez, were two among the many who gave their lives for the faith in the East.

MARTYRS OF JAPAN

(D. 1632)

🔥

MARTYRS

Martin was born in Zaragoza, Spain, circa 1592. Ordained an Augustinian priest, he was sent to Japan where the Order conducted missions. Melchior Sanchez, also an ordained Augustinian priest, was born in Granada, Spain, in 1599. Both men had served in the Augustinian mission in Manila, the Philippines. With the deaths of missionaries in Japan in 1629, Martin and Melchior were sent out as replacements. They disguised themselves as merchants and carried out their labors among the Christians in the mountains near Nagasaki.

When Melchior became ill, the missionaries went to the city seeking medical assistance. They were arrested by the military forces of Iemitsu Tokugawa, a formidable foe of Europeans and the Church. Iemitsu was relentless in pursuing Catholic missionaries and the faithful, and cruelty and prolonged horrors were the hallmarks of imprisonment during his reign. Imprisoned in Nagasaki, Martin and Melchior were subjected to almost inhuman tortures before being martyred by being burned alive on December 11, 1632.

Pope John Paul II beatified Martin and Melchior on April 23, 1989, announcing: *"Dear brothers and sisters, the new Blesseds Martin and Melchior are mature fruits of the missionary and evangelizing spirit that has character-*

ized the Church in Spain. Born into the bosom of deeply Christian families and Saragossa and Granada, they left everything to follow Christ. These two martyrs, glory of the Church and the Augustinian family, should be a challenge and a stimulus that arouses in Spanish families that Christian vitality which enables the message of salvation to reach the farthest corners of the earth. May these values not be lost! May such a witness of faith which honors and exalts Spanish history not be forgotten!"

John Souzy and Companions

Many priests of France refused to support or even recognize the edicts of the French Revolution and its authorities. They took an oath that brought persecution to the Church, despite the dangers apparent in such a decision. As a result of their refusal, in 1794, 829 priests and religious were arrested and forced to board two slave ships anchored in the Charente River, near Rochefort. The Martyrs of La Rochelle, also called the Martyrs of Pontini di Rochefort, included Blesseds John Souzy, Gabriel Pergaud, and sixty-two companions.

MARTYRS OF LA ROCHELLE

(D. 1794)

MARTYRS

These holy and religious exiles (officially they were considered such, but the deportation was not to a place but to a passage) were crowded into small boats. They sailed in darkness and in inhumane and unsupportable conditions, aggravated by the fact that every morning the crew burned coal (tar), which made the air unbreathable. During the journey, they were forced to remain below decks without food or water. In addition, they were subjected to brutalities and the mockery of the sailors. Every prayer and every sign of faith were forbidden. Nearly all of the martyrs were stricken by contagious diseases. Deprived of all medical assistance, many prisoners served as nurses for their companions. Among the martyred were:

John Souzy 🔥 A priest from La Rochelle, he was named vicar general of the victims when they were deported. John died after ten months and was buried on Madame Island. His companions included thirteen priests from French dioceses and twelve members of religious congregations.

Gabriel Pergaud 🔥 An Augustinian martyr of La Rochelle, Gabriel was born on October 29, 1752, at Saint-Priest-la-Plaine (Creuse), France. He entered the Canons Regular of St. Augustine and took his vows in 1769. Ordained, Gabriel served in many capacities, including prior of the abbey of Beaulieu, (Côtes-d'Arnior). A man of faith and character, he opposed the extreme measures of the government and with sixty-two others, including Blessed

John Baptist Souzy, was placed into the holds of barges anchored near Rochefort. He reportedly died on July 21, 1794, along with 574 other victims.

Pope John Paul II beatified these martyrs on October 1, 1995, declaring:

"This morning, dear brother and sisters, we are thinking of sixty-four French priests who died with hundreds of others on the 'decks of Rochefort.'"

. . . . *"They gradually let themselves be identified with the sacrifice of Christ, which they celebrated by virtue of their ordination. Here they are offered to our gaze as a living symbol of the power of Christ, who acts in human weaknesses."*

Sisters of the Sacred Heart of Jesus

The Spanish Civil War claimed the lives of countless Catholics, bequeathing a heritage of hope and courage to succeeding generations. Two victims of the violence and hatred were Sisters of the Sacred Heart of Jesus in Madrid: Blesseds Rita Dolores Pujatte Sanchez and Frances of the Sacred Heart of Jesus Aldea Araujo. Both were elderly and infirm, but neither was spared.

MARTYRS OF MADRID

(D. 1936)

MARTYRS

Rita Dolores Pujatte Sanchez was born in Aspe, Spain, on February 19, 1853, the daughter of Antonio Pujatte and Luisa Sanchez. She had four siblings and was raised in the faith. As a young woman, Rita Dolores was a catechist and charity worker and a tertiary Franciscan. In 1888, she entered the Sisters of Charity of the Sacred Heart of Jesus, becoming Superior General in 1900 and serving until 1928. Rita Dolores retired to St. Susanna's College in Madrid, and by 1936 she was infirm and blind.

Frances of the Sacred Heart of Jesus Aldea Araujo was born in Somolinos, Spain, on December 17, 1881. Orphaned when young, Frances was a boarding student at St. Susanna's until she entered the congregation at age eighteen. A teacher, Frances served as assistant and then General Secretary of the Sisters of Charity of the Sacred Heart of Jesus.

On July 20, 1936, the revolutionary military forces attacked St. Susanna's College, and Rita and Frances were allowed to leave because of their age. Taking refuge in a nearby apartment, the sisters were taken prisoners by the rebels two hours later. They were brought forcibly to a site near Canillejas, a suburb of Madrid, and there they were shot. An autopsy performed the next day reported that their remains had not stiffened and emitted a fragrant perfume. In 1940, their bodies were exhumed as part of the opening of their Cause. Their remains still had not decomposed, and had life-like appearances. In 1954, the remains of Rita and Frances, still incorrupt, were enshrined in the college of the congregation.

Pope John Paul II beatified Rita and Frances as martyrs on May 10, 1998, declaring: *"The supreme commandment of the Lord had taken deep root during the years of their religious consecration, which they lived in fidelity to the congregation's charism."* The Holy Father added: *"Their example is a call to all Christians to love as Christ loves, even amid the greatest difficulties."*

Marianist Educators of Ciudad Real

The Spanish Civil War claimed victims of many religious Orders and congregations. In September, 1936, three Marianists, Carlos Eraña Guruceta, Fidel Fuido, and Jesús Hita, shared in this martyrdom in Ciudad Real, Spain.

MARTYRS OF THE MARIANIST CONGREGATION

(D. 1936)

MARTYRS

Carlos Eraña Guruceta was born in Arechavaleta (Guipuzcoa), Spain, on November 2, 1884. He entered the Marianists, and made his perpetual vows in 1908. Carlos assumed teaching assignments in the congregation's educational institutions and was principal in several schools. He was at the Colegio de Nuestra Señora de Pilar in Madrid when civil war exploded across Spain.

In 1936, Carlos went to Alcaros, Ciudad Real, where he had served originally. He discovered many other Marianists in hiding, as the religious Orders of Spain had been suppressed. Carlos began to aid these fellow religious, enlisting the assistance of former students in amassing the necessary havens and funds. He continued working until September 6, when he was arrested by troops of the "Popular Army."

The former seminary in the city had been turned into a prison, and Carlos was taken there. He remained a captive for twelve days, standing as a model of faith and true resolve. On September 18, in the company of seven laymen, Carlos was taken into the seminary yard and shot to death.

Jesús Hita was born in Calahorra, Spain, on April 17, 1900. He entered the Marianists and was accepted as a lay brother, making his final vows on August 26, 1928.

During the war, Jesús was at the Colegio de Nuestra Señora del Pilar in Madrid, but went to Ciudad Real to teach during the summer. In the summer of 1936 anticlerical militias were taking over religious facilities and seizing members of religious Orders. Jesús was forced to seek refuge with a Catholic family in the town to avoid arrest. Seeing the desecration and persecutions, Jesús practiced penitential acts in reparation. He was arrested and executed on September 25, with Blessed Juan Pedro, Pablo María, and two priests. Their bodies were thrown into a well.

Fidel Fuido was born in Yécora, Spain, on April 24, 1880, and entered the Society of Mary, making his final vows in 1904. Fidel then taught at Colegio Nuestra Señora del Pilar in Madrid, from 1910-1933. A respected archaeologist with a doctorate in history, Fidel was in the Ciudad Real at the Marianist college when the persecution of the Church began. Forced out of his seminary which was converted into a prison, Fidel was arrested in a small boarding house and held prisoner for two months. He was set free but then arrested again and taken to the seminary, where he was executed at dawn on October 17.

Pope John Paul II beatified the Marianist Martyrs on May 7, 1995, declaring: *"As Marianists they learned how to love Our Lady intensely and . . . with gentleness they went to their martyrdom, the supreme act of surrender to Jesus and Mary, and like others before them, they died forgiving, thus certain of following the footsteps of Christ himself."*

Lay and Religious Martyrs of the Spanish Civil War

Also called the Martyrs of Daimiel, the Passionist Martyrs, led by Niceforo of Jesus and Mary Tejerina, were victims of the anti-Catholic rebel forces in the Spanish Civil War. This group of twenty-six martyrs was composed mostly of young men between the ages of eighteen and twenty-one studying at the Passionist formation house in Daimeil, Spain. The six priests, four lay brothers, and fifteen Passionist students were under the direction of Niceforo.

MARTYRS OF THE PASSIONIST CONGREGATION

(D. 1936)

MARTYRS

On the night of July 21, 1936, the Daimiel monastery was surrounded by armed rebel militia and the occupants were forced to evacuate to a local cemetery. Destined for immediate execution or to be buried alive, the Passionists were spared by the local mayor. Even so, the students and their directors bid one another goodbye, knowing full well the fate that awaited those charged with the crime of "being religious."

Father Niceforo was an inspiration to the students and the Passionist family. On the night when they were arrested, he declared: "Beloved sons and brothers, this is our Gethsemane. In its weak part, nature faints away and loses courage. However, Jesus Christ is with us. He is going to give us himself who is strength for the weak. An angel comforted Jesus. It is Jesus Christ himself who will comfort and sustain us. In a few moments we shall be with Christ. Inhabitants of Calvary, go on and die for Christ! It is my task to encourage you, but I myself am encouraged by your example!"

Niceforo was killed in Manzanares on July 23, 1936, with five students: José Estalayo Garcia, Epifanio Sierra Conde, Fulgencio Calvo Sanchez, Abilio Ramos Ramos, and Zacarias Fernandez Crespo. On the same day in Carabanchel Bajo, Father Germano Perez Gimenez, Father Felipe Valcabado Granada, and Brothers Anacario Benito Nozal and Felipe Ruiz Fraile died with students Maurilio Macho Rodriguez, José Oses Sainz, Julio Mediavilla Concejero, José Ruiz Martínez and Laurino Proano Cuesta.

On July 25, 1936, Father Pedro Lergo Redondo was executed at Urda with Brother Benito Solana Ruiz and student Feliz Ugalde Iruzun. Father Juan Pedro Bengoa Aranguren and Brother Pablo Leoz Portillo were martyred on September 25 at Carrion de Calatrava.

On October 23, 1936, the remaining martyrs, Father Ildefonso Garcia Nozal, Father Justiniano Cuesta Redondo, and students Enfracio de Celis Salinas, Tomas Cuartero Garcia, Honorino Carracedo Ramos, and José Cuartero Garcia were killed in Manzanares.

Pope John Paul II beatified the Martyrs of the Passionist Congregation on October 1, 1989, declaring:

"The majority of them, young men between eighteen and twenty-one years of age, lived dreaming of the priesthood, but the Lord ordained that their first Mass should be their own holocaust. Now we exalt them and give glory to Christ, who has associated them to the Cross. 'The Lord loves the just . . . and sustains the orphan and widow, the way of the wicked he thwarts. The Lord reigns for ever' (Ps 145[146]:9-10)."

Martyrs of the Piarist Congregation ❦ See Martyrs of the Scalopian Congregation.

Lay Defenders of the Pope

The valiant nation of Poland has long withstood invasions, occupations, and repression conducted by military forces of neighboring lands. Throughout the terrible ordeals of each new assault, the faith of the Polish people is tried anew, and in each episode of tragedy the Church has survived and offered the faithful new witnesses for Christ.

MARTYRS OF PODLASIE

(D. 1874)

MARTYRS

Blessed Vincent Lewoniuk and twelve companions were Byzantine-rite Catholics living in Podlasie, in the eastern region of modern Poland. In 1874, Czar Alexander II of Russia, was in control of that part of Poland, and he intended to suppress the eparchy of Chem, thus incorporating all Eastern-rite Catholics loyal to the pope into the Orthodox Church.

On January 24, 1874, soldiers arrived in Pratulin, where Vincent Lewoniuk and the people heard that the parish was to become Orthodox. The people rejected the Order, despite promises of favors from the czar and threats for disobedience. The officer in charge, quite disturbed by the spontaneous demonstration and the zeal, ordered his soldiers to prepare their weapons.

The people knelt in the street, singing hymns and repeating: "It is sweet to die for the faith." The martyrs were all laymen, most of them married with families, and they were between the ages of nineteen and fifty, most in their twenties. All thirteen were shot to death before their horrified families and friends. The bodies were buried by the Russians, and the families were forbidden to show them any honor. Czar Alexander II suppressed the eparchy of Chem the following year, but he did not erase the glory of the martyrs or the faith.

Pope John Paul II beatified Vincent and his twelve companions on October 6, 1996, and His Holiness greeted a group of Ukrainian pilgrims, declaring: *"I urge you to imitate their courageous perseverance in the faith and to follow their fervent devotion to the Blessed Virgin."*

Dionysius Pamplona and Companions

The Scalopians or Piarists, also called the Clerks Regular of the Pious Schools, were founded in 1597 by St. Joseph Calasanctius or Calasanz. In 1621, the Scalopians were made a religious congregation by Pope Gregory XV (r. 1621-1623). Called by some the Poor Clerks of the Mother of God, or the Paulines, the Scalopians were true pioneers in the apostolate of education. As a result, their houses and institutions in Spain drew the wrath of the revolutionaries during the Spanish Civil War.

MARTYRS OF THE SCALOPIAN CONGREGATION

(D. 1936)

MARTYRS

Blessed Dionysius Pamplona and twelve Scalopian companions died as a result of their dedication. Dionysius was a priest, born in 1868 in Calamocha, Teruel, Spain. He was director of the Peralta de la Sol School in Huesca and performed other roles for the congregation. In 1936, Dionysius was arrested as a priest, but he escaped from prison in order to go to the parish church to consume all of the consecrated hosts, endangered by the atheist militias. Recaptured, he was martyred on July 25, 1936, near Monzon prison. His companions were:

Emmanuel Segura A priest and educator. He was born in 1881 in Almonacid de la Sierra in Saragossa province, Spain. Emmanuel was a novice master in Peralta del Sol. He was martyred on July 23, 1936.

David Carlos ♥ A Scalopian brother from Asorta, Navarre, Spain. He was offered his freedom if he would abandon his religious habit but refused. David was slain on July 28, 1936.

Enrico Canadell ♥ A native of Olot, Gerona, Italy, born in 1890. He was ordained as a Scalopian and was especially devoted to the Holy Eucharist. Enrico was martyred near Castelfullit on August 17, 1936.

Faustino Oteiza ♥ A priest and educator, born in Aygui, in Navarre, in 1890. He was particularly devoted to the Blessed Virgin. He was slain on August 9, 1936.

Florentino Felipe ♥ A Scalopian lay brother, he was born in Alquierzar, in Huesca, Spain, in 1856. Imprisoned for two weeks, Florentino was suffering from a severe stomach ailment at the time of his arrest. He was martyred on August 9, 1936.

Matteas Cardona ♥ A newly ordained Scalopian priest, born in Vallibona, Castellón, Spain, in 1902. He was devoted and calm throughout his ordeal, martyred on August 20, 1936, near his hometown.

Francesco Carceller ♥ A member of a devout family, he was born in Forcall, Castellón, Spain, in 1901. He was an ordained priest and a dedicated educator. Francesco was martyred on October 2, 1936.

Ignazio Casanovas ♥ Born in Igualada, Barcelona, Spain, in 1893, he was noted for his piety and goodness. He was slain on September 16, 1936.

Carlo Navarro ♥ A newly ordained Scalopian priest, Carlo was born in Torrente, Valencia, in 1911. He was martyred on September 22, 1939, calling out: *Viva Cristo Rey*, "Long live Christ the King" and invoking the Virgin Mary.

José Ferrer ♥ A Scalopian priest who was born in 1904 in Algemesi, Valencia, Spain. He served as an organist in the cathedral of Albarracín and was noted for his deep piety. José died on December 9, 1936.

Juan Agramunt ♥ A Scalopian priest and educator, he was born in 1907 in Almazora, Castellón, Spain. Kept in prison for weeks, he was martyred on August 13, 1936.

Alfredo Parte ♥ A Scalopian priest from Cirreluelo de Bricia, Bourgos, Spain, he was singled out for a terrible martyrdom, dying on December 27, 1936, after refusing to abjure the faith and his membership in the Scalopians.

Pope John Paul II beatified the Martyrs of the Scalopian Congregation on October 1, 1995, declaring: *"Dionysius Pamplona and his companion martyrs were not the heroes of a human war, but teachers of youth, who, because of their status as religious and teachers, faced their tragic destiny as authentic witnesses to the faith, giving us with their martyrdom the last lesson of their life."*

Victims of the Spanish Civil War

During the Spanish Civil War, entire communities were closed by the godless revolutionary militias, but the religious did not abandon their vocations. Mother Angeles de San José Lloret Martí and her sixteen companions belonged to the such a determined religious congregation.

Members of the Sisters of Christian Doctrine, these nuns continued their life of prayer even after their Generalate convent was closed by going into hiding. They were discovered and arrest, and spent four months in where they calmly and openly lived as a devout community. They even knitted jerseys for their captors. Mother Angeles de San José and her nuns were martyred as a community in the fall of 1936.

Pope John Paul II beatified Mother San José and her companions on October 1, 1995, declaring: *"Mother Angeles de San José gathered in a single apartment members who had no families or friends to take them in. There they lived fraternal charity, discovering how persecution, poverty, and suffering are all ways that lead to God."* The Holy Father said also: *"These sisters, practicing what they had so often passed on in teaching catechism, spent their last few months sewing clothes for those who put an end to their lives. Their death then and their glorification now proclaim the power of the risen Christ and the need to dedicate oneself to the task of evangelization. With them, the communities of Valencia and Cataluña add new names to their martyrology."*

MARTYRS OF THE SISTERS OF CHRISTIAN DOCTRINE

(D. 1936)

MARTYRS

Martyrs of Spain See **Martyrs of the Hospitallers of St. John of God.**

Faithful Confessors

In 1989, Pope John Paul II received a large group of pilgrims from Thailand, the famed Siam of the past. These devout Catholics had arrived in Rome to celebrate the beatification of the first martyrs of their nation, which the Holy Father visited in 1984.

The Martyrs of Thailand were seven native Catholics slain in December, 1940, in Songkhon, a com-

MARTYRS OF THAILAND

(D. 1940)

MARTYRS

munity of rice farmers on the Mekong River. During that era, foreign missionaries were being exiled from the region and no religious or cultural pluralism was tolerated. The local police coerced many into abjuring the faith, going door-to-door in each village seeking religious sympathizers.

Philip Siphong 🌿 Called "the man of oak," he was the lay religious leader of Songkhon, and he followed behind the police, restoring the faith throughout the village. Born in Nonseng in 1907, he married Maria Thong and had five children. In Songkhou, Philip taught in the school and was a catechist, replacing the exiled parish priest as leader. He was arrested because of his zeal and success and was shot in a woods near the village on December 16.

Sister Agnes Phila 🌿 A member of the Congregation of the Lovers of the Cross, she led the remaining six martyrs in their ordeals. Born in Ban in 1909, she became a teaching sister of her congregation. Sister Agnes served in various capacities and was appointed superior of the Songkhon Catholic school in 1932. She served faithfully, and during the persecution she encouraged the local Catholics in the faith. Sister Agnes wrote a defense of the faith before dying, stating: "You may kill us, but you cannot kill the Church and you cannot kill God."

With her was Sister Lucia Khambang, who was sent to Songkhon in 1940. Born in Viengkuk in 1917, she had entered the Lovers of the Cross Congregation in 1931. Sister Lucia died on December 26. Agatha Phutta, who was an unmarried woman born in 1881, helped in the kitchen of the mission. Refusing to deny the faith, she was martyred at age fifty-nine. Mission aides Bibiana Khamphai, age fifteen, and Maria Phon, age fourteen, were slain at the local cemetery.

Cecilia Butsi 🌿 The last of the Thai martyrs, she was just sixteen when she was martyred. She spoke openly at a public meeting, defying the police and defending the faith. She died with the others.

Pope John Paul II beatified the Martyrs of Thailand on October 22, 1989, declaring: *"Today, Mission Sunday, we celebrate the beatification of the holy Martyrs of Thailand. In union with the whole Church, we give thanks to the most Blessed Trinity for the witness and example that those martyrs have given to the entire Christian world. It is significant that their generous sacrifice was made within a Christian community that while still young, was prepared to bear witness to Jesus Christ and to the power of his love with full self-giving: 'You shall be my witnesses . . . to the end of the earth' (Acts 1:8)."*

Victims of the Spanish Civil War

These blesseds were victims of the Spanish Civil War, a reign of terror designed to suppress the faith and to rid Spain of all religious influences. The Communist-led militias and rebel groups attacked convents, monasteries, and seminaries, alarming the various religious houses. Many Orders and congregations moved their communities to safer locales, sometimes abandoning their houses or leaving such institutions in the care of a small group of religious.

MARTYRS OF THE VISITATION ORDER

(D. 1936)

MARTYRS

The Martyrs of the Visitation Order were six members of the Madrid convent who remained in the house while other religious of the Order withdrew to Oronoz. Sister María Gabriela de Hinojosa was in charge and found the nuns a relatively safe place. A neighbor, however, reported them to the revolutionary authorities, and the nuns were arrested. When they were first interrogated, the Visitation nuns rejoiced because they knew "martyrdom is not far off." The following night they were taken in a van to a remote, vacant area. They were all shot to death on November 18, 1936, except for Sister María Cecilia Cendoya Araquistain, who fled when her closest companion fell. She surrendered moments later and was executed by a firing squad five days later in Vallecas, a suburb of Madrid. The Martyrs of the Visitation Order are:

María Gabriela de Hinojosa Naveros, (born in Ahlama, Grenada, on July 24, 1872); Josefa María Barrera Izaguire (born in El Ferol, La Coruña, May 23, 1881); Teresa María Cavestany y Anduaga (born in Puerto Real, Cadiz, July 30, 1888); María Angela Olaizola Garagarza (born in Azpietia, Guipúzcoa, November 12, 1893); María Engracia Lecuona Aramburu (born in Oyarzun, Guipúzcoa, on July 2, 1897); María Inés Zudaire Galdeano (born in Echávarri, Navarre, on January 28, 1900); and María Cecilia Cendoya Araquistain (born in Azpietia, Guipúzcoa, on January 10, 1910).

Pope John Paul II beatified the Martyrs of the Visitation Order on May 10, 1998, announcing that the Church rejoiced in raising these martyrs to honors of the altar. The Holy Father said:

"We are all advancing towards the goal (the heavenly Jerusalem), where the saints and martyrs have preceded us down the centuries. On our earthly pilgrimage these brethren of ours, who passed victoriously through 'great tribulations' serve as an example, incentive and encouragement to us."

The first Australian raised to the honors of the altars of the Church, Blessed Mary of the Cross MacKillop embodies the finest attributes of Christian Charity. The Land Down Under was opened by the British and used as a penal colony.

MARY OF THE CROSS MACKILLOP

(D. 1909)

EDUCATOR

Catholics, labeled "criminals," were transported to Australia, but in the early days were deprived of benefits of the faith. Still, the Church endured, and Mary of the Cross MacKillop stands as the symbol of centuries of loyalty to Catholic beliefs and traditions. Her congregation, the Sisters of St. Joseph and of the Sacred Heart, perform the traditional educational apostolate in several lands as a result of her spiritual vision and her stamina.

Mary of the Cross was born on January 15, 1842, in Fitzroy, Australia, of Scottish parents and was baptized Mary Helen. Her father aided her education, and Mary developed skills in teaching and social guidance. Father Julian Tenison Woods became her spiritual director, and in 1866 he asked Mary to assume the leadership of a group of women dedicated to educating Catholics in the region. Mary of the Cross was trained in the religious life and took her final vows in 1869, receiving her convent name. Four years later, Father Woods was removed from control of the congregation in Adelaide. By this time, Mary of the Cross had recruited 127 sisters and had opened 34 schools.

The local bishop excommunicated Mary of the Cross for disobedience and dispensed forty-seven sisters from their vows. The following year, near death, the bishop absolved the excommunication and apologized to Mary of the Cross. The Holy See intervened and the congregation resumed its labors. In 1873, Mary of the Cross made efforts to stabilize her community even more by going to Rome. The constitutions were accepted there in 1875, and Mary of the Cross became superior general. She traveled across Europe seeking financial aid and aspirants for her congregation and she worked to enlist support from the Australian hierarchy. As late as 1887, Rome had to intervene again to keep the Sisters of St. Joseph and of the Sacred Heart free of diocesan -evel control by certain bishops. In 1888, the congregation, called the Josephite Sisters, was finally approved by the Holy See and by Pope Leo XIII (r. 1878-1903). Though Mary of the Cross had been replaced as superior general, she was once again elected to that office.

Mary of the Cross continued to serve the local Catholic populations, showing special concern for the Aborigines. The eucalyptus was her special emblem, as Mary of the Cross also fostered conservation. Mary of the Cross saw her sisters spread throughout Australia, New Zealand, and Peru. She died on August 8, 1909, in Sydney.

Pope John Paul II beatified Mary of the Cross on January 19, 1995, honoring her as a pioneer in the religious and educational apostolates; a woman who endured suffering to bring graces to her native land and to Australia's aboriginal population.

Missionary Canon Regular of Tibet

High in the Himalayas, on the rooftop of the world, sits Tibet, a small Buddhist nation isolated from the world by its geography and religious tenets until Communist China invaded in 1950. Maurice Tornay, an Augustinian Canon Regular, was one of the few Europeans to reach the small kingdom in the snowy crests before it became a possession of China. He journeyed there as a missionary, and he gave up his life as a martyr

Maurice was born on August 31, 1910, in La Rosiére, in the canton of Valais, Switzerland. Educated at St. Maurice Abbey, Maurice entered the Canons Regular of Grand St. Bernard in 1931. He was solemnly professed in 1935 and volunteered for the missions. The following year, he was sent to Weixi, Yunnan, China. There he finished his theological studies and was ordained in Ha Noi in 1938. He served as a catechist in Houa-Lo-Pa until 1945.

MAURICE TORNAY

(D. 1949)

MARTYR

In that year, Maurice was assigned to Yorkalo, in Tibet. Established as the local pastor, Maurice faced opposition from the Buddhist lamas of the region. They forced him into exile, confiscating his church and rectory. Maurice went to Pamé, where he served Catholic traders and encouraged fidelity among the Catholic Tibetans. Maurice continued his mission despite suffering from stomach ulcers, a condition that he had developed in his younger years.

As a last resort, Maurice journeyed to Lhasa to seek tolerance from the Dalai Lama to save his Catholic faithful. He and his servant were ambushed on the road and slain on August 11, 1949 in To Thong.

Pope John Paul II beatified Maurice on May 16, 1993, declaring:

"Brothers and sisters, let us implore the Holy Spirit. The Church and world need families, which like the Tornay family, will be the forges where parents hand on to their children Christ's call to the Christian life, priestly or religious. Let us offer thanks to the seeds of hope in that Asian land. The mission and suffering of Father Tornay, and of his predecessors in the Foreign Mission Society of Paris and the Canons of the Grand Saint-Bernard, are silently bearing fruit in a slow maturation. We cannot fail to rejoice in the respectful dialogue between Tibetan and Catholic monks in order to discover him

who is the Way and the Truth and the Life. Vocations are coming, as we can see by the recent ordination of one of our blessed's students; Christians will continue the work of Father Tornay who wanted to teach children and lead them to holiness; a holy life alone is worth being lived."

Melchior Sanchez 🔥 **See Martyrs of Japan.**

Ecuadorian Educator, the "Rose of Baba and Guayaquil"

Suffering purifies and clarifies the human vision when it is accepted with grace. The Rose of Baba and Guayaquil, Blessed Mercedes of Jesus Molina, stands as an insignia of that truth today. She not only inspires her native Ecuador but the entire world with her wisdom and spiritual dedication. An educator, missionary, and foundress, Mercedes of Jesus was raised to the altars of the Church by Pope John Paul II during his apostolic visit to Ecuador.

MERCEDES OF JESUS MOLINA

(D. 1883)

FOUNDRESS

Mercedes of Jesus was born in Baba, Ecuador, in 1828. Having matured through difficulties and suffering, she chose consecration to Christ as her true vocation. In Guayaquil, she began an apostolate as a laywoman by teaching orphans and aiding the abandoned. Slowly her labors took her among the Jibaro Indians, the natives of the region, long misunderstood and ill-treated. Mercedes of Jesus also became protectress of the abandoned children in Cuenca.

She was joined by other fearless, dedicated women, and on Easter Monday, 1873, with the approval of the bishop of Riobamba, Mercedes of Jesus started the Congregation of the Sisters of Maríana of Jesus, also called the Maríanites. Her spiritual daughters embraced her apostolate of education, care of orphans and the local Jibaros, and the service of the needy and the abandoned. Pope John Paul II called her "a model for living." She died, exhausted from her labors and mourned by the people of her native land, on June 12, 1883.

Pope John Paul II beatified Mercedes of Jesus on the Las Samanes Esplanade in Guayaquil, on February 1, 1985, announcing:

"Mother Mercedes was captivated by the poverty of the Child of Bethlehem, by the suffering on the pained face of the Crucified. She wanted to be simply and clearly love for suffering, according to the motto recounted in early biographical notes. 'As much love for as many sufferings as there are in the world;' to practice charity toward all those who, in poverty, suffering, and abandonment, reflected the mystery of the poor child of Bethlehem or of Christ suffering on Calvary. She was mother and educator of orphans, a poor missionary and peacemaker among the Indians, foundress of a religious family. To her spiritual

daughters she transmitted her same spirit. . . . This was love without limits, able to bring aid and comfort, as Mother summarized in her constitutions, 'to as many afflicted hearts as there are in the world.' "

Victim of the Spanish Civil War

The blood of the early martyrs nurtured the faith on alien soils, and in the modern world the martyrs stand as symbols of fidelity and hope even in the darkness of lunatic ideologies or violence. Blessed Mercedes Prat y Prat stands as an insignia of faith in the terrible era of the Spanish Civil War.

She was born in Barcelona, Spain, on March 6, 1880, the daughter of Juan and Teresa Prat y Prat, who both died while Mercedes was still a child. Skilled in the domestic arts, Mercedes started her ministry by teaching such activities to poor girls in Barcelona. In 1904, Mercedes entered the Society of St. Teresa of Jesus, and as a member of the community taught and labored as an artist.

When the Spanish Civil War broke upon the society, and Mercedes and her nun companions had to leave the convent to take refuge with families or friends. Mercedes started toward the society's residence, but was halted by four members of the revolutionary militia. They demanded to know if she was a religious, and she joyously admitted her status. Arrested, Mercedes was executed by firing squad the following day, July 24, 1936.

MERCEDES PRAT Y PRAT

(D. 1936)

MARTYR

Pope John Paul II beatified Mercedes on April 29, 1990, declaring: *"Her great love for God and neighbor brought her to engage in the apostolic work of catechesis and in Sunday school. Besides her prudence, Mercedes distinguished herself by her virtue of fortitude which was especially clear in the way she serenely met dangers and suffered persecution. Her love for her neighbor showed itself above all in her act of pardoning those who shot her."*

Victim of Dachau

The infamous Dachau concentration camp stands today as a stark, weather-beaten symbol of the horrors of Nazi barbarism. The barracks, extermination buildings, and crematoriums are a constant reminder of the untold suffering of thousands upon thousands. Yet even as the physical presence that is

MICHAEL KOZAL

(D. 1943)

MARTYR

Dachau rots and molders, the spiritual radiance of the men and women who died excruciatingly at the hands of their Nazi captors — martyrs of many faiths — will not be dimmed by the ravages of time or season.

Blessed Michael Kozal died in Dachau concentration camp. He was a bishop of Poland singled out for imprisonment and death by the Nazis because of his fervor and faith. He was born at Ligota (Nowy Folwark), in Poland, on September 27, 1893. Raised staunchly in the faith, Michael studied for the priesthood, and after completing his seminary training was ordained in 1918. He was then assigned to various parishes, teaching as well in diocesan secondary schools. Michael also served as a seminary instructor for twelve years.

Two weeks before the invasion of Poland and the start of World War II, Michael was consecrated a bishop. He served as an auxiliary and then as bishop of Wloclawek. Because of his status and academic background, Michael was arrested by the Nazis as soon as their forces occupied his region. He was confined at first to a convent, but in 1941, he was sent to Dachau Concentration Camp. There he learned of the suffering being endured by Catholics in his native land, and there he offered his own life to save his fellow countrymen. Michael celebrated Mass whenever possible and comforted other prisoners during his camp ordeal. On January 26, 1943, he was given a lethal injection by his Nazi tormentors.

Pope John Paul II beatified Michael as one of the martyrs of the faith in Warsaw, Poland, on June 14, 1987, praising this bishop for his courage and generosity in declaring himself a willing victim of love for the Polish people. Michael was honored for being a prelate of such holiness that he was singled out by the Nazis as an enemy of their godless regime.

Jesus of Mexico

"Long live Christ the King," has long been the anthem of the martyrs of the Latin nations of the world. The valiant men and women dying at the hands of the godless have called out their marvelous salute as they surrendered their lives. *Viva Cristo Rey* were the last words uttered by Miguel Augustine Pro the martyred Jesuit priest of Mexico.

MIGUEL AUGUSTINE PRO

(D. 1927)

MARTYR

Miguel Augustine Pro was born in Guadalupe de Zacatecas on January 13, 1891, to a prosperous, devout family. His father was a mining engineer. In August, 1911, Miguel entered the novitiate of the Jesuits at Michoacán, taking his first vows but then having to flee the country in 1914. Miguel went to Granada, Spain, and then to Belgium to continue his studies and was ordained on August 31, 1925.

After his ordination, Miguel returned to Mexico despite the fact that the revolutionary government banned all religious practisces in the land. Miguel labored in Mexico, resorting to disguises and the use of safe houses provided by devout families. He administered the Sacraments, taught catechetics, and supported the poor while avoiding government forces.

On November 18, 1927, Miguel was arrested with his brother, Roberto, and was charged with the ridiculous and false crime of attempting to assassinate the president of Mexico. A stay of execution was arranged, but it was too late to save Miguel. Roberto was spared, but Miguel was executed by a firing squad on November 23. He died saying: "Long live Christ the King" (*Viva Cristo Rey*).

from *Faces of Holiness*

Father Miguel Pro

When Miguel was buried, thousands of the faithful defied the authorities by making a public display of mourning. There were vast crowds marching behind the coffin, and more than five hundred automobiles formed the procession to Miguel's final resting place. At the funeral, an elderly woman mourner had her sight miraculously restored.

Pope John Paul II beatified Miguel on September 18, 1988, announcing:

"At the beatification of Father Miguel Augustine Pro, a Jesuit priest, whose virtues we today exalt and propose to the People of God, is a reason for joy for the universal Church, especially for the Church in Mexico. He is a new glory for the beloved Mexican nation, as well as for the Society of Jesus. His life of sacrificing and intrepid apostolate was always inspired by a tireless evangelizing effort . . . Neither suffering nor serious trouble, neither the exhausting ministerial activity, frequently carried out in difficult and dangerous circumstances, could stifle the radiating and contagious joy which he brought to his life for Christ and which nothing could take away (cf. Jn 16:22). Indeed, the deepest root of self-sacrificing surrender for the lowly was his passionate love for Jesus Christ and his ardent desire to be conformed to him, even unto death."

The spirit of St. Francis of Assisi continues in the world, interpreted in each new age by holy men and women who have caught the fire of his devotion. Blessed Modestino Mazzarella is another Franciscan luminary who brought the spiritual legacy of St. Francis alive in his own era.

MODESTINO OF JESUS AND MARY MAZZARELLA

(D. 1854)

RELIGIOUS

Modestino was born at Frattamaggiore, Naples, Italy, on September 5, 1802, baptized Dominic. Raised in a humble, working-class family, he served as an altar boy and attended parish services. At age eighteen, Modestino was sponsored by Bishop Agostino Tommasi in the seminary. In 1821, the death of this patron forced Modestino to study at home.

One year later, Modestino entered the Franciscans at Grumo Nevano and was sent to the novitiate of Santa Lucia, in Naples. He was professed in 1824 and ordained a priest on December 22, 1827, in Aversa. His assignments in the Order were varied, and he served as superior in two Franciscan houses. Then, in 1839, he was transferred to Naples to serve in Santa Maria della Sanità, a parish in a slum area of the city.

A devotee of Our Lady of Good Counsel, Modestino worked night and day to care for the sick and the poor. He was a marvelous champion of the faith, inspiring spiritual and moral resolve in his apostolate. Even in the dreaded cholera epidemic of 1854, Modestino went out to the people, caring for the victims of the disease. He died of cholera on July 24, 1854.

Pope John Paul II beatified Modestino on June 29, 1995, announcing: " *'For you are my hope, O Lord; my trust, O God, from my youth' (Responsorial Psalm, 70 [71]: 5). Thus sings the Church which is constantly enlivened by the breath of the Holy Spirit. Today this is echoed by Blessed Modestino of Jesus and Mary, a priest of the Franciscan Order of Friars Minor, an outstanding witness to God's mercy, who instilled hope in Southern Italy during the first half of the last century. From boyhood, God was pleased to reveal to him the mysteries of the kingdom of heaven (cf. Mt 11:25; Gospel acclamation), leading him to discover the authentic value of the person who is fulfilled through generous devotion to the poor and crucified Christ in the gift of self to others. Father Modestino lived in a society of marginalization and moral suffering, and was able to share fully the expectations and anxieties of the weakest, responding to the deep need for God found in his brothers and sisters who thirsted for justice and love. He thus became a leaven of renewal and a living sign of hope. The hand of the Lord was truly upon him, making him a minister of mercy and comfort to every social class, especially through his diligent, patient celebration of the sacrament of Reconciliation. Father Modestino was a true 'universal brother': everyone could rely on him, finding someone who would listen, welcome, and share. This love led him to give of his very self, and he did not hesitate to expose himself to the threat of death in order to help his brothers and sisters struck by a cholera epidemic. Indeed, he shared their fate to the very last, dying as a victim of love."*

Ecuadorian of the Hidden Way

Not every blessed has been a religious. Not every saint has been a martyr. Some have been friends of God in hidden ways, living life obscurely by serving the needs of others and attaining perfection. Narcisa de Jesus Martillo Morán was just such a friend of God.

NARCISA DE JESUS MARTILLO MORÁN

(D. 1869)

LAY MYSTIC

Narcisa was born in Daule (Nobol), a small village in the diocese of Guayaquil, Ecuador, in 1833, the fifth of nine children of Pedro and Josef Morán. Her parents died while she was very young, and she moved to Guayaquil to work as a seamstress to help support her brothers and sisters. Narcisa de Jesus was maturing spiritually, and she spent hours in prayer and penance during this period of her life, drawn to Christ.

Sometime about 1865, she moved to Cuenca, and there the bishop invited her to enter the Carmelite cloister. However, Narcisa believed she was called upon to remain a laywoman. She returned to Guayaquil for three years and then went to Lima, where she took up residence in a Dominican convent. Narcisa was not a religious, but she was allowed to remain within the convent and to attend the religious ceremonies conducted there.

Narcisa was prayerful and intensely recollected, maintaining a profound spiritual union with Christ. She served as a catechist for children and adults, and she visited the poor sections of Guayaquil to teach the families there about the faith. Her life was a hidden one of devotion, service, and recollection. She died in Lima, Peru, on December 8, 1869, at the age of thirty-six. Her obscurity ended with her death, as pilgrims began devotions at her tomb, and her Cause was opened in 1889.

Pope John Paul II beatified Narcisa on October 25, 1992, declaring her a glory of Ecuador and praising her devotion to Nazareth and the mysteries of Calvary.

The call to the religious life is a wondrous grace, perhaps overlooked by the modern world. Countless men and women have responded generously to Christ's invitations, and their dedication has benefited people everywhere. At the age of nine Nazaría Ignacia heard the call to the religious life and she answered: "I will follow you, Lord, as closely as a human creature can."

NAZARÍA IGNACIA OF ST. TERESA OF JESUS MARCH MESA

(D. 1943)

FOUNDRESS

She was born in Madrid, Spain, on January 10, 1889, one of eighteen children of Juan and Nazaría Mesa Ramos March y Reve. When she received her First Communion at age nine, Nazaría knew that she was destined to be a religious. Her family's move to Mexico in 1906 did not alter Nazaría's resolve or her zeal.

In Mexico, Nazaría was encouraged by local religious in her efforts to evangelize the people of her area. Day after day she went to the poor sections to teach the faith and conduct catechism classes. In time she attracted other young women, and with them, Nazaría went to Oruro, Bolivia.

On December 23, 1912, Nazaría founded the Missionary Crusaders of the Church at Oruro. Her congregation grew rapidly, and Nazaría was able to establish houses in Argentina, Uruguay, and Spain. Her vision of carrying Christ's banner into a troubled world formed the members of her congregation and attracted dedicated young women of many walks of life. They opened soup kitchens and aided the poor in cities and mining camps. On two occasions her life was threatened, once in a violent persecution in Bolivia in 1932, and again in the Spanish Civil War in 1936. Her motto was "For Christ . . . for the Church . . . for souls," and she died in Buenos Aires, Argentina with those words on her lips, on July 6, 1943. Her remains were enshrined in her community at Oruro.

Pope John Paul II beatified Nazaría on September 27, 1992, declaring: *"Blessed Nazaría Ignacia of St. Teresa March Mesa . . . was drawn interiorly by the message of the prophet Isaiah, which she heard: 'The Lord . . . has sent me . . . to heal the brokenhearted' (61:1). Moved by this apostolic concern, she founded in Bolivia the Missionary Crusaders of the Church, with whom she meant to 'go out into the streets' to meet people, to be in solidarity with them, to help them, especially if these people were covered with sores of material need, as was Lazarus, the poor man in the Gospel (cf. Lk 16:21), but primarily to bring them to God."*

Niceforo of Jesus and Mary Tejerina 🌿 **See Martyrs of the Passionist Congregation.**

Founder of the Sisters of the Child Jesus or Holy Child

The friends of God have a way of finding one another on their earthly sojourns, using human friendships as a strengthening bond and as an impetus for greater service. St. John Baptist de la Salle encouraged Blessed Nicholas Roland, and aided his Cause after Nicholas's death.

NICHOLAS ROLAND
(D. 1678)
🌿
FOUNDER

Nicholas was born in Reims, France, on December 8, 1642. Educated in the faith and virtues, Nicholas received the grace of a religious vocation at an early age. He attended the Jesuit College in Reims, and went to Paris to complete his studies in philosophy and theology. He returned to Reims and was made a canon of the cathedral. There Nicholas served with St. John Baptist de la Salle, acting as the saint's spiritual director and encouraging him in his ministry.

Nicholas also understood the need for a religious congregations to foster educational institutions particularly designed to shelter and to aid in the development of young women. In 1670, Nicholas began to recruit dedicated women to establish such a congregation. He founded the Sisters of the Child Jesus or Holy Child with two educators and worked diligently to counsel and guide the new community. Nicholas also labored to provide constitutions for the congregation and to obtain the necessary papal approbation which was given on May 9, 1678, to St. John Baptist and Archbishop Le Tellier.

Nicholas died on April 26, 1678, the victim of an epidemic in Reims. He named St. John Baptist de la Salle the executor of his will. The saint revered Nicholas for his holiness and his concern for the young of his era.

Pope John Paul II beatified Nicholas on October 16, 1994, announcing:

"This morning, dear brothers and sisters, we are forcefully reminded of the mystery of Redemption. Yes, we have 'a great high priest who has passed through the heavens' (Heb. 4:14). He is Christ Jesus, the crucified Lord, risen and living in glory. He was the soul of Nicolas Roland's activity. During his short but spiritually intense life, he continually allowed the Redeemer to use him to accomplish his mission as high priest. Conformed to the person of Christ, he shared his love for those he guided to the priesthood, in order to 'receive

mercy' (Heb. 4:16) for them: 'Jesus' immense love for you,' he used to say, 'is even greater than your infidelity.' This unfailing faith and hope in the merciful love of the Incarnate Word led him to found the Congregation of the Sisters of the Infant Jesus. They would consecrate themselves to the apostolate of educating and evangelizing poor children. Indeed, he admirably said: 'Orphans represent us to Jesus Christ in his childhood.' "

Scientist and "Pilgrim of the World"

This blessed was the Apostle of Hildesheim, called a "Pilgrim of the World" by a contemporary. A bishop, eminent anatomist, and geologist, he is also revered as Niels Stensen or Nikolaus Stens.

NICOLAUS STENSEN

(D. 1686)

BISHOP

He was born in Copenhagen on January 11, 1638, the son of Lutherans, Sten Peterson and his wife, Anna Nielstochter. Educated locally, Nicolaus entered the university of Copenhagen, where he became famous as a scientist for his discovery of important aspects of the thyroid gland. At the university of Leiden, Nicolaus made further discoveries concerning glands, muscles, the heart, and the circulatory system.

In 1664, Nicolaus was denied a chair, a position of academic importance, at the university of Copenhagen. He received his doctorate in medicine from Leiden and then went to Paris for two years, gaining fame for his research in embryology and the anatomy of the brain. He went to Florence, Italy, to continue his academic career and was well-received there by the grand duke of Tuscany. While in Florence he converted to Catholicism, entering the Church on November 4, 1667. Ferdinand II, Archduke of Tuscany, gave Nicolaus a warm welcome into the faith and enthusiastic support. His conversion came as a result of his attendance at a Livorno Corpus Christi procession, which moved him deeply.

By 1669, Nicolaus was back in Denmark, where King Christian IV gave him the rank of Royal Anatomist. By 1674, Nicolaus was again in Florence. There he was appointed by Cosimo III as tutor to Prince Ferdinand. Nicolaus was also studying for the priesthood and was ordained in 1675. Two years later he was consecrated a bishop, and he labored almost a decade in the northern missions of Germany, in Hanover. A vibrant preacher, he brought countless soul back into the faith as the suffragan bishop of Munster. He then became the vicar apostolic of the Hanover area until his death on December 5, 1686, at the age of forty-eight.

His remains were enshrined in a vault in the basilica of St. Lawrence. The diocese of Hildesheim has always venerated Nicolaus, and many have been blessed by his intercession on their behalf.

Pope John Paul II beatified Nicolaus on October 23, 1988, announcing:
"... *at a distance of centuries, there reaches us, as it were, a cry from all those whose death is recorded in the Book of Life. Through their lives full of the Spirit of Christ, united to his paschal mystery . . . blessed son of the Danish land! You enliven the choir of those great people who have preceded you on the way to holiness. With them you cry: 'He who is mighty has done great things for me.' This cry of yours is heard in heaven and on earth. May it be received in the hearts of your brothers and sisters today and cause in them an abundant harvest of good, in faith, charity, and communion."*

Maronite Scholar and Mentor of St. Sharbel

The Maronite rite of the Church has a long and splendid history of faith and loyalty. The raising of St. Sharbel Maklouf to the altars of the Church recently introduced the Maronites to the faithful around the world. Blessed Nimatullah Youssef Al-Hardini, a teacher of St. Sharbel, was a pioneer in the same spiritual traditions.

He was born in Hardin, Lebanon, in 1808, and four of his brothers entered the monastic orders of the Maronite Church. Nimatullah entered the Lebanese Maronite Order in 1828 and was sent to St. Anthony Monastery in Qozhaya, near the Qadisha, the "Holy Valley," for two years. There he became known for his love of the Blessed Sacrament.

After his profession, Nimatullah was assigned to the monastery of Sts. Cyprian and Justina in Kfifan, where he studied philosophy and theology. After his ordination as a priest, he became director of the scholasticate, and St. Sharbel was one of his students. Nimatullah was a model religious, believing community life led to perfection.

NIMATULLAH YOUSSEF KASSAB AL-HARDINI

(D. 1859)

RELIGIOUS

He had great devotion to the Virgin Mary and honored her as the Immaculate Conception. In 1845, the Holy See appointed Nimatullah a general assistant of the Order. He served in this capacity for two years, declining an appointment as Abbot General.

Nimatullah came down with pneumonia in December, 1859, at the monastery of Kfifan and died on December 14. He held an icon in his hands as he died, commending his soul to Mary. Pope John Paul II beatified Nimatullah on May 10, 1998, announcing: *"Blessed Al-Hardini is a model of Christian and monastic life for the Maronite community and for all Christ's followers in our time. As a man of prayer he calls his brothers and sisters to trust in God and to commit all their efforts to following Christ, in order to build a better future."*

Victim of Dachau

The first Catholic priest to die in a Nazi concentration camp was a victim of petty officials who believed that they had the right to violate moral codes and to punish anyone who did not support their programs and their privileges.

OTTO NEURURER

(D. 1940)

MARTYR

Otto Neururer, the first priest martyr of the Nazis in a prison camp, was a pastor who tried to safeguard the sanctity of marriage. For this he died of "extreme punishment" in Buchenwald.

Otto was born on March 25, 1882, in Piller, Austria, the twelfth child of an industrious peasant family. His father died when Otto was still young, and his mother had to operate the family farm and mill while raising her children. She was prone to depression, and Otto grew up rather timid as a result.

He attended the minor seminary at Brixen, demonstrating a brilliant intellect and many virtues. In the diocesan seminary, Otto completed his studies for the priesthood and was ordained, celebrating his first Mass in Piller, his hometown. He was then assigned as a curate or teacher in several parishes, finally going to Götzens, near Innsbruck.

By the time Otto arrived in Götzens, the Nazis had invaded and had set up vast political governments in this Tirol region. A reign of terror began, but Otto did not withdraw or show timidity in his priestly duties. At Götzens, he advised a young woman not to marry a divorced man with an evil reputation. The man was enraged when he discovered Otto's involvement and went to his close friend the *Gauleiter,* the leading Nazi official of the Tirol region. Otto was arrested for slander to the detriment of German marriage and was sent to Dachau concentration camp. He was then moved to Buchenwald, where he endured hideous tortures.

He comforted and aided his fellow prisoners throughout his ordeal and remained steadfast in the faith and in prayer. Then a prisoner asked to baptized. Otto suspected a Nazi trap, as such ceremonies were forbidden in the camp. It was a trap, and two days later Otto was transferred to "a bunker of extreme punishment." Otto was hung upside down until he died on May 30, 1940. His ashes are enshrined in Götzens.

Pope John Paul II beatified Otto as a martyr on November 24, 1996, stating:

"The simple parish priest, Otto Neururer, gave his witness to Christ's truth, by defending the sanctity of Christian marriage in the most difficult and dangerous circumstances, and for this reason he was imprisoned by the Gestapo. In the concentration camp, it was his sense of priestly duty that spurred him to give lessons in the faith, despite the severe prohibition of the camp authorities. As punishment, he was hung upside down until he died. The two mar-

tyrs, Otto Neururer and Jacob Gapp, offer us all, in an era which would like to make Christianity something optional and relativize all obligations, a witness of uncompromising loyalty to Jesus' truth, where it always shines as such. Thus, they can be our heavenly intercessors as patrons of courageous preaching and of the holiness of marriage and priestly service." (See also Jacob Gapp.)

Foundress of the Daughters of Mary

The Piarists, or Scalopians, have long pioneered educational apostolates, attracting men and women of formidable faith and fortitude. Paula Montal (Farnes) was a woman of these virtues, and her vision enabled countless others to dedicate their lives to the same ministry.

She was born in Arenys de Mar, near Barcelona, Spain, on October 11, 1799, the daughter of Ramon and Vicenta Fornes Montal. Raised in a seaside village, Paula's childhood appears to have been difficult, and she became prayerful and recollected, aware of the suffering of others.

PAULA MONTAL

(D. 1889)

🔥

FOUNDRESS

At the age of thirty, still unmarried and devout, Paula realized the grace of a religious vocation and went with a friend, Inez Busquets, to Gerona, where they opened a school to provide the young with proper education and spiritual guidance. The school was a success, prompting Paula to establish a college in May, 1842, and a third educational institute in 1846.

On February 2, 1847, she founded the Daughters of Mary, taking the religious name of Paula of St. Joseph of Calasanz. Three companions joined her in this holy foundation, with Paula providing the vision and leadership for attracting other young women and for expanding the congregation's educational efforts.

The Daughters of Mary, "the Pious School Sisters," received papal approval from Pope Pius IX (r. 1846-1878) in May, 1860. Five years later, Queen Isabel II (r. 1833-1868) of Spain recognized the Daughters of Mary as well. The daughters arrived in the United States in 1954.

Paula, exhausted by her labors and aware of the fact that she had spent her life in the service of Christ and Spain's children, died faithful to the Piarist rule at Olesa de Montserrat on February 26, 1889. She was declared venerable in 1988. Pope John Paul II beatified Paula on April 18, 1993, praising her for following in the footsteps of St. Joseph Calasanz and for bringing a profound charism to the Piarist of Scalopian spirit. Her life of service and devotion was honored.

The titled and privileged of the world often do not offer themselves to the service of others in need. Secure in their own circles and enclaves, many wealthy people of social or inherited ranks do not respond to the ills of the poor. Pauline von Mallinckrodt thus stands as a contradiction to her own aristocratic background and as a symbol of Christian love overcoming social divisions.

PAULINE VON MALLINCKRODT

(D. 1881)

FOUNDRESS

Pauline was born in Minden, Westphalia, Germany, on June 3, 1817, a member of the noble ranks of her society. Her father was a Lutheran, and her mother a solidly practicing Catholic. Pauline was the oldest of four children, and her brother, Herman, became a famous Catholic political leader.

Raised in the comforts and opportunities of the aristocratic world, Pauline was taught the faith by her mother. She learned as well the basic requirements of service and was shown the incredible depths of suffering of her era. Pauline responded generously to these sufferings by opening a school for infants and the blind at Paderborn. Innovative and alert to the needs of her charges, Pauline molded the letters of the alphabet so that her students could learn to read with their handicaps.

Realizing that simple laywomen could not expand and renew the apostolate that she had started, Pauline offered her facilities to St. Sophie Barat. St. Sophie Barat was unable to assume the responsibility for the school because of political turmoil and prior commitments. Pauline thus came to a critical juncture in her life of service, and she responded again with generosity.

On August 21, 1849, Pauline founded the Sisters of Christian Charity — also called the Daughters of the Blessed Virgin Mary of the Immaculate Conception — and was soon joined by other faithful women who realized the need for such sacrifices. The congregation was approved by Pope Pius IX (r. 1846-1878) on February 21, 1863.

A short time later, Bismark and other German leaders forced the congregation out of Germany. The anti-Catholic *Kulturkampf* (the program in German lands that sought to subordinate the Church to the will of the State) was in operation at the time and was set on limiting the Catholic influence. Pauline went to Belgium when her Paderborn school was closed, and so she established a house near Brussels. She labored endlessly to expand her community, visiting the United States in 1873 and 1879. Her sisters began their teaching ministry in America as a result of her visit.

Pauline remained faithful to Christ and to the impaired, the needy, and the young until her death from pneumonia at Paderborn on April 30, 1881. Her noble and devout manners and her indomitable dedication won many to her apostolate in the Old and New Worlds.

Pope John Paul II beatified Pauline on April 14, 1985, praising her untiring efforts and the spiritual legacy that she left for dedicated souls in the apostolates of truly caring for those in need.

Foundress of the the Daughters of the Immaculate Conception

The "first saint who grew up in Brazil," Pauline was declared blessed by Pope John Paul II in her native land, while thousands of the faithful rejoiced and prayed. She may have come from Italy, but she was raised in Brazil and in Brazil her spiritual awareness was formed and allowed to blossom.

Pauline was born in Vigola Vattaro (Trento), Italy, on December 16, 1865. Her hometown was under Austrian control at the time; today it is part of Italy. When she was ten years old, Pauline's family moved to Brazil, and there she continued her Catholic life, desiring to dedicate herself to Christ. At age fifteen, she and a companion moved into a shack to look after a woman dying of cancer. The Daughters of the Immaculate Conception, founded by Pauline, grew out of that first act of mercy, and she became Sister Pauline of the Heart of Jesus in Agony. The bishop of Curetiba approved of the congregation in 1885. Pauline was elected for one term as Superior General but then returned to caring for the sick.

PAULINE AMABILIS VISENTEINER

(D. 1942)

FOUNDRESS

In time, stricken with diabetes, Pauline lived in seclusion and prayer in the motherhouse. She went blind and lost an arm because of the disease, and she died on July 9, 1942.

Pope John Paul II beatified Pauline in Florianopolis (São Paulo), Brazil, on October 18, 1991, announcing:

"What most distinguished the life of the saints is their ability to awaken the desire for God in those who have the joy of being around them. Their generous correspondence to divine grace is therefore rewarded with a constant inclination towards God who is desired, known, loved, and praised. It is precisely in this light that the Servant of God is presented to us as we prepare to recognize her solemnly among the blessed in the kingdom of heaven. 'Think of what is above' (Col 3:2). This was precisely the gift lived to the highest degree by Mother Pauline. She was able to convert all her words and actions into a continual act of praise to God. In her youth she asked God for the grace to enter religious life with the single goal of loving and serving him in the best way possible. Accept-

ing the Will of God led her to a constant self-renunciation, facing every sacrifice in order to fulfill the divine plan, especially in the particularly heroic period when she was deposed as Superior General of the Congregation she had founded. The fruit of this great love of God was the charity which the Servant of God lived from her childhood until the last moment of her earthly life in regard to all those who lived with her. In her spiritual testament she wrote: 'I exhort you to have among yourselves holy Charity, especially towards the patients in the Holy Houses (the elderly) in the hospices, etc. Have great consideration for the practice of holy Charity.' This is why, in the Hospital of Vigolo she and her first companion received the title of 'nurse.' This being-for-others is the background for her whole life."

Peter Ruiz de los Paños y Angel ❧ **See Martyrs of the Diocesan Worker Priests**.

Founder of the Teresian Association

Some individuals grasp the inevitability of death with good grace. This recognition of the limitations on mortal existence does not alarm them but teaches them to live each day as if it were the last one allotted to them. Pedro (Peter) Povedo Castroverde is reported to have lived the spirituality of a martyr, which means that he understood the need to use each hour of each day to accomplish the tasks before him. A Carmelite tertiary, Pedro inculcated the rich Carmelite spiritual heritage into every aspect of his life, inspiring the faithful in his native land.

PEDRO (PETER) POVEDO CASTROVERDE

(D. 1936)

PRIEST

Pedro was born in Linares, Spain, on December 3, 1874, and during his youth he developed a contemplative spirituality, uniquely combined with an awareness of the active apostolate necessary in the world. In 1889, he entered the diocesan seminary in Jaen. When his family experienced financial difficulties, he transferred to the diocese of Guadix, Granada, where the bishop gave Pedro a scholarship. The young man completed his studies and was ordained a priest on April 17, 1897.

He taught in the seminary, and in 1900 finished his licentiate in theology in Seville. Pedro returned to Guadix where he began his many charitable works, later going to Madrid. In 1906, he was named a canon of the Basilica of Covadonga, in Asturias, and became an active apostle of Catholic education. He joined the Third Order Carmelites and supported Pope Pius XI's apostolic constitution, *Provida Mater Ecclesia*.

In 1911, Pedro opened St. Teresa of Ávila Academy, which became the foundation of a secular institute, called the Teresians, in Madrid in 1911. The Teresians combined the contemplative and active apostolate in seeking to bear witness to the world. Peter taught his followers to work without ceasing to imbue the modern world with mystical truths. The Teresian Institute spread throughout Europe, Asia, Africa, and South America. In 1921, Pedro was appointed a chaplain of the Royal Palace in Madrid, and three years later he received papal approval of the Teresians, also called the Teresian Association. Pedro died in Madrid on July 28, 1936.

Pope John Paul II beatified Pedro on October 10, 1993, announcing:

"Father Pedro Povedo Castroverde, founder of the Teresian Association, who was . . . able to give his own witness to the point of shedding his blood. His highest aspiration was always to respond, like Jesus, to the Father's Will. 'Lord, may I think what you want me to think,' we read in his writings; 'may I desire what you desire me to desire; may I speak as you want me to speak; may I work as you want me to work' (Diario, 15 March 1933). . . . From the prophet Isaiah we heard: 'The hand of the Lord will rest on this mountain' (25:10a). Indeed, at the feet of the Santina in Covadonga, spurred by his deep love for the Virgin Mary, the new blessed found the inspiration for his apostolic desires that focused on promoting the evangelizing presence of Christians in the world, mainly in the field of teaching and culture, with a spirit of profound ecclesial sensitivity, of unreserved fidelity and generous surrender."

Franciscan Missionary

The splendor of the spiritual legacy of St. Francis of Assisi is revered by people of all faiths, and many, following in his footsteps, have been likened to him in the modern age. One such follower was Peter of St. Joseph Betancur, also called Betancourt, a Franciscan tertiary, called "the St. Francis of the Americas." He was a so-called minstrel of Christ who changed the lives of all who knew him and benefited from his generosity.

Peter was born in Villaflores, on the island of Tenerife, on May 16, 1619. A descendant of the Canary Island conqueror, Juan de Betancur, Peter was raised as a simple shepherd. He spent his youth in the field and pastures, where he developed an intense prayer life and union with Christ.

At the age of thirty-one, Peter left Tenerife and his shepherd's life to go to Guatemala. After a long and arduous journey, Peter arrived in Guatemala City, where

PETER OF ST. JOSEPH BETANCUR

(D. 1667)

FOUNDER

he was befriended by the local Franciscans and Jesuits. There he started studies for the priesthood at the Jesuit College in San Borgia, though he later withdrew. Still drawn to the religious life, Peter took private vows and became a Third Order Franciscan, taking the name Peter of St. Joseph.

In 1658, he moved to the vacant hut of the famous mystic Maria de Esquivel. He also founded the hospital, Our Lady of Bethlehem, a hostel, schools, and an oratory, all designed to aid the needy. Organizing the many generous young men who followed him, Peter founded the Hospitaler Bethlehemites to provide adequate medical care and Christian charity. He rented a house in a part of Guatemala City called "Calvary" and established his hospital there, supporting the hospital and his other charitable institutions by begging on the streets. Peter wore a Franciscan habit as he entered poor sections of the city to build chapels and shrines for the local families, and he promoted devotions and prayed for the souls in Purgatory.

Beloved and revered, Peter started the custom of gathering children for the recitation of the Franciscan Rosary on each February 18th. He also started the popular *Posada* celebrations that continue today throughout South America. On April 25, 1667, Peter, "the St. Francis of the Americas," died in Guatemala City. His Cause was opened in 1709.

Pope John Paul II beatified Peter on June 22, 1980, honoring the humility, dedication, and service of the blessed, all of which reflected Franciscan joy, trust, and delight in caring for God's own.

Founder of the Sisters of the Holy Family

The priestly vocation has evolved over the centuries, impacted by the needs of various eras and by the generosity of the men called to serve God and the Church in this honored role. In recent times the exploits and deeds of some priests have dazzled the faithful. Peter Bonilli not only inspired his own parishioners but received honors from Pope St. Pius X because he brought a willing heart to his labors and an intense devotion to the Holy Family of Nazareth.

PETER BONILLI

(D. 1935)

PRIEST

Peter was born on March 15, 1841, to Sebastian and Maria Allegretti Bonilli in San Lorenzo Trebiani (di Trevi) in Umbria, Italy. He was brought up in a devout family and received the grace of a priestly vocation, entering the local seminary. Upon completing his studies, Peter was ordained in 1863.

He was then sent to Cannaiola, where he would serve as a pastor for more than three decades, sharing the trials and tribulations of the Catholic people of that region. Peter had great devotion to the Holy Family and tried to dedicate himself to the daily needs of his parish. He was alert to the changing moral attitudes of his age and did not turn aside from the most vulnerable of society.

In 1884, Peter started "the Little Orphanage of Nazareth" in Cannaiola. There he took care of orphaned young girls and abandoned boys. Peter attracted many generous souls who aided him in this apostolate. With some of these devout women he started a congregation, called the Sisters of the Holy Family. Attracting more dedicated members, Peter was able to expand his ministries.

In 1893, he opened a hospice for the deaf and the blind. The Sisters of the Holy Family took over the operation of this institution and moved it to Spoleto. Peter followed, going to Spoleto to supervise operations. He was already famous as an apostle of charity and as a spiritual director, and in Spoleto he was made a canon of the cathedral and the rector of the regional seminary. Pope St. Pius X honored him in 1908. Peter, exhausted by his many labors, died in Spoleto on January 5, 1935.

Pope John Paul II beatified Peter on April 21, 1988, declaring:

"He understood that it was necessary to be present in the flock, also to give his life which would look after and nourish them in whatever situation, even that of sharing times of danger, going into unhealthy places and the humblest and most despised areas. He remained for thirty-five years in a parish in the most depressed area of the Diocese of Spoleto, where religious and moral conditions were exceptionally poor and disheartening, marked by degrading profanity, licentiousness, gambling, and drunkenness. A generous imitator of Christ the Good Shepherd, Father Bonilli lavished his charity on all who needed assistance. Experienced since childhood in the sufferings, hardships, humiliations, and needs of the country people, he devoted himself to 'nourishing' his people and leading them to more fertile pastures (cf. Ps 22[23]:2). He who 'knew his flock' wished to find suitable food for it. . . . He also guided them in his own experience of prayer, so that they might find pasture in contact with God and in the Eucharist. In particular, he saw in the family the basis of the renewal of society and ecclesial life. 'To be a family, to establish the family, to build up the family,' was his motto and program. The family, every family, ought to have its vocation and mission renewed according to the example of the Holy Family."

Missionary to the Lepers

As Blessed Damien de Veuster sacrificed himself in Hawaii, this blessed, Peter Donders, spent his life caring for victims of Hansen's Disease — lepers. Leprosy, an age-old scourge, struck terror into the hearts of each new generation of the world — from biblical times through the ages of inventions and progress. The labors of Peter Donders and Blessed Damien took away the terror, revealing the

PETER DONDERS

(D. 1887)

RELIGIOUS

suffering patients as human beings afflicted with pain and facing certain death.

Peter was born in Tilburg, in the Netherlands, on October 27, 1805, a child of Arnold and Petronella Donders. While still quite young, Peter and his brother, Martin, had to leave school to aid the family by working for extra income. Peter had received the grace of a priestly vocation, and eventually he would concentrated all of his energies on earning a seminary degree.

He worked in a factory to earn money and then took a position as a servant in the local seminary. At age twenty-six, he applied to the Franciscans, Jesuits, and Redemptorists, but was refused. He had centered on a foreign missionary vocation, inspired by the chance reading of the Annals of the Propagation of the Faith.

While studying at Herlaar, Peter received financial aid from a patron which enabled him to complete his priestly studies. He was ordained in 1840 for the missions in Surinam (Dutch Guiana). One year later he was sent to Paramibo, where he served until 1865. By 1850, he had baptized 1,200 plantation workers. During the epidemic of 1851, Peter displayed superhuman energies and concern for victims until falling ill himself.

When he recovered, Peter went to Batavia to care for the lepers, and his outstanding labors earned him an invitation to join the Redemptorists. He was received into the congregation and was given the opportunity to be reunited with his beloved lepers in Batavia again. Peter was always dedicated and loving in caring for the victims of leprosy. He even learned to play musical instruments to bring his patients moments of comfort and consolation.

He was not handsome, but he radiated Christ's compassion. A contemporary stated that Peter's "beauty was mainly within." He labored in Batavia until his death on January 14, 1887. He was interred in Batavia.

Pope John Paul II beatified Peter on May 23, 1982, praising the blessed for his authentic evangelical life in imitation of Christ. The Holy Father stated:

"We can say that he was an apostle of the poor. In fact, he was born into a poor family and had to lead the life of a worker before he could pursue his priestly vocation. He dedicated his whole priestly life to the poor. . . . In addition, he is an invitation and an incentive for the renewal and reflourishing of the missionary thrust which in the last century and in this one has made an exceptional contribution to the carrying out of the Church's missionary duty. Joining the Congregation of the Most Holy Redeemer late in life, he practiced in an excellent way what St. Alphonsus proposed as an ideal for his religious: imitate the virtues and examples of the Redeemer in preaching the divine word to the poor."

Founder of the Brothers of Charity of Mary Help of Christians

Today, men and women who have achieved their material goals in the world, those who have reached a certain pinnacle of success, are beginning to ask themselves if life does not offer something beyond their scope and vision. Blessed Peter Friedhofen stands as a marvelous insignia of human endeavors open to all humans, in all their fullness. Pope John Paul II said that Peter demonstrated *"a love that knew no limits in its universal sacrifice of self."*

PETER FRIEDHOFEN

(D. 1860)

FOUNDER

Peter was born on February 25, 1819, in Weitersburg, Germany, near Koblenz, the sixth of seven children born to a poor family. Peter's father died one year later, adding to the burden of the family: The children had to find work and extra income as soon as they were able to enter the marketplace.

Peter and his older brother Jacob traveled to various villages in the region working as chimney sweeps. Peter often sang Marian hymns while he worked high above the ground, and even invited the children who watched from the street to join in. When his brother died, Peter tried to care for his widowed mother and eleven children but was unable to manage the burden physically or financially. His desire had always been to aid the sick and the suffering, particularly children, and he was led to dedicate himself to their care. He started charitable projects for them in Adenau, Cochem, and Wittlich. He also built a shrine for the Blessed Virgin Mary to foster Marian devotions.

The Brothers of Charity of Mary, Help of Christians, also called the Brothers of Mercy, evolved from Peter's first charities, and the constitution of the congregation was approved by Bishop Arnoldi of Trier on July 2, 1848. The congregation was adapted to the Alexian Brothers' rule, and Peter and his first companion, Karl Marchand, were trained by the Alexians at Aachen.

Peter opened his first house on June 21, 1850, and wore the habit of the congregation after March 25, 1851. After many trials and difficulties, he opened other houses, aided by the bishop of Trier and the president of the Rhineland. The congregation served the sick and needy, and it expanded throughout Europe and into Brazil, China, and Malaysia. Peter directed the increasing demands and the swelling membership of his congregation until his death at age forty-one from tuberculosis on December 21, 1860, in Koblenz. He was buried with honors in Trier.

Pope John Paul II beatified Peter on June 23, 1985, declaring:

" *'The love of Christ constrains us' — this is what St. Paul avows of himself. It was this same love that constrained the newly-beatified Peter Friedhofen at the age of thirty to consecrate his life totally to God and to the service of the sick. Although himself poor and in bad health, he gave up his lay calling as a chimney-sweep, in order to make a new start out of his religious conviction and his burning love of neighbor. He saw the wretched situation of uprooted, sick and needy people, and recognized his own apostolic mission. Thus, he founded in 1850 the community of the 'Brothers of Charity of Mary Help of Christians' with the task of serving God in poor, sick, and old people."*

Patron of the Deaf

When wars and revolutions crash upon cities and nations, innocent men, women, and children are caught up and made to suffer without cause. The handicapped or disabled suffer doubly, and this was particularly true in the French

PETER FRANCIS JAMET

(D. 1845)

🔥

PRIEST

Revolution that unleashed untold terrors upon all. Blessed Peter Jamet, a priest of France, did not allow the horrors of the French Revolution to cause him to abandon the handicapped and the mentally ill around him. He was their father, and he stayed resolutely at their side, even when hiding from authorities.

He was born in Fresnes, France, on September 13, 1762, where he was raised with a deep reverence for the faith by a devout family. While growing up, Peter received the grace of a priestly vocation and became aware of the suffering of the handicapped in his region. He entered the local seminary, where he completed his studies for the priesthood. Ordained in 1787, Peter was assigned to the position of chaplain and confessor to the convent of the Sisters of the Good Savior. The French Revolution began taking a toll on Catholic institutions at the same time, and Peter and other priests were ordered to take an oath of allegiance to the anti-Catholic state authorities. He refused to take such an oath in good conscience and, as a result, had to seek shelter and a ministry conducted in secret.

Peter had started his apostolate of caring for the handicapped and mentally ill sometime before having to hide from the authorities, and he continued this ministry by assuming a disguise. The terrors unleashed in his region of France did not stop him from caring for vast numbers of handicapped individuals. In seclusion or disguise throughout this period, Peter wrote a sign language dictionary for his deaf and mute charges. He wrote 10,000 entries but did not complete the masterwork before his death.

When the French Revolution came to an end, Peter went to Caen University, where he was revered. He served as rector of the university there from 1822-1830. He combined this role with his care of the handicapped and then spent the remaining years of his life dedicated solely to these patients. He died on January 12, 1845.

Pope John Paul II beatified Peter on May 10, 1987. At his beatification ceremony, two hundred deaf mutes signed the entire proceedings. Peter was praised as a father of the needy and an individual who could not be terrorized into abandoning the people entrusted to him by Christ.

Victim of Japanese Military

The islands of the Pacific became well-known in World War II as Americans and their allies fought and died to rid the region of the forces of Japanese occupation. Yet, in the newspapers, little was mentioned about the native peoples living on these island battlegrounds where titanic forces fought their global war. Even fewer realized that Catholics died as martyrs on these islands. Blessed Peter To Rot, a native of one of these island battlegrounds, was martyred for the faith he refused to deny.

PETER TO ROT

(D. 1945)

MARTYR

Peter was born in Rakunai, New Britain, an island off the northeast coast of Papua New Guinea, in 1912. His father was To Puia, the chief of his village, and his mother was Maria Ia Tumul. Peter's father had invited missionaries to his village, and he and his family were baptized. Peter was trained as a catechist of the Catholic Faith at a young age, and was trained to administer at the local school. He also conducted prayer services and instructional sessions to aid missionaries, and in 1933, Peter took up the role of chief catechist in his own village. He married Paula Ia Varpit, a former student, and the couple had three children.

When the Japanese military forces arrived in New Britain to occupy the region, they interned the missionary priests, and Peter, harassed as a possible objector, was arrested several times. The Japanese tried to win the favor of the local populations by legalizing polygamy and making resistance to this legislation a punishable offense, and when their efforts failed, the military authorities insti-

from *Faces of Holiness*

Peter To Rot

tuted rules and regulations designed to limit the Catholic presence. Peter openly opposed the regulations, knowing that he had to witness for the faith. As a result, he was arrested again, and singled out for harsh treatment. Realizing the danger he was in, Peter asked his wife to bring him his good clothes — he wanted to go to God properly attired.

About a month before the Japanese surrendered to the Allied forces in the Pacific region, thirty-three-year-old Peter was taken to a hut in the secluded Vunaiara region. There he was given a lethal injection and was held down while he died in agony. The next day his body was returned to his village for burial.

Pope John Paul II beatified Peter in Port Moresby, Papua New Guinea, on January 17, 1995, declaring the heroic virtue of this devout catechist who dared the wrath of the occupying military forces in order to fulfill his commitment as a Christian by fostering the faith in a time of peril.

Foundress of the Congregation of the Mothers of the Helpless and of St. Joseph of the Mountain

This blessed founded a congregation so attuned to the needs of the abandoned and vulnerable that they were called "Mother of the Helpless" by the bishop of Málaga, Spain. Petra of St. Joseph Perez Florida brought all of the her energies and zeal to this apostolate and matured spiritually in undertaking heroic programs of charity.

PETRA OF ST. JOSEPH PEREZ FLORIDA

(D. 1906)

FOUNDRESS

She was born in Málaga, Spain on December 7, 1845, and was raised in a devout family. Her childhood was a time of preparation for the apostolate, as she recalled: "I thought about nothing else but becoming a nun." Petra also suffered for the poor, understanding their heartache when their pleas for aid were met with indifference.

Petra started begging for the poor, an activity that her father opposed vehemently. In time she was able to enlist his support, and she began living with three companions who desired to aid her in ministry to the poor. In 1880, the Congregation of the Mothers of the Helpless and of St. Joseph of the Mountain was the result of this first effort. The bishop of Málaga, watching Petra and her companions, proposed the congregation's title.

In 1895, Petra began working on Montaña Pelada, a royal sanctuary of St. Joseph of the Mountain in Barcelona. The church was dedicated in 1901. Guiding her growing communities and promoting more efforts for the poor, Petra continued her labors until her death in Barcelona on August 16, 1906.

Pope John Paul II beatified Petra on October 16, 1994, declaring her heroic virtues and praising her for being consumed by divine love.

Lay Role Model for Youth

The role models paraded before today's young people are certainly unique in the annals of human history. Such models attain superstar rank usually because of their involvement in the entertainment industry, sports, and business. They are lauded for their accomplishments on the stages of the world, not for their spiritual or mental achievements. For this reason, Pier (Peter) George Frassati, lovingly called Pier Giorgio in Rome, stands as a remarkable contradiction to the surperstars of this era.

PIER (PETER) GEORGE FRASSATI

(D. 1925)

LAY APOSTLE

He was born in Turin, Italy, on April 6, 1901, the son of Alfredo and Adelaide Amelia Frassati. His father was a senator of Italy, ambassador to Germany, and the founder of the *La Stampa* magazine. Pier and his younger sister, Luciana, were educated in the faith, although their parents were not devout.

He demonstrated many virtues and a certain spiritual maturity even as a child. As an adult he chose a mining career, a lifestyle that brought him close to the poor, and he aided them with charitable gifts and service through the St. Vincent de Paul Society. Pier was a daily communicant and had great devotion to the Blessed Virgin Mary. He was also athletic, outgoing, and a charming companion to people of all classes. Peter was an avid skier and mountain climber, who met life with cheerfulness and joy.

When asked why he performed so many acts of charity, Pier replied: "Jesus comes to visit me each morning in Holy Communion. I return his visit to him in the poor."

In June, 1925, Pier contracted polio while visiting an abandoned sick person, and he faced the terminal illness with calm, patience, and holy resolve. He wrote just before his death that "We should always be cheerful. Sadness should be banished from

Pier Frassati

from Faces of Holiness

all Christian souls. . . . Even in the midst of intense physical suffering it is one of joy." The last thing he wrote displayed his charity, in that he asked for medication for an ill friend who was unable to afford the needed dosage. He died in Turin on July 4, 1925, mourned and revered for his special union with Christ and his remarkable joy. Literally thousands came to pay their respects, remembering his personal kindness.

Pope John Paul II beatified Pier on May 20, 1990, announcing:

" 'Sanctify Christ as Lord in your hearts. Always be ready to give an explanation to anyone who asks you for a reason for your hope' (1Pt 3:15). . . . In our century, Pier Giorgio Frassati, whom I have the joy of declaring blessed today in the name of the Church, incarnated these words of St. Peter in his own life. The power of the Spirit of Truth, united to Christ, made him a modern witness to the hope which springs from the Gospel and to the grace of salvation which works in human hearts. . . . Thus he became a living witness and courageous defender of this hope in the name of the Christian youth of the twentieth century. Faith and charity, the true driving forces of his existence made him active and diligent in the milieu in which he lived, in his family and school, in the university and society; they transformed him into a joyful, enthusiastic apostle of Christ, a passionate follower of his message and charity. The secret of his apostolic zeal and holiness is to be sought in the ascetical and spiritual journey which he traveled; in prayer, in persevering adoration, even at night, of the Blessed Sacrament, in his thirst for the Word of God, which he sought in Biblical texts; in chastity lived as a cheerful, uncompromising discipline; in his daily love of silence and life's 'ordinariness.' It is precisely in these factors that we are given to understand the deep well-spring of his spiritual vitality."

Virgin Victim

PIERINA (PETRINA) MOROSINI

(D. 1957)

MARTYR

Women in countries occupied by military forces are often the victims of physical attacks. Blessed Pierina Morosini's rapist/murderer took from the world an exquisite young soul who had dedicated herself as a Bride of Christ.

She was born in Fiobbo di Albino on January 7, 1931, the eldest and only daughter of a farm family. Raised in the faith, she was trained to take responsibility and to serve others. Pierina helped her mother with household duties, and when she was old enough, she started working in a local cotton mill.

Very devout, she attended Mass daily and aided the local parish as a member of the Catholic Action organization. Pierina

from *Faces of Holiness*

Pierina Morosini

also took private vows of poverty, chastity, and obedience, probably hoping to embrace the religious life in time.

On April 6, 1957, Pierina was raped and beaten to death by an assailant. The people of the village were horrified by the violent crime, especially since Pierina's personal holiness and singular devotion to Christ were well-known in the region. Pierina's funeral was one of the largest ever held in that part of Italy, and she was laid to rest in her hometown. Today, a small monument with her picture at the place her body was found has replaced the wooden cross put up by her father and brothers.

Pope John Paul II beatified Pierina on October 4, 1987, as a young woman who symbolizes purity in this modern world of rampant violence and suffering. Her personal vows and her daily service were honored as acts that graced her family and neighbors, and her death as a true martyrdom.

Co-Founder of the Scalopians

The Scalopians, or Piarists, have become internationally famous through the centuries because of their labors, and many of their congregation, including martyrs, are being raised to the honors of the altars of the Church. Peter of the Nativity Casani, one of the founding companions of the Scalopians, the Pious Schools Congregation, is one of the foremost examples of the Scalopian friends of God.

Peter was born in Lucca, Italy, on September 8, 1570, the only son of Gaspar and Elizabeth Drogo Casani. His father was not religious and was openly opposed to Catholic devotions, but Peter was dedicated to the Blessed Virgin Mary at an early age. In 1591, when his mother died, he realized that he had a religious vocation and turned his back on the world to study for the priesthood.

PIETRO (PETER) CASANI

(D. 1647)

FOUNDER

In 1594, Peter entered the Congregation of the Blessed Virgin, impressing his superiors with holiness and dedication. He completed his religious and seminary training and was ordained in the Lateran Basilica in Rome on September

23, 1600. He worked in the congregation's various institutions until he met St. Joseph Calasanz, who was involved in a religious and social revolution — forming special schools for the poor. The religious of the Blessed Virgin of Lucca undertook the ministry of the Pious Schools, and the Congregation of the Mother of God was founded. When the two congregations were recognized by the Holy See in March, 1617, Peter became a Clerk Regular of the Mother of God of the Pious Schools. He was invested by Cardinal Benedetto Giusitiniani on March 25.

Peter served as the first novice master, demonstrating extraordinary concerns about religious formation and the educational apostolate. He taught that "patience and prayer are enough." He served as a leading figure in the expansion of the congregation, in time becoming the provincial superior of Genoa and Naples and commissary general of Moravia. Peter also served the Scalopians or Piarists as an assistant superior general for twenty years, bringing a quiet resolve and commitment to that post in the congregation. Peter died in Rome on October 13, 1647, mourned by his fellow religious and all who benefited from the heroic performance of his religious duties.

Pope John Paul II beatified Peter on October 1, 1995, stating: *"Pietro Casani, a native of Lucca, joined Joseph Calasanz in 1614 'to educate' Roman children 'in piety and letters.' Open to love of neighbor and dedicated to the education of poor children, he said before his death: 'Much can be accomplished by patience and prayer.' "*

Philip Ripoll Morata ✤ **See Felipe Ripall Morata**.

Philip Munarriz ✤ **See Martyrs of Barbastro**.

Philip Rinaldi ✤ **See Filippo Rinaldi**.

Philip Siphong ✤ **See Martyrs of Thailand**.

Philip Smaldoni ✤ **See Filippo Smaldone**.

PIUS CAMPIDELLI

(D. 1889)

✤

VICTIM SOUL

Passionist Victim of Love

Age is not a factor in the science of the saints. Almighty God demonstrates again and again that the very young can respond to grace with generosity and with an ardor that astonishes the world. Blessed Pius Campidelli was one of the young holy ones, destined to shine forever for the glory of God and as a shimmering jewel of the Passionist Congregation.

He was born in Trebbio, near

Rimini, Italy, on April 29, 1868, and was baptized Luigi on the same day. The fourth of six children, he was the son of Joseph and Filomena Belpani Campidelli, farmers of the region. Pius's father died of typhoid fever in 1874 and an uncle came to the farm to help with the heavier work. Pius labored on the farm, a tract of land that demanded the time and energies of the entire family. He managed to attend school and served as an altar boy, becoming devoted to the prayer life after his First Communion at age ten.

Two and a half years later, Pius and his family attended a Passionist mission. He applied for admission to the congregation and was accepted in 1882, taking the religious name Pius of St. Aloysius Gonzaga. Pius took his first vows on April 30, 1884, and began studying for the priesthood. In 1871, he received the tonsure and minor orders at San Entizio, near Viterbo.

It was then discovered that Pius was in the last stages of tuberculosis, doomed to an early death by the ravages of the disease. Pius accepted the medical prognosis with serenity, declaring that he was a willing victim of love for the Church. Surrounded by the Passionists, whom he thanked for their concern and care, Pius died in Casale on November 2, 1889.

Pope John Paul II beatified Pius on November 17, 1985, declaring that the boy of only fourteen years of age was advanced spiritually. The Holy Father praised Pius for offering his life and honored the new blessed for his spirit of penance, Christ-like ideals, and for his serenity. The Holy Father honored Pius in the International Youth Year, declaring: *"It is fitting that this year should see him honored and put before all young people as a model and an inspiration."*

Trappist Oblate

Blessed Rafael Arnáiz Barón was given a very short span of life on earth, but during his time, he functioned on spiritual and intellectual levels unknown by most. His existence was quite simply a quest for the "Absolute," a continual seeking after unity with God. Recognized early on as a remarkably gifted soul, Rafael left a profound spiritual legacy for his native land.

Rafael was born in Burgos, Spain, on April 9, 1911, the eldest of four children in a prominent family. Raised devoutly and developing spiritual maturity at an early age, Rafael was educated by the Jesuits and then studied architecture in Madrid. He was described by contemporaries as being lively, extroverted, and artistic.

At age eighteen, Rafael realized that the religious life was his goal. He started an intense prayer life, even while involved in the secular world. In 1933, after completing mili-

RAFAEL ARNÁIZ BARÓN

(D. 1938)

🔥

MYSTIC

tary service, Rafael joined the Trappists at San Isidro de Dueños Monastery. Shortly after joining he was found to be suffering from diabetes mellitus, and he was forced to return home to recuperate properly. Stabilized, Rafael returned to the Trappists as an oblate, unable to assume regular monastic roles because of his illness. After suffering another attack of the disease, he died on April 26, 1938, at age twenty-seven.

Rafael was a writer of profound spiritual and ascetical works. These writings spread quickly throughout Spain, and his grave at San Isidro Monastery became a pilgrimage site.

Pope John Paul II beatified Rafael on September 27, 1992, declaring:

" 'Fight the good fight of faith,' the second reading urges us, and adds: 'Take firm hold on the everlasting life to which you were called when, in the presence of many witnesses, you made your noble profession of faith' (1Tm 6:12). With great joy we can proclaim today that the new blessed born in Spain incarnated in [his] life these words of St. Paul. Blessed Rafael Arnáiz Barón incarnated them in his brief but intense monastic life as a Trappist, being an example, especially for young people, of a loving and unconditional response to the divine call. 'God alone!' he often repeated in his spiritual exercises."

Polish Conventual Franciscan

Some heroic souls have lives that are measured well beyond their own brief existence. Rafael Melchior Chylinski represents not only the spiritual perfection that results from grace and union with God, but also Poland's fight for independence.

RAFAEL
MELCHIOR
CHYLINSKI

(D. 1741)

RELIGIOUS

Rafael was a noble, born in Wysoczka, Poland, on January 8, 1690. Though raised in an era of self-indulgence and extravagance, he turned his back on his hereditary rights and privileges to become a Conventual Franciscan. As a Franciscan priest he attained a remarkable degree of holiness and became known as a patron of the poor. During the terrible epidemic of Krakow in 1736, Rafael, living in Lageiewniki, part of Lodz, cared for the sick without sparing himself by receiving victims of the plague and offering them shelter and medical aid.

Rafael remained faithful to his religious vows, emanating a resolve and piety that inspired others. He died at Lagiewniki on December 2, 1741.

Pope John Paul II beatified Rafael on June 9, 1991, in the square of Farmer's Park in Warsaw, announcing:

"Father Rafael was never a deputy, a Member of Parliament. He chose the vocation of a poor son of St. Francis, but his witness is very similar. His life

was hidden, hidden in Christ; it was a protest against the conscience, the atti-
tude and the self-destructive behavior of the nobility in those Saxon times, and
we know how the story ended. But why does Providence remind us of this to-
day? Why only now has this process matured through all the signs of earth and
heaven, and we can proclaim Father Rafael blessed? Look for the answer to
this question. We are searching for an answer to this question. The Church does
not have the answers at hand; the Pope does not want to suggest any interpre-
tation to you. All of us, 35 million Poles, should reflect together on the meaning
of this beatification in the year of our Lord 1991."

Bishop of Veracruz, Mexico

In the early eras of Christianity, the saints suffered persecutions and exile because of their zeal and influence on the faithful. In the modern era, Rafael Guizar Valencia, "the Bishop of the poor," suffered the same trials as his spiritual ancestors.

Rafael was born in Cotija, Michoacan, Mexico, on April 26, 1878. Receiving the grace of a religious vocation, he entered the seminary at Zamora and completed his priestly studies. He was ordained on June 1, 1901, and started his ministry with exceptional zeal — just four years later Rafael was appointed apostolic missionary and spiritual director of the seminary.

The revolutionary government in control of Mexico at the time was anti-Catholic and widespread in its denunciation of the faith. To combat this evil, Rafael published *La Nación*, a periodical that kept the faithful informed and inspired. He was

RAFAEL

GUIZAR

VALENCIA

(D. 1938)

BISHOP

singled out for harassment as a result and had to move to Mexico City, where he disguised himself as a junk dealer so that he could move about freely to minister to those in need. Rafael was sentenced to death by the Mexican courts, in absentia, and he left the country to work in Cuba and in the United States.

He was consecrated the bishop of Veracruz, Mexico, in 1919, and started revitalizing the diocese, writing a catechism of Christian doctrine and rebuilding the seminary. That seminary was later confiscated by the government. Rafael then moved his program for priest formation to Mexico City, where it was operated successfully for fifteen years. He sold all that he had during this period to nurture the poor. At the same time he was suffering from cardiac problems, diabetes, obesity, and phlebitis.

Forced into exile again, Rafael worked in the United States, Cuba, and Colombia. He finally made the dramatic decision to return to Veracruz and continue his apostolate. Taken ill from overwork, he died in Mexico City on June 6, 1938.

Pope John Paul II beatified Rafael on June 29, 1995, proclaiming:

"He carried out his apostolate as a priest and Bishop amid almost constant persecution and situations of danger. For many years he had no fixed residence, yet no difficulty prevented him from fulfilling his missionary tasks. He said repeatedly: 'I will give my life for the salvation of souls,' like the Good Shepherd. Those who knew him said there was no power or obstacle which could weaken his evangelizing zeal. Teaching catechism and giving popular missions were the focus of his activity. His native Mexico, the United States, Guatemala, and Cuba were to benefit from his pastoral zeal. His spirituality was based on eucharistic devotion and love of the Virgin Mary. Fostering priestly vocations, administering the sacraments, particularly Penance and Matrimony, regularizing many common-law unions, preaching the word of God, as well as constant devotion to prayer also made him a man of faith and action who was concerned for the salvation of souls."

Foundress of the Institute of the Holy Guardian Angels

This new blessed, Rafaela Ybarra, experienced the joys and sorrows of the world and put her energies to the service of others and to the glory of God. A respected and beloved figure in the Church of Spain, she was called "the Widow of Villalonga" and the "Mother."

RAFAELA YBARRA

(D. 1900)

❧

FOUNDRESS

Rafaela was born in Bilbao, Spain, on January 16, 1843, to a noble and pious family. As was the custom then, she was married quite young, but her husband passed away within a short time. Always drawn to the service of the Church, she decided, after much prayerful reflection, that she was called by God to devote her life to an apostolate of service to others.

This commitment to service manifested itself in a very specific way. She established a new religious congregation, the Institute of the Holy Guardian Angels. Under her care, the young women who joined the institute labored to found hospitals, maternity homes, and programs designed to give comfort, protection, and hope to the many children who were left without parents through disaster, neglect, abandonment, or social upheaval. Rafaela also administered programs to aid the poor of all ages and to relieve the suffering found throughout Spain among the needy, the suffering, and the chronically ill and forgotten souls. Her work continued right up until her death in Bilbao on February 23, 1900.

Pope John Paul II beatified Rafaela on September 30, 1984, announcing

"Her unconditional dedication to God and others in the different circumstances of her life is admirable . . . From the Cross and prayer she was able to draw strength to offer herself on the altars of Christian love."

Maronite Virgin and Victim Soul

The Maronite Church has a long history of faithful service and spiritual splendor. St. Sharbel is already known to the faithful of the modern world, as is his teacher, Blessed Nimatullah Youssef Kassab al-Hardini. Yet another Maronite mystic and joyful victim of divine love has been raised to the honors of the altar. She is Rafka, or Rafqa ar-Reyes, also called Rebecca de Himlaya.

Rafka was born in the mountain village of Himlaya, Lebanon, in 1832, called Petra Ar-Rayes at her Maronite baptism. Raised by devout Maronite parents, Rafka lost her mother at age seven. She was raised by a stepmother and received the grace of a religious vocation.

In 1853, Rafka entered the Marianist Sisters and was given the name Anissa in religion. She taught young girls in the congregation's schools from 1856-1871, but was drawn more and more to the contemplative life. In that year, the Marianist Congregation was dissolved, an event that

RAFKA (REBECCA) DE HIMLAYA

(D. 1914)

MYSTIC

allowed Rafka to enter the Maronite Order of St. Anthony, and she became a member of the community of St. Simeon. She was given the name Rafqa in her new community.

On Rosary Sunday, 1885, Rafka prayed to become a victim of divine love. She was struck blind that night and endured terrible pain in her right eye. That eye was eventually removed in an operation without an anesthetic. Rafka had hemorrhages from her eye two or three times a week ever after as a result, yet this suffering did not stop her from performing all of her normal convent duties. She did the washing, baking, and weaving, and even memorized the Divine Office so that she could join her sister religious in choir services.

In 1897, Rafka was assigned to the monastery of St. Joseph of Gerabta. There

from *Faces of Holiness*

Blessed Rafka de Himlaya

she suffered paralysis from disarticulation of her bones. She developed sores and abscesses and still prayed: "For the glory of God, in union with Christ's passion." Rafka continued to pray and to face death with the same calm and spirit of joyful surrender. Rebecca said: "I am not afraid. I have been waiting for my Lord for a long time." She died on March 23, 1914, at As-Sahr. More than 2,600 miracles were reported at her tomb.

Pope John Paul II beatified Rafka on November 17, 1985, declaring:

"Blessed Rafka de Himlaya was truly 'salt of the earth and light of the world,' a mission that is incumbent upon all the disciples of Christ. Having inherited the many rich ecclesiastical and monastic traditions of Lebanon, the new blessed left to her country and to the Church in return the mysterious flavor of an existence totally impregnated by the spirit of Christ the Redeemer. She is indeed like a light 'on a mountain top.' One could also apply to her the beautiful verse from Psalm 92: 'The just flourishes like the palm tree, like a cedar of Lebanon shall he grow!' "

Victim of Sachsenhausen

The Nazis threatened the Church in Germany long before they began their horrifying assault on Europe and the world. Like all dictatorships, the Nazis relied on terror, lies, and the ruination of the righteous in order to strengthen their grip on Germany. Anyone who dared to oppose them faced harsh retaliation, sometimes with imprisonment and death. Rupert Mayer understood what his opposition to this recognized evil would bring, and he willingly paid the ultimate price for Christ.

RUPERT MAYER

(D. 1945)

MARTYR

Rupert was born in Stuttgart, Germany, on January 23, 1876. He was the son of Kolumban and Maria Schaürer Mayer, raised devoutly in the Catholic Faith and well educated. He entered the seminary and after some years of study was ordained on May 2, 1899. A year later he entered the Society of Jesus.

The Jesuits sent Rupert to Lichtenstein to study and then assigned him to the Society's various apostolates. He became chaplain during World War I and was severely wounded. When he recovered, Rupert went on to serve as a chaplain of a Sodality and conducted a mission for travelers.

He saw the troubled condition of Germany in the beginning of the 1930's and tried to warn the faithful of the coming disasters. As a result, the Nazis warned Rupert to cease his sermons and attacks in 1933. Although they threatened him with severe retaliations, Rupert was not cowed by their words. He continued to attack the Nazis from the pulpit and in 1936 was arrested for his activities for a brief period. He did not allow the Nazis to silence him completely, however, and he earned their enmity.

On November 3, 1939, Rupert was sent to Sachsenhausen concentration camp, where he experienced severe abuse and torture. He was there only a short time when he was sent to Ettal Abbey. Rupert was detained in the abbey until Germany surrendered to the Allied forces. He returned to Munich at the war's end, on May 11, 1945. Exhausted by his sufferings, Rupert died on November 1, 1945 in Munich. He was buried in the Sodality Church in Munich, revered for his heroism in opposing the brutal Nazi regime.

Pope John Paul II beatified Rupert on May 3, 1987, praising him as a steadfast priest who understood that the Church could not survive the new barbarism of the world without champions who risked life and limb to reverberate Catholic truths in the world.

Salvator Lilli of Cappadocia and Companions ❦ See Martyrs of Armenia.

Foundress of the Sisters of the Poor

The saints of the Church inspire the faithful and sometimes aid in the formation of generous souls in new generations. For Blessed Savina Petrilli, the role of St. Catherine of Siena was paramount to her spiritual apostolate and she bequeathed a heritage of devotion and service as a response to Christ's love.

Savina was born in Siena, Italy, on August 29, 1851, where she was raised in a pious home and introduced at age ten to the life of St. Catherine of Siena. Savina began to practice devotion to Christ in the Eucharist and to Christ Crucified. She also became aware of the needs of the poor. The Children of Mary Sodality in her parish aided in her formation, and her parish priest was an active confessor and spiritual guide.

In 1869, Savina made a pilgrimage to Rome. In an audience with Pope Pius

SAVINA PETRILLI

(D. 1923)

FOUNDRESS

IX, Savina was told by the Holy Father to walk in St. Catherine's footsteps. She returned home to pray, and in 1872 she confided to her dying sister, Emilia, that she planned to found a religious congregation. She approached the archbishop of Siena with the same aspiration, and in 1873 this prelate instructed Savina to draw up rules for a community to be called the Sisters of the Poor.

One year later, Savina and her companions moved into a small apartment and cared for an abandoned baby, the first of many. Savina faced severe trials, but her Sisters of the Poor received diocesan approval and approbation from the Holy See in 1875. New foundations were made in Italy and Brazil, and then in

Argentina and Italy. In 1922, Savina was diagnosed with malignant cancer. She continued work until her death on April 18, 1923.

Pope John Paul II beatified Savina on April 24, 1988, declaring:

"You are my God . . . I extol you with my life, with all my strength, Mother Savina seems to say, but I extol you by gathering before you, my God, the most neglected brothers and sisters seeking along the ways of the world all those whom people despise, in order to lead every person to the joy of the banquet of the Kingdom. Therefore I extol you by extending the work of the Sisters of the Poor to the most neglected areas of the earth and the most difficult working conditions, so that everyone may find joy and peace and 'give thanks to the Lord, for he is good; for his kindness endures forever' (Ps 117[118]:29)."

Catechist of the Slaves

This blessed was honored in his lifetime as "the Catechist of the Slaves," but he is also revered as one of the kindest, most gentle human beings ever to walk upon the earth. His name in the world was Jean-Bernard Rousseau, and his name in religion became synonymous with the virtues of the Christian faith. The Holy Father went to the Island of Réunion to declare this to the world.

SCUBILION

(D. 1867)

RELIGIOUS

Scubilion was born Jean-Bernard Rousseau in Anny-Côte (Tharaigeau), France, on March 22, 1797. His Burgundian family was very devout, and Scubilion performed labors for his local parish, including the activities of a catechist. Dedicated and eager to serve others, he received the grace of a religious vocation and applied to the Christian Brothers. He entered the Paris Christian Brothers novitiate in 1822, receiving the religious name of Scubilion. In the decade following his profession, he served in the Christian Brothers' schools in France where he was much loved by his students because he was kind and treated everyone who came to him with dignity and respect.

That Christ-like presence would change the lives of men and women in a distant land when Scubilion was assigned to the island of Réunion in the Indian Ocean. In 1833, he accepted this missionary assignment and sailed to Réunion, where he would remain for thirty-four years. The people to whom Scubilion would dedicate his time and energies on Réunion were the enslaved natives. As he began to work with them, he was stunned when he realized that no one had given them any level of education or catechism. Scubilion, bringing his kindly manner and his profound sense of worth of individual human beings into his mission, began classes for the slaves.

The slaves came to Scubilion in the evenings, after long hours of labor and ill-treatment. He provided Catholic doctrine on many levels, designed to interest the slaves and to prepare them for reception of the sacraments. When the slaves were emancipated in 1848, they turned to Scubilion to guide them through their transition to freedom.

During his last years, Scubilion was exhausted and ill, but he labored in the local parish, winning all to Christ. He died at Sainte-Marie, Isle de Réunion, on April 13, 1867, revered by the islanders.

Pope John Paul II beatified Scubilion on May 2, 1989 on Réunion, proclaiming: *"The love of God and the love of neighbor were inseparable in him. In the eyes of everyone, he shone with a power of love that revealed the God of Love. He was light, as Christ wished it: 'You are the light of the world.' He allowed himself to be enlightened by Jesus Christ and he enlightened others in the light of Jesus Christ by this example and in particular, by his catechesis among the slaves."*

Italian Chaplain and Military Priest

The unsung heroes of the military history of any nation are the chaplains who serve with distinction in war and in peace. America has an honor roll of distinguished "padres": Blessed Secondo Pollo stands as Italy's symbol of the chaplaincy corps.

Secondo Pollo was born in Caresanablot, Italy, near Vercelli, on January 2, 1908. He was raised in a devout family and trained in reverence for the Blessed Sacrament and the Blessed Virgin. Secondo received as well the grace of a religious vocation and entered Montecrivello seminary. He was then sent to the Pontifical Lombard Seminary in Rome and was ordained upon completing his studies.

SECONDO POLLO

(D. 1941)

MARTYR

After ordination, Secondo was assigned to Montecrivello but also served in surrounding parishes. There he taught catechetical classes to children, using a stable as a classroom in one parish. He rejoiced in being a parish priest, but he was assigned as spiritual director for the major seminary of the archdiocese, where he earned a reputation as a preacher and confessor. In September 1936, Secondo was named archdiocesan chaplain to the Italian Youth of Catholic Action and went to serve as a chaplain in the local prison.

In 1940, Secondo was named administrator of a parish in Larizzate. One year later he was drafted as a military chaplain. Assigned to the Val Chisone battalion of the Alpine Regiment, he was sent to Montenegro, where he served with honor. On December 26, 1941, Secondo was fatally wounded while caring for the fallen on the battlefield. He said: "I am going to God, who is so good." Secondo bowed his head and died.

Pope John Paul II beatified Secondo Pollo on May 23, 1998, in Vercelli, Italy, with 20,000 faithful in attendance. The Holy Father declared:

"The secrets of Father Secondo's ascent to the peaks of holiness were two: continual rootedness in God through prayer, and the most tender devotion to our heavenly Mother, Mary. . . . Let us give thanks to the Lord for the gift of this blessed and for all the saints and blesseds who, in Christ, the one Mediator of Salvation, build a 'bridge' between God and the world by reflecting and radiating heaven's brightness upon humanity making its pilgrim way on earth."

Canon Regular of the Lateran of Corpus Christi

During the 1400s, Europe was a seething, troubled continent plagued by epidemics and political and religious confrontations. Out of this chaos arose holy men and women with unique talents and graces who dedicated themselves to serving their neighbors and the Church. Stanislas Kazimierczyk was one of the spiritual giants of this historical period. Almost forgotten through the centuries, Stanislas has been introduced to the faith, revered for his great austerity and his ministerial zeal.

STANISLAS KAZIMIERCZYK

(D. 1489)

RELIGIOUS

He was born in 1433 in Casimiria, at the time a part of modern Krakow, Poland. Stanislas was the son of a devout couple: Soltyn Matthias and his wife, Hedwige. He was educated in the local schools, displaying a certain brilliance, and attended Jagiellion University. Stanislas earned a doctorate with honors.

In 1456, he entered the Canons Regular of the Lateran of Corpus Christi, taking his vows as a religious. Stanislas completed his novitiate, was educated for the priesthood, and was then ordained. His austerity and mortification were attracting people even then, and he assumed many roles in the community. Stanislas served as a preacher, master of novices, and sub-prior in his monastery.

His devotion to the Blessed Virgin Mary and the Passion of Christ distinguished Stanislas, but he centered his priestly life on the Holy Eucharist, drawing his strength from the Blessed Sacrament. Stanislas became famous as a peacher, confessor, and spiritual director. He was also a powerful foe of the Wycliffe and Hus heresies.

His written spiritual sermons and lectures have survived in part, although a collection of his homilies was destroyed in World War II. These display his generous concern for the poor and sick, as well as his towering intellect and spirituality. Stanislas died in Casmiria on May 3, 1489. He was buried in the church of Corpus Christi.

Pope John Paul II beatified Stanislas on April 18, 1993, praising him as a glory of Poland and the Church, a giant of the intellect and faith who helped to preserve his nation's Catholic heritage.

Teresa Benedicta of the Cross 🔥 **See Edith Stein**.

Victim of Nazis

Nazi atrocities during World War II took many forms, and innocent men and women died as a result of raids and military forays. Teresa Bracco, a young Italian woman, was caught up in a German retaliatory attack and assaulted. She resisted, as she had always declared: "I would rather be killed than give in,' and her defense of her purity cost her life.

Teresa Bracco was born in Santa Giulia on February 24, 1924, the daughter of Giacomo and Anna Pera Bracco, Catholic farmers. The family was pious, reciting the Rosary each evening, and Teresa learned her devotions in her home. She was also taught the faith by the local parish priest, Father Natale Olivieri, who gave her religious books. Teresa was well-behaved in school and attended Mass each day. Her inspiration was St. Dominic Savio.

TERESA BRACCO

(D. 1944)

MARTYR

In the fall of 1943, guerrilla warfare began in the Acqui region of Italy, Teresa's home. The local people watched these clashes between the partisans and German troops and tried to avoid becoming involved. On July 24, 1944, however, the partisans fought the Germans on the road between Cairo Montenotte and Cortemilia. The next day, the Germans began punitive assaults on the region, entering Santa Giulia on August 28, 1944. The Germans believed Santa Giulia was a partisan stronghold and put repressive measures into place.

Three young women, including Teresa, were taken prisoner in the town. Teresa was dragged to a deserted area by one of the Germans. Resisting and trying to escape, she enraged her attacker who choked the young woman and then shot her, shattering her skull. Teresa had been killed for the simple reason that she would not surrender her purity.

Pope John Paul II beatified Teresa on May 24, 1998, in Turin's Piazza Vittorio, and the people of the Piedmont attended in large numbers. At the ceremony, the Holy Father declared:

"To young people in particular, I hold up this young woman whom the Church is proclaiming blessed today so that they may learn from her clear faith, witnessed to in daily commitment, moral consistency without compromises and the courage of sacrificing even life if necessary, in order not to betray the values that give it meaning."

Teresa Garcia y Garcia 🔥 See Martyrs of Guadalajara.

Foundress of the Third Order Carmelite Sisters

One of the hallmarks of the Christian faith is joy, the reflection of Christ's Redemption and Mercy. Blessed Teresa Maria of the Cross Manetti was not only a mirror of such joy but was renowned for what her contemporaries called her "angelic innocence," a quality that touched the lives of thousands through her Carmelite apostolate.

TERESA MARIA OF THE CROSS MANETTI

(D. 1910)

MYSTIC

She was born Teresa Adelaida Cesina Manetti on March 2, 1846, at San Martino a Campo Bisenzio, near Florence, Italy. She was the daughter of Salvatore and Rosa Bigali Manetti, who called her "Bettina." The family was quite poor, and Teresa Maria was not well-educated, but she displayed a beautiful radiance of joy and innocence.

In 1865, Teresa and other young women started a house of devotion and retreat, and she became a Third Order Discalced Carmelite, taking the name Teresa Maria of the Cross. On December 7, 1888, Teresa and twenty-six other virgins received the habit of the Discalced Carmelites, founding the Third Order Carmelite Sisters, in Florence. The Holy See approved the congregation in 1904.

A hallmark of Teresa Maria's spirituality was her devotion to the Blessed Sacrament and to the Passion of Christ. She experienced many spiritual and mystical graces and displayed heroic virtue in the many trials facing her new religious foundation.

Teresa Maria died in Campo Bisenzio on April 23, 1910, mourned by all who had come into contact with her. Her Cause was approved in 1937. Pope John Paul II beatified Teresa Maria on October 19, 1986, honoring her founding, her Carmelite spirituality, and her mirroring of Christ in a troubled time.

Foundress of the Congregation of the Little Sisters of Divine Providence

The loss of a loved one can lead to despair, to desolation, or to an awakening of Divine Love and the acute sense of the needs of others. Teresa Grillo Michel used loss and sorrow as purifying agents in her life, awakening from her mourning to the wisdom of the chosen soul.

TERESA GRILLO MICHEL

(D. 1944)

FOUNDRESS

She was born in Alessandria (Spinetta Marengo), Italy, on September 25, 1855, the fifth child of Giuseppi and Maria Antonetta Parvopassau Grillo. Her father was the chief physician at the Civil Hospital of Alessandria and her mother was a member of an illustrious local family. She was baptized Maddalena.

Her father died while she was still young, and Teresa and her family moved to Turin. She attended the school operated by the Ladies of Loretto in Lodi, and upon graduation was introduced to society in Alessandria. On August 2, 1877, Teresa married Giovanni Michel and they moved to several towns before finally settling in Naples. Giovanni died of sunstroke in 1891, and Teresa went through the ordeal of profound and lasting grief.

Restored through spiritual reading and the help of family members, Teresa embarked on a new apostolate. She opened her home to children and the needy, and in 1893 sold her house to purchase a building on the Via Fa'a di Bruno (honoring that blessed). This was called the Little Shelter of Divine Providence.

On January 8, 1899, Teresa and eight companions received the habit of the Congregation of the Little Sisters of Divine Providence. She spent the remaining years of her life guiding her rapidly spreading congregation, which at her death had twenty-five houses in Italy, nineteen in Brazil, and seven in Argentina. Blessed Luigi Orioni asked her to accept the apostolate in Argentina in 1927. Teresa made eight voyages to Latin America to establish hospitals, nurseries, homes for the aged, orphanages, and schools. She lived to see her congregation approved by the Holy See in 1942. Teresa died in Alessandria on January 25, 1944.

Pope John Paul II beatified Teresa on May 24, 1998, in Turin's Piazza Vittorio, announcing: *"She was called by the Lord to spread love, especially among the poor. . . . This generous daughter of Piedmont follows in the steps of the saints and blesseds who, down the centuries, have brought the world the message of divine love through active service to their needy brethren. Let us thank God for the living witness given by the holiness of this woman. . . ."*

Foundress of the Sisters of Providence of St. Mary-of-the-Woods

The frontiers of America drew countless noble souls into the wilderness in this nation's infancy. They brought the "Good News" of Christ into raw and uncharted lands as missionaries, followed by courageous women who arrived to establish schools and the stable society needed in the wilds. Mother Théodore-Anne-Thérèse Guerin, the founder of the Sisters of Providence of St. Mary-of-the-Woods, depending solely upon Divine Providence on the frontier, where she influenced others with her heroic faith and spirit of dedication.

THÉODORE-ANNE-THÉRÈSE GUERIN

(D. 1856)

FOUNDRESS

Théodore-Anne-Thérèse was born in Etables, France, on October 2, 1798, the daughter of Laurent and Isabelle Guerin. Baptized the next day, Théodore-Anne-Thérèse received her First Holy Communion at the age of ten. On the day of her First Communion, she announced her desire to become a nun, and she spent hours in prayer. Then, on September 6, 1825, she received the habit of the Sisters of Providence at Ruillé-sur-Loire, making her final vows on September 5, 1831. She became Sister Théodore in the convent.

During her novitiate, Theodore suffered from a serious illness, probably smallpox, and the medicines administered to her at that time severely damaged her digestive system, leaving her physically frail for life. Yet she continued her vocation, serving the various schools of the congregation and receiving the Medal of Honor in Angers for her teaching methods. Théodore also studied medicine and cared for the sick poor.

At the request of the bishop of the diocese of Vincennes, Indiana, in 1839 Théodore led five Sisters of Providence into the American frontier. They arrived at Saint-Mary-of-the-Woods, Indiana, on October 22, 1840. There, Théodore established the motherhouse and novitiate of the congregation, starting with a chapel made of logs. While learning English and adapting to the American lifestyle, Theodore began her first academy for young girls. The first student arrived on July 4, 1841.

Théodore opened schools as well in Jasper, Indiana, St. Mary-of-the-Woods Village, and at St. Francisville, Illinois. She also founded two orphanages and pharmacies to serve the poor. Theodore faced poverty, fires, persecution by local Protestants, and the separation of her house from the congregation in France. She remained steadfast and resolute, declaring: "Have confidence in the Providence that so far has never failed us. The way is not yet clear. Grope always slowly. Do not press matter; be patient, be trustful."

Théodore's final illness began Holy Week in March, 1856. Writing her final words, she rejoiced: "I am obliged to keep to my bed. What a beautiful week to be upon the Cross. O good Cross, I will love thee with all my heart." She died on May 14, 1856, and was buried in the Church of the Immaculate Conception at Saint-Mary-of-the-Woods.

Pope John Paul II beatified Mother Théodore on October 25, 1998, in Rome, declaring: *" 'The Lord stood by me and gave me strength to proclaim the word fully' (2 Tm. 4:17). In these words to Timothy, St. Paul looks back across the years of his apostolic ministry and affirms his hope in the Lord in the face of adversity. The words of the apostle were engraved on Mother Théodore Guerin's heart when she left her native France in 1840 with five companions to face the uncertainties and dangers of the frontier territory of Indiana. Her life and work were always guided by the sure hand of Providence, in which she had complete confidence. She understood that she must spend herself in God's service, seeking always his will. Despite initial difficulties and misunderstandings, and subsequent crosses and afflictions, she felt deeply that God had blessed her Congregation of the Sisters of Providence, giving it growth and forging a union of hearts among its members. In the congregation's schools and orphanages, Mother Théodore's witness led many young boys and girls to the loving care of God in their lives. Today she continues to teach Christians to abandon themselves to the providence of their heavenly Father and to be totally committed to doing what pleases him. The life of Blessed Théodore Guerin is a testimony that everything is possible with God and for God. May her spiritual daughters and all who experienced her charism live the same spirit today."*

Founder of the Disciples of the Divine Master

The work of Don Alberione brought life and hope to thousands of faithful in Italy, and it attracted the lifelong commitment of the Blessed Timothy Ciaccardo. Timothy was one of the modern holy men and women who understood the power of the media in the world, and he used it to promote the Church's social apostolates.

TIMOTHY

GIACCARDO

(D. 1948)

FOUNDER

Timothy was born on June 13, 1896, at Narzole, Cueneo, Italy, and was baptized Giuseppe Domenico Giaccardo the same day. At an early age he met Don Alberione, the Founder of the Society of St. Paul. Devout, Timothy entered the seminary of the diocese of Alba, but in 1917 transferred to the Society of St. Paul knowing full well that joining an as-yet-unapproved society could result in his not being ordained. He joined anyway, and two years later, on October 19, 1919, Timothy was ordained the first priest of the Society.

In 1926 Father Giaccardo was sent to found the first house of the congregation in Rome. He faced the difficulties with a spirit of faith and prayer, accepting his roles as teacher, confessor, spiritual director, and adminstrator. He was also the editor of a weekly periodical *The Voice of Rome*. After a decade serving in Rome he was named the superior of the motherhouse in Alba, where his calm reserve and prayers were needed in directing the growing congregation. In 1946, Timothy was called back to Rome where he was appointed Provincial Superior for the Society of St. Paul in Italy and the Vicar General of the Pauline Family.

Timothy was revered for his intense spiritual life and endless activities. Offering his own life so that the Disciples of the Divine Master might be approved as a separate religious congregation, his intention was obviously received as he was stricken with acute leukemia and died on January 34, 1948, just twelve days after celebrating a Mass of thanksgiving with the members of the new congregation. He was buried in the lower crypt of the Basilica of Mary, Queen of Apostles, beside the house which he had founded.

Pope John Paul II beatified Timothy on October 22, 1989, declaring:

"In the face of a world in which the faith encounters difficulties and insidious ideas of every kind which threaten the very survival of many souls, Timothy Giaccardo, the first disciple of Don Alberione, interpreted fidelity to his own priestly vocation as proclaiming the Gospel through the press, thereby having an ever broader and deeper effect on his brothers and sisters. Thus he proposed to spread the Gospel and the Church's teaching through the modern means of social communications, which he saw as the principal and typical apostolate of the modern world. All, this was to be in absolute fidelity to the Church's magisterium in a spiritual life nourished daily through eucharistic adoration and devotion to Our Lady, in the persuasive example of his humility and meekness which made him so beloved by the entire Pauline family, which today, seventy-five years after its foundation, finds in him a model in continuing the mission entrusted to it by Don Alberione."

Carmelite Victim of Dachau

TITUS

BRANDSMA

(D. 1942)

MARTYR

Tyranny does not distinguish in its victims, and the Nazi persecution of men and women of all ages and faiths is a vivid testimony to twentieth-century tyranny at its worst. Blessed Titus Brandsma, a small, energetic, holy Carmelite paid the ultimate price for his beliefs and vocal exposure of the Nazis and their perfidious lies. Pope John Paul II recognized Titus's courage and intellectual honesty, calling him *"a man of our century."*

Titus Brandsma was born on February 23, 1881, at Bolsward, the Netherlands, baptized Anno Sjoerd. Titus displayed an intellectual brilliance even at a young age, and he earned his doctorate at twenty-eight.

After entering the Carmelites and receiving the religious name of Titus, he announced that he had reached his spiritual home. His brilliance and dedication were recognized, and Titus was assigned as a professor at the Catholic University of Nijmegen. He would serve in this capacity for nineteen years, becoming an authority on mystical theology.

Titus earned fame as well as a journalist and author. He lectured in the United States and was well-received because of his scholarship and his evident holiness. Alarmed by the Nazi propaganda and military power, Titus began to speak out against the anti-Semitic laws passed in Germany. In 1935, he warned that Catholic newspapers could not print Nazi propaganda in good conscience. This stand brought him to the attention of the Nazis, who called him "that dangerous little friar."

When the Nazis invaded the Netherlands, they jailed Titus and kept him confined. The SS and the Gestapo interrogated him and they offered him solitude in a monastery if he would make a statement that Catholic papers could publish Dutch Nazi Party proclamations. When he refused, he was punished. An SS official declared that: "Brandsma is genuinely a man of character and firm convictions." The SS decided that the sixty-one-year-old Titus needed to be silenced. He was sent to Amersfoort Prison in Holland and then to Dachau concentration camp. There he worked as a laborer, managing to console his fellow prisoners even as his health was nearing a state of collapse. He lived by the simple motto: "They who want to win the world for Christ must have the courage to come in to conflict with it."

Hospitalized in the dreaded medical facility which conducted horrifying experiments on prisoners, Titus was condemned to death because he was too ill for further tests. A prisoner serving as a nursing aide prepared a lethal injection, and Titus gave her his Rosary. He received the poison on July 16, 1942. Three days later his body was placed in the Dachau crematorium, and his ashes were deposited into a mass grave. The nursing aide who administered the injection testified at Titus' Cause.

Pope John Paul II beatified Titus on December 3, 1985, speaking of the terrible trial of this "dangerous little friar" who answered hate with love:

" 'The souls of the righteous are in the hands of God' (Wis. 3:1). The Church listens to the word of God today, 3 November, the Sunday after the solemnity of All Saints and after the day commemorating all the faithful departed. The Church listens to this word on the day that she raises to the glories of the altar Titus Brandsma, son of the Netherlands and a religious of the Carmelite Order. Once again, a man who passed through the torments of a concentration camp — in this case, Dachau — is raised to the glories of the altar. A man who 'was punished,' in the words of today's liturgy (Wis. 3:4). And precisely in the midst of this 'punishment,' in the midst of a concentration camp, *which remains the shameful blot upon this century, God found Titus Brandsma worthy of himself (cf. Wis. 3:5). Today the Church rereads the signs of this divine approval and proclaims the glory of the Holy Trinity, professing with the author of the Book of Wisdom: 'The souls of the righteous are in the hand of God, and no torment will ever touch them.' And yet, Titus Brandsma suffered torments; in the sight of men he was punished. Yes, God tested him. The ex-deportees of the concentration camps know very well what a human Calvary were those places of affliction. Places of great trial for men and women. The trial of moral force . . . in this regard, perhaps, we are best spoken to by today's Gospel, which recalls the commitment to love our enemies. The concentration camps were organized according to the program of disdain for man, according to the program of hate. Through what trials of conscience, of character, of heart must have passed a disciple of Christ who recalled his words concerning the love of one's enemies! Not to answer with hate, but with love. This is perhaps the greatest trial of man's moral strength."*

Sister of Mercy of the Holy Cross

In this age when men and women blame their childhood sufferings, the social environment, or their own family members for their mistakes, Blessed Ulricha Nisch stands as a refreshing example of human daring: She blamed no one for her childhood experiences. She did not hug such tragedies to herself. Ulricha understood that she was to endure in silence, sometimes buffeted by trials, and always hidden.

ULRICHA NISCH

(D. 1913)

RELIGIOUS

Ulricha, also revered as Francisca Nisch, was born on September 18, 1882, at Obersdorf-Mittelbiberach on the Ress River of Germany. Ulricha was illegitimate and was raised for the first six years of her life by her grandmother and godmother. Her parents married after her birth, and at age seven she went to live with them. As the oldest child of a poor family, Ulricha had to assume household duties. She was a prayerful young woman, even as she performed her chores or attended the local school.

When she was old enough, Ulricha was sent to various regions in Germany and then to Switzerland to work as a domestic servant. In Rorschach, Switzerland, she became ill and was placed in a hospital operated by the Sisters of Mercy of the Holy Cross of Ingenhohl. Ulricha received the grace of a religious vocation through this contact and entered the congregation on October 17, 1904, at Hegne, Germany. She was professed on April 24, 1907.

Her domestic experiences led to assignments in the kitchens of the convent in Bühl and in St. Vincent's in Baden-Baden. Spiritually, Ulricha had great devotion to the Cross and the Holy Eucharist. She was a profoundly holy religious, and more and more religious and laypeople are becoming aware of the profound truths of her silent mystical way. Suffering physically, she made no complaint, and reported no discomfort. She predicted the way she would die hidden, saying: "God wills that I die as I have lived." Ulricha collapsed and was diagnosed with advanced tuberculosis. She died in Hegne on May 8, 1913. No one was at her bedside as she breathed her last, as even her nurse had been called away.

Pope John Paul II beatified Ulricha on November 1, 1987, and at the ceremony she was revered as a holy woman of the "Little Way" of the spirit. Ulricha was honored as a soul that lived the true spiritual union in a profound and hidden manner, unnoticed by the world.

Foundress of the Ursulines of the Sacred Heart

The family has long been hailed as the "cradle of the faith and vocations," and the Ledochowska family of Poland stands as a symbol of the truth of the adage. Blessed Ursula Ledochowska was the sister of St. Theresa Ledochowska. These sisters' dedication, zeal, and endurance brought graces and good to thousands of their contemporaries, and their vision provided the modern world with continuing service.

Ursula was born in Loosdorr, Austria, on April 17, 1865, and baptized Julia as the daughter of Count Anthony Ledochowska and his wife. She was raised devoutly, undertaking many charitable projects while still young. In 1873, the family moved to St. Poelten after suffering a financial reverse. In February of 1885, Ursula's father died of smallpox, and the family was aided by an uncle, Cardinal Lebo, who was in Rome.

URSULA LEDOCHOWSKA

(D. 1939)

FOUNDRESS

Receiving the grace of a religious vocation, Ursula founded the Ursulines of the Sacred Heart, also called the Gray Ursulines. Ursula submitted the rule and constitutions of the congregation to Pope Benedict XV (r. 1914-1922) for approval. The actual motherhouse is in Pniewy, Poland, but the Holy See asked Ursula to make her permanent residence in Rome. There her example inspired many Catholic institutions. She died on May 29, 1939, in her convent on the Via del Casalet in Rome, mourned by Romans and the people of Poland.

Pope John Paul II beatified Ursula in Poznan, Poland, on June 20, 1983, announcing that her vision and devotion enabled countless souls to witness for Christ and to provide Christ's charity to all in need.

Carmelite Victim of the Spanish Civil War

The simple phrase, "Come on, our reward is waiting for us," became the rallying cry for a group of martyrs in the Spanish Civil War. The woman who called out those words of encouragement was Victoria Diez y Bustos de Molina, who died with the same inexhaustible joy that she exhibited while she served Christ on earth.

VICTORIA DIEZ Y BUSTOS DE MOLINA

(D. 1936)

❦

MARTYR

Victoria was born in Seville, Spain, on November 11, 1903, the only child of a devout family. Victoria was raised modestly and became a teacher. She also studied art and demonstrated many abilities. Her life, however, was formed by her profound faith and by a desire to help others.

When Victoria met Blessed Peter Posedo Castroverde, she recognized the opportunity to fulfill her heart's desire. She joined Blessed Peter's newly formed Teresian Association and began training in the Carmelite spiritual way. Her first assignment was as a teacher in Cheles, a small town near the Portuguese border. A year later she returned to Seville, where she was able to aid her family. She taught at Hornachuelos until 1936, when the Church there was brutally attacked.

On August 11, 1936, Victoria was arrested and taken to the town hall and then to a makeshift prison. She was calm and kind to her companions, displaying her joy and her profound beliefs. At daybreak, Victoria and seventeen others were escorted to an abandoned mine shaft at Rincón and cruelly martyred. Victoria encouraged the others with her promise of their "reward." Her last words were "Long live Christ the King."

Pope John Paul II beatified Victoria on October 10, 1993, saying:

"Victoria Diez y Bustos de Molina . . . was able to incarnate the spirituality of the Teresian Association where she made her total gift to God, pronouncing these words: 'If it is necessary to give one's life to be identified with Christ, our divine model, from now on I no longer exist for the world because my life is Christ and to die is gain.' This blessed is an example of openness to the Spirit and apostolic fruitfulness. She was able to sanctify herself in her work as a teacher in a rural community, at the same time helping out in parish activities, particularly in catechesis. The happiness she transmitted to all was a faithful reflection of that unconditional surrender to Jesus, which led her to the supreme witness of offering her life for the salvation of many."

Model Laywoman of Madagascar

Few Americans know anything about Madagascar, an island located off the southeast coast of Africa, which today is called the Malagasy Republic. In 1989 Pope John Paul II went to Madagascar to raise to the altars the glory of the Church of Madagascar, Victoria Rasoamanarivo.

Victoria was born to a leading Malagasy family in Tamanarive in 1848. Her maternal grandfather was the prime minister for many years, and other relatives held high offices. The Jesuit missionaries and the Sisters of St. Joseph of Cluny educated Victoria, who asked to become a Catholic. She was baptized Victoria on March 1, 1863. Her faith was tested when King

VICTORIA RASOAMANARIVO
(D. 1894)

LAY RELIGIOUS

Radama II was overthrown and the missionaries were persecuted, but she remained loyal to the Church.

On May 13, 1864, Victoria married the son of the prime minister, who openly abused her to the point that even the young man's father counseled divorce. Victoria refused and stayed true to her marriage vows until 1887, when her husband died.

Four years before, the French Catholic missionaries had been expelled, and Victoria had used her influence to keep the churches open and schools in operation. She was present in 1886 when the missionaries returned and turned over a prosperous Catholic community to their care.

Victoria spent six hours a day in prayer and cared for the poor and the sick. Her later years brought many illnesses, but she remained a powerful protector of the Church, revered by all. Victoria died on August 21, 1894, and was declared venerable in 1983.

Pope John Paul II beatified Victoria on April 30, 1989, at Antananarivo, declaring:

"Today, we honor a woman who loved Christ authentically, a woman who remained faithful to the Word of the Lord: Victoria Rasoamanarivo. The Church recognizes her sanctity, with her brothers and sisters of this land who admire her example, and count on her intercession. The Church in Madagascar and the Church throughout the world greet her as one in whom God dwells, as a sister to whom one remains close in the mysterious reality of the communion of saints. Victoria has lived the gift of faith intensely, from the time of her Christian initiation as a catechumen. She received the Spirit of Christ. Throughout her life she knew how to keep the living memory of the Word of Jesus (cf. Jn 14:26). With the power of the 'Counsellor,' she found the courage for a fidelity

without weakness. In the depth of her being, Victoria remained constantly in God's presence. All were struck by the intensity of her prayer. Familiar with the presence of God, she knew how to draw others into intimacy with the Lord. Like the Blessed Virgin Mary, she advanced daily in the pilgrimage of faith. Had she not given to the Catholic Union the maxim: 'Let us sanctify ourselves first; then we shall see to sanctifying others'? The witness of her action shows well that it is not a question of a piety that was closed in on itself. On the contrary, Victoria did not think that she could bring the Good News to her brothers and sisters without opening her whole being to the power of grace. That is why, in the midst of her activities and cares, she always found much time for prayer. . . . We pray to Victoria that she may help the sons and daughters of Madagascar to receive the gift of faith in the generous way she received it; we ask her to draw her Malagasy brothers and sisters to put their whole life in the light of Christ which enlightens the baptized, guides their decisions, supports them in difficulty, and accompanies them in joy."

Bishop Victim of Communists

The Christian reverence for all human life and for the purity of women have long been hallmarks of the faith. In the past decades, heroic men and women have stood against both Nazi and Communist oppression in order to safeguard such reverence. Blessed Vilmos Apor, the martyred bishop of Hungary, faced both the Nazis and the Communists, and he gave his life to defend the women and young girls in his care.

VILMOS APOR

(D. 1945)

🌿

MARTYR

He was born on February 29, 1892, the sixth child of a noble Hungarian family. His father died when Vilmos was very young, and his mother raised her children quite devoutly. Vilmos was educated by the Jesuits and then entered the seminary. He was sent to Innsbruck, Austria, where he earned a doctorate in theology.

Vilmos was ordained a priest for the diocese of Nagyváradon on August 2, 1915. He performed ministerial apostolates in the diocese and served for a brief time as a military chaplain. Throughout his ministries, Vilmos displayed a love of the poor and a fine sense of the religious life as he sponsored religious communities and parochial life.

On February 24, 1941, Vilmos, appointed a bishop by Pope Pius XII (r. 1939-1958), was consecrated for the diocese of Györ. His episcopal motto summed up his apostolate: "The Cross strengthens the weak and makes gentle the strong." Vilmos would need graces and resolve, as Hungary was ravaged by war.

When Vilmos read the racial laws enforced by the Nazis, he put himself in danger by protesting against them and by working with the Popular Democratic Catholic Party in resisting the Nazis until the war's end. Russian troops then occupied Hungary, and new horrors began for the faithful.

On Good Friday, 1945, Russian troops demanded that Vilmos turn over the one hundred women and young girls who had taken refuge in the cellar of his episcopal palace. In confrontation, the bishop was shot by a Russian officer, and the troops fled the scene. Vilmos had saved the women from repeated rapes by the Russian soldiers, but he knew that he had done so at the cost of his own life. He was operated on for wounds to his hand, forehead, and stomach, but he died of his wounds on Easter Monday, April 2, 1945. He was buried in the Carmelite church and his Cause was opened immediately. Vilmos's remains are now is enshrined in the cathedral of Győr.

Pope John Paul II beatified Vilmos on November 9, 1997, proclaiming:

"The intimate sharing in the mystery of Christ, the new and perfect Temple in whom full communion between God and man is realized (cf. Jn 2:21), shines forth in the pastoral service of Blessed Vilmos Apor, whose life was crowned with martyrdom. He was the "parish priest of the poor," a ministry which he continued as a Bishop during the dark years of the Second World War, working as a generous benefactor of the needy and the defender of the persecuted. He was not afraid to raise his voice to censure, on the basis of Gospel principles, the injustices and abuses of power towards minorities, especially towards the Jewish community. . . . The heroic witness of Bishop Vilmos Apor honors the history of the noble Hungarian nation and is held up today for the admiration of the whole Church. May it encourage believers to follow Christ in their lives without hesitation. This is the holiness to which all the baptized are called!"

Passionist Bishop of Bulgaria

The atheist political systems of the modern world target the friends of God. Such holy men and women stand as constant symbols of faith, and as such they represent the redemptive love of Christ amid the horrors of modern tyranny. Vincent Eugene Bossilkov, the martyred Passionist bishop of Bulgaria, was targeted as a friend of God by the Communists of his native land.

He was born in Belene, Bulgaria, on November 16, 1900, to a Latin-rite Catholic family. Educated at local schools, Vincent entered the Passionist seminary at age eleven. He studied then at Nikopol, and in Belgium, and later in the Netherlands. In 1919, he received the Passionist

VINCENT

EUGENE

BOSSILKOV

(D. 1952)

MARTYR

habit and the religious name of Eugene of the Sacred Heart. His final vows were in 1923, and he was ordained on July 25, 1926. This was followed by theological studies in Rome leading to his doctorate.

In 1933, Vincent returned to his diocese, where he became secretary to the bishop and a priest of the cathedral. He asked to be made a parish priest and was sent to Bardaski-Gheran. Vincent served as the official orator for the 250th anniversary of the Catholic uprising against the Turks in 1938.

Following World War II and the invasion of Rusian Communist troops into Bulgaria, Vincent was appointed bishop of Nikopol. He was consecrated in 1947 and made a *ad limina* visit to

Blessed Vincent Eugene Bossilkov

Rome, the following year. Pope Pius XII (r. 1939-1958) encouraged Vincent in his apostolate, giving him blessings. Soon after, the apostolic delegate, or representative of the Holy See, was expelled from Bulgaria by the Communists, who also exiled all foreign missionaries and tried to crush Catholics who maintained allegiance to Rome. Throughout 1950-1951, Vincent and other Church leaders suffered severe persecutions.

Vincent and Bishop Romanov, the elderly Catholic exarch, were arrested on July 16, 1952, while on vacation near Sofia. Vincent was imprisoned, tortured, and tried from September 29 to October 3 in a typical Communist-sham court procedure. He was executed on November 11, 1952, in Sofia prison, and his body was dumped into a common grave. He had seen his own peril and had assured friends and a relative: "Don't worry about me; I am already clothed with God's grace and have remained faithful to Christ and the Church."

Pope John Paul II beatified Vincent on March 15, 1998, declaring that the martyred bishop has become *"the Church's radiant glory in his country,"* and that Vincent was *"a fearless witness to the Cross of Christ. . . ."*

Victim of the Spanish Civil War

As Spain anguished in the throes of the Civil War, thousands of priests and religious were hunted down and slain. The toll was horrifyingly high, and some communities were obliterated by martyrdom. Other religious and priests survived because the Spanish laity came to their aid. Despite the perils of such assistance, Spanish laymen and women rescued religious and kept them safe from the terrible ordeals being visited upon the Church by the Communist-inspired revolutionary militias. Vincent Vilar David was just such a heroic layman, and he died as he had lived, imbued with the virtues of Christ.

Vincent was born in Manises, Valnecia, Spain, on June 28, 1889, the youngest of eight children in the David family. He was educated in the Scalopian or Piarist Schools and studied engineering in Valencia.

VINCENT VILAR DAVID

(D. 1937)

❧

MARTYR

Vincent labored as an industrial engineer in the family ceramics firm, was active in civic affairs, married Isabel Rodes Reig, and was involved in parish activities and in Catholic youth groups. Thus, Vincent was well prepared to render service to the Church when the Spanish Civil War engulfed that nation. He maintained his devout routines, and he openly declared his faith as he gave shelter to priests and religious. These activities brought him to the attention of the rebel authorities, who arrested him. On February 14, 1937, Vincent said goodbye to his wife, who told him: "See you tomorrow!" His wife and others heard shots ring out and knew that Vincent had been murdered.

Pope John Paul II beatified Vincent on October 1, 1995, stating: *". . . Blessed Vincent Vilar David, who with his martyrdom crowned his life of total dedication to God, to his neighbor, and to the promotion of justice in the world of work . . . enriched the martyrology of Valencia. His prayer and deep devotion to the Eucharist nourished his whole life, so that his work bore the stamp of God's presence."*

Vincent Lewoniuk and Companions ❧ **See Martyrs of Podlasie.**

Genoa, Italy, was long overshadowed by the great maritime city of Venice, and so it is often forgotten that the Genoese were also the builders of a proud ocean-going power. In the seventeenth century, Genoa enjoyed much prestige and served as one of Italy's many repositories of culture and art. It was in this era that Blessed Virginia Centurione Bracelli began her apostolate of mercy.

VIRGINIA CENTURIONE BRACELLI

(D. 1651)

FOUNDRESS

Virginia was born the daughter of the doge, the aristocratic ruler of Genoa on April 2, 1587. She was raised in splendor; hers was a world of rank and privilege. At home in the faith and in the palatial abodes of the nobility of that era, Virginia married Gasparo Grimaldi Bracelli, and they resided in Genoa as a couple of prominence until his death in 1625.

Virginia began a series of charitable programs and many were astonished by her Christ-like concern for those in want. Virginia opened a home called "St. Mary of the Refuge" for needy children in Genoa. She attracted supporters and co-workers in this apostolate, as her willingness to sacrifice her aristocratic comforts to aid those abandoned by society were an inspiration to all who felt the call to give their lives for Christ. When Virginia had formed a group of dedicated women for her apostolate, she adopted a Franciscan rule and founded the Daughters of Mount Calvary. She was aided by Marquess Emmanuele Brignole, who gave her a second residence.

In time the Daughters of Mount Calvary would receive residences in Rome from Popes Pius VII (r.1800-1823) and Gregory XVI (r.1831-1846). Virginia died in Genoa, mourned by nobles and commoners, on December 15, 1651. Pope John Paul II beatified Virginia on September 22, 1985, in Genoa before a tumultuous crowd of the faithful. The Holy Father declared that the life of the new blessed reflected her city's heritage of Catholicity, and Genoa's splendid vision. Virginia was honored as a woman whose love crossed all boundaries of society.

Founder of the Ursuline Daughters of Mary Immaculate

The timeless visions and virtues of the saints of the past still inspire, still guide the generous souls of new eras. Zeferino was such a soul, and the saint that inspired him to heroic acts of charity was Angela Merici. As early as 1855, Zeferino was celebrating her feast day and using her life as model for young women of his own time.

Zeferino was born in Verona, Italy, on September 24, 1813, the older of two sons of Antonio and Angela Frattini Agostini. Four days later, he was baptized in the church of Sts. Nazarius and Celsus. His father was a doctor, and the family was devout and involved in the local parish, where Zeferino would begin his priestly ministry. His mother, widowed while still young, raised Zeferino and his brother. She was revered in the area for her gentleness and spiritual awareness.

ZEFERINO AGOSTINI

(D. 1896)

❧

FOUNDER

Receiving the grace of a religious vocation, Zeferino studied at the local schools and then the diocesan seminary. On March 11, 1837, he was ordained to the priesthood by the bishop of Verona and celebrated his first Mass in the local parish of Sts. Nazarius and Celsus. He was assigned there as an assistant priest, teaching Christian doctrine and directing parish activities for local young men. He became the pastor in 1865. Sts. Nazarius and Celsus was large and served the poverty stricken section of the city, and Zeferino carried out his ministry alone. The overwhelming tasks facing him did not deter Zeferino, who had recourse to hours of prayer and devotion in order to foster his apostolic zeal. He focused on the education of the young women of the parish, speaking always of St. Angela Merici and celebrating her feast day.

When three young women came to Zeferino to offer themselves as religious for the service of the poor, he founded a Pious Union of Sisters devoted to St. Angela Merici. That rule was approved by Bishop Ricabona in 1856. In that same year, Zeferino opened a school for destitute girls. The women involved in this apostolate entered Zeferino's newly founded Congregation of Ursulines, Daughters of Mary Immaculate, and they made their first vows on September 24, 1869. Zeferino cautioned them in 1874, saying: "Do not be dismayed by toil or suffering, nor by the meager fruit of your labors. Remember that God rewards not according to results but efforts." He lived according to that great spiritual truth until April 6, 1896.

Pope John Paul II beatified Zeferino on October 25, 1998, in Rome, declaring: *"He stands before us today as a humble, steadfast witness to the Gospel in the latter half of the nineteenth century, a fruitful period for the Church in Verona. His faith was steadfast, his charitable work effective, and ardent was the priestly spirit that distinguished him."*

INDEX OF SAINTS AND BLESSEDS

Hita, Jesús, 300
Hoa, Simon, 63
Hoan, John, 60
Ho-Dinh-Hy, Michael, 62
Hogg, John, 286
Holiday, Richard, 286
Horner, Nicholas, 287
Houben, Charles of Mount Argus, 122
Hunt, Thomas, 287
Hunt, Thurston, 287
Huong, Lawrence, 61
Huy, Augustine, 57
Ibañez de Erquicia, Dominic, 51
Imbert, Lawrence, 53
Ingleby, Francis, 287
Iruzun, Feliz Ugalde, 302
Isidore Gagelin, Francis, 59
Jablonska, Maria Bernardina, 245
Jaccard, Francis, 59
Jamet, Peter Francis, 330
Jansoone, Frederick, 165
Jarrige, Catherine, 120
Jearney, John, 296
John of Dukla, 36
Joubert, Eugénie, 148
Jugan, Marie of the Cross, 271
Kafka, Maria Restituta, 246
Kalinowski, Raphael (Jozef), 75
Karlowska, Maria, 247
Kazimierczyk, Stanislas, 346
Kern, Jacob, 186
Khambang, Lucia, 306
Khamphai, Bibiana, 306
Khang, Joseph, 60
Kim, Andrew, 53
Kim, Agnes, 53
Kim, Columba, 53
Koan, Paul, 62
Kolbe, Maximilian, 67
Kolping, Adolph, 86
Kostistk, Jeremiah of Valachia, 189
Kowalska, Maria Faustina, 248
Kozal, Michael, 311
Kozka, Caroline, 119
Krizin, Marek, 54
Kuen, Jacques, 52
Lac, Paul, 62

Lambert, Matthew, 295
Lambton, Joseph, 287
Lament, Boleslawa Maria, 115
Lampley, William, 287
Laval, Francis de Montmorency, 160
Laval, Jacob Desiré, 187
Lazarus of Kyoto, 51
Le Bouteiller, Marthe, 279
Leclerq, Solomon, 290
Ledochowska, Ursula, 355
Lego, John, 289
Lego, René, 289
Leisner, Karl, 215
Lentini, Dominic, 136
Lewoniuk, Vincent, 302
Leziniana, Matthew Alonzo, 62
Lichtenburg, Bernard, 112
Loan, Luke, 61
Longo, Bartholomew, 108
Lopez, Marciano José (Filomeno), 282
Lowe, John, 287
Lucci, Anthony, 102
Ludlam, Robert, 287
Lumbreras, Martin of St. Nicholas, 297
Luu, Joseph, 61
MacKillop, Mary of the Cross, 308
Magallanes, Christopher, 124
Magdalen of Canossa, 44
Malla, Ceferino Gimenez, 121
Manetti, Teresa Maria of the Cross, 348
Manyanet y Vives, Joseph, 204
March Mesa, Nazaría Ignacia of St. Teresa of Jesus, 316
Marchand, Joseph, 61
Marchisio, Clemente, 127
Marello, Joseph (Giuseppe), 205
María of the Angels of St. Joseph (Marciana Valtierra Tordesillas), 291
María Pilar of St. Francis Borgia (Jacoba Martinez Garcia), 291
Martí, Mother Angeles de San José Lloret, 305
Martillo Morán, Narcisa de Jesus, 315

Martinez, José Puiz, 302
Martinez, Valerio Bernardo, 280
Martyrs of Almeria, 280
Martyrs of Armenia, 280
Martyrs of Asturias (Turon), 281
Martyrs of Barbastro, 283
Martyrs of England, Scotland, and Wales, 285
Martyrs of Ethoipia, 288
Martyrs of France, 289
Martyrs of Guadalajara, 290
Martyrs of Ireland, 294
Martyrs of Japan, 297
Martyrs of Japan (d.c. 1630), 50
Martyrs of Korea, 52
Martyrs of Kosice, 54
Martyrs of La Rochelle, 298
Martyrs of Madrid, 299
Martyrs of Podlasie, 302
Martyrs of Thailand, 305
Martyrs of the Diocesan Worker Priests, 284
Martyrs of the French Revolution, 290
Martyrs of the Hospitallers of St. John of God, 292-294
Martyrs of the Marianist Congregation, 300
Martyrs of the Passionist Congregation, 301
Martyrs of the Scalopian Congregation, 303
Martyrs of the Sisters of Christian Doctrine, 305
Martyrs of the Visitation Order, 307
Martyrs of Vietnam, 55
Marzorati, Samuel, 288
Matulaitis (Matulewicz), George, 171
Maubant, Philibert, 53
Mayer, Rupert, 342
Mazzarella, Modestino of Jesus and Mary, 314
Mazzucconi, John Baptist, 193
McKenraghty, Maurice, 296
Medina Olmos, Emmanuel, 280
Meeham, Charles, 287

Sanchez, Fulgencio Calvo, 302
Sanchez, Melchior, 297
Sancho de Guerra, María Josefa, 259
Sandys, John, 287
Santamaria, Grimoaldo, 176
Sargeant, Richard, 287
Sarkander, Jan, 32
Sarnelli, Gennaro Maria, 168
Satellico, Maria Crucifixa, 260
Scalabrini, John Baptist, 195
Scherer, Maria Theresa, 260
Schinina, Maria, 261
Schöffler, Augustine, 57
Schuster, Ildephonse (Alfredo), 181
Schwartz, Anton Maria, 103
Scott, Mountford, 287
Scotus, John Duns, 192
Scrosoppi of Udine, Luigi (Aloysius), 224
Scubilion, 344
Segura, Emmanuel, 303
Serra, Junípero, 214
Shihozuka, Vincent, 51
Siedliska, Maria of Jesus, 262
Silvestrelli, Bernard Maria, 113
Simon de Longpré, Marie Catherine, 272
Simpson, Richard, 287
Siphong, Philip, 306
Smaldone, Filippo, 152
Snow, Peter, 287
Southerne, William, 287
Souzy, John, 298
Spenser, William, 287
Spinelli, Francis, 162
Spinola y Maestre, Marcellus, 229
Sprott, Thomas, 287
Stangassinger, Gaspar (Kaspar), 168
Stein, Edith, 21
Stensen, Nicolaus, 318
Stepinac, Aloysius, 90

Stollenwerk, Maria Helen, 263
Sugar, John, 287
Sutton, Robert, 287
Sykes, Edmund, 287
Talbot, John, 287
Tansi, Cyprian (Iwene), 128
Taylor, Francis, 296
Tejedor, Cyril Bertrand, 282
Tejerina, Mary, 301
Tekakwitha, Kateri, 216
Teresa of the Child Jesus and St. John of the Cross (Eusebia Garcia y Garcia), 291
Thanh, John Baptist, 60
Thé, Nicholas, 62
Thévenet, Mary of St. Ignatius (Claudine), 66
Thi, Joseph, 61
Thi, Peter, 63
Tho, Martin, 61
Thomson, William, 287
Thorpe, Roger, 287
Thules, John, 287
Thwing, Edward, 287
Tinh, Martin, 61
Tinh, Paul, 62
Tirry, William, 296
To Rot, Peter, 331
Toan, Thomas, 65
Tomasi, Joseph Maria Cardinal, 41
Tomonaga, Jacob Kyshei, 51
Tong Buong, Paul, 62
Tornay, Maurice, 309
Tovini, Giuseppe (Joseph), 173
Trach, Dominic, 58
Trichet, Marie-Louise of Jesus, 276
Trieu, Emmanuel, 58
Troiani, Maria Catherine of St. Rose, 265
Trong, Andrew, 57
Trung, Francis, 59
Truszkowska, Angela Maria, 97

Tschiderer Von (Zu) Gleifheim, John, 196
Tsiou, James, 52
Tuan Peter, 63
Tuy, Peter, 63
Uy, Dominic, 58
Uyarra, Evencio Ricardo, 280
Uyen, Joseph Peter, 61
Vaillot, María Anna, 289
Valencia, Rafael Guizar, 339
Van Hanh Dieu, Dominic, 58
Van, Peter, 63
Vannini (Adelaides), Josephine, 212
Vaz, Joseph, 209
Venard, Théophane, 55, 64
Vendramini, Elizabeth, 144
Venegas de la Torre, María of Jesus, 266
Ventaja, Diego, 280
Versiglia, Luigi (Aloysius), 225
Vicuña, Laura, 219
Vinh, Stephen, 64
Visenteiner, Pauline Amabilis, 323
Von Mallinckrodt, Pauline, 322
Watkinson, Thomas, 287
Webley, Henry, 287
Weiss, Liberatus, 288
Wharton, Christopher, 287
Whittaker, Thomas, 287
Wiaux, Mutien-Marie, 72
Woodcock, John, 287
Woodfen, Nicholas, 286
Wrenno, Roger, 287
Yaxley, Richard, 287
Ybarra, Rafaela, 340
Yen, Vincent, 65
Yi Kwong-hai, John, 54
Yi Yon-hui, Mary, 54
Yu Tae-Chol, Peter, 54
Zapico, Julian Alfredo (Vilfridio Fernández), 282
Zubero, Dominic Iturrate, 137